Library of
Davidson College

The Old Saxon Language

Berkeley Models of Grammars

Irmengard Rauch
General Editor

Vol. 1

PETER LANG
New York • San Francisco • Bern • Baltimore
Frankfurt am Main • Berlin • Wien • Paris

Irmengard Rauch

The Old Saxon Language

Grammar, Epic Narrative, Linguistic Interference

PETER LANG
New York • San Francisco • Bern • Baltimore
Frankfurt am Main • Berlin • Wien • Paris

Library of Congress Cataloging-in-Publication Data

Rauch, Irmengard.
 The Old Saxon language : grammar, epic narrative, linguistic interference / by Irmengard Rauch.
  p. cm. — (Berkeley models of grammars ; vol. 1)
  Includes bibliographical references and index.
  1. Old Saxon language—Grammar. I. Title. II. Series.
PF3994.R38   1992   429'.5—dc20   92-20320
ISBN 0-8204-1893-5   CIP
ISSN 1061-6055

Die Deutsche Bibliothek-CIP-Einheitsaufnahme

Rauch, Irmengard:
The Old Saxon language : grammar, epic narrative, linguistic interference / Irmengard Rauch. - New York ; Berlin ; Bern ; Frankfurt/M. ; Paris ; Wien : Lang, 1992
 (Berkeley models of grammars ; Vol. 1)
 ISBN 0-8204-1893-5
NE: GT

Cover Design by James Brisson

The paper in this book meets the guidelines for permanence and durability of the Committee on Production Guidelines for Book Longevity of the Council on Library Resources.

© Peter Lang Publishing, Inc., New York 1992

All rights reserved.
Reprint or reproduction, even partially, in all forms such as microfilm, xerography, microfiche, microcard, offset strictly prohibited.

Printed in the United States of America.

GERALD, CHRIS, GREG

Contents

Plate I   *Ms. C Fit 1: lines 1-18a*   xvii

Plate II   *Ms. M Fit 2-3: lines 117-179a*   xviii-xix

Plate III   *Ms. S Fit 7: lines 558b-582a;*
           Fit 8: lines 675-683a; lines 692-698   xx-xxi

Plate IV   *Versus de Poeta & interprete huius codicis*   xxii

Plate V   *Map of Old Saxon Speech Area*   xxiii

Introduction   xxv

Symbols and Abbreviations   xli

Chapter One
Reading an Old Saxon Text;
Early Cognitive Decisions;
The Verb in the Lexicon;
The Strong Verb Dictionary Finder Chart

1. The Old Saxon Text: Narrative Discourse   1
2. The OS Sentence, Grammatical Constituents, Lexicon   2
3. The Verb in the Lexicon   3
   3.1 The Fundamental Identifying
       Form (FIF) of the Verb   3
   3.2 Strong, Weak, Modal Auxiliary,
       Anomalous Verb Types   4

3.3 Strong Verb ABLAUT   5
　　　　3.3.1 The Strong Verb Dictionary Finder Chart   6
　　　　3.3.2 Variation in the Seven Strong Verb Sets   12

Chapter Two
After the First Search; Diachronic Synchrony
and Linguistic Explanation; Linear Syntax:
Independent Sentence; Pragmatic Strategies;
Nonlinear Micro-syntax: Morphology;
Inflection of Verb Present Tense

4. Linguistic Generalization in Diachronic Synchrony   19
5. Completing the Search   23
6. Linear Syntax: The Independent Sentence   24
　　6.1 The Independent Declarative Sentence:
　　　　 (X)VbSO   24
　　6.2 The Unmarked Interrogative and the Unmarked
　　　　 Imperative Sentence: (X)VbSO   25
　　6.3 The Marked Independent Sentence:
　　　　 (X)SVbO and (X)SOVb   26
　　6.4 Textual and Pragmatic Strategies
　　　　 in Linear Syntax   27
7. Nonlinear Micro-syntax: Morphology   31
8. Inflection of Verb Present Tense Indicative   35
　　8.1 Present Tense Indicative Suffix   35
　　8.2 Present Tense Plural Types: Membership
　　　　 and Root Modifications   36
　　　　8.2.1 The -(*a*)*d* Plural Verbs   37
　　　　8.2.2 The -*un* Plural Verbs   38
　　　　8.2.3 Anomalous Verbs   39

Chapter Three
Propositional Meaning and Valence;
The Noun and its Grammatical Categories;
Inflection of the Masculine Strong Noun;
Inflection of the Neuter Strong Noun

9.	Propositional Meaning and Valence	43
10.	The Argument(s)	46
	10.1 The Noun and Its Categories	46
11.	The Inflection of the Masculine Strong Noun	48
	11.1 Masculine Strong Noun Suffix	48
	11.2 Masculine Strong Noun Plural Types: Root and Suffix Variations	50
	11.2.1 Masculine Strong Noun ø-Plural Subset Contaminations; Anomalies	52
12.	The Inflection of the Neuter Strong Noun	53
	12.1 Neuter Strong Noun Suffix	53
	12.2 Neuter Strong Noun Plural Types: Root and Suffix Variations	54
	12.2.1 Neuter Strong Noun ø-Plural Subset Contaminations; Anomalies	56

Chapter Four
Primary Evidence in Reading the OS Text;
Graphemics and the Interpretation
of Desinences; Inflection of the Feminine
Strong Noun; Inflection of the Masculine,
Neuter, and Feminine Weak Nouns

13.	Graphemics	57
	13.1 Graphic Variation	58
	13.2 Reading the Inflectional Syllable: Reality in Diachronic Synchrony	59
14.	The Inflection of the Feminine Strong Noun	63
	14.1 Feminine Strong Noun Suffix	63
	14.2 Feminine Strong Noun Plural Types: Root and Suffix Variations	65
	14.2.1 Feminine Strong Noun *i*-Plural Subset Contaminations; Anomalies	67
15.	The Inflection of the Trigender Weak Noun	68
	15.1 Trigender Weak Noun Suffix	68

15.2 Trigender Weak Noun: Root
and Suffix Variations　　　　　　　70

Chapter Five
Hearing the Old Saxon Text;
Articulatory/Acoustic Features of the Sounds;
Systematic Segmental Phonemes;
Suprasegmental Phonemes;
Alliterative Verse Form; Syllable

16. Sounds in Historical Language　　　　　73
    16.1 Articulatory Phonetics　　　　　　74
        16.1.1 Consonant　　　　　　　　　75
        16.1.2 Vowel　　　　　　　　　　　77
    16.2 Acoustic Phonetics　　　　　　　　79
        16.2.1 Consonant　　　　　　　　　80
        16.2.2 Vowel　　　　　　　　　　　82
17. The Old Saxon Sound System　　　　　　83
    17.1 Segmental Phonemes of Old Saxon　85
    17.2 Old Saxon Systematic Phonemes　　85
    17.3 Suprasegmental Phonemes of Old Saxon　88
        17.3.1 Old Saxon Alliterative Verse Form　88
        17.3.2 Word Stress Phonemes　　　91
        17.3.3 Syntactic Stress　　　　　93
    17.4 Old Saxon Syllable　　　　　　　　96

Chapter Six
Sorting out the Graphemic Variation;
Heliand and *Genesis* Manuscripts;
Latin Prefaces; Old Saxon Speech Area,
Dialects and Megadialects;
Phonemic, Allophonic, Graphemic Fit

18. The Sound:Symbol Fit　　　　　　　　　99
19. Time/Space Setting of the Primary
    Old Saxon Data　　　　　　　　　　　100

19.1	The *Heliand* Manuscripts	100
19.2	The Role of the Latin *Heliand* and *Genesis* Prefaces	101
19.3	Dialects and Megadialects	103
	19.3.1 The Old Saxon Speech Area	103
	19.3.2 *Heliand* Dialects and Register	105
	19.3.3 Old Frisian, Old English, Old High German Megadialect Interference	108
19.4	Phoneme, Allophone, Grapheme	112
	19.4.1 /p/	113
	19.4.2 /b/	113
	19.4.3 /f/	114
	19.4.4 /m/	115
	19.4.5 /w/	115
	19.4.6 /t/	116
	19.4.7 /d/	117
	19.4.8 /th/	118
	19.4.9 /s/	120
	19.4.10 /n/	120
	19.4.11 /l/	121
	19.4.12 /r/	121
	19.4.13 /k/	122
	19.4.14 /g/	124
	19.4.15 /x/	125
	19.4.16 /j/	126
	19.4.17 /h/	127
	19.4.18 /ī/	128
	19.4.19 /ū/	128
	19.4.20 /i/	128
	19.4.21 /u/	129
	19.4.22 /ẹ/	129
	19.4.23 /ọ/	130
	19.4.24 /ẹ̄/	131

19.4.25 /ǭ/	131
19.4.26 /e/	131
19.4.27 /o/	133
19.4.28 /ə/	134
19.4.29 /a/	134
19.4.30 /ā/	135
19.4.31 Diphthongs	135
19.5 Old Saxon Systematic Phones	137

Chapter Seven
Configurating the Morphology;
Nonlinear Macro-syntax;
Subcategorization Rules in the Predicate,
Argument, Modality Constituents

20. Nonlinear Macro-syntax	139
21. Subcategorization Rules	140
22. Predicate Constituent	140
22.1 Simple Nominal Complement	143
22.2 Complex Nominal Complement	145
22.3 Case Transformed to Prepositional Phrase	147
22.4 Adverbial Complement by Case or Case Transformed to Prepositional Phrase	149
22.5 Infinitive Complement	151
22.6 Present Participle Complement	153
22.7 Preterite Participle Complement	154
22.8 Sentence Complement	155
23. Argument Constituent	156
23.1 Article Determiner	157
23.2 Quantifier Determiner	157
23.3 Possessive Pronoun Determiner, Intensifier Pronoun, Possessive Noun	158
23.4 NP Expansion by Adjective	159
23.5 NP Expansion by Sentence	160
24. Modality Constituent	162

24.1	Tense	162
24.2	Mood	170
24.3	Aspect	176
24.4	Polarity	179
24.5	Diathesis	182

Chapter Eight
The Lexicon: Derivation and Compounding;
Nonnoun Nominal Inflection;
Weakly Stressed Vowels;
Inflection of the Verb Preterite Tense;
Inflection of the Imperative and Subjunctive

25.	Noninflectional Morphology	185
	25.1 Derivation	187
	25.2 Compounding	189
26.	The Inflection of Nonnoun Nominals	191
	26.1 Trigender Strong Nonnoun Nominal Suffix	192
	26.1.1 Trigender Pronoun	194
	26.1.2 Trigender Strong Adjective	199
	26.1.3 Trigender Weak Adjective	201
	26.1.4 Nonfinite Verb	203
27.	Weakly Stressed Vowels	205
28.	Inflection of Verb Preterite Tense Indicative	207
	28.1 Preterite Tense Indicative Suffix	208
	28.2 Preterite Tense Plural Types	209
	28.2.1 The Nondental Preterite	210
	28.2.2 The Dental Preterite	211
	28.2.3 Anomalous Verbs	214
29.	The Inflection of the Nonindicative Verb Moods	214
	29.1 The Imperative	214
	29.2 The Subjunctive	215
	29.2.1 Present	215
	29.2.2 Preterite	216
30.	Further Linear and Nonlinear Syntax Rules	218
	30.1 Linear Order	218

30.1.1 The Dependent Sentence	218
30.1.2 Lexical Category Phrases	219
30.2 Occasional Optional Congruence Rules	221

Selected Readings — 223
Old Saxon

Heliand: Fits I, II, VII, VIII, XXXII, XXXVII, XXXVIII, XXXIX, LII, LIII	225
Genesis Fragment	250
Minor Documents: Charms, *Psalm V.9.* Explication	251

Latin

Prose Preface(s)	253
Verse Preface	255

Old High German

Charm Against Worms	257
Notker: *Psalm V.9.* Explication	257
Tatian: Luke 1.5-25	257
Otfrid: 1, 17	258
Muspilli	262

Old English

Genesis Passages	267
Cædmon	273

Old Saxon Glossary — 277

Latin Glossary — 315

Old High German Glossary — 333

Old English Glossary	357
Linguistic Technical Terms	373
Selected Bibliography	401
Index	409

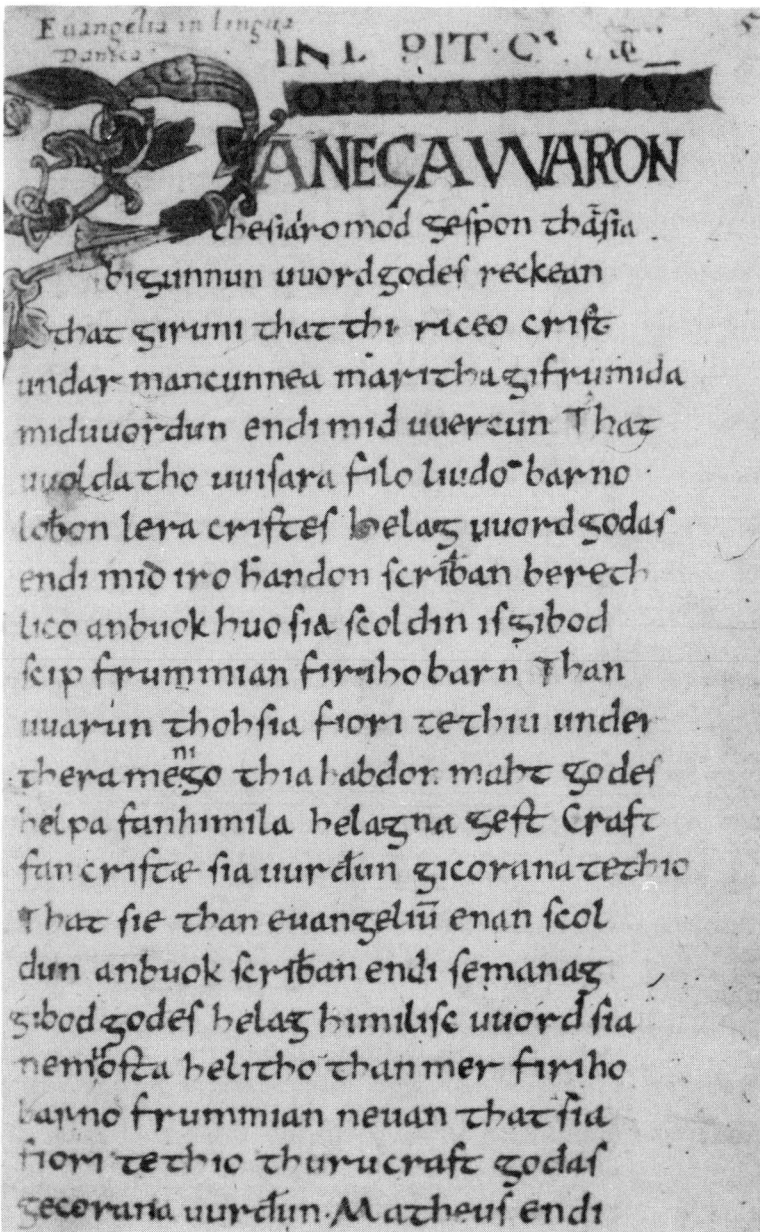

Plate I   Ms. C Fit 1: lines 1-18a

uualdanda uuerde endi thin uuord so self. thin thionost is im an
thanke that thu sulica githahti haues an is ones craft Ic is engil
bium gabriel bium ic hetan. the gio for goda standu and uuard
for them alouualdon. ne si that he me an is arundi huarod sendean uuillea. Nu hiet he me an theran sid faran. hiet that ic
thi gicudd. that thi kind gibores fon thinera aldero idis odan
scoldi uuerdan an theséro uueroldi uuordun spahi. That ni scal an
is liua gio lides an bitan uuines an is uueroldi. so habed im uurdgi-
scapu metod gimarcod. endi mahtig god. het that ic thi thoh sagdi
that it scoldi gi sid uuesan heuan cuninges. het that git it
heldin uuel tuhin thurh treuua. Quad that he im tiras so filu
an godes rikea forgeuan uueldi. He quad that the godo gumo
Iohannes te namon hebbean scoldi. gibod that git hetin so
that kind thar is quami. quad that it Krist es gisid an be farc
uundun uuerold uuerdan scoldi. is selbes sunies. en di quad
that sie sliumo herodan is bod skepi bede quamin. Zacharias tho gi mahalda endi uuid selban sprac drohtines engil endi
im thero dadeo bigan uundron thero uuordo. Huuo mag that
gi uuerdan so quad he after an aldre. It is une al to lat so tegi-
uuinnanne so thu mid thinun uuordun gi spriskis huuanda uuit

habdun aldres or efno tuentig uuintro. an uncro uueroldi. er thiu
quam thit uuif temi. than uuarun uuit nu at samna an sibun tia uuin
tro gibenkeon endi gibeddeon. sidor ic siemi te brudi gecos. so uuit ther
an uncro iugudi gigirnan nimohtun. that uuit erbiuuard egan mostin
fodean an uncun flettea. nu uuit sus gifrodod sint. habad unc eldi
binoman ellandadi. that uuit sint an uncro siuni gislekit endi an uncun
sidun lat. flesk is unc ant fallan fel unscom. is unca lud giliden
lik gitrusnod. sind unca andbari odorlicaron mod endi megincraft
so uuit giu so managan dag uuarun an thesero uueroldi. so mi thes uun
dar thunkit. huuo it so giuuerdan magi. so thu mid thinun uuordun
gispricis. Tho uuard that heuencuninges bodon harm an is mode
that he is giuuerkes so uundron scolda. endi that ni uuelda gihuggean
that im mahtig helag god. so alajungas so he fon crist uuas selbo gi
uuirkean of he so uueldi. Skerida im tho te uuitea. that he ni mahte
enig uuord sprekan gimahlien mid is muda. er than thi magu
uuirdid fon thiuuo aldero idis erl afodit kind iung giboran cunnies
goder uuanum te thesero uueroldi. than scalt thu eft uuord sprekan
hebbean thinaro stemna giuuald. ni tharft thu stum uuesan len
gron huila. Tho uuard it san gilestid so giuuordan te uuaron
so thar an them uuiha gisprak engil thes alouualdon. uuard ald
gumo spraca bilosit thoh he spahan hugi bari an is breostun.
Bidun allan dag that uuerod for them uuiha. endi uundrodun
alla bihuui he thar so lango lof salig man suuido frod gumo fran
sinun thionon thorfti. so thar er enig thegno nidedaz than sie

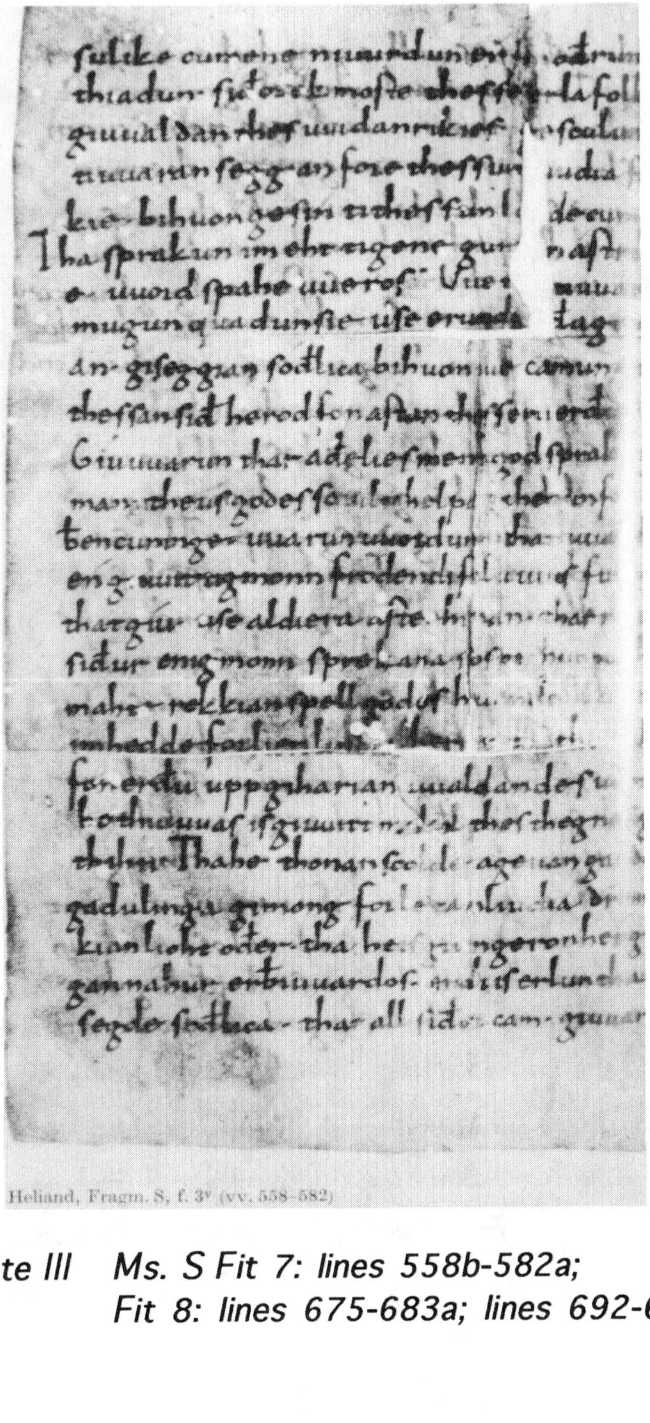

Plate III   Ms. S Fit 7: lines 558b–582a;
Fit 8: lines 675–683a; lines 692–698

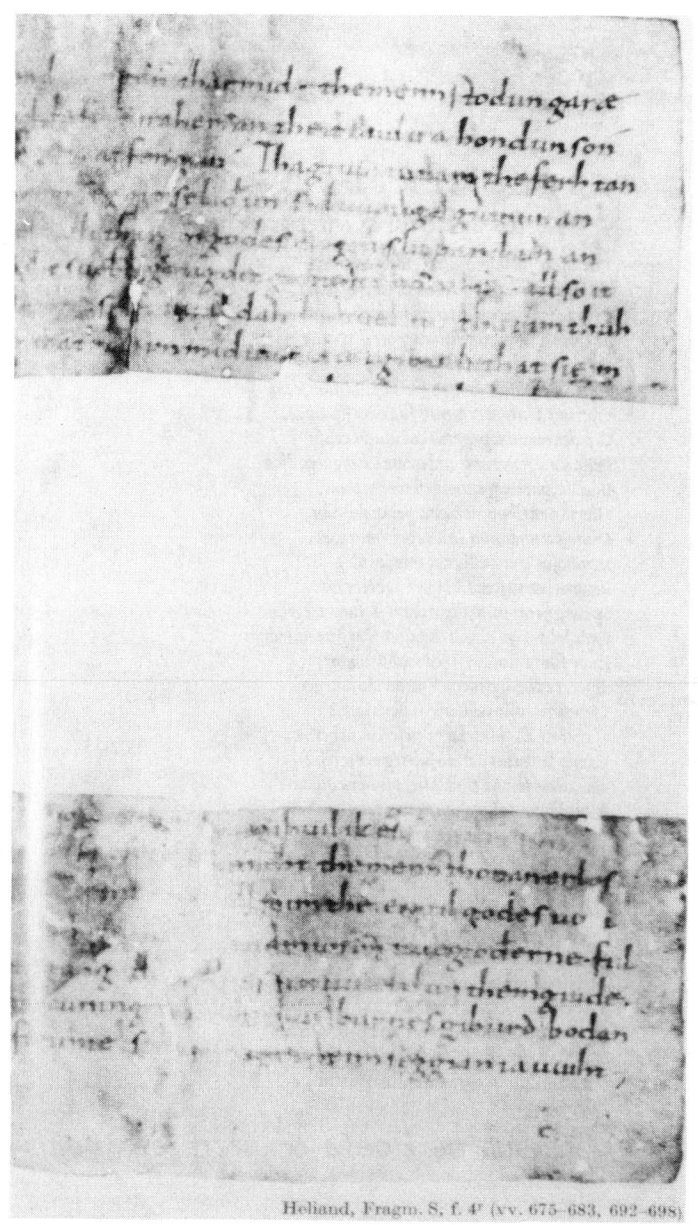

Plate III   Ms. S Fit 7: lines 558b-582a;
Fit 8: lines 675-683a; lines 692-698

94 TESTES VERITATIS TEMPORVM
Versus de Poeta & interprete huius codicis.

Fortunam studiumq; uiri lætosq; labores,
Carmine priuatam delectat promere uitam,
Qui dudum impresso terram uertebat aratro,
Intentus modico, & uictum quærebat in agro,
[Contentus casula fuerat, cui culmea testa,
Postesq; accliues sonipes sua lumina nunquam
Obtriuit, tantum armentis sua cura studebat.]
O fœlix nimium proprio qui uiuere censu
Præualuit, fomitemq; ardentem extinguere diræ
Inuidiæ, pacemq; animi gestare quietam.
Gloria non illum, non alta palatia regum,
Diuitiæ mundi, non dira cupido mouebat.
Inuidiosus erat nulli, nec inuidus illi.
Securus latam scindebat uomere terram.
Spemq; suam in modico totam statuebat agello :
Cum sol per quadrum cœpisset spargere mundum
Luce sua radios, atris cedentibus umbris,
*Menare, pro ducere, uox Italica est. Egerat exiguo paucos * menando iuuencos
Depellens tecto uasti per pascua saltus.
Lætus & attonitus larga pascebat in herba,
Cumq; fatigatus patulo sub tegmine, fessa
Conuictus somno tradidisset membra quieto :
Mox diuina polo resonans uox labitur alto,
O quid agis Vates, cur cantus tempora perdis?
Incipe diuinas recitare ex ordine leges,
Transferre in propriam clarißima dogmata linguam.
Nec mora post tanti fuerat miracula dicti.
Qui prius agricola, mox & fuit ille poeta :
Tunc cantus nimio Vates perfusus amore,
Metrica pòst docta dictauit carmina lingua.
Cœperat à prima nascentis origine mundi,
Quinq; relabentis percurrens tempora secli,
Venit ad aduentum Christi, qui sanguine mundum
Faucibus eripuit tetri miseratus Auerni.

Plate IV Versus de Poeta & interprete huius codicis

Plate V Map of Old Saxon Speech Area

Introduction

The Old Saxon Language: Grammar, Epic Narrative, Linguistic Interference (*OSL*) breaks with traditional grammars of historical languages in several significant ways. It is written for the neophyte as well as for the seasoned scholar. On the one hand, it takes language students by the hand in introducing them to fundamental general linguistic concepts, to which students of historical German and English frequently do not have access. At the same time, it introduces students specializing in non-Germanic linguistics to approach the basic structure of a historical Germanic language. On the other hand, the *OSL* proceeds very much within the best Berkeley tradition to prompt the learning student to intellectually comingle with researching faculty. Thus, many of the most sophisticated research problems enveloping the study of Old Saxon are addressed.

The seasoned researcher, however, will not find the familiar traditional anchors of a historical Germanic grammar. Instead of a standard phonology, morphology, syntax layout in the presentation of the grammar, the *OSL* is largely dictated by cognitive strategies needed to unravel a sentence or larger piece of Old Saxon discourse semantically. In fact, the semantic focus pervades the entire grammar. No claim is made, however, as to the consecutive or simultaneous functioning of given perceptual strategies in the reading of a historical Germanic text.

The *OSL* thus deals early on with the semantic significance of verb ABLAUT morphology (Chap. I), as well as with the pragmatic meaning of the linear placement of the verb in the discourse (Chap. II). Only later (Chap. V and VI) does it address the phonology of Old Saxon, so assiduously pursued in traditional scholarship. Fascinating though it be, (it is by no means neglected in the *OSL*; cf. below), the sound component of Old Saxon is simply not one of the first challenges the reader of the language encounters in seeking the meaning of a piece of text.

The Old Saxon specialist will miss another familiar traditional anchor of a historical grammar, its genetic grounding. It is argued in the *OSL* (Chap. II: 4, Chap. IV: 13.2) that neither the average native Old Saxon nor many of today's readers of an Old Saxon text were or are etymologists, i.e., knowledgeable in the genetic facts of the language; and yet the former were able to communicate and the latter can learn the structure of Old Saxon.

Nowhere is the anchoring in genetic facts more entrenched in historical Germanic than in the inflectional morphology, which is, to be sure, the guts of the grammar. Witness the comfort with which the bulk of the Old Saxon inflectional morphology can be readily synopsized and visualized in three genetically formatted charts (pages xxviii-xxxiii), which emulate the paradigms of traditional grammars such as Gallée 1910 and Holthausen 1921 (the latter distinguishes analogical variants by semicolon).

Although the *OSL* refers to genetic fact as a learning aid, e.g., to distinguish the prehistoric umlaut rule from the historic umlaut rule (Chap. I: 3.3.1, 3.3.2 and Chap. II: 4) or as an articulation device with traditional grammars, e.g., the genetic stem class identifications of the Old Saxon nouns (Chap. II: 11.1, 12.1 and Chap. IV: 14.1, 15.1), it approaches the inflectional morphology as a diachronic synchrony. By diachronic synchrony is meant

Synopsis of Inflectional Morphology

STRONG DECLENSION

NOUNS

		a-stems			ō-stems Fem.	Masc. (short)
		Masc.	Neut. (short)	(long)		
Sg.	N.	dag	graf	word	geba,-e	hugi
	G.	dages,-as	grabes	wordes	geba;-e,-u	huges,-ies
	D.	dage,-a	grabe	worde	gebu,-o;-a	hugi;-ie
	A.	dag	graf	word	geba,-e	hugi
	I.	dagu,-o	grabu	wordu	...	hugi;-iu
Pl.	N.A.	dagos,-as; -a	grabu	word	geba	hugi;-ios
	G.	dago	grabo	wordo	gebono,gebo	hugio,-eo
	D.	dagum,-on	grabum	wordum	gebum,-on	hugium,-ion

STRONG DECLENSION

ADJECTIVES

		Masc.	Neut.	Fem.
Sg.	N.	blind	blind	blind
	G.	blindes,-as	blindes,-as	blindara,-era
	D.	blindum;-omu,-emu	blindum;-omu,-emu	blindaru,-eru
	A.	blindan,-na	blind	blinda,-e
	I.	blindu,-o	blindu,-o	...
Pl.	N.A.	blinde,-a	blind;-e,-a	blinde,-a
	G.	blindaro	blindaro	blindaro
	D.	blindum	blindum	blindum

		WEAK DECLENSION			
i-stems (long)	Fem.	Masc.	Neut.	Fem.
gast	fard	hano,-a	herta,-e	tunga,-e
gastes	ferdi	hanen,-an;-on	herten,-an;-on	tungun,-an,-on
gaste	ferdi;-iu	hanen,-an;-on	herten,-an;-on	tungun,-an,-on
gast	fard	hanon;-an	herta,-e	tunga,-e
...	...	...	...	...
gesti	ferdi	hanon;-un,-an	hertun;-on	tungun,-on,-an
gestio	ferdio	hanono	hertono	tungono
gestium	ferdium	hanon;-un	hertun,-on	tungun,-on,-an

WEAK DECLENSION			'who'	'what'
Masc.	Neut.	Fem.	Masc.	Neut.
blindo,-a	blinda,-e	blinda,-e	hwē, hwie	hwat
blinden,-an;-on	blinden,-an;-on	blindun	hwes	hwes
blindon;-en,-an	blindon;-en,-an	blindun,-on,-an	hwem(u)	hwem(u)
blindon,-an	blinda,-e	blindun,-on,-an	hwena,-e	hwat
...		...	(Neut. Instr. hwī, hwiu;	
blindun,-on,-an	blindun,-on,-an	blindun,-on,-an	hweo, hwȫ)	
blindono	blindono	blindono		
blindum,-un	blindum,-un	blindum,-un		

		Sg.	Dual	Pl.	Third Person	
					PERSONAL	
					Masc.	Neut.
P R O N O U N S	N.	ik, ek	wit	wĭ, we	hĕ, hie; hĭ,	it, et
	G.	mīn	unkero	ūser	is, es	is, es
	D.	mĭ, me	unk	ūs	imu,-o; im	imu,-o; im
	A.	mik, mĭ	unk	ūs	ina,-e	it, et
	N.	thŭ	git	gĭ, ge	sia, sea, sie	siu; sea
	G.	thīn	...	euwar, iuwaro	iro, ira, era	iro, ira
	D.	thĭ	ink	eu, iu	im	im
	A.	thik, thĭ	ink	eu, iu	sia, sea, sie	siu; sea

		u-stems	nd-stems	root-stems
M I S C. N O U N S	Sg. N.	sunu,-o	friund	man(n)
	G.	sunies,-eas,-es	friundes,-as	mannes,-as
	D.	suno,-u;-ie,-i	friunde,-a	man; manne
	A.	sunu,-o	friund	man(n)
	I.	...	...	...
	Pl. NA	suni	friund;-os,-a	man(n); mēn
	G.	sunio,-o	friundo	manno,-a
	D.	sunun,-iun	friundun,-on	mannun,-on

Fem.	Masc.	Neut.	Fem.
	DEMONSTRATIVE		
siu, sia, sea	(these)	thit	thius
ira,-e; iru,-o	theses	theses	thesara;-o,-oro
iru, iro; ira	thesumu;-on	thesumu;-on	thesaru,-o,-oro
sia, sie, sea	thesan,-en	thit(Inst.thius)	thesa
sia, sea, siu	these,-a	thius	thesa,-e
iro,-a, era	thesaro,-oro	thesaro,-oro	thesaro,-oro
im	thesum,-on	thesum,-on	thesum,-on
sia, sea, siu	these,-a	thius	these,-a
r-stems	DEFINITE ARTICLE		
brōðer,-ar	thē̆, thie	that	thiu; thia
brōðer,-ar	thes,-as	thes,-as	thera;-o
brōðer,-ar	them,-u,-o	them,-u,-o	theru,-o;-a
brōðer,-ar	thena, thana	that	thia,-ea,-ie,the
...	...	thiu	...
gibrōðer,-ar	thea,-ia,-ie,thē̆	thiu; thea	thea,-ia,-ie,thē̆
...	thero,-a	thero,-a	thero,-a
gibrōðarum	thē̆m, thē̆n	thē̆m, thē̆n	thē̆m, thē̆n

			Strong	Weak 1 (short)	Weak 1 (long)
VERBS	**Present Tense**	Indic. Sg.1	grīpu,-o	fremmiu	hēliu
		2	grīpis	fremis	hēlis
		3	grīpid,-t;-ð	fremid,-t;-ð	hēlid,-t;-d
		Pl.	grīpad,-t;-ð	fremmiad,-ð	hēliad;-ð
		Subj. Sg.1	grīpe,-a	fremmie	hēlie
		2	grīpes,-as	fremmies	hēlies
		3	grīpe,-a	fremmie	hēlie
		Pl.	grīpen,-an	fremmien	hēlien
	Imp.	Sg.	grīp	fremi	hēli
		Pl.	grīpad,-t,-ð	fremmiad,-ð	hēliad,-ð
		Infin.	grīpan	fremmian	hēlian
		Gerund	grīpanne	fremmianne	hēlianne
		Part.	grīpandi	fremmiandi	hēliandi
	Past Tense	Indic. Sg.1	grēp	fremida,-e	hēlda,-e
		2	gripi	fremides,-as	hēldes,-as
		3	grēp	fremida,-e	hēlda,-e
		Pl.	gripun,-on	fremidun,-on	hēldun,-on
		Subj. Sg.1	gripi,-e	fremidi	hēldi
		2	gripis	fremidis	hēldis
		3	gripi	fremidi	hēldi
		Pl.	gripin	fremidin	hēldin
		Part.	gigripan,-en	gifremid,-t	gihēlid,-t

Weak 2	Preterite-Present	'be'
makon	wēt	bium, biun
makos	wēst	bis(t)
makod,-t;-ð	wēt	is(t)
mako(ia)d,-t;-ð	witun	sind(un)
mako(ie),-gea	witi	sī
makos	witis	sīs
mako(ie)	witi	sī
mako(ia)n	witin	sīn
mako	- - -	wis, wes
mako(ia)d,-t;-ð	- - -	wesað,-t
mako,-(ia)n,-gean	witan	wesan,-en
makonne	witanne	wesanne
mako(gea)ndi	witandi	wesandi
makoda,-e	wissa	was
makodes,-as	- - -	- - -
makoda,-e	wissa	was
makodun,-on	wissun,-on	wārun
makodi	wissi	wāri
makodis	wistis	wāris
makodi	wissi	wāri
makodin	wissi	wārin
gimakod,-t	giwitan	- - -

CLASSES OF STRONG VERBS

	Inf	Pret.1Sg.	Pret.1Pl.	Past.Part.	Pres.3Sg.
I	grīpan	grēp	gripun	gigripan	grīpid
II	biodan	bōd	budun	gibodan	biudid
	lūkan	lōk	lukun	gilokan	lūkid
III	bindan	band	bundun	gibundan	bindid
	helpan	halp	hulpun	giholpan	hilpid
IV	beran	bar	bārun	giboran	birid
V	geban	gaf	gābun	gigeban	gibid
VI	faran	fōr	fōrun	gifaran	ferid
VII	haldan	held	heldun	gihaldan	heldid
	lātan	lēt	lētun	gilātan	lātid
	hētan	hēt	hētun	hētan	hētid
	hrōpan	hriop	hriopun	gehrōpan	hrōpid

Introduction

ongoing variation and/or change within the Old Saxon language era (Chap. II: 4).

The critical difference in traditional inflectional morphological approaches and in that espoused for the Old Saxon data in the *OSL* is that with the latter approach the Old Saxon inflectional morphology emerges typologically primarily as a base form inflection rather than as a stem inflection in the sense of Wurzel (1987: 64). Case and number in Old Saxon noun inflection proceed from the nominative singular of the noun, which is the fundamental identifying form (FIF) of the noun. Old Saxon nouns, with few exceptions, display a nominative singular base in ø (Chap. III: 11.2.1 and 12.2, 12.2.1; Chap. IV: 14.2, 14.2.1 and 15.2). The price paid for attainment of a generalized base inflection in ø in the feminine strong noun (Chap. IV: 14.1) and in the feminine and neuter weak noun and adjective (Chap. IV: 15.1; Chap. VIII: 26.1.3) is the introduction of a subtractive feature V̶ (barred vowel), whereby the final vowel of the FIF syncopates in given oblique cases and numbers.

Ahistorical as well is the presentation of the sounds of Old Saxon in the *OSL* (Chap. V and VI). The genetic provenance of each sound is not traced; rather the phonological space it occupies within the sound system, as hypothesized for *Heliand* and *Genesis* ninth/tenth century Old Saxon, is determined. An Old Saxon sound occupies a relative position within a sonority continuum (Chap. V: 17.2) which is based on various types of evidence, in particular, the graphemic evidence (Chap. V: 16).

On the one hand, traditional grammars, e.g., Holthausen 1921 or Gallée 1910, attempt to harness the rampant graphic variation characteristic of this Old Saxon sound evidence through genetic derivation. On the other hand, a more recent treatment of phonology such as that of Klein 1985 extracts phonemes at the cost of intertwining the relationships among the graphs, and accordingly the phones of the system.

Illustrative of this issue is the allographic/allophonic swarming evident in the three distinct categories posited by Klein (1985: 1076) as the Old Saxon phonemes /iu, ia, ę̄/. The *OSL*, while recognizing the phoneme /ę̄/ (Chap. VI: 19.4.22), configurates it with the diphthong represented by graphic <ie>, which in turn configurates with <ia> (Chap. VI: 19.4.31). Just as the sounds of Old Saxon can be scaled on a sonority continuum, so the graphs of Old Saxon can be considered interrelated and, indeed, in scalar relationship. Observe in the chart (page xxxvii) a given set of graph/digraph data (with reliance on statistics from Page 1952) for nine Old Saxon words, three each traditionally assigned to /iu, ia, ę̄/, respectively:

Introduction

xxxvii

liuhtian 'light'	u 1C		iu 3M 2C	io 1M	eo 1C				
sniumo 'quickly'			iu 7M 7C	io 1C				i 1C	
liudi 'people'	u 1C	eu 1M	iu 110M 120C	io 2C	eo 2C				
thiod 'nation'			iu 2C	io 73M 61C	eo 8M 14C	ie 24C	ia 3M		
liof 'dear'				io 27M 28C	eo 8M 3C	ie 13C	ia 2M	i 1C	
hlier 'cheek'					eo 1M	ie 2C		ea 1M	
mēda 'reward'					eo 1C	ie 11C			e 10M 2C
hier 'here'						ie 135C		i 36M 6C	e 85M 12C
thĕ̄/thie 'the'						ie M some C many	ea M some	i C few	e M many C some

| u | eu | iu | io | eo | ie | ia | ea | i | e |

The data of the three subsets evolve a continuum which is cognitively a center-periphery schema. Central to the series or network is the <eo> area where the three categories actually overlap. Chaining the family resemblance outward to the left shows but one feature difference, raising or lowering of one of the digraph components <eo, io, iu, eu, u> of *inliuhtian, sniumo, liudi*, with the highest frequency member <iu> central to this first subset or subseries. The subseries extension to <i> is a somewhat spurious metonymic/synecdochic extension. The broadest digraph subset is the <iu, io, eo, ie, ia, ea, i> subseries of *thiod, liof, hlier* with highest frequency in the <io, eo, ie> range as central. This second subseries could show extension by one feature, but for <eo> to <ie>. If <ie> and <ea> were interchanged, the family resemblance would be intact, but notice the frequency of <ea> for this second subset. The fact that the <io> subseries extends better to the right is significant in sharing space with subset three. Subseries three digraphs chain well enough, although this subseries of *mēda, hier, thie/thĕ* would pattern better with <ie> at the center with <e>. On the other hand, if <ie> stays as originally shown, then it, along with <eo> and <io>, becomes central to combined subsets two and three, reflective of mutual encroachment on one another's space, although they do not resemble one another well yet in *Heliand* and *Genesis* Old Saxon, with <eo> beside <ie>, as noted above. However, the resemblance of <ie> to <eo> and <io> assures diphthongization for OS <ie>, certainly in ms. C (cf. Chap. V: 19.3.3; Rauch forthcoming a).

Chapter VII of the *OSL* represents the first substantial syntactic component in an existing Old Saxon grammar, while Old Saxon lexical derivation and compounding are addressed in Chapter VIII. The *OSL* is self-contained in its inclusion of ample selected readings from the Old Saxon *Heliand*, *Genesis* and minor documents, as well as selected parallel Old High German and Old English passages. The Old English *Caedmon* text interlaces thematically with the Latin Prefaces to the *Heliand* (cf. Chap. VI: 19.2). Although the *OSL* provides a Latin glossary, as well as Old Saxon, Old High German, and Old English glossaries for the selected passages, the reader may wish to refer to Magoun 1948 for an English translation of the Latin Prefaces.

Permission has been granted to reprint selected readings: from Ferdinand Holthausen, *Altsächsisches Elementarbuch* 2. ed. rev. (1921), published by Carl Winter Universitätsverlag; from Otto Behaghel, *Heliand und Genesis* 8. ed. rev. W. Mitzka (1965), and 9. ed. rev. B. Taeger (1984) published by Max Niemeyer Verlag; from Samuel Moore/Thomas A. Knott, *The Elements of Old English* 10. ed. rev. J. R. Hulbert (1955), published by George Wahr Publishing Co., as well as from Wilhelm Braune/Karl Helm, *Althochdeutsches Lesebuch* 14. ed. rev. E. A. Ebbinghaus (1965), published by Max Niemeyer Verlag. Further permissions were granted: for Plate III, which is reprinted from Bernhard Bischoff, "Die Straubinger Fragmente einer Heliand-Handschrift" in *Beiträge zur Geschichte der deutschen Sprache und Literatur* 101 (1979): 171-180, published by Max Niemeyer Verlag; for Plate IV, reprinted from Irmengard Rauch, "The *Heliand* Versus 5-7 Again" in *Folia Linguistica: Acta Societatis Linguisticae Europaeae* (1968): 39-47, published by Mouton & Co.; for Plate V, reprinted from Joachim Hartig, "86. Soziokulturelle Voraussetzungen und Sprachraum des Altniederdeutschen (Altsächsischen)" in W. Besch et al. ed. *Sprachgeschichte: Ein Handbuch zur Geschichte der deutschen Sprache und ihrer Erforschung* 2/2 (1985) 1069-1074, published by Walter de Gruyter & Co.; Plate V was originally published by Karl Wachholt Verlag in *Niederdeutsch: Sprache und*

Literatur, Eine Einführung, 1: *Sprache* (1973) edited by Jan Goossens.

I am grateful to the John Simon Guggenheim Memorial Foundation and to the National Endowment for the Humanities for their support in my researching and writing of this book, the inaugural volume for the Lang series *Berkeley Models of Grammars*.

Symbols and Abbreviations

{ }	set inclusion
( )	possibility or optional; in paradigm or rule does not signal parentheses
[ ]	phone; semantic/syntactic feature
< >	graph
/ /	phoneme; not to be confused with slash signaling mutually exclusive alternatives
*	nonexistent data; reconstructed data
~	alternating with; alternation
ø	zero
>	becomes
<	comes from
X	any element other than S or Vb
∝	+ or -
acc.	accusative case
adj.	adjective
adv.	adverb
advbl.	adverbial
anom.	anomalous
art.	article
aux.	auxiliary
C	consonant
Co	coda
comp.	complement
conj.	conjunction
cop.	copula(tive)
D	determiner
dat.	dative case
ess.	essive

FD	final devoicing
fem.	feminine gender
FIF	fundamental identifying form
FVb	finite verb
fut.	future
GC	grammatical change
gen.	genitive case
Gmc.	Germanic
hist.	historic(al)
hw	question word
IE	Indo-European
imp.	imperative mood
indic.	indicative mood
inf.	infinitive
instr.	instrumental case
intrans.	intransitive
loc.	locative case
M	modality
masc.	masculine
mod. aux.	modal auxiliary
ms(s).	manuscript(s)
MV	voicing of consonants medially in voiced surrounds
N	nasal consonant
neg.	negative
neut.	neuter gender
Nn	noun
nom.	nominative case
noml	nominal
NP	noun phrase
Nu	nucleus
O	object
OE	Old English
OF	Old Frisian
OHG	Old High German
OS	Old Saxon

Symbols and Abbreviations

OSL	*The Old Saxon Language: Grammar, Epic Narrative, Linguistic Interference*
On	onset
p.	person
part.	participle
pat.	patient
perf.	perfect
pl.	plural number
posiv.	positive
PP	prepositional phrase
prehist.	prehistoric
prep.	preposition
pres.	present (tense)
pret.	preterite (tense)
pron.	pronoun
qual	qualifier
R	resonant
S	subject
sent.	sentence
sg.	singular number
SScR	syntactic subcategorization rule
str.	strong
subj.	subjunctive mood
subst.	substantive
SuR	suprasegmental rule
σ	syllable
trans.	transitive
V	vowel
Vb	verb
voc.	vocative case
VP	verb phrase
wk.	weak

Chapter One

Reading an Old Saxon Text;
Early Cognitive Decisions;
The Verb in the Lexicon;
The Strong Verb Dictionary Finder Chart

1. The Old Saxon Text: Narrative Discourse

The primary data for Old Saxon (OS) is the *Heliand*, a ninth/tenth century narrative epic with 5983 alliterative lines extant; and the *Genesis*, a ninth century narrative epic with 337 alliterative lines extant (cf. further Chapter VI: 19.1). Accordingly, the reader has at his/her disposal a substantial, coherent text whose macro-structure s/he cognizes through successive semantic and pragmatic decisions. The reader thereby discovers the narrative propositional and modal content of the macro-text. S/he analyzes the interrelatedness of cognitive constituents such as topicalization, reference, sequence. Finally, the reader concentrates on individual sentences and their immediate connectedness, i.e., the micro-text. Again s/he engages in a series of cognitive decisions ultimately focussing on the syntactic, morphological, and phonological components of the grammar; again s/he is processing propositional or inferential content. While the discourse of the macro-structure entails mainly text linguistics, the discourse of the micro-structure entails largely sentence linguistics. Together these elements comprise the grammar of a language. (On the distinction between and among the concepts text, discourse, and narrative see Rauch 1981, 1983a.)

2. The OS Sentence, Grammatical Constituents, Lexicon

Basic to the entire grammar is the word, the linguistic entity which plays a major role in expressing propositional content of both the macro- and microstructure. For the reader of a second language, be it a contemporary or a historical language, immediate although partial access to the words of the language is the lexicon. The lexicon in the *OSL* is limited to data occurring in the selected readings to this grammar.

The OS proposition at the sentence level consists of a relation or predicator and its argument(s). Consider, e.g., the OS sentence

(1) *Ic is engil bium.*
'I am his angel.'

The relation is '(am) (his) angel' and the argument is 'I' (cf. Chap. III: 9). The reading, or the understanding, of the semantic and pragmatic content of the proposition entails making decisions about the linear and nonlinear syntax of the sentence. While the linear syntax deals largely with word order, the nonlinear syntax includes a predicate constituent, a modality constituent, and an argument constituent (cf. Chap. III: 9). These three constituents in turn subsume other parts of the grammar such as the morphology and the phonology.

The reader makes decisions concerning the linear and nonlinear syntax in conjunction with decisions for identifying the lexicon. An OS word is listed in the lexicon in its fundamental identifying form (FIF), together with its grammatical specifications and glosses. A word such as *engil* occurring syntagmatically, i.e., in a narrative chain, as in the sentence above, is paradigmatically homophonous, i.e., with its FIF, which is also *engil*, in the lexicon. The word *bium*, on the other hand, requires decisions on the part of the reader whereby s/he comes to associate it with its FIF *wesan* in the lexicon. The word *bium* is suppletive relative to its FIF, i.e., although *bium* shares the gloss 'be' with *wesan*, its form is quite different from *wesan*.

3. The Verb in the Lexicon

The predicate constituent normally houses a verb form; the search for the FIF of the verb is one of the earliest decision-making processes facing the reader of OS.

3.1 The Fundamental Identifying Form (FIF) of the Verb

The OS verb is composed morphologically of a stem plus an ending (cf. Chap. II: 7). It is listed in the lexicon in a FIF, the infinitive, which is signalled by the suffix *-an*, *-en*, or *-n* added to the verb stem, thus, e.g., *niman* 'take,' *nerian* 'save.' The anomalous verbs *dōn* 'do,' *gān* 'go,' *stān* 'stand,' and verb stems ending in *-Co-*, e.g., *makon* 'make' (known genetically as class 2 weak verbs; cf. Chap. II: 8.1), have an *-n* suffix.

The infinitive is the fundamental identifying form of all verbs listed in the lexicon. In order to arrive at the lexical meaning, the reader of OS must be able to extrapolate a paradigmatic infinitive form from the syntagmatic finite form found in the text. S/he may encounter an infinitive form syntagmatically in conjunction with a finite form or as a gerund (cf. Chap. VIII: 26.1.4). This Chapter, however, considers the infinitive for its paradigmatic role as the FIF of the verb in the lexicon.

3.2 Strong, Weak, Modal Auxiliary, Anomalous Verb Types

The lexicon indicates each verb by (Vb); its type is marked as strong (str.), weak (wk.), modal auxiliary (mod. aux.), or anomalous (anom.). The designation anomalous is used instead of the term athematic and/or irregular; modal auxiliary replaces the traditional term preterite-present (cf. Chap. II: 8.2.2, 8.2.3). The traditional terminologies strong and weak verb are retained in many synchronic grammars, as they are here. This designation is based on the formation of the preterite tense. Verbs which form their preterite by a dental suffix are termed weak; verbs which do not are termed strong. The modal auxiliary as well as the anomalous verbs *dōn* 'do' and *willian* 'will' have weak preterites, while the anomalous verb *wesan* 'be' has a strong preterite. Weak verbs are subcategorized by the sign 1, 2, 3 in the lexicon, reflective of their genetic subclasses (cf. Chap. II: 8.2). The subcategories are dispensable in a synchronic grammar; it must, however, be remembered that the stem form of class 2 weak ends in *-o* with an infinitive suffix of merely *-n*. Strong verbs are subcategorized into seven classes (I through VII), a classification indispensable to synchronic and genetic grammars of OS (cf. sect. 3.3.2 below).

3.3 Strong Verb ABLAUT

Once the decision has been made that a syntagmatic form is paradigmatically a verb as signalled by its present or preterite suffix inflection, decisions concerning its lexical meaning are initiated by recourse to the lexicon or glossary. If the syntagmatic or finite form is not identifiable with an infinitive in the lexicon, it is likely that the finite form belongs to a verb with vocalic root alternation, called ABLAUT. ABLAUT is a characteristic sign of strong verbs, i.e., those verbs which do not form their preterites by means of a dental suffix. Since OS is primarily a suffix language, the suffix can identify a verb as weak or strong, with the exception of the set of eleven modal auxiliary verbs, which must be memorized (cf. Chap. II: 8.2.2). While a weak verb form will usually be read, excepting the modifications described in Chap. II: 8.2.1, as having a root identical with the root of its infinitive and hence its FIF in the lexicon, a strong finite verb form will usually be read as having an altered root in its FIF in the lexicon. Such root alternation is not without limits and control (cf. sect. 3.3.2 below). The alternations can be systematized and conveniently memorized in seven ABLAUT sets. Most Germanic (Gmc.) grammars treat the strong verb in terms of these seven sets, in which syntagmatic or finite forms of a strong verb in a text can be extrapolated from any one of four possible fundamental alternating vowel forms (ABLAUT): (a) the infinitive, (b) 1.3 person preterite singular, (c) preterite plural, and (d) the preterite participle. The infinitive fundament (a) provides the root for itself (cf.

Chap. VIII: 26.1.4); the present tense indicative (cf. Chap. II: 8.1) and subjunctive (cf. Chap. VIII: 29.2); the imperative (cf. Chap. VIII: 29.1); and the present participle (cf. Chap. VIII: 26.1.4). The 1.3 preterite singular (b) provides the base only for the indicative (cf. Chap. VIII: 28.1). The preterite plural (c) provides the base for the plural and the second person singular indicative (cf. Chap. VIII: 28.1), as well as for the preterite subjunctive of all persons and numbers (cf. Chap. VIII: 29.2). The preterite participle (d) provides the base for itself (cf. Chap. VIII: 26.1.4).

3.3.1 The Strong Verb Dictionary Finder Chart

Since the change in root vowel (ABLAUT), minus any prefix or suffix, would effect a change in meaning, e.g., (a) *nim-*, (b) *nam-*, (c) *nām-*, (d) *num-* (cf. set IV), the alternation is known as a morphophonemic alternation, i.e., the meaningful alternation of a phoneme within a morpheme. Synchronically, verb ABLAUT serves to signal secondarily (the inflectional endings being the primary sign) tenses, moods, persons, and numbers, thus showing OS to be essentially a suffix language.

Finite or syntagmatic verb forms occur then with any of the vowels in the chart below, termed the strong verb dictionary finder chart. Column (a) contains the FIF by which the verb is listed in a lexicon; it is the point of reference for the lexical meaning of any syntagmatic verb form with vowels occurring in (a), (b), (c), or (d).

Verb ABLAUT; Finder Chart: 3.3 - 3.3.2

	(a)	(b)	(c)	(d)
I	ī	ē̄	i	i
II	iu/io//ū	ǭ	u	o
III	e/i	a	u	u/o
IV	e/i	a	ā	u/o
V	e/i	a	ā	e
VI	a	ō	ō	a
VII	a//ā//ę̄	e//ę̄	e//ę̄	a//ā//ę̄
	ǭ//ō̄	io	io	ǭ//ō̄

A few salient characteristics of these seven sets will reduce the burden on the reader's memory. The root consonants following the root vowel in the four fundamental forms of set III tend to be a resonant (R = *l, r, m, n*) plus another consonant (C); set IV tends to have the root vowel followed by a resonant only, in all four fundamental forms; set V, which displays root vowels common with sets III and IV, has a root vowel followed by a non-resonant consonant in its four fundamental forms. The single slash vowel alternatives in sets II, III, IV, and V are synchronic reflexes of a genetic phonological rule whereby the high vowel *u* of the root is lowered to *o* before a mid or low vowel *a, e, o* unless a nasal consonant (N) intervenes, and the mid vowel of the root *e* is raised to *i* before a high vowel *i, u,* or a *j*, as well as before an intervening nasal consonant. This genetic phonological rule is called a prehistoric umlaut rule in which the vowel of a root syllable is mutated by the vowel of a following syllable. The same genetic rule would allow the collapse of columns (c) and (d) of sets II and III. The distinctions $\bar{e̞} : \bar{e̝}$ and $\bar{o̞} : \bar{o̝}$ (cf. Chap. VI: 19.4.22-25), indicated in neither the readings nor the lexicon, are collapsed for the sake of recognition simplicity to $\bar{e}$ and $\bar{o}$, thus yielding a revised strong verb dictionary finder chart with examples, as follows:

Verb ABLAUT; Finder Chart: 3.3 - 3.3.2

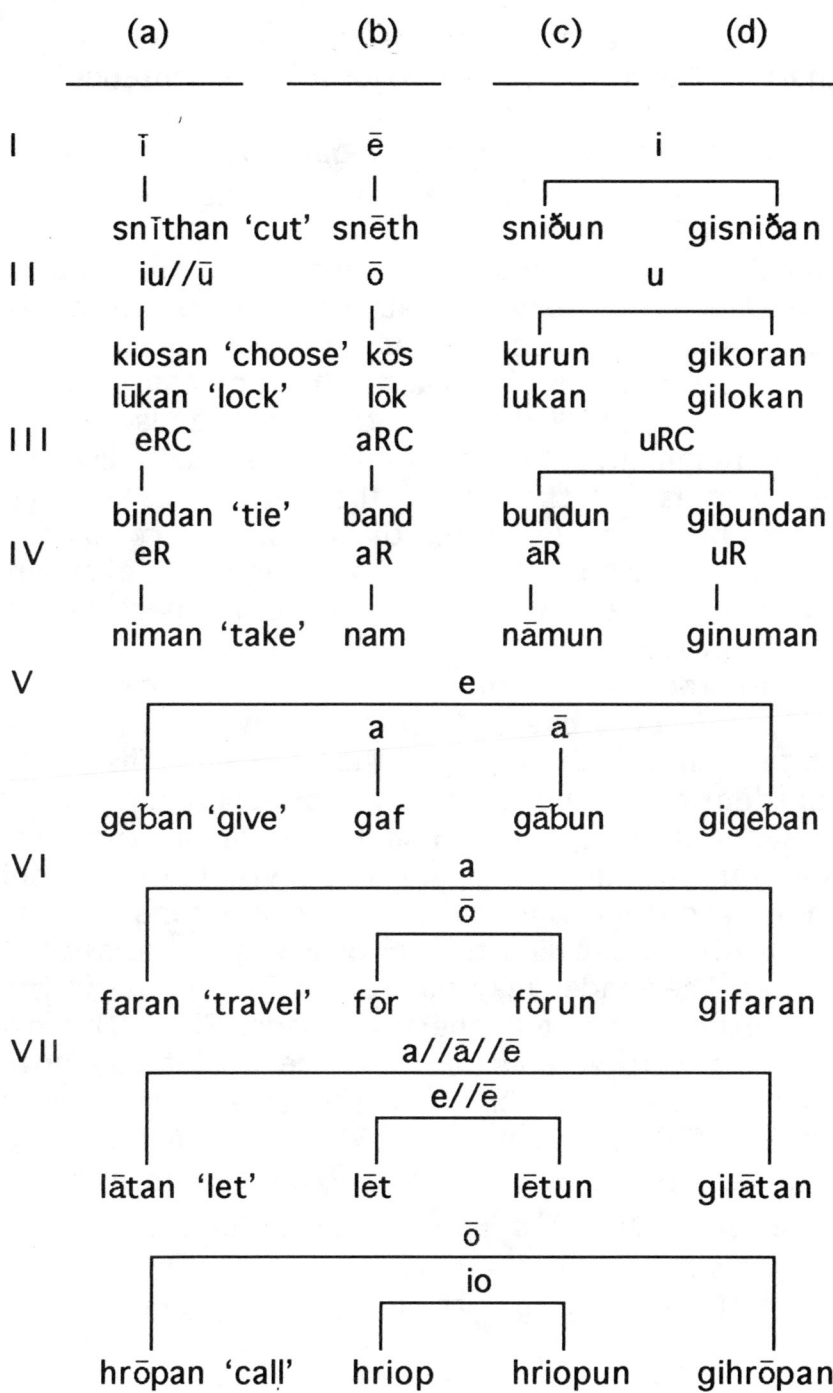

The application of this strong verb dictionary finder chart is illustrated in the following OS sentence.

(2) *Gaf it is jungarun forð.*
'He gave it to His disciples.'

Since the unmarked word order of the declarative sentence in OS is verb-first (Chap. II: 6.1), the reader may initially consider *gaf* as a possible verb form. S/he observes that the vowel *a* of the root can occur in sets III, IV, V, VI, or VII. Because the *a* of *gaf* is not followed by a resonant, the reader eliminates sets III and IV as possibilities for the FIF of the verb in ascertaining its lexical meaning. By means of the dictionary finder chart, i.e., the shape of the root vowel and its following root consonant, the reader has reduced his/her decisions to three possibilities.

In order to narrow these possibilities, additional rules can be observed which apply to the dictionary finder chart. Genetically, other vocalic characteristics for identifying the vocalic morphophonemic alternation (ABLAUT) are quite prominent; however, their reflexes are not strongly transparent or visible synchronically. Other accompanying consonant characteristics can also be helpful in deciding the FIF of a syntagmatic word such as *gaf*. The reader may opt for an FIF **gafan*, which s/he will observe is not in the OS lexicon. Since the existent *gaf* is a word without a suffix, the reader can now have recourse to a synchronic consonantal rule of final devoicing (FD) (cf. Chap. VI: 19.5). The FD of the consonants *b, ƀ, d, ð, g, ɣ, j* to *p, f, t, þ, k, x, ç* suggests to the reader a FIF *geƀan* which is listed in the lexicon as belonging to set V and having the meaning 'give.' The signs of the ABLAUT and FD in *gaf* are merely phonological indications of its identity. These indications, as well as the syntactic indication of first-place position of *gaf* in the sentence, are accompanied by morphological (zero suffix, cf. Chap. VIII: 28.1) and pragmatic indications (narrative discourse features, cf. Chap. II: 1.4), to corroborate the reader's decision that 'gave' is the relation in the sentence in which the arguments are 'he,' 'it,' and 'disciples' (cf. Chap. III: 9).

The FD rule should not be confused with another consonant alternation that the reader may observe in all but set IV of the seven strong verb classes. It is a voiced:voiceless consonant alternation, called grammatical change (GC), which can be observed on the dictionary finder chart in the sample words for sets I and II in the forms of columns (a) (b) on the one hand, and the forms of columns (c) (d), on the other hand. The fact that the consonant *th* alternates with the consonant *ð* of of set I, and that the consonant *s* alternates with the consonant *r* of set II is due to a phonological genetic rule known as Verner's Law. In other examples of GC, the consonant *h* alternates with the consonant *g* or *w*, and the consonant *f* alternates with the consonant *ƀ*. Synchronically, GC, as does ABLAUT, serves to signal secondarily (the inflections are the primary signs) tenses, moods, persons, and numbers; it, too, is therefore a morphophonemic alternation. The term grammatical change, without recourse to linguistic genetics, identifies the alternation, i.e., there is no implication as to the direction of the change synchronically. There is also no synchronic phonological distinction between, e.g., a GC *f* and a FD *f*, nor between a GC *ƀ* and a *ƀ* which obtains through the OS rule of medial voicing of fricatives (MV), which voices *f, þ, s, x* to *ƀ, ð, z, ɣ* (cf. Chap. VI: 19.5).

3.3.2 Variation in the Seven Strong Verb Sets

The ABLAUT vowel, the root shape, (e.g., whether the root ends in R), the effects of the prehistoric umlaut rule, GC, and FD can be obscured primarily by one or more of the following factors: historical umlaut (cf. Chap. I: 3.3.2), variation in OS graphemics (Chap. VI: 19.4), MV, and/or more general language factors such as analogy, megadialect interference, scribal error. On occasion factors are only mere conjecture since the OS language of the *Heliand* and *Genesis* texts dates from a millennium ago (cf. Chap. VI: 18 for types of evidence).

Historical umlaut refers to the palatalization of a root vowel *a, ā, o, ō, u, ū,* generally by an *i* or *j* in the suffix of the word. MV is the opposite partner to the FD rule in that *f, p, s, x* are voiced internally in voiced surrounds (cf. Chap. VI: 19.5). Nevertheless, graphic confusion can obscure the functioning of a rule, e.g., *lesan* 'read,' set IV col. (a) does not indicate graphically the MV of *s*. Variations in the seven strong verb sets as evidenced in the *Heliand* and *Genesis* texts include those discussed immediately below. (For evidence from minor documents cf. Gallée 1910, Holthausen 1921):

Set I: ABLAUT: *ē* (col b.) occurs rarely as *ā, arās* 'arose,' as *ei, skreid* 'went,' (megadialect interference, cf. Chap. VI: 19.3.3), or as *ǣ, arǣs* 'arose' (graphic variation, cf. Chap. VI: 19.4.24).

GC: *w* (col. c) occurs also as *h, farlihi* 'gave' (analogy); *ð* (cols. c,d) occurs also as *d, snidi* 'cut,' *giliden* 'went,' as *th, mithun* 'avoided,' *gilithan* 'went' (graphic variation and/or analogy, cf. Chap. VI: 19.4.7, 19.4.8).

FD: *th* (col. b) occurs also as *d, mēd* 'avoid,' as *ð, screð* 'went' (graphic variation and/or analogy, cf. Chap. VI: 19.4.7, 19.4.8).

MV: (col. a) rarely signalled except for *ð* which occurs also as *d, mīdan* 'avoid,' as *th, līthan* 'go' (graphic variation and/or analogy, cf. Chap. VI: 19.4.7, 19.4.8).

Set II: ABLAUT: *io* (col. a) occurs also as *eo, teoh* 'pull' 2 sg. imp. (graphic variation, cf. Chap. V: 19.4.31), as *iu, tiuh* 2 sg. imp. (prehist. umlaut by analogy), as *eu, hreuwan* 'rue' (constrained prehist. umlaut by analogy to 2 sg. ind., cf. Chap. I: 3.3.1); *ō* (col. b) occurs as *au* in *hrau* 'rued' (constrained monophthongization, cf. Chap. V: 19.3.3).

GC: *g*, graph <g>, (col c) occurs also as *h, tuhin* 'reared' (analogy).

FD: *h* (col b) occurs also as *g*, graph <g> *bidrōg* 'deceived' (analogy); *t* (col. b) occurs also as *d, hlōd* 'grew' (analogy and/or graphic variation, cf. Chap. VI: 19.4.7).

MV: rarely signalled; *b* (col. a) occurs as *w* in *hiowandi* 'lamenting.'

Set III: ABLAUT: *i* (col. a) occurs also as *e, sweltid* 'dies' (analogy and/or phonetic, cf. Chap. VI: 19.4.20); *e* (col. a) occurs also as *i, hilf* 'help' 2 sg. imp. (prehist. umlaut by analogy); *u* (col. c) occurs also as *a, wardun* 'became' (analogy); *u* (col. c) also occurs as *i, wirði* 'became' (historical umlaut, cf. Chap. V: 19.4.21).

GC: *ð* (col. c) occurs also as *d, wurdun* 'became,' as *th, wurthan* 'became'; *ð* (col. d) occurs also as *d, fundan* 'found' (graphic variation and/or analogy, cf. Chap. VI: 19.4.7); g (cols. c,d) occurs as *h, bifulhan, bifolhen* 'commanded' (analogy).

FD: *f* (col. b) occurs also as *ƀ, huarƀ* 'went'; *th* (col. b) occurs also as *d, ð, t, ward, warð, wart* 'became'; *h* (col. b) occurs also as *g*, graph <g>, *gibarg* 'hid' (graphic variation and/or analogy, cf. Chap. VI: 19.4.15).

MV: *ð* (col. a) occurs as *d, th, werdan, werthan* 'become' (graphic and/or analogy, cf. Chap. VI: 19.4.7, 19.4.8).

Root shape: *findan* 'find' (col. a) occurs also as *fīdan*; *antfand* 'perceive' (col. b) occurs also as a quasi weak preterite *antfunda*. Geminate root consonants tend to simplex in final position (col. b) *bigann* and *bigan*. A small subset has the resonant before the root vowel, thus *bregdan* 'weave,' *brestan* 'bust,' *fregnan* 'ask'; *bifelhan* 'command' (col. a) occurs also as *bifelahan* (epenthesis, cf. Chap. VIII: 27); *befilliu* 1 sg. pres. occurs.

Set IV: ABLAUT: *e* (col. a) occurs as *u kuman* 'come'; *i* (col. a) occurs also as *e neman* 'take,' *u* (col. d) occurs also as *o binomana* 'taken' (graphic, cf. Chap. VI: 19.4.21).

Verb ABLAUT; Finder Chart: 3.3 - 3.3.2

GC, FD, MV not applicable to resonants which characterize set IV.

Root shape: *kuman* 'come' has initial cluster *qu-* (cols. b,c) *quam, quāmun* 'came'. A small subset has resonant before the root vowel followed by *k*, thus *sprekan* 'speak,' *wrekan* 'avenge;' with *k* only *stekan* 'pierce'.

Set V: ABLAUT: *e* (col. a) occurs also as *i*, *giƀ* 'give' 2 sg. imp. (prehist. umlaut by analogy).

GC: *w* (cols. c, d) occurs also as *h*, *gisāhun* 'saw,' *gisehan* 'seen' and as *ø*, *gisaun, giseen* (analogy and *h-* drop, cf. Chap. VI: 19.4.17); *ð* (col. c) occurs also as *d, th quādun, quāthun* 'said' (graphic variation and/or analogy, cf. Chap. VI: 19.4.8).

FD: *th* (col. b) occurs as *d, ð, t, quad, quað, quat* 'said,' also in sandhi with *he* 'he' as *t(h), quathe* (graphic variation and/or cliticization, cf. Chap. VI: 19.4.8); *f* (col. b) occurs also as *ƀ, giƀ* 'give' 2 sg. imp. (graphic variation, cf. Chap. VI: 19.4.3).

MV: rarely signalled except for *ð* (col. a), which occurs also as *d, th, queden, quethan* 'say' (graphic variation, cf. Chap. VI: 19.4.8).

Root shape: *h-* drop can occur in *sehan, sean* 'see' (cf. Chap. VI: 19.4.17). A small subset consisting of *liggian* 'be,' *sittian* 'sit,' and *biddian* 'ask' have an infinitive stem ending in *i* and they inflect in the 2.3 sg. pres. indic. tense, for which the fundamental form is col. a, with a simplex root consonant *bidis* 'ask,' *sitit* 'sits'; a single root consonant is also projected for their sg. imp. (not attested). *wesan* 'be' has an anomalous present indicative (cf. Chap. II: 8.2.3) and present optative (cf. Chap. VIII: 29.2.1); it has no preterite participle (col. d).

Set VI: ABLAUT: *a* (col. a) occurs also as *e*, *afhebbian* 'raise' (hist. umlaut, cf. Chap. I: 3.3.2); *ō* (cols. b,c) occurs also as *uo*, *huof* 'raised,' *asluogin* 'murdered' (dialect, cf. Chap. VI: 19.3.2).

GC: *ƀ* (cols. c, d) occurs also as *b*, *afhōbi*, *afhaben* 'raised up' (graphic variation, cf. Chap. VI: 19.4.3).

FD: *f* (col. b) occurs also as *ƀ*, *ahuoƀ* 'raised up'; *h* occurs as *g*, graph <g>, *log* 'blamed' (graphic variation and/or analogy, cf. Chap. VI: 19.4.15).

MV: *ff* (col. a) occurs also as *bb afhebbian* 'raise up' (geminate *b* is not only voiced but also stopped, cf. Chap. VI: 19.4.2).

Root shape: *h-* drop can occur in *aslahan* (col. a) *aslaan* 'murder' (cf. Chap. VI: 19.4.17). A small subset consisting of *swerian* 'swear,' **hlahhian* 'laugh,' *heffian* 'raise,' **afseffian* 'notice,' **skeppian* 'create,' **steppian* 'step' have an infinitive stem ending in *i* and the latter five inflect in the 2.3 sg. pres. indic. tense, for which the fundamental form is col. a, with a simplex root consonant (2 sg. not attested) *ahabið*

Verb ABLAUT; Finder Chart: 3.3 - 3.3.2 17

'raises up.' A single root consonant is also projected for their sg. imp. (not attested). The verb *standan* 'stand' (col. a) has preterites (cols. b,c) without root *n*, thus *stōd, stōdun* 'stood' although *stuond* (col. b) also occurs.

Set VII: ABLAUT: *a* (col. a) occurs also as *e gengit* 'goes' (hist. umlaut, cf. Chap. I: 3.3.2); *e* or *ē* (cols. b, c) occurs also as *ie, fieng* 'caught,' *hieldin* 'held' (dialect, cf. Chap VI: 19.3.2), as *i, anwillun* 'streamed out' (megadialect interference, cf. Chap. VI: 19.3.3). Instead of *ō* (col. a) *io, eo, ea* occur in *griotandi* 'crying' (graphic and/or phonetic, cf. Chap. VI: 19.4.31); *io* (cols. b, c) occurs also as *eo, ie, hreop, hriep* 'called' (graphic variation and/or phonetic, cf. Chap. VI: 19.4.31).

FD: Questionable *k* occurs as *g, feng* 'caught' (cf. graphemics and phonology, Chap. VI: 19.4.14).

MV: *ð* (col. a) occurs also as *d, skēdan* 'separate' (graphic variation and/or analogy, cf. Chap. VI: 19.4.8, 19.4.7).

Root shape: *gihauwan* 'hit' (col. a) has a preterite *heu* (col. b) with *w-* drop (cf. Chap. VI: 19.4.5). Geminate root consonants also occur simplex (col. b) *fel* 'fill' (graphic and phonetic, cf. Chap. VI: 19.4.11). The verb *fāhan* 'catch' (col. a) has fundamental forms (b), (c), (d) with root *n feng, fengun, gifangan*; **hāhan* 'hang' (col. a) has form (d) with root *n bihangan. wōpian* 'cry' and *sāian* 'sow' have an infinitive stem ending in *i; sāian* 'sow' (col. a) also occurs as *sehan* (hist.

umlaut, glide switch, cf. Chaps. I: 3.3.2, VI: 19.4.16, 19.4.17). *obarsāian* 'sow over' (col. a) has a preterite *obarseu* and a weak preterite *sāida* (cf. Chap. VIII: 28.2).

Chapter Two

After the First Search; Diachronic Synchrony and Linguistic Explanation; Linear Syntax: Independent Sentence; Pragmatic Strategies; Nonlinear Micro-syntax: Morphology; Inflection of Verb Present Tense

4. Linguistic Generalization in Diachronic Synchrony

In observing a sentence such as

(3) *Hwat quiðis thu umbi gōdon?*
'What do you say about a Good One?'

the reader of the OS text sets out to identify the FIFs of the words signalling the relation or predicator and the argument(s) of the proposition. The decisions confronting the reader in a first lexical search for the FIF of a verb form, commonly included in the predicate constituent, were outlined in Chap. I: 3. Following those suggested guidelines for verb identification, the reader will have concluded that *quiðis* is listed in the lexicon as the FIF *queðan* with the meaning 'speak.' The difference in root vowel *e* and *i* need not be memorized, since the reader expects or can predict this difference from the rule which allowed him/her to conclude the paradigmatic *queðan* from the syntagmatic *quiðis*, namely the prehistoric umlaut rule which functions in strong verb set V, column (a). Such a rule is a generalization which affects many other words not only of strong verb set V, but also of other verb sets, and, in fact, of other word types, e.g., nouns. The utility of a linguistic generalization for the reader of the OS text is then beyond doubt.

The results of the prehistoric umlaut rule were described (Chap. I: 3.3.1) as "synchronic reflexes of a genetic phonological rule whereby the high vowel *u* of the root is lowered to *o* before a mid or low vowel *a, e, o* unless a nasal consonant (N) intervenes, and the mid vowel of the root *e* is raised to *i* before a high vowel *i, u*, or a *j*, as well as before an intervening nasal consonant." Two questions are immediately pertinent to the formulation of such a generalization: Why is this rule designated as prehistoric? and secondly, Why does it appear to indicate a process? The reader of the OS text approaches the data as belonging to one fixed time frame in history, i.e., ninth/tenth century. S/he assumes s/he is learning a certain language of a certain time; this is the implication in the term synchronic. The reader, accordingly, does not need to view the data in terms of ancestry or descendants. Doing so, however, is what is usually meant by the term diachronic. In the *OSL* a stand is taken for a **diachronic synchrony** inasmuch as the concept of a time frame in which language data are static is a fiction. Synchronic variation entails diachrony, i.e., process or change at least from one linguistic moment to the next. The term diachronic, then, in the *OSL* is appropriate to any meaningful data change or variation, regardless of whether it is within the OS time frame, prior to it, or subsequent to it. Accordingly, the term diachronic as equated solely with an ancestor stage of OS is dysfunctional in the *OSL*.

Diachronic Synchrony: 4

Older language stages for OS are usually proposed as (North-) West Germanic, Germanic, Indo-European, Indo-Hittite. Instead of designating these languages as diachronic relative to OS, the *OSL* terms them as genetic since diachrony is also inherent in OS without recourse to ancestry or descendants. The designation genetic has a second compelling reason: it does not necessarily imply a parent relationship between, e.g., OS and Indo-European; genetic can also be considered a sibling relationship. Usually the labels (North-) West Germanic, Germanic, Indo-European, Indo-Hittite are understood as Proto- or parent languages which are reconstructed hypothetically upon data from the sibling members of the Proto- set. Such a Proto-language generally implies an earlier linguistic data time frame. Since it is a hypothetical construct, a Proto-language is, however, devoid of real time and, in fact, actual linguistic data. Trubetzkoy (1939) suggests that Proto-languages are fictions, and that it is more reasonable to view actual sibling languages as related through a set of common characteristics or features, rather than by a common nonexistent but hypothetical parent. An exception to this might be the case of Proto-Romance, if Vulgar Latin can be construed as the embodiment of Proto-Romance, since Vulgar Latin does indeed have linguistic flesh and blood. In the case of OS, the language features which it shares with its immediate siblings, e.g., Old High German and Old English, to comprise a West-Germanic Proto-language, certainly would attest to the megadialect similarities and differences rather than to temporal precedence, since these languages offer data which are roughly coterminous. Again, the language characteristics shared by OS and Gothic, an East Germanic language attested some 300 to 400 years earlier, certainly bespeak megadialect or genetically laterally related features, rather than a parent-child relationship. To be sure, the Gothic:OS lateral relation is between an older attested and a younger attested sibling; the linguist can rightfully take into consideration some features of Gothic not shared with the West Germanic dialects but shared with other Indo-European languages in data older than OS as possibly indicating age or language development from one era into the next. The purposeful use of the term genetic grammar in the *OSL*, then, attempts to put in perspective the fact that all language data are diachronic and dialectal, and that the reader of the OS text learns the grammar of OS primarily for itself, not as a repository for a set of correspondences hypothetically reconstructed as ancestor stages of OS. The conclusion is that the process statement is appropriate not only for a language studied genetically, but also for a language studied synchronically, yielding a diachronic synchrony.

Why, however, is the prehistoric umlaut rule designated as prehistoric? The *e:i* and the *u:o* alternations observed by this rule could simply be designated as such, namely as given alternations. Yet, it is to be noted that the prehistoric umlaut rule differs in kind from the historic umlaut rule (Chap. I: 3.3.2). The term prehistoric implies that the rule functioned prior to actual textual discourse data or evidence. The reader of OS sees the results of the functioning of the rule in the distribution of *e:i* and *u:o* in the actual data. The results are by and large invariant in the *Heliand* and *Genesis* texts, so that the linguist considers the rule as no longer functioning, unproductive, at the time of the writing of these texts. The linguist therefore allocates the rule to the prehistory of the texts, termed genetic in the *OSL*. In the case of the historic umlaut rule, the alternation between, e.g., *a* and *e*, the results are mixed, i.e., variant in the actual data. However, in this *a:e* alternation, *a* in an umlaut setting is not necessarily signalled as *e*, so

Linear Syntax; Pragmatics: 5 - 6.4 23

that the linguist considers the historic umlaut rule as one which is still ongoing or productive during the recording of the OS textual evidence. The linguist thus allocates this rule to the recorded period (history) of the texts, termed synchronic in the *OSL*. Observe the process wording of this diachronic synchrony rule as given in Chap. I: 3.2.2 : "palatalization of a root vowel *a, ā, o, ō, u, ū* generally by an *i* or *j* in the suffix of the word."

The value of the terms prehistoric:historic, unproductive:productive, invariant:variant, genetic:synchronic in labeling linguistic data in a given sentence, is in minimizing the reader's task. Linguistic explanation in the form of significant rules or generalizations eases the burden on the memory of the reader. The purpose, then, of recourse to genetic rules in learning OS is not at all understanding prehistory, but it is rather understanding OS itself.

5. Completing the Search

The first search makes accessible to the reader of OS the lexical meaning of such a word as *quiðis* in sentence (3) *Hwat quiðis thu umbi gōdon?* of Chap. II: 4 above. It does not, however, give the meaning of the inflection *-is* of the verb. This is part of the grammatical and in particular of the morphological meaning which is learned in the inflectional morphology subsumed by nonlinear syntax (cf. Chap. II: 7 below). Other factors such as the position of the word in the sentence and, in turn, the sentence in the larger discourse also account for some of the meaning of the word in the text. These are the considerations of linear syntax (cf. Chap. II: 6 below). All components of the grammar, whether phonological, morphological, or syntactic, study a paradigmatic linguistic unit for its syntagmatic or narrative discourse use. The study of pragmatics forms an overlay on or intersects all the components of the grammar. The reader thus achieves the "fine tuning" of the meaning of a word.

6. Linear Syntax: The Independent Sentence

The independent sentence can be declarative, interrogative, or imperative. The most common or frequent word order to express these three language functions is designated as unmarked (cf. Chap. I: 3.3.1); less common word order for each function is designated as marked.

6.1 The Independent Declarative Sentence: (X)VbSO

The unmarked word order of the OS independent declarative sentence is clearly (X)VbSO order, where X signifies any word other than the verb (Vb) or the subject (S); O is the sign for the object. Without introductory word, however, SVb word order is frequent, although it is slightly less than twice as frequent as VbS word order. XSVb word order is the least frequent order in independent declarative sentences. It is found less than one-third as often as VbS order, less than one-fifth as often as SVb order, and less than one-seventh as often as the predominant XVbS word order. On balance, the (X)SVb word order occurs approximately two-fifths less frequently than the (X)VbS word order.

Linear Syntax; Pragmatics: 5 - 6.4 25

XVbSO: **Ni gābin ina** *thesa* **liudi** *thi.*
'These people would not bring Him to you.'

VbSO: **Lēdid** *up thanan her hebencuning thea hluttaron* **theoda** *an that langsame lioht.*
'The exalted King of Heaven leads upwards from thence the pure people into the long-lasting light.'

6.2 The Unmarked Interrogative and the Unmarked Imperative Sentence: (X)VbSO

The unmarked order of the OS independent interrogative or independent imperative sentence is (X)VbSO. Most interrogative sentences utilize X; this X is commonly an *hw-* word. Imperative or command sentences frequently, although not necessarily, employ an overt subject:

Interrogative: **Scal** *ik im sibun siðun iro* **sundea** *alāten?*
'Shall I forgive them their sin seven times?'

Imperative: **Erod** *gi arme* **man**, **dēliad** *iwan* **ōdwelon.**
'Support ye poor people! Share your riches!'

6.3 The Marked Independent Sentence: (X)SVbO and (X)SOVb

Of the (X)SVb independent declarative sentences (cf. Chap. II: 6.1 above) less than one-twentieth have (X)SOVb order, which is strongly marked. (X)SOVb order is also more marked for the independent imperative sentence than is the marked (X)SVbO order. (X)SOVb order is almost nonexistent for the OS independent interrogative sentence, while (X)SVbO is the marked order:

(X)SVbO:
Declarative: *That **friðdubarn tholode wrēðes willeon**.*
'The Child of Peace tolerated the will of the grim one.'

Imperative: *Simlun **gi** fasto te gode berad iuwa **breostgithāht**.*
'Always direct you your mind firmly to God.'

Interrogative: *"Te hwī gi **wārlogon**," quað he, "**fandot mīn** sō frōkno?"*
'"Why do you hypocrites," said He, "tempt me so keenly?"' (Sehrt 1966 lists *wārlogon* as nominative, not vocative.)

(X)SOVb:
Declarative: *Hi **gewald habda** togeanna tēcan.*
'He had the power to show signs.'

Imperative: *Nio **gi** an thesumu lande thiu*

Linear Syntax; Pragmatics: 5 - 6.4 27

>lēs lēra mīna wordun ni wīsiad.
>'Nevertheless make known with words my teaching in this land.'

Interrogative: *Bihwī thu hēr dōpisli fremis undar thesumu folke?*
'Why do you perform baptism here among these people?'

6.4 Textual and Pragmatic Strategies in Linear Syntax

In discussing the reader's approach to the OS text, the independent sentences (1) *Ic is engil bium* (Chap. I: 2), (2) *Gaf it is jungarun forð* (Chap. I: 3.3.1), and (3) *Hwat quiðis thu umbi gōdon?* (Chap. II: 4) were observed with a view to extrapolating meaning for the syntagmatic verb in the relation of each sentence. Thus far, the approach to the meaning yielded by the lexical FIF was shown; so, e.g., the reader knows that *quiðis* (sent. 3) belongs to the FIF *queðan* meaning 'say.' S/he can further observe that *quiðis* linearly follows an *hw-* word which is the unmarked syntagm for an interrogative sentence (Chap. II: 6.2). Added to the gloss 'say' then, is the functional meaning "question." From the first search the reader also knows the meaning of *gaf* (sent. 2) as 'gave.' According to its linear syntax (VbO), *gaf* can have either declarative or interrogative function; its preterite tense meaning (cf. col. b of Strong Verb Dictionary Finder Chart, Chap. I: 3.3, 3.3.1) precludes a possible imperative meaning. The decision as to the functional meaning of sentence (2) can only be made by recourse to its setting in its greater discourse (*Heliand und Genesis*, Behaghel 1965, 11. 2852-2857):

>That folc stillo bēd
>sat gesīδi mikil; undar thiu he thurh is selbes craft,
>manno drohtin, thene meti **uuīhide**,
>hēlag hebencuning, **endi** mid is handun **brak**,
>**gaf** it is iungarun forδ, **endi** it sie
>>undar themu gumskepie hēt
>
>dragan endi dēlien.

>'The people waited quietly,
>a great crowd was sitting; meanwhile He through
>His own power, the Lord of men, blessed
>the food, the holy King of heaven, and
>with His hands He broke (it), He gave it
>to His disciples, and He ordered that they
>bring it and divide it among the
>multitude.'

Sentence (2) clearly does not convey interrogative meaning; it is one of a series of narrative statements. As a declarative sentence it is to be compared, then, with sentence (1) where the finite verb *bium* 'am' linearly follows its subject. SVb is marked position for any function in OS (cf. Chap. II: 6.3). To ascertain the positional meaning of *bium*, sentence (1) must also be observed in its wider discourse (*Heliand und Genesis*, Behaghel 1965, 11. 116-122):

>"Thīna dādi sind," quaδ he,
>"uualdanda uuerδe endi thīn word sō self,
>thīn thionost is im an thanke, that thu sulica
>>githāht habes

an is ēnes craft. Ic is engil bium,
Gabriel bium ic hētan,   the gio for goda standu,
anduuard for them alouualdon,   ne sī that he me
                        an is ārunði huarod
sendean uuillea."

                    "Your deeds are," said he
"pleasing to the Lord, and your words as well.
your service is appreciated by Him, since you
have such faith in His power alone. I am
His angel. Gabriel am I called, who ever
stands before God, present before the
Almighty, unless He might want to send
me somewhere on His errand."

Again, the greater discourse or macro-structure reveals the declarative meaning of the sentence; it is one of a series of uttered assertions.

The next task for the reader is to decide why declarative meaning is conveyed by differential linear syntax in sentences (1) and (2). Both sentences are overtly constative, i.e., they describe an event or state of affairs. Sentence (1), however, is less **implicitly performative** than is sentence (2), since it is a direct quotation indicative of performing the act of speaking, explicitly introduced in the wider narrative speech situation of sentence (1) by *quað he* 'said he.' In contrast, sentence (2) can be considered implicitly performative by virtue of the *Heliand* author's act of recounting events to his readers, which he does throughout his text. The *quað he* syntagm associated with sentence (1) is then another speech act beyond or within that of the author's narration. To be sure, many other discourse features such as 1 sg. and present tense of sentence (1) contrasting with 3 sg. and preterite tense of sentence (2) contribute to the different text meaning of the two declarative sentences. At issue here, however, is why declarative sentences (1) and (2) employ SV and VO word order, respectively, and how their linear syntax interdigitates with the constative:performative speech act difference observed above.

Direct quotations, according to Ries (1880: 31), occur more frequently in the unmarked declarative order (X)VbSO than in the marked orders. The SV order with the intervening predicate noun *engil* of sentence (1), placing *bium* last in the sentence, is accordingly striking by its marked order. The linear dynamic of the self-introduction, self-identification of Gabriel to Zacharias certainly conveys a meaning of directness, of straightforwardness. The components of the comment 'am His angel' are inverted so that the position of *engil* before *bium* lends definiteness to the predicate noun. Whether metrical (cf. Chap. V: 17.3.1) considerations, namely that *engil* houses the key alliteration of the entire line, influenced the position of *bium*, or whether the desired pragmatic meaning of the sentence is accountable for the placement of *engil* into the principal stress position of the linear syntax can only be answered by the *Heliand* author. Either or both strategies certainly affect the textual meaning of sentence (1) and accordingly aid in the fine tuning of the meaning of the syntagmatic *bium*.

Finally, the question arises: What are the textual meanings of the OS unmarked (X)VbSO linear order, as represented in sentence (2) *Gaf it is jungarun forð.* One of the most common functions of the strategy of VO linear order in the *Heliand* is concatenation or continuation in a narrative sequence. Sentence (2) expresses one of a series of actions enumerated in the particular narrative scenario of which it is a part. The semantic linkage of sentence (2) with the immediately preceding sentence is strengthened by virtue of the position of *gaf* directly contiguous to the preceding sentence *endi mid is handun brak*. The concatenation meaning of this pragmatic strategy follows Behaghel's two universal linguistic generalizations, which hold that semantically related linguistic units are contiguous or adjacent in their linear syntax (Behaghel Rule 1), and that old information precedes new information in a sentence (Behaghel Rule 2) (cf. Behaghel 1932). The meaning of old information in *gaf* of sentence (2) refers to the fact that the verb represents an action which is part of a series of actions before it, and that it is consequent to those actions, even if the actions in themselves are new. *Gaf* in concatenative or conjunctive first position links sentence (2) to the preceding sentence, as the conjunction *endi* 'and' of that preceding sentence containing the verb *brak* 'broke' functions to link it with the preceding sentence containing the verb *wīhide* 'blessed.' The action subsequent to *wīhide*, *brak* and *gaf*, which is *hēt* 'ordered,' is linked to *gaf* by another occurrence of the conjunction *endi*. That *gaf* is an alliterating word does not necessarily require its first position in the half line in which it occurs; accordingly, pragmatic rather than metrical constraints account for the VO linear order of sentence (2). This common concatenative function, which thus enhances the textual meaning of *gaf*, interdigitates, however, with several other pragmatic strategies functional in the OS texts (cf. Rauch 1981a).

7. Nonlinear Micro-syntax: Morphology

If the linear syntax, in particular the textual and paradigmatic strategies in the linear syntax of a grammar (cf. Chap. II: 6.4), is accountable for the fine-tuning of the reading of the meaning of, e.g., *bium*, *gaf*, *quiðis*, whose lexical meaning the reader ascertained in the first search (Chap. I: 3), the nonlinear syntax is the place for the adjustment of the paradigmatic meaning of these words into their gross syntagmatic meaning. Although the reader has arrived at the decision that, e.g., *quiðis*, through its FIF means 'speak,' s/he has only identified the meaning of that part of the word usually embodied in the root of the word.

Mophology deals directly with the paradigmatic (derivation/compounding) and syntagmatic (inflection) composition of all parts of the word, and the relationship of these parts to one another. The morphology of a word together with the most immediate interrelationship of a word to another word in the proposition, frequently expressed in subcategorization rules, comprise the nonlinear micro-syntax and the nonlinear macro-syntax, respectively. Subcategorization or selection rules express the immediate bonds, grammatical agreements, between and among the relation and the arguments of a sentence (cf. Chap. III: 9). Thus, e.g., in sentence (3) *Hwat quiðis thu umbi gōdon?*, the reader will decide that *quiðis* and *thu* are congruent by their respective morphologies. The identification of *quiðis* with *thu* is not at all totally insured by its linear syntax (cf. Chap. II: 6-6.4 above); specifically, the individual composition or morphology of each of the two words interlocks. The more explicit the grammatical information expressed by the nonlinear syntax, the less explicit the meaning of the linear syntax. This correlation is a universal principle of all language, namely, that there is a trade-off in the work of the two syntaxes. As noted in Chap. I: 3.3 and 3.3.1, OS is an inflection or suffix language, i.e., a substantial portion of the grammatical meaning of a word is signalled by the inflectional suffix of a word.

A word in a syntagm consists of a root, a stem, and an inflection which is the suffix. The inflection is variable in the syntagm; its study comprises inflectional morphology. The root is that largely invariable part of the word which embodies the essential lexical meaning of a word; its most frequent syllable shape is in OS consonant-vowel-consonant (CVC), as is characteristic of an Indo-European language. The stem of a word is the root plus an invariable phonological increment. For example, the FIF forms of the verb, the infinitives, discussed in Chap. I: 3.1 above, *niman* 'take,' *nerian* 'save,' and *makon* 'make,' display the roots *nim-*, *ner-*, *mak-*, respectively. The stem of *nerian* is *neri-*, that of *makon* is *mako-*, while that of *niman* remains *nim-*, or, in other words, the stem *nim-* is homophonous with its root. The suffixes *-an*, *-n*, however, are not inflectional suffixes; they are invariable derivational suffixes. These suffixes simply signal the word class meaning of a word paradigm, in this instance the paradigm of the infinitive (cf. Chap. VIII: 26.1.4). Derivational suffixes, as well as prefixes, are part of noninflectional morphology, which also includes compounding of words (cf. Chap. VIII: 25; 25.2).

ABLAUT, discussed in Chap. I: 3.3, is integral to both derivational and inflectional morphology, since it conveys both derivational and inflectional meaning. For example, the ABLAUT or vocalic root alternation between *geƀa* 'gift' and *gaf* 'gave' or between *barn* 'child' and *beran* 'to bear' help identify the first words of each set as belonging to the noun paradigm, while the second member of each set belongs to the lexical category verb. This use of ABLAUT to supply word classes is subsumed under derivational morphology. Similarly, the use of ABLAUT to supply the word paradigm infinitive (cf.

above), e.g., *beran* 'bear,' in contrast to the word paradigm preterite participle, e.g., *giboran* 'borne,' properly belongs to derivational morphology. However, the use of ABLAUT to distinguish between verb forms in syntagm is subsumed by inflectional morphology. Thus, while the ABLAUT of 1 sg. pret. *bar* 'I bore' is of derivational import relative to the ABLAUT of 1 sg. pres. *biru* 'I bear,' the ABLAUT of 1 sg. pret. *bar* is of inflectional import relative to that of 2 sg. pret, *bāri* 'you have borne,' because the members of the latter ABLAUT set (*bar:bāri*) are variable within one and the same preterite paradigm, while the members of the former ABLAUT set (*bar:biru*) represent two separate word paradigms, viz., the preterite and the present paradigms, respectively. Noninflectional as well as inflectional morphology contributes to the productive system of a language; aided by the linear syntax and the phonology, the dynamic within the morphology is responsible for the creation of new words in a language (cf. Chap. VIII: 25).

In reconsidering the word *quiðis*, it remains for the reader to decide the meaning of the *-is* inflectional suffix. In the case of *bium* and *gaf* the reader observes that both verbs have a CVC syllable shape and accordingly signal a so-called zero inflection. By means of the approach outlined for the use of the Strong Verb Dictionary Finder Chart (Chap. I: 3.3.1), the reader associates *gaf* with the preterite tense and its inflections (cf. Chap. VIII: 28), while s/he associates *quiðis* with the present tense and its inflections (cf. Chap. II: 8.2.1 below). The present tense form of *bium* resists identification via the Strong Verb Dictionary Finder Chart, since it is a suppletive form of *wesan* 'be,' one of a small set of anomalous verbs (cf. Chap. I: 2), and as such must be memorized (cf. Chap. II: 8.2.3 below).

Morphology; Present Indicative: 7 - 8.2.3   35

8. Inflection of Verb Present Tense Indicative

Present and indicative are the tense and mood categories of the verb which are constant throughout inflectional paradigms so designated. Together with aspect, polarity, and diathesis, the semantic-syntactic structure of inflectional paradigms is treated in the modality constituent of the nonlinear syntax of the *OSL* (cf. Chap. VII: 25). Paradigmatically variable in the present indicative inflection of a verb are the further grammatical categories of person, 1, 2, 3, and verb number, singular and plural.

8.1 Present Tense Indicative Suffix

The present tense indicative inflections of the strong and weak verbs (cf. Chap. I: 3.2; II: 8), which include all OS verbs but a set of anomalous verbs (cf. II: 8.2.3 below), fall into one of two sets according to their plural suffix:

		-(a)d Plural	*-un* Plural
Sg.	1	-u	-ø
	2	-(i)s	-(s)t
	3	-(i)D	-ø
Pl.		-(a)D	-un

The present tense suffixes are added to the stem of the infinitive, the FIF of the verb, minus *-an*, *-en*; in the case of infinitive final *-on* the stem is minus *-n* only. Stems thus ending in *-o* add only *-s*, *-d* to the 2 sg., e.g., *bedos* 'you pray,' 3 sg. and the pl., e.g., *tholod*; the 1 sg. is identical to the FIF or infinitive, e.g., *tholon* 'to suffer' or 'I suffer' (cf. Chap. VIII: 26.1.4). Similarly, stems ending in -*i* add only -*s*, -*d* to the 2 sg., e.g., *habis* 'you have,' 3 sg. *habit* 'he has'. The -*st* 2 sg. suffix occurs in *kanst* 'you can,' *farmanst* 'you disdain,' *wēst* 'you know' (cf. II: 8.2 below for membership in -*(a)d* and -*un* plural sets).

Present tense suffixes are liable to OS graphic variation. *D* represents an archigraph for the occurring graphs <d>, <t>, <ð>, <th> (dialect, Chap. VI: 19.3.2; phonology, Chap. VI: 19.4.7). Graph lowering of <u, i> can occur as <o,e>, which, in turn, can occur as <a>; thus, e.g., 2 sg. -*is* suffix can occur as <-*is*, -*es*, -*as*> (graphemics, cf. Chap. IV: 13.2; dialect, Chap. VI: 19.3.2; phonology, Chap. VIII: 27). The -*(a)d* 2.3 pl. suffix can occur with nasal, thus *gornonð* 'you lament,' *tholond* 'they suffer' (megadialect interference, cf. Chap. VI: 19.3.3). The 3 sg. *libod*, *libot* 'he lives' occurs only for *libbian*, while the 3 pl. *libbiot* 'they live' occurs beside *libbiat*. The 3 pl. *folgod*, *folgot* 'they follow' occurs also as *folgoiad*, *folgoiat* (cf. megadialect, Chap. VIII: 26.1.4). As can be observed, the distinctions among strong verbs and the various types of weak verbs in their dental plural present indicative suffixes are minimal; these distinctions are further lessened by graph lowering.

8.2 Present Tense Plural Types: Membership and Root Modifications

All OS verbs except the anomalous verbs of Chap. II: 8.2.3 below thus add one of the two sets of suffixes to their root stems to express present tense:

	-(a)d Plural			-un Plural
Sg.1	gibu 'give'	neriu 'save'	makon 'make'	skal 'should'
2	gibis	neris	makos	skalt
3	gibid	nerid	makod	skal
Pl.	gebad	neriad	makod	skulun

As observed in Chap. I: 3.2, the distinction of the OS verb as strong or weak actually rests on its preterite formation (cf. Chap. VIII: 28). The *-(a)d* plural present indicative paradigm represents genetically the weak classes 1,2,3 and the seven strong verb sets. The *-un* plural present indicative paradigm represents genetically the modal auxiliary verbs, known genetically as the preterite-present verbs.

8.2.1 The *-(a)d* Plural Verbs

Verbs whose stems end in *-i* include a small set of strong verbs from classes V, VI, and VII, listed in Chap. I: 3.3.2, and the weak verb sets 1 and 3. The *-ad* plural verb stems ending in *-i* alternate geminate root consonants in 1 sg. and in the pl., with simplex root consonant in 2.3 sg. in roots with short vowel followed by no other consonants but the simplex. Roots ending with root consonant *-r* or with root consonant *-ð* do not show this alternation even if they have short root vowel. Thus OS has simplex consonant throughout the paradigm *nerian* 'save,' but geminate (by nature, i.e., genetically) throughout the paradigm *merrian* 'hinder'. Other short vowel *-ad* plural verbs with stem ending in *-i*, but with no simplex:geminate consonant alternation, are *fellian* 'fell,' *antkennian* 'perceive,' *kussian* 'kiss,' **rittian* 'carve,' *thrukkian* 'press'. The consonant gemination is largely secondary to the suffix in distinguishing the inflections of the present tense -*ad* plural verbs. Present tense roots of ABLAUT sets II, III, IV, V with root vowels *iu//u* or *e* are liable to the prehistoric umlaut rule, thus *giƀu* 'I give' but *geƀad* pl. (cf. Chaps. I: 3.3.1, 3.3.2). Present tense inflections of ABLAUT sets VI and VII with root vowel *a*, *ā* are liable to the historic umlaut rule in the 2.3 sg., e.g., *slehit* 'he kills,' but *slahad* pl. (cf. Chap. I: 3.3.1, 3.3.2, and Chap. VI: 19.4.26, 19.4.30). The verb *hebbian* 'have' and *seggian* 'say' have root vowel *a* in the 2.3 sg., thus *haƀis* 'you have.' However, *e* also occurs in 2 sg. *segis*. Conversely *a* occurs also in 1 sg. *habbiu* and 2.3 pl. *habbiad* (*e* forms attest to historical umlaut, cf. Chap. I: 3.3.2).

8.2.2 The -*un* Plural Verbs

Verbs with a -*un* plural present indicative constitute a set of eleven verbs in OS which occur with high frequency and must be memorized.

The -*un* plural verbs, known as modal auxiliary verbs, fall into two subsets. One set with invariable root vowel throughout its fundamental forms (cf. I: 3.3) contains the modal auxiliaries *mōtan* 'must, may' and *ēgan* 'own'; for the latter only the plural is extant in the present indicative. Of the remaining nine auxiliaries with variable root, alternation of the root vowel between the singular and the plural occurs in *witan* 'know,' with root *ē* in the sg. alternating with root *i* in the pl., and in *dugan 'be of use' with root *ō* in the sg. alternating with root *u* in the pl. A sg. root *a*, pl. root *u* alternation occurs in the present indicative of *thurƀan 'need,' *kunnan 'can,' *skulan* 'shall,' *mugan* 'be able'. Of the remaining three verbs, two attest to only sg. forms with root *a* in the present indicative, *(gi)durran* 'dare' and **farmunan* 'disdain'. The final verb **unnan* 'grant' occurs with the prefixes *gi-* or *af-* and has no attested present indicative. The vowel alternation in the second subset is only redundantly functional as a plural marker, since the *-un* suffix signals plural. The consonant alternation in the sg. *tharf*:pl. *thurbun* (cf. grammatical change, Chap. I: 3.3.1), in the sg. *maht*:pl. *mugun* (cf. final devoicing, Chap. VI: 19.5), in the sg. *kan*:pl. *kunnun* are also secondarily functional as tense signs. The 2 sg. *scealt* 'you should' also occurs (megadialect interference, cf. Chap. VI: 19.4.13).

8.2.3 Anomalous Verbs

Of very high frequency are the three anomalous verbs *wesan* 'be,' *dōn* 'do' and *willian* 'will'.

	wesan 'be'	**d(u)ŏn 'do'**	**willian 'will'**
Sg. 1	bium/n 'be'	d(u)ŏm/n	williu
2	bist	d(u)ŏs	
		Sg. 2/3	wili
3	is(t)		
	Sg. 3/Pl.	d(u)ŏt	
Pl.	sind		williat

The indicated variations in the *wesan* paradigm are mostly dialect determined (cf. Chap. VI: 19.3). Further, *biun* occurs also as *bion* (graph lowering, cf. II: 8.1 above); *bist* occurs also as *bis*; *sind* occurs also as *sint*, *sinð* (final devoicing and/or graphic, cf. Chap. VI: 19.5), as *sindun* (analogy with *-un* plural), and as *sīn*. Note the <m> ~ <n> variation (cf. Chap. III: 12.1).

The indicated variations in the *d(u)ōn* 'do' paradigm are mostly dialect determined (cf. Chap. VI: 19.3.2). The forms with *uo* have short *o* always; *d(u)ōt* occurs also as *d(u)ōd*; 2 sg. *duoas*, 3 sg. *dōit*, and 2.3 pl. *duat* also occur. Note the <m> ~ <n> variation (cf. Chap. III: 12.1).

The root vowel in the *willian* paradigm occurs also as *e* in the present indicative except for the 2.3 sg. (dialect, cf. Chap. VI: 19.3.2). One occurrence of ø root vowel occurs in 1 pl. *williat* (graphic or scribal error, cf. Chap. VI: 18). The single root consonant in the 2.3 sg. also occurs geminate. *williu*, 1 sg., is subject to optional graph lowering (cf. Chap. VI: 19.4.26) or loss of stem ending *i* or of final *u* yielding such forms as *willeo*, *wellu*, *wille*; *willek* also occurs (cliticization). The 2 sg. occurs also as *willis* (analogy, cf. *-(a)d* pl.), *wilt* (analogy, cf. *-un* pl.), and *wil*. The 3 sg. occurs also as *wilit* (analogy, cf. *-(a)d* pl. and *wil* (analogy, cf. *-un* pl.). The stem ending *i* of *williat*, pl., is subject to possible graph lowering, e.g., *willeat* 2 pl. (cf. Chap. IV: 13.2) or to possible loss *wellat* 1 pl. The suffix *-at* of *williat*, pl., occurs also as *d* (cf. Chap. VI: 19.4.7), as *a* 3 pl., and as *-ant* 2 pl. (cf. megadialect interference, Chap. 19.3.3).

In addition, the verb *stān* 'stand' represents an anomalous, but also very fragmentary paradigm. *stān* yields a 2 sg. *stēs*, 3 sg. and 3 pl. *stād*. The 3 sg. also occurs as *stēd* (dialect, cf. Chap. VI: 19.3.2), as once occurring *set*, and once occurring *steid*. The final *d* occurs also as *t* and *ð* (cf. Chap. VI: 19.4.7). Only a 3 sg. present indicative *begēd* 'traverse, commit' in a non-*Heliand* document is extant (Bede *Homily*). The meaning of *stān* is otherwise expressed in OS by the regular strong verb *standan* (ABLAUT set VI). A possible OS *gān* does not occur in the *Heliand* and *Genesis* data; instead OS *gangan* (ABLAUT set VII) occurs.

Chapter Three

Propositional Meaning and Valence;
The Noun and its Grammatical Categories;
Inflection of the Masculine Strong Noun;
Inflection of the Neuter Strong Noun

9. Propositional Meaning and Valence

Cognition of the pragmatic meaning of the three sentences (1) *Ic is engil bium*; (2) *Gaf it is jungarun forð*; (3) *Hwat quið is thu umbi gōdon?* (cf. Chap. II: 6.4) requires at the same time perception of their propositional meaning. Early in the *OSL* (cf. Chap. I: 2), sentence (1) was defined as a proposition consisting of the relation or predicator '(am) (His) angel' and the argument 'I.' While sentence refers to a grammatically structured string of one or more words yielding a complete thought, a proposition emphasizes the semantic structure of the complete thought conveyed in the sentence. A sentence is an exocentric construct, i.e., neither the predicator nor the subject argument dominates or substitutes for the meaning of the entire sentence; both are coequally required. Thus, e.g., in sentence (1) neither *Ic* nor *(is) engil (bium)* independently yields the complete thought. While *Ic (is) engil (bium)* and *Ic (bium) (is) engil* display two different sentence meanings pragmatically (cf. Chap. II: 6.4), they attest to the same propositional meaning, which is commonly signified in predicate calculus as $E(i)$, that is,

ENGIL (ic). The copula *bium* is in identity or equative relation and accordingly is subsumed in the predicator *engil*. The possessive *is* 'his' relates to *engil* in a second proposition, in which *engil* is the argument and *is* is the predicator. We notice then that a predicator which ascribes to an argument an action or state can be from among various lexical categories, e.g., noun, adjective, pronoun, preposition, verb, although conjunctions and articles do not serve as predicators. The argument, on the other hand, is from a nominal or substantive category and refers to persons, places, or things.

Arguments are not necessarily in exocentric relationship with a predicator. Thus in sentence (2) *Gaf it is jungarun forð* 'He gave it to His disciples' *jungarun* is in endocentric relation to the predicator *Gaf* since *jungarun* is subordinate to *Gaf* in the nonlinear syntax predicate constituent where *Gaf* is self-sufficient. The propositional meaning of sentence (2) is signified in predicate calculus as G (*h, i, j), that is, *GAF* (*he, it jungarun*). Although the subject argument [in sentence (2) the nonovert *he* 'he' with anaphoric reference to *heƀencuning* 'King of heaven' in the immediately preceding discourse] is not subordinate to the predicator, it nevertheless is in case relationship, i.e., syntactic-semantic interaction or bond, with the predicator. As such, the subject argument plays a role in the predicate constituent and is considered in the nonlinear syntax with all other arguments interacting semantically with the predicator of a given sentence. The *OSL* also treats nominal phrases independently of the predicator, as nominals together with their modifications in the nonlinear syntax argument constituent (cf. Chap. VII: 23).

While predicate calculus subverts grammatical categories and pragmatic meaning, on the one hand, it exploits logical meaning and highlights the state or action (predicator) asserted about a given nominal or nominals [argument(s)]; on the other hand, predicators are "operators by means of which simple propositions are constructed out of names, i.e., nominals" (Lyons 1977: v. 1: 148). The understanding of the nature of a simple proposition offers insight into the contributions of the different types of meaning in cognizing the OS sentence, i.e., the micro-propositional meaning of a sentence in contrast with the grammatical meaning of a sentence and micro- and macro-pragmatical meaning of a sentence. Predicate calculus also indicates well the degree of valence of the given predicator, i.e., the number of actual or potential arguments of a given predicator. Thus in sentence (1) *engil* has a degree of one or is a so-called one-place predicate or monovalent, viz. *ic.* (N.B. Predicate refers to any potential predicator.) *Gaf* of sentence (2) is a three-place predicate or trivalent, viz. **he, it, jungarun.* *Quiðis* of sentence (3) *Hwat quiðis thu umbi gōdon* 'What do you say about a Good One?' is also potentially a three-place predicate. Only two arguments are realized here, thus Q (*th, hw*) viz. QUIÐIS (*thu, hwat*); an indirect object or patient argument is not expressed.

In two out of the three sentences above, a verb form served as the predicator, which is the most commonly systematized predicate category. The predicate constituent in the *OSL* is cognized in terms of a verb form as predicator, even in sentences containing an equative verb [cf. sentence (1) above]. Furthermore, as observed in Chapter II: 7, OS is an inflection or suffix language in which the grammatical-semantic bonds between the predicator and the arguments demonstrate a substantial degree of iconicity in their inflectional morphology, i.e., they reciprocally mirror their grammatical-semantic interrelationship. In the nonlinear macro-syntax the bond between subject argument and predicator is considered one of concord, while that between nonsubject arguments and predicator is understood in terms of governance (collectively congruence). Since the former relationship is exocentric and the latter is endocentric (cf. above), this viewpoint certainly is a viable one. However, predicate calculus subject and nonsubject arguments alike are bonded syntactically and semantically to the predicator (cf. Chap. VII: 22), by means of iconic linkages inflectionally symbolized. In Chapters I and II the verb predicator was cognized as pivotal to the meaning of an OS sentence. We proceed below to the inflectional morphology of the arguments commonly embodied in the noun.

10. The Argument(s)

Because of the propositional nature of a sentence, the reader instinctively and/or by learned reading strategies searches for the meaning of the arguments interacting with the verb predicator in a given OS sentence. S/he cognizes the argument(s) of a proposition by perceptions similar to those s/he employs in identifying the verb predicator (cf. Chap. I: 3). In particular, the reader is intent on disambiguating various arguments from one another relative to the predicator, i.e., determining the particular grammatical-semantic bond of each argument with the verb.

10.1 The Noun and Its Categories

Arguments are nominals or substantives, frequently nouns whose grammatical meaning is bonded to the predicator chiefly through inflectional morphology. Just as with a verb form, the reader interprets the noun in syntagm to consist of a root, stem, and inflection which is the suffix (cf. Chap. II: 7). To ascertain the lexical meaning of a noun the reader has recourse to the lexicon which lists the noun in its FIF, with its grammatical specifications and glosses (cf. Chap. I: 2). As with the verb (Chap. I: 3.2), the noun is designated strong (str.) or weak (wk.); again for the purpose of articulation with other more traditional grammars, these designations are employed in the *OSL*. Genetically, the weak:strong classification refers to stem sets by which nouns with genetic stem-formant in *-n* are distinguished as weak (cf. Chap. IV: 15.1). A further grammatical category of the OS noun is gender, a property assigned to the noun as an additional grammatical marker both for paradigmatic classification in sets and for syntagmatic bonding. Thus, e.g., the masculine accusative singular *n*-stem is distinguished from the neuter accusative singular *n*-stem by a different suffix. The possible adjectives which bond with *n*-stems of either gender in syntagm will mirror their individual servitude or bond to either noun, each through its particular inflectional suffix. The noun grammatical categories of stem set and grammatical gender are genetically fixed, although some nouns are heteroclitic, i.e., belong to more than one stem set, e.g., OS *sunna* 'sun,' weak and strong, and/or have multiple gender designation, e.g., OS *bōk* 'book,' feminine and neuter. The noun grammatical categories of number: singular and plural, and case: nominative, accusative, genitive, dative, instrumental display paradigmatic variability via the inflection of the noun. These instantiate or embody syntactic-semantic bonds with the predicator; case in particular indicates the degree and kind of valence set determining the syntactic-semantic structure of a verb predicator. Terms such as nominative are grammatical convenience classifications retained for articulation with traditional grammars; the semantic relevance of the cases is studied in the nonlinear syntax of the predicate constituent (cf. Chap. VII: 22). Genetically instantiated cases such as locative and vocative are not considered in the inflectional morphology; they are, however, observed in the semantics of the nonlinear syntax.

11. The Inflection of the Masculine Strong Noun

11.1 Masculine Strong Noun Suffix

The masculine strong noun, i.e., masculine noun sets excluding the masculine weak noun known genetically as n-stems, (cf. Chap. IV: 15.1) is inflected as follows:

	Singular	Plural
Nom. Acc.	-ø	-os/i/ø
Gen.	-es	-(i)o
Dat.	-e	-(i)un
(Instr.)	-u	

The masculine inflectional suffixes are added to the stem of the noun as evidenced in the nominative singular, which is the FIF of the noun in the lexicon, i.e., the noun nominative singular is equated with the noun stem; it serves as the basis of identification in grammars and lexicons. The plural nominative-accusative suffix distinguishes three sets of strong masculine nouns; the ø-plural has three subsets. The i of the genitive and dative plural is germane to the plural of i-plural nouns and as such can be cognized as signaling the plural rather than case. The nominative-accusative would then be understood as a stem ending in -i with a ø-plural suffix.

How the native Old Saxon internalized the segmentation of root, stem, and inflectional suffix remains an unanswered question. The language learner and reader of the OS text exploits various strategies of syncretization in cognizing inflectional paradigms; no claim is made to one particular or absolute viewpoint.

The masculine strong noun inflectional suffixes as well as stem vowels, i.e., noninflectional suffix to the root, are liable to Old Saxon graphic variation. Graph lowering of <u, i> to <o, e> can occur, thus, e.g., dat. pl. *-iun* sequence, whether belonging to the *-os* plural set or to the *i*-plural set, can occur as <-ion or -eon>. The graphic dat. pl. *-um* rarely occurs (cf. Chap. III: 12.1). Graph lowering of <o, e> to <a> can occur; thus, e.g., gen. sg. *-es*, dat. sg. *-e*; nom. pl. *-os* can occur as *-a(s)*. A dat. pl. *-an* shows progressive lowering from u>o>a. Less frequent graph raising of <e, o> to <i, u> occurs, e.g., in dat. sg. *muodi* 'mood,' gen. pl. *lidu* 'limb.'

The instrumental singular is generally limited to the *os*-plural type and to the ø-plural subset with possible ø-dat., instr. sg. (cf. Chap III: 11.2, 11.2.1 below). For articulation with traditional grammars, it is to be observed that the *-os* plural genetically reflects the Gmc. **a-* and **ja-*stems, the *i*-plural reflects genetically the Gmc. long syllable **i-*stems (roots with V̄C, V̆CC, or polysyllabic roots), whereas the ø-plural reflects genetically the Gmc. **wa-*, short syllable *i-* (roots with V̆C), **u-*, **r-*, **nd,-* and root stems. In synchronic grammar these nine genetic stem classes are hardly distinguishable; in fact, the Old Saxon masculine strong noun is remarkably uniform in case inflections across genetic stem sets, making these latter irrelevant to the functioning of *Heliand* Old Saxon. Such uniformity is achieved through syncretism, i.e., the merger of linguistic units. While signs of genetically stem-unique case inflections are observable, the above (Chap. III:

10.1) mentioned heterocliticity observable in the suffix variations discussed below (Chap. III: 11.2, 11.2.1) attests to the ongoing syncretism and resultant destruction of the genetic stem class distinctions.

11.2 Masculine Strong Noun Plural Types: Root and Suffix Variations

With the exception of kinship terms, **all** OS masculine strong noun types inflect the same in the singular; their plural inflection differs only in the nominative-accusative plural according to three types, the ø type showing three subsets. N.B. The genitive/dative plural of the *i*-plural type is syncretized with the genitive/dative plural of the *os-* and the ø-plural types (cf. Chap. III: 11.1 above).

	os-Plural		i-Plural	ø-Plural
Sg. Nom. Acc.	dag 'day'	hirdi 'shepherd'	gast 'guest'	friund 'friend'
Gen.	dages	hirdies	gastes	friundes
Dat.	dage	hirdie	gaste	friunde
Instr.	dagu	hirdiu		
Pl. Nom. Acc.	dagos	hirdios	gesti	friund
Gen.	dago	hirdio	gestio	friundo
Dat.	dagum	hirdiun	gestiun	friundun

The root of any masculine strong noun may be subject to word final devoicing of fricatives or stops, or to medial voicing of fricatives which is sometimes signalled graphemically, e.g., *dag ~ dages* 'day' but *hof ~ hoƀes* 'courtyard.' A syllable final devoicing rule applies in polysyllabic roots which can alternate epenthetic or

Masculine Strong Noun: 11 - 11.2.1

medial vowel with ø, e.g., *diubal ~ diufles* 'devil' (cf. Chap. VIII: 27). Degemination, i.e., simplification of geminate consonants applies optionally to stems not ending in *-i*, e.g., dat. pl. *mannun*, but nom. sg. *man*. The root of *i*-plural nouns is liable to historical umlaut in all cases of the plural. (For other root modifications not directly related to the inflection of a masculine strong noun, see Chap. VI).

Variations which signal not simply graphic raising or lowering (cf. 11.1 above) occur in addition to the displayed paradigmatic suffixes. They exhibit further cross-fertilization or contamination leading to the neutralization of historically relatively distinct stem classes. Such variations for the three plural formations of the masculine strong noun as evidenced in the *Heliand* and *Genesis* texts include those discussed immediately below (for evidence from minor documents cf. Gallée 1910, Holthausen 1921).

The *os-* nominative/accusative plural can occur as *-a*, e.g., *slutila* 'keys.' The *os*-plural masculine noun stems ending in *-i* can occur with ø dat. sg. e.g., *sinweldi* 'large forest'; further, syncopation of the stem-*i* before vowel can occur, thus, e.g., nom. pl. *herdos* 'shepherds' (the root *e* variation aside, cf. Chap. VIII: 27). On the other hand, an *os*-plural masculine noun stem not ending in *-i* can occur with an *i*, so, e.g., dat. sg. *sithie* 'path.'

The *i-* nominative/accusative plural which evinces this *-i* on the plural stem of the genitive and dative, also yields genitive and dative plurals with syncopated *i*, thus, e.g., *liudo, liudun* 'people.' A rare *-in* dat. pl. can occur, e.g., *liudin*. An instr. sg. with *-i*, *-u*, *-iu*, or ø can occur, e.g., *wihtiu* 'thing.'

The ø nominative/accusative plural occurs also with an *-os* or *-on* nominative/accusative plural, e.g., *wīgandos, wīgandon* 'warriors.' The nom. acc. sg. *-(i)o* occurs, thus *hēleando, hēlendio, hēlandi* 'savior;' gen. sg.

neriandan, neriend(i)en occur. A gen. pl. *-oro, -ero, -i* can occur, e.g., *helendero* 'saviors;' with an intrusive *-i*, a gen. sg./gen. pl./dat. pl. can occur, e.g., gen. sg., *waldandies* 'ruler,' *hatandiero* 'haters,' *hettendiun* 'enemy;' a ø suffix occurs on a dat. sg., e.g., *waldand* 'ruler.' The nom. acc, pl. *mēn* 'man' occurs.

11.2.1 Masculine Strong Noun ø-Plural Subset Contaminations; Anomalies

Particularly revealing evidence for a diachronic synchrony (cf. Chap II: 4), i.e., obvious language change in progress, are *Heliand* and *Genesis* data evincing the interplay or contamination of genetic stem types inclining toward, and thus subsumed as subsets of the ø-plural masculine strong noun.

	ø-Plural +Nom.Sg.-u	ø-Plural +Dat.Instr.Sg.ø	ø-Plural +ø Sg.
Sg. Nom. Acc.	sunu 'son'	hugi 'mind'	fader 'father'
Gen.	sunies	hugies	
Dat.	sunie	hugi(e)	
(Instr)		hugi(u)	
			↓
Pl. Nom. Acc.	suni	hugi	
Gen.	sunio	hugio	*
Dat.	suniun	hugiun	faderun

The ø-plural with a nom. sg. in *-u* occurs with stem final *i* in all cases but the nom. sg. A dat. sg. syncretized to the nom. sg. can occur, thus *sunu*, or with stem final *i*, thus *suni*. A gen. and a dat. pl. can occur without stem final *i*, *suno, sunun*, respectively (cf. Chap. VIII: 27).

Neuter Strong Noun: 12 - 12.2.1

The ø-plural with possible dat. instr. sg. in *-ø hugi*, (cf. Chap. VIII: 27), can occur with nom. acc. pl. *-o(s)*, thus *grurio* 'fear,' *hornselios* 'building adorned with horns.' The gen. sg. can occur without stem-final *i*, thus *metes* 'food.'

The ø plural with ø sg. is unattested in the gen. pl. To this set belong kinship terms.

A small, fragmented subset of masculine strong nouns with no attested plural have a *u* (or lower graph<o>) stem vowel, e.g., *sēu* 'sea,' *ēo* 'law,' which alternates with its homorganic semivowel, the glide *w*, in the gen. and dat. sg., thus *sewes, ēwe*. A gen. and dat. sg. with syncopated *w* can occur, e.g., *sees, sēe*, respectively.

12. The Inflection of the Neuter Strong Noun

12.1 Neuter Strong Noun Suffix

The neuter strong noun, i.e., all types but the neuter weak nouns, the latter identified genetically as the *n*-stems (cf. Chap. IV: 15.1), is inflected as follows:

	Singular	Plural
Nom. Acc.	-ø	-u, -ø
Gen.	-es	-o
Dat.	-e	-un
Instr.	-u	

It is to be observed that the neuter strong noun inflection is identical with the masculine strong noun in the singular. In the plural the neuter strong noun has a possible nominative/accusative *-u* suffix, but no *-i* plural suffix. The genitive plural *-o* and dative plural *-un* of the strong neuter noun coincide with those of the strong masculine noun, if the -*i* of the *i*-plural masculine strong noun is perceived as a plural rather than as a case suffix (cf. Chap. III: 11.1 above).

The common *Heliand* and *Genesis* graphemic variation rules (cf. Chap. IV: 13.2) of lowered <i, u> to <e, o> and lowered <e, o> to <a>, as well as the raised <a> to <e or o> and of <m> as <n> apply to the strong neuter noun stem and inflectional suffixes (cf. also Chap. III: 11.1 above).

The instrumental singular is generally limited to the *u*-plural type and to a small subset of the ø-plural which displays a possible ø-dat. instr. sg. (cf. Chap. III: 12.2, 12.2.1 below).

The strong neuter noun *u*-plural reflects genetically the Gmc. short syllable **a*-stems (roots with V̆C), while the strong neuter noun ø-plural suffix reflects genetically the Gmc. long syllable **a*-stems (roots with V̄C, V̆CC, or polysyllabic roots), **ja-*, **wa-*, **i-*, **u-*, and **s*-stems. Clearly, these genetic stem types have merged considerably in the diachronic synchrony of OS grammar; the variations and contaminations (cf. Chap. III: 12.2, 12.2.1) further attest to their strong syncretism (cf. Chap. III: 11.1).

12.2 Neuter Strong Noun Plural Types: Root and Suffix Variations

All OS neuter strong noun types inflect the same in the singular and in the genitive and dative plural. Two neuter strong noun types are distinguished on the basis of a nominative/accusative plural suffix in -*u* or in -ø; the ø-type with two subsets (cf. Chap. III: 12.2.1 below). **Note the near complete coincidence of the neuter**

Neuter Strong Noun: 12 - 12.2.1

strong noun inflectional suffixes with those of the masculine strong noun.

	u-Plural	ø-Plural	
Sg. Nom. Acc.	graf 'grave'	hros 'horse'	kunni 'kin'
Gen.	grabes	hrosses	kunnies
Dat.	grabe	hrosse	kunnie
(Instr.)	grabu	hrossu	kunniu
Pl. Nom. Acc.	grabu	hros	kunni
Gen.	grabo	hrosso	kunnio
Dat.	grabun	hrossun	kunniun

The root of any neuter strong noun is liable to final devoicing of fricatives or stops, and to medial voicing of fricatives, which can be signalled graphemically, thus, *graf ~ grabe*. Polysyllabic roots tend to alternate epenthetic or medial vowel with ø, e.g., *mahal ~ mahle* 'law court.' Degemination to simplex consonant of stems not ending in -*i* applies, e.g., *hros*. (For other root variations not directly relevant to the inflection of strong neuter nouns see Chap. VI).

While the graphemic lowering and raising rules apply generously in the various cases but for the nom. acc. sg. of the strong neuter *u*-plural type nouns, nongraphemic variation is infrequent; a gen. pl. can occur with inserted -*i*, thus *aldarlagio* 'life time.'

The ø-plural strong neuter noun *hūs* 'house' occurs also with a ø-dat. sg. A ø-plural strong neuter can occur with *u*- in the nom. acc. pl., thus *nettiu* 'net.' On the other hand, ø-plural strong neuter nouns with stems in -*i* can occur with syncopated -*i* in the gen., dat., and instr. sg., thus, *kunnes* 'kin,' *rīke* 'kingdom' and *gesiðu* 'multitude,' respectively. A dat. sg. stem vowel -*i* without case inflection can occur, e.g., *kunni*, and a dat. sg. with *-u* occurs in *thiustriu* 'darkness.'

Some ø-plural strong neuter nouns with geminated root consonant plus stem vowel-*i* display a contracted root (haplology of -CV) in the nom. sg., which alternates freely with the noncontracted form, thus, *net* 'net' beside *netti*; other such nouns are: *bed* 'bed,' *bil* 'sword,' *firiwit* 'curiosity,' *flet* 'room,' *gimet* 'measure,' *giwit* 'wisdom,' *inwid* 'evil,' *wig* 'horse.'

12.2.1 Neuter Strong Noun ø-Plural Subset Contaminations; Anomalies

A small fragmented subset of neuter nouns with ø-plural suffix have a *u* (or lower graph <o>) stem vowel, e.g., *hrēo* 'corpse,' *beo* 'harvest,' which alternates with its homorganic semivowel, the glide *w*, in the gen. sg., e.g., *hrewes* and the gen. pl., e.g., *bewo* 'harvest;' *knio* 'knee' has a dat. pl. *kneohon* (cf. Chap. VI: 19.4.5). In the case of *balu* 'ruin,' gen. sg. *baluwes*, the alternation is *u ~ uw* (cf. Chap. III: 11.2.1 above).

A small subset of strong neuter nouns with ø-plural can occur with a -ø dat. and instr. sg., thus *gumscepi* 'crowd.' A nom. acc. sg. without stem-final *i*, *gibodskip*, and a gen. sg. with ø, *gibodskepi* 'command.' Nouns included in this subset are *urlagi* 'war,' *halsmeni* 'necklace,' and several compounds with second element -*scipi* (Chap. III: 11.2.1 above).

Strongly anomalous is the neuter strong noun nom. acc. sg. *fehu* 'cattle,' with a gen. sg. *fehes*, dat. sg. *fehe*, instr. sg. *feho*. With the nom. acc. sg. as an exception, *fehu* obviously inflects as expected for a masculine strong noun. No plural is attested.

Chapter Four

Primary Evidence in Reading the OS Text;
Graphemics and the Interpretation
of Desinences; Inflection of the Feminine
Strong Noun; Inflection of the Masculine,
Neuter, and Feminine Weak Nouns

13. Graphemics

Since the principal evidence which the reader of a historical text utilizes in cognizing the text is the written data, familiarity with OS orthographic habits as rendered in standard editions of the *Heliand* and *Genesis* is invaluable. This is particularly the case in OS because of the richness of the variations in spelling both for consonants and vowels, and both in root and affix syllables. The focus on orthography in the *OSL* is linguistic rather than paleographic, which would study the Carolingian minuscle and uncial, together with peculiarities such as <ę æ>, employed in the OS *Heliand* and *Genesis* manuscripts (cf. plates of *Heliand* manuscripts xvii-xxi; Gallée 1910: §7-11, Holthausen 1921: §32-37).

Standard *Heliand* and *Genesis* editions employ <a b ƀ c d ð e f g h i k l m n o p q r s t u v x y z> and combinations thereof. Graph <æ> while only footnoted in the Sievers (1978) edition, e.g., *bærhtero* 'bright,' is not indicated in any way for OS data in the Behaghel edition (1965). Observe that neither <j> nor <w> are manuscript Old Saxon, although both graphs are standardly employed in OS grammars and dictionaries; the *OSL* renders manuscript <i g> and <u uu vu vv> as such, and not as <j> and <w>, respectively, only in citing OS in-text data, not in linguistic sentences or paradigms. Thus, e.g., *jungar(un)* 'disciples' of linguistic sentence (2) is spelled with <j> in Chap. I: 3.3.1, Chap. II: 6.4, and in the OS glossary, while it is spelled with <i> in the quoted line 2857 from the Behaghel edition in Chap. II: 6.4 and in the quoted line 3107 of the Old Saxon Selected Readings. Note that the manuscript cluster <qu> is not rendered through linguistic <kw>.

13.1 Graphic variation

Variation between and among graphs is rampant in all syllables of an OS word. The variations may be free, i.e., not influence meaning, e.g., the adverb *simlon* ~ *simblon* ~ *simnon* ~ *sinnon* 'always,' showing variations which represent common phonetic iconisms or assimilations. In addition they may be phonologically significant, e.g., graph lowering of the strong masculine dative singular <e> desinence to <a> indicative of an open *e* sound, perhaps also indicative of end syllable weakening (cf. Chap. III: 11.1 and Chap. VIII: 27). They may be iconically produced in the syntagm, e.g., *te gidruogi dadi* 'as a deception might have done,' in which the<i> of the noun copies the <i> of the verb, or *reginugiscapu* 'fate,' where the final <u> iconically induces medial <u> (cf. Chap. VIII: 27). Finally, graphic variation may represent meaning, signifying distinct morphemes, e.g., accusative singular *hell* 'hell' with affective meaning alternating with *hellia* (cf. further Rauch 1987).

Graphic Variation: 13 - 13.2   59

13.2 Reading the Inflectional Syllable: Reality in Diachronic Synchrony

Graphic variation in the OS inflectional syllable appears particularly volatile. Consider the title and main character of the OS epic data, *hēliand* in the nominative singular:

> hēlandi
> hēlandeo
> hēlendi
> hēleand
> hēland
> hēleando
> hēlendio

Both in medial and inflectional syllable, graphic variation abounds. Once the FIF has been recognized, the reader concentrates on disambiguating the desinence, i.e., the inflectional suffix. The *OSL* classifies *hēliand* as a masculine strong ø-plural noun (cf. Chap. III: 11.2). The <-(V)o> variation (occurring three times) as well as the <-i> variation (two occurrences) then require explanation, since the former could be paradigmatically interpreted as a genitive plural; the latter could be read as a rare dative singular in which <e> is raised to <i> (cf. Chap. III: 11.1). Since *hēliand* shows expanded genitive plural in *-ero* (cf. Chap. III: 11.2), and since the syntax requires subject meaning, the <-(V)o> desinence can only be interpreted as iconic with that of the FIF of a masculine weak noun (cf. Chap. IV: 15.2 below). In the case of the <-i> desinence, the syntax again dictates a nominative inflectional suffix; the <-i> may be the result of <o> apocope in a <-Vo> desinence. The working hypothesis of the *OSL* is that the naive native speaker of OS did communicate effectively regardless of the seeming graphemic rummage which informs the OS data.

To be sure, the extreme possibility of viewing OS as a pidgin or creole type language should not be overlooked (cf. Chap. VI: 19.3.2).

The standard grammars, Gallée (1910) and Holthausen (1921), appeal not infrequently to scribal error. Thus, e.g., Gallée (§ 314.5) writes of the genitive plural *lidu* 'limb': "ist wohl fehlerhaft." This <u> desinence (instead of expected <io>) can be accounted for by <i> syncope (cf. Chap. III: 11.1). Accordingly, on the basis of extant forms, the *OSL* assigns *lið* to the strong masculine *i*-plural nouns (cf. Chap. III: 11.2) and not to the ø-plural subset type *sunu* 'son' as Gallée and Holthausen do.

The genitive singular strong *OSL* ø-plural feminine *bedu* 'prayer' is attributed by Holthausen (1921: §283.3) to analogy with the dat. sg. desinence. Such iconism may be a causal factor; however, dialect and/or scribal habit may also be factors: ms. C uses the *bedu*, ms. M *bede*, the latter considered megadialect, i.e., Old Frisian habit compared to the expected *beda* (cf. Chap. IV: 14.2). Ms. M also attests to a *bede* dative singular which can be iconic with the genitive singular; or it can be viewed as graphic lowering of <u> to <o> to <a>, often interpreted as weakening of end syllable (cf. Chap. VIII: 27) plus graphic raising <a> to <e>. In fact, both the genitive and the dative singular desinences of strong *OSL* ø-plural feminine nouns vary the graphs <u, o, a, e> (cf. Chap. IV: 14.2 below). These graphic variations heighten the degree of probability in decision making for the hermeneutic task facing the reader of OS. To be sure, such decisions are resolved in traditional grammars by appeal to genetic origin or reconstruction. Thus, e.g., Holthausen (1921: §282) quite unambiguously differentiates a genitive singular <-a> and a dative singular <-u> from all other graphic variants in his genetically labeled "ō-Stämme" plural feminine noun paradigm (=*OSL* ø-plural). The somewhat facetious question which presents itself is how the ongoing communication of the native Old Saxon was possible without the benefit of genetic language insights. The *OSL* assumes that such communication was indeed possible (cf. above); the *OSL*, accordingly, takes the viewpoint that the second language learner of OS can read the OS data successfully without recourse to genetic facts (cf. Chap. II: 4), and that s/he is, in fact, engaging in "historical interlanguage" learning (cf. Rauch 1988).

Framed another way, the challenging question speaks to what the native Old Saxon, and by implication the second language learner of OS, cognizes when confronted with an array of graphic variations. A few additional cases in point will serve to prioritize the descriptive/explanatory options facing the OS linguist. The strong feminine *i*-plural noun *tīd* 'time' also shows a nom. pl. *tīda* which can be genetically linked with the strong *OSL* ø-plural feminine nouns with a FIF with stem ending -a. Alternatively, the -a of *tīda* can be linked with OS graphic lowering from <i> to <e> and from <e> to <a> (cf. 14.1 below). The decision requires a judgment as to whether the reader (native Old Saxon or second language learner) cognizes the noun as belonging to a paradigmatic class or whether s/he perceives the graphic and/or phonological variation, and thus iconism, in the inflection. The answer is quite independent of the teleological explanation offered by Sievers (1878: 505.n.106) of the scribal iconically produced <-a> embedded in syntagm with (*Ne sint*) *mīna* (*noh*) ... *cumana* 'my times (are not yet) come' (cf. sect. 13.1 above). Remarkably, Holthausen (1921: § 283.4) maintains that the <-i> variation, *thiedi*, for the dat. sg. strong ø-feminine *thiodu* 'folk' follows the genetic "*i*-Deklination," while the <-a> variation, *thioda*, belongs "wohl zu einem mask. oder neutr. *a*-Stamme." Such statements indirectly impute to the OS native speaker trained linguistic etymological abilities. Nor is it the case that for the most part the current second language learner is etymologically sophisticated. Moreover, Holthausen overlooks the fact that a feminine gender paradigm is unambiguously targeted by the preceding determiner in the noun phrase syntagm, which in Indo-European languages generally plays the role of servitude. Thus we read *thesaro thioda, theru thiedi* 'these, the people,' with tell-tale feminine inflection of the article. The dat. sg. variant *thioda* also occurs with the feminine article *thesare*.

To be sure, the single, anomalous dat. sg. *theson thioda*, with masculine/neuter determiner, is, according to Gallée (1910: §308.2) either scribal error or indicative of nascent gender change to neuter in accord with Middle Low German and Middle Netherlandic. Appeal to future linguistic history on the basis of one form is as tenuous as appeal to genetic history in a grammar focused on diachronic synchrony. This is not at all to deny that some OS nouns straddle gender types and/or noun pardigm types (cf. e.g., Chap. IV: 14.1, 14.2 below). It does, however, speak directly to the immediate perception of graphic variants by the reader of the OS text. Although the reader may gradually extrapolate from the confusion of desinential graphs, neutralizations, and syncretisms in noun inflectional morphologies of the diachronic synchrony, his most immediate, superficial (surface) extrapolation is simply cognition of the graphic lowering phenomena of, most commonly, <i, u> to <e, o>, and in turn, to <a>, which, for its part, can be found raised to <e, o>. Chapter VI presents the after-the-fact linguistic formulations of graphic variation attributable to phonological change, dialect, and/or megadialect interference.

14. The Inflection of the Feminine Strong Noun

For a general introduction to the "Noun and Its Categories" see Chap. III: 10.1.

14.1. Feminine Strong Noun Suffix

The feminine strong noun, i.e., all types but feminine weak nouns, known genetically as *n*-stems (cf. sect. 15.1), is inflected as follows:

	Singular	Plural
Nom. Acc.	-ø	-ø/i
Gen.	-ø/i	ⱽ-on-/i- ⁄ o
Dat.	ⱽ-u/ø/i	ⱽ-/i- ⁄ un

In contrast with the masculine and neuter inflectional suffixes (cf. Chap. III: 11.1, 12.1), the feminine desinences appear at first sight proliferated, in particular, in the singular. As with the masculine and neuter strong nouns, the nominative singular serves as the FIF; the nouns of all three genders are read as -ø suffix nominative singular desinences. One of the costs of this generalization, as well as other valuable generalizations in cognizing the inflection of the feminine strong noun, is the introduction of a subtractive feature into the morphology, viz., ⱽ, the dative singular ⱽ-u, genitive plural ⱽ-ono, and dative plural ⱽ-un. (Slash separates mutually exclusive alternatives; broken slash indicates 1) the addition of element right of the broken slash to elements with a right suspension mark left of the broken slash, 2) a mutually exclusive alternative. Thus, in the strong feminine genitive plural -*ono*, -*io*, and

-*o* desinences are indicated.) V̵ signals that the final vowel of the FIF, the nominative/accusative singular, syncopates before the dative singular -*u*, the genitive plural -*ono*, and the dative plural -*un* desinences. The genitive and dative singular *i*-suffix is germane to feminine strong nouns with nom. acc. pl. *i*-suffix and, as to be expected, the *i* of the genitive and the dative plural are germane as well to the *i*-plural type. Another cost of preserving the vital ø suffix nominative/accusative singular FIF which links all of the inflectional noun morphology of the nonlinear syntax to the lexicon is the subversion of the possible, almost complete syncretization of strong feminine *i*-plural nouns with the strong feminine ø-plural nouns having ø genitive and dative singular inflectional suffixes. The genitive/dative singular ø-suffix shows remarkable lack of overt inflection for the feminine strong noun. To be sure, on further study the feminine strong noun impresses, then, as moving toward syncretism in its singular. But for the -*ono* genitive plural suffix, the strong feminine noun plural case suffixes overlap with those of the masculine and neuter strong nouns. In sum, the dative singular V̵-*u* and the genitive plural V̵-*ono* suffixes which belong to one and the same type of noun, (cf. Chap. IV: 14.2 below), and the syncretization of cases in the singular typify the strong feminine noun. Such syncretization bears witness to the functioning of inborn abductive reasoning underlying the cognition of an OS sentence, whether by a native speaker or second language learner/reader of OS (cf. Chap. II: 4). Furthermore, the strong feminine noun attests to no instrumental case suffix.

The feminine strong noun inflectional and stem suffixes, however, show the graphemic variation so characteristic of *Heliand* and *Genesis* OS data (cf.Chap. III: 11.1, 12.1; IV: 13.2). <i, u> vary with lower <e, o>, <a> varies with raised <e, o>, and <m> with <n>. A dat. sg. <u>

can be found as <a>, thus *thioda* 'folk,' and a nom. pl. <i> occurs as <a>, thus *tīda* 'times.' The reader of an OS text cognizes these as instances of progressive graphic lowering <u> to <o> to <a> and <i> to <e> to <a>, respectively (cf. Chap. IV: 13.2 above). The dat. sg. *thiudu* 'folk' also occurs as *thiode* and *thiedi*; accordingly the reader can conceptualize either of these as graph raising from a lowered <a>.

Genetically, the ø-plural with dat. sg. ∀-*u* and gen. pl. ∀-*ono* strong feminine noun reflects the Gmc. *$\bar{o}$-, *$j\bar{o}$-, and *$w\bar{o}$- stems. The remaining feminine strong noun ø-plurals, all with ø-suffixes throughout the singular cases, reflect genetically the Gmc. *$\bar{\imath}n$-, *r-, and short syllable *$\check{\imath}$- (roots with $\check{V}C$) stems. The *i*-plural reflects genetically the Gmc. long syllable *i-stems (roots with $\bar{V}C$, $\check{V}CC$, or polysyllabic roots), *u-stems and root stems. The classification into two plural sets as well as the lively variations and contaminations to be noted (Chap. IV: 14.2, 14.2.1 below) attest to the ongoing syncretism of stem types and cases in the OS strong feminine noun (cf. Chap. III: 11.1).

14.2 Feminine Strong Noun Plural Types: Root and Suffix Variations

The OS strong feminine noun inflection is remarkable for its relative uniformity of desinences; the vertical arrows in the graph below readily indicate such syncretization. In addition, the dat. pl. of the two feminine strong noun types, based on the nominative/accusative plural suffix, coincide; they coincide as well with the strong masculine and the strong neuter noun types (cf. Chap. III: 11.2, 12.2).

The strong feminine noun ø-plural type with dat. sg. -*u* has a gen. pl. suffix expanded by -*on*, thus -*ono*. But for this observation the gen. pl. of the two feminine strong noun types coincide; they coincide as well with the strong masculine and the strong neuter noun types (cf. Chap. III: 11.2, 12.2). The feminine strong noun *i*-plural type has one subtype (Chap. IV: 14.2.1 below) which reveals further syncretization with the strong masculine and neuter noun desinences.

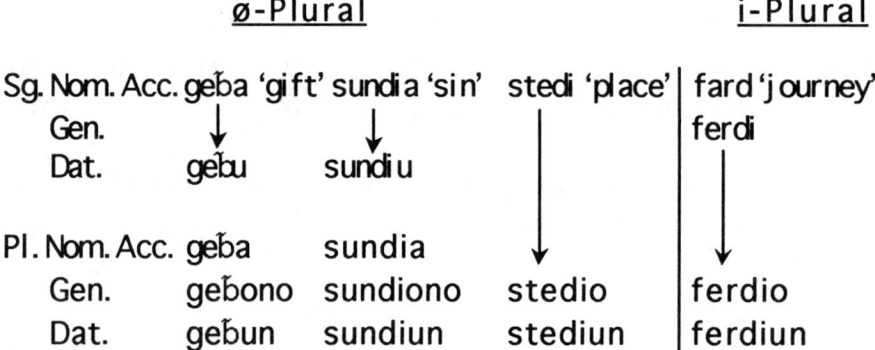

The strong feminine noun root is liable to the rules of word final devoicing of fricatives or stops, and to medial voicing of fricatives which may be signalled graphically, e.g., *burh* ~ *burges* 'city.' Degemination of stem final consonants occurs, e.g., acc. sg. *hel* ~ dat. sg. *helliu* 'hell' (cf. below). The root of *i*-plural nouns is liable to historical umlaut in all cases but the nom. sg. (For other root variations not directly related to the inflection of the strong feminine noun see Chap. VI).

Beside graph lowering and/or raising (cf. 14.1 above), variations in the inflection of strong feminine ø-plural nouns with dat. sg. -*u* and gen. pl. -*ono*, include a possible nom. acc. sg. and a gen. dat. sg. in V́, thus *hwīl* 'time,' and *helli* 'hell,' respectively. A dat. sg. and gen. pl. with V́-Ø, e.g., *thiod* 'folk' occur. A gen. sg. V́-*u* occurs, e.g., *bedu*

Feminine Strong Noun: 14 - 14.2.1

'prayer' as well as a dat. sg. and a gen. pl. in Ø, *scola* 'group' and *seliða* 'houses,' respectively. Stems without stem vowel *i*-, e.g., *stemna* 'voice,' can occur with expanded stem, thus dat. sg. *stemniu*, while a stem with *-i*, e.g., *hellia* 'hell' can occur with syncopated *i*, thus gen. sg. *hella*. A contracted root occurs [haplology of -CV(V)] in e.g., acc. or dat. sg. *hel(l)*, or gen. sg. *thi* 'maid' with non-contracted nom. sg. *thiwa/thiwi*. Both of these last nouns evince an anomalous gen. sg., thus, *thiun* and *helliun*. An anomalous dat. sg. *stemnun* and an anomalous nom. acc. pl. *sundiun* also occur. Such *n*-forms show ongoing contaminations with the OS weak feminine noun (cf. Chap. IV: 15 below).

Strong feminine ø-plural nouns, with all cases of the singular in ø, can have a nom. sg. in *-a*, thus *blindia* 'blindness,' a nom. and dat. ag. in *-u*, thus *meginstrengiu* 'great power,' and *finistriu* 'darkness,' respectively. Further a dat. sg. ¥-*u* occurs, thus *menigo* 'crowd.' *giswester* 'sisters' has an anomalous dat. pl. *gisustruonion*.

Strong feminine *i*-plural nouns, with *i* represented in all cases but the nominative/accusative singular, show variations which include a gen. sg. and a dat. sg. *-ø* suffix, e.g., *tīd* 'time' and *craft* 'power,' respectively. A dat. sg. *-iu*, thus *brūdiu* 'wife' also occurs.

14.2.1 Feminine Strong Noun i-Plural Subset Contaminations; Anomalies

Not only does the feminine strong noun bear witness to confusion, i.e., syncretization between and among the genetic stem types (cf. 14.1 above), but it also evinces multiple data pointing to the neutralization of grammatical gender inflectional suffixes. Neutralization in progress is effectively indicated by the gen. sg. in -*es*; many of the strong feminine nouns inflected as follows are, accordingly, heteroclitic, e.g., *craft* 'strength' which is feminine as well as masculine. The reader of an OS text has reference, then, to more than one inflectional paradigm.

i-Plural + Gen. Sg. -(i)es

Sg. Nom. Acc.   burg 'city'
    Gen.   burg(i)es
    Dat.   burg(i)

Pl. Nom. Acc.   burgi
    Gen.   burg(i)o
    Dat.   burg(i)un

The possible (*i*) accounts for many of the variations occurring in this subset. A nom. acc. pl. can occur in -ø, thus *magað* 'maiden' (cf. Chap. VIII: 27), *naht* 'night.'

15. The Inflection of the Trigender Weak Noun

15.1 Trigender Weak Noun Suffix

The weak noun suffixes for all three genders are identified genetically as *n*-stems for the obvious reason that -*n* occurs in most of its inflectional cases. The reader of an OS text cognizes the *(V)n* suffix as an inflectional suffix synchronically, while genetically these are viewed as *Vn* stem increments (for distinction between stem and inflectional suffix cf. Chap. III: 10.1, Chap. II: 7). All weak nouns are inflected as follows (N.B. The dative is ordered prior to the genitive in the plural):

Trigender Weak Noun: 15 - 15.2

	Masculine	Neuter	Feminine
Sg. Nom.	-ø	-ø	-ø
Acc.	-n	↓	∀-un
Gen. Dat.	↓	←---- ∀-on	↓
Pl. Nom. Acc.		⟶	↓
Dat.	↓	←---- ∀-on	←
Gen.	-no	←---- ∀-ono	←

Note again that the FIF or base form is the nominative singular form to which the inflectional suffix is added. For the feminine and neuter, except the neuter accusative singular, the subtractive feature ∀ signals that the final vowel of the FIF, the nominative singular, syncopates before the desinences. The arrows which indicate complete (full line) or partial (broken line) coincidence in desinence, are to facilitate recognition for the learner of OS; they by no means indicate derivation or origin, whether genetically or synchronically. They do, however, show the enormous syncretization of the weak inflectional suffix both within and across genders. Certainly the dative and genitive plural know no gender distinction. The genitive plural suffix is most unambiguous and therefore identifiable. The nominative singular suffixes of all genders, and the accusative singular neuter suffix find their identity in lack of *-n*, yet the OS graphic lowering and raising rules can obscure their gender distinctions except in the neuter accusative singular. Indeed, the bulk of the weak noun inflectional suffixes which are in *(V)n* can lose gender and number discreteness through the effects of graphic variation, whether in stem vowel or inflectional vowel, especially among <u>, <o>, <a>, <e> (cf. Chap. IV: 13.2). Effects of graphic <m>, <n> variation are seen mostly in the dat. pl.; they are not impossible elsewhere, e.g., gen. sg. fem. *thiernum* 'servant.' Notice the lack of an instrumental case in the trigender weak nouns.

15.2 Trigender Weak Noun: Root and Suffix Variations

The weak noun of all three genders is readily recognizable to the reader of an OS text by its nasal suffix in the nominative plural and the oblique cases, but for the neuter accusative singular. As far as the strong nouns are concerned, a suffix with nasal is familiar to the reader only from the dative plural of all OS strong noun types and from the genitive plural of feminine ø-plural strong nouns with a dative singular in V-u. Observe that the OS weak noun has only three gender types, which have no subtypes. There is but one nominative/accusative plural type for each gender; the feminine and neuter plural coincide.

	Masculine	Neuter	Feminine
Sg. Nom.	herro 'lord'	herta 'heart'	tunga 'tongue'
Acc.	herron	↓	tungun
Gen. Dat.	│	herton	│
Pl. Nom. Acc.	│	hertun	│
Dat.	↓	herton	↓
Gen.	herrono	hertono	tungon
			tungono

The weak noun is not susceptible to root modifications relevant to its inflection. (For other root modifications not directly associated with the inflection of the weak noun see Chap. VI).

Roots with -i stem suffix, e.g., *willio* 'will,' can occur with syncopated *i*, thus nom. sg. masc. *willo*. Contrarily, roots without stem suffix -*i* can undergo epenthesis, e.g., acc. sg. masc. *brunnion* 'well.' Apocope of -*n* occurs, e.g., in the gen. sg. masc. *herro* 'lord,' dat. sg. fem. *quenu* 'wife.'

As an exception, the vocative singular (cf. Chap. III: 10.1) is overtly distinct from the nominative singular in voc. *frō* 'lord,' nom. sg. *frōho* (cf. Chap. VI for root modifications).

Chapter Five

Hearing the Old Saxon Text;
Articulatory/Acoustic Features of the Sounds;
Systematic Segmental Phonemes;
Suprasegmental Phonemes;
Alliterative Verse Form; Syllable

16. Sounds in Historical Language

The reader of a historical text, obviously not a native speaker, stands mute, so to speak, before the text whose actual speech sounds have died away centuries ago. Nevertheless, the reader has at his/her disposal several types of evidence which allow varying degrees of probability for approximating the sounds of a now dead language such as Old Saxon. As noted in Chapter IV, the principal evidence is the graphemic data; its interpretation is aided by metrical evidence, loan evidence, comparative evidence with other languages or with other time frames in its own history, and typological and universal evidence (cf. further Penzl 1972, Rauch 1990). Although the sounds of a language are not in and of themselves meaning-bearing, the supposed articulation and acoustic analysis of historical data lend an aura of reality to the dead language when spoken and heard by the contemporary reader.

16.1 Articulatory Phonetics

From the viewpoint of the production of sound, the human head and neck metaphorically constitute a musical instrument. Besides observing that sounds emanate from the mouth, or in the case of nasalized sounds, the nose, or both, upon touching the head, e.g., at the temples, crown, the cheeks of the face, or the throat at the larynx or Adam's apple in the course of speaking, one can feel the vibrations of sound. For its use in sound the respiratory air stream is modified in the larynx, the pharynx (the tube-like cavity above the larynx leading into the back of the mouth and the nose), the mouth, with teeth, tongue, palate, uvula, the lips, and the nose. Thus, there are many movable parts on this "human musical instrument" which shape the individual sounds.

On the one hand, the sounds produced are not radically different from one another; on the other hand, a division into consonants and vowels is common in articulatory description. Sounds are, however, different enough to be discrete both in paradigm and in syntagm (cf. 17 below). Quite fundamentally, the respiratory air passes relatively unimpeded, i.e., unobstructed, enroute to emission through the mouth and/or nose in the articulation of a vowel, whereas the obstruction, whole or partial, of respiratory air from the lungs enroute to emission through the mouth and/or nose characterizes a consonant (cf. further below). The consonantal and vocalic material is subsumed under segmental phonology, in distinction to suprasegmentals, which refers to sound material such as pitch, stress, and juncture affecting more than one segmental sound (cf. sect. 17.3).

Jesperson (1926) proposed a scale of sonority for consonants and vowels whereby the sounds are ranked according to the degree of openness in the vocal tract through which the air travels and the vibration or nonvibration of the vocal cords or folds during phonation. Thus the vowel sound *a* is the most sonorous, while the consonants *p, t, k* are the least sonorous, with all other sounds ranging on a continuum between. From this viewpoint vowels and consonants are not totally different entities.

16.1.1 Consonant

A description of the physical articulation of consonants includes the type and degree of obstruction of the air stream in the production of a given consonant; this parameter is the manner of articulation of the consonant. If the airflow is completely obstructed, a stop consonant results, such as *p* of OS *pīna* 'pain,' where the air stream is cut off by the lips. If the air is impeded but continues through the vocal tract and out of the mouth, the sound is a continuant, a designation which includes nonstopped consonants as well as vowels. Continuant consonants, however, experience some obstruction, friction, or continuous noise which distinguish them from vowels. If the lips do not close entirely, but some air leaks or sifts through the lips and/or the teeth yielding audible friction, an *f* as in OS *fīf* 'five' may result, a sound which is properly termed fricative. A fricative of the *s*-type is a sibilant as in OS *sið* 'path.' Still other continuant consonants with less friction than fricatives are liquid consonants such as *l* as in OS *līð* (neut.) 'drink' and *r* as in OS *rīki* 'rule, kingdom.' Because the air passes along the sides of the tongue in shaping *l*, it is subclassed a lateral consonant. OS *r* is most frequently subclassed a trill, resulting from the vibration of the tip of the tongue. The nasal consonants *m* and *n* as in OS *mīdan* 'avoid' and OS *nīð* 'hatred,' respectively, are also produced with lessened obstruction of the air. They are not continuants per se since the air flows through the nose rather than the mouth, but they do form a natural class (a set whose members share one or more features) with liquids, a class called resonants, since they approach vowels on the scale of sonority, in contrast to stops and fricatives, which form the obstruent class. Two further consonants, *w* and *j* as in OS *wundar* 'wonder' and OS *jungaro* 'disciple,' respectively, are continuant consonants as well; they constitute the phonetic class glide and are considered the consonantal counterpart of the vowels *u* and *i*, respectively. Finally, the continuant, breath *h* as in OS *hungar* 'hunger,' will also be considered a glide in the *OSL*.

Consonants thus become more sonorous as they approach vowels on a continuous scale. A second parameter which plays a role in determining degree of sonority of a consonant is the action of the vocal folds, which vibrate in the production of a voiced consonant. Thus, e.g., the voiced counterpart of the OS stop *p* is OS *b* as in *bīdan* 'wait.' The resonants and glides are by definition voiced, as are the vowels. Accordingly, vowels are most sonorous, followed by glides, liquids, nasals, voiced fricatives, voiced stops, voiceless fricatives, with the voiceless stops the least sonorous.

A third parameter that places a consonant in a natural class is its place of articulation in the vocal tract, i.e., the physiological part of the "human musical instrument" which directly shapes the air stream in the production of a given consonant. The flow of air can be impeded at the outermost area of the vocal tract, the lips; a consonant thus formed is bilabial, e.g., *p* of OS *pīna* 'pain,' *b* of OS *bīdan* 'wait,' or *m* of OS *mīdan* 'avoid.' Directly behind the upper lip, the upper teeth join the lower lip in the shaping of a labiodental such as *f* in OS *fīf* 'five.' The teeth may also be joined by the very mobile tongue, the front of which, when placed between the teeth during articulation, yields interdental consonants, e.g., *þ* as in OS *thīn* 'your.' Consonants produced with the front of the tongue touching the alveolar ridge just behind the upper front teeth are alveolar, e.g., *t* and *d* as in OS *tīd* 'time,' *n* and *d* in OS *nīð* 'hatred,' *l* in OS *līð* 'drink.' The roof of the mouth from the area behind the alveolar ridge, viz. the palate, to the back of the mouth, where the roof of the mouth is called the velum, ending in a pendant fleshy lobe, the uvula, may also serve as a contact area for various parts (center, back) of the tongue. Thus, consonants shaped by the tongue in juxtaposition with the palate are palatal, e.g., *j* as in OS *jungaro* 'disciple,' while consonants shaped by the tongue in contact with the velum are velar, e.g., *k* or *ng* as in OS *kuning* 'king.' In the case of *w* as in OS *wundar* 'wonder,' the tongue approaches the velum, but the lips are rounded instead of spread; accordingly *w* can be labeled the composite labiovelar. The consonant *h* as in OS *hungar* 'hunger,' is noisy breath produced through constriction of the glottis, the opening between the vocal folds, hence it may be termed a glottal consonant. In chameleon-like fashion *h* copies the place of articulation and hence the shaped air of its contiguous vowel (cf. sect. 16.1.2). In fact, *h* can be understood as a voiceless vowel immediately preceding the voiced vowel; it may, therefore, be viewed as a transitional or glide consonant.

16.1.2 Vowel

Vowels are most sonorous on the scale of sonority (cf. 16.1); all OS vowels are voiced, i.e., the vocal folds are in a state of vibration. The physical articulation of vowels requires the shaping of the air stream in the mouth by means of raising and lowering the tongue, fronting or retracting it, and by rounding or spreading the lips. As with consonant formation, the vocal tract from the lips to the back of the throat of the "human musical instrument" can be pinpointed as places of articulation for vowels; they are termed tongue positions. Thus, in the articulation of *ī* in OS *īsarn* 'iron,' the tongue is arched forward under the palate, resulting in a palatal or front vowel, while *ū* as in OS *ūt* 'out' requires the bunching of the tongue back in the vicinity of the velum to produce a velar or back vowel. The tongue in fairly neutral or central position produces a central vowel such as *a* in OS *all* 'all'. Along with tongue position, the height of the tongue (tongue height) in the mouth modifies the air stream used to shape a vowel. Thus, the tongue bunches high toward the palate or the velum in the articulation of the *ī* and *ū,* respectively, whereas it is relatively flat or low in the articulation of *a*. Accordingly, tongue height in shaping the breath stream is described as high, mid, low or close, half-close, half-open, open. A third parameter which distinguishes vowel formation is the rounding or spreading of the lips. Back vowels such as *ū* in OS *ūt* and *ō* in OS *ōðar* form a natural class in articulation through the rounding of the lips. The *i* of OS *fisk* 'fish' is articulated with spread lips, however, the first *i* of OS *firiston* 'first' may have been articulated with rounded lips (cf. Chap. VI: 19.4.21). Finally the degree of muscular tension in the tongue, cheeks, and jaw also shapes or colors a vowel. For example, more muscular tension is required to keep the tongue high and front in the articulation of *ī* in OS *īsarn* 'iron' than in the articulation of *i* in OS *fisk* 'fish,' the first accordingly labeled tense, the second lax. Often tense and lax are concomitant with long and short vowel duration, respectively, and/or with relative closeness and openness, respectively.

16.2   Acoustic   Phonetics

Whereas articulatory phonetics concentrates on the physiology of the "human musical instrument" in the shaping of sound, acoustic phonetics concentrates on the physics of those shaped sounds as perceived by the ear and as measured on machines. Sound is waves in the air produced by vibration emanating from various parts of the "human musical instrument" as they shape the respiratory air. The frequency per second of the vibration (a complete cycle from rest) yields the specific pitch of a sound. The intensity or loudness of a sound is determined by the amplitude of the vibration; i.e., the distance from rest to the furthest point reached. Intensity plays a role, although not the sole role, in stress. Frequencies and intensity of sound waves can be analyzed, whether by the ear or machine, e.g., the sound spectrograph, as a spectrum with an x-axis and a y-axis respresenting frequency and intensity, respectively. The distinguishing quality (timbre) of a sound is determined by its frequencies, which appear as concentrations of acoustic energy or vertical bands of energy called formants. Acoustically vowels are periodic vibrations while consonants represent nonperiodic vibrations, technically noise. As consonants ascend the scale of sonority (cf. sect. 16.1 above) they are composed of both nonperiodic and periodic vibrations.

In vowel formation the dominant formants reflect resonance chambers in the "human musical instrument," such as the pharynx and the mouth. Thus, formant 1 with low frequency is spread far apart from formants 2 and 3 with higher frequencies in the pronunciation of *ī* as in OS *īsarn* 'iron,' while formant 2 strongly approaches (lowers in frequency) formant 1 which moves (raises frequency) slightly toward formant 2, and formant 3 moves (lowers frequency) slightly toward formants 1 and 2 in the pronunciation of *a* as in OS *all* 'all.' The spatial concentration of formants in the case of *a* characterizes it as [+compact], in contrast to *i* which is [+diffuse] since the formants are more spread out. Analogously, frequency predominance and location help characterize consonants acoustically; thus, *t* of OS *tīd* 'time' is [+diffuse] and *k* of OS *kuning* is [+compact]. Again, we observe no absolute distinction between consonants and vowels.

16.2.1 Consonant

As indicated in sect. 16.2 above, acoustic classification of sounds is based on binary features, thus, e.g., OS *ī* and *t* are [+diffuse] but [-compact]. This is only one of a bundle of features which characterize each sound. Feature theory displays a proliferation of acoustic features since those first proposed by Jacobson, Fant and Halle 1952. Accordingly the twelve acoustic features used in the *OSL* may have alternate names and/or may be employed in configurations (with or without additional features) differing from those suggested here. The objective is disambiguation of each sound, which may be achieved by proposing any number of configurations of features. Some acoustic feature configurations are more realistic (more refined) analogues to the articulatory features (cf. sect. 16.1) than are other acoustic feature configurations of the same sound. High priority is placed on simplicity and naturalness in choosing distinctive feature networks to account for phonological fact. The basic sonority distinction between a consonant and a vowel is as follows: A consonant which is not a glide is [+consonantal]; a resonant is not only [+consonantal] but also [+vocalic], e.g., *m* in OS *mīdan*; a glide is [-consonantal] and [-vocalic], e.g., *w* in OS *wundar*; all other consonants are [-vocalic], e.g., *b* in OS *bīdan* 'wait.'

Acoustic features of place include [+diffuse] in the case of labials and dentals, with hyponyms bilabials, labiodentals and interdentals, alveolars, respectively, as, e.g., *p* of OS *pīna* 'pain' and *þ* of OS *thīn* 'your.' The acoustic feature [-diffuse] is appropriate to velars, subsuming palatals and velars, as, e.g., *k* of OS *kuning* 'king;' its opposition feature [+compact] is largely redundant in the description of the OS consonants and hence will be unspecified. The opposition pair [grave:acute] characterizes the broad class dentals as [-grave], e.g., *þ* of OS *thīn* 'your,' in distinction to the broad set labials and the narrow set velars, e.g., *p* of OS *pīna* 'pain' and *k* of OS *kuning* 'king,' respectively, as [+grave]; the palatal *j* as in OS *jungaro* 'disciple' is [-grave]. The feature [+flat] refers to lip-rounding such as occurs in *w* of OS *wundar* 'wonder;' the opposing member of the feature set is [+plain].

Acoustic features of manner which distinguish stops from continuants are [-continuant] as for *p* of OS *pīna* 'pain' versus [+continuant] for *f* of OS *fīf* 'five;' the opposing feature is [interrupted]. The acoustic feature [strident], as opposed to [mellow], distinguishes labiodentals from bilabials, dentals (alveolars) from interdentals, and uvulars from velars, e.g., alveolar *s* of OS *sīn* 'his' is contrasted as [+strident] with interdental *þ* of OS *thīn* 'your' as [-strident]. The feature [tense], as opposed to [lax], characterizes aspiration as found, for example, subphonemically, i.e., nondistinctively on the initial voiceless stops in OS, thus *p* of *pīna* 'pain,' which is symbolized phonetically as [p^h]. The feature [+tense] may also describe the relative tenseness of a voiceless consonant when compared with its voiced counterpart, thus the *p* of *pīna* 'pain' relative to the *b* of OS *bīdan* 'wait,' where tension is concomitant and nondistinctive. The acoustic features [+voice] and [-voice] distinguish, as noted above, e.g., the *p* of OS *pīna* 'pain' from the *b* of OS *bīdan* 'wait.' Finally, the feature [+long] may refer to geminate consonants.

16.2.2 Vowel

Acoustically, vowels are designated as [+vocalic] and [-consonantal]. The feature set [diffuse:compact] signifies high tongue height and low tongue height, respectively, thus the *ī* of OS *īsarn* 'iron' and the *a* of OS *all* 'all,' the first [+diffuse], the second [+compact]. Palatal or front vowels (tongue position) are [+acute], e.g., *ī* of OS *īsarn* 'iron,' while velar or back vowels are [+grave], e.g., *ū* of OS *ūt* 'out.' The lip-rounding of *ū* in OS *ūt* is designated as [+flat], the opposition feature being [plain]. All OS vowels are [+continuant] and [+voice], which are accordingly redundant features. The acoustic feature set [strident:mellow], which refers to the degree of turbulence or noise of a consonant, is not germane to vowel description. The acoustic feature pair [tense:lax] distinguishes a more close vowel from a more open vowel, e.g., *ī* of *īsarn* 'iron' from *i* of *fisk* 'fish,' where degree of vowel tension is concomitant with degree of vowel strength. However, the two long *ē*'s, e.g., of OS, *lēt*

Systematic Phonemes (Chart): 17 - 17.2

's/he allowed' and *lẽð* 'evil,' are disambiguated on the basis of the features [+tense] and [-tense], respectively. While *ē̜* of OS *lēt* 'allowed' can be distinguished from short *ę* as in OS *lęsad* 'they gather,' as [+tense] and [-tense] respectively, *ē̜* of OS *lẽð*, being [-tense], must be distinguished from *ę* of OS *lęsad* 'they gather' by a twelfth acoustic feature for OS, viz. [+long] for *ē̜* with [-long] for *ę*. The acoustic feature [nasal] is not distinctive in the phonological system of OS which follows.

17. The Old Saxon Sound System

Old Saxon, as every other language, is a system or network of relationships both within a particular component of the grammar, e.g., the phonology, and across the components of the grammar, e.g., phonology and semantics. The study of the articulatory and acoustic features of OS defines a particular sound by describing both what it is and what it is not relative to other sounds in the OS language. Thus, a sound is defined by similarities and differences in a system; it derives its existence from the system which it inhabits. A sound disambiguated from every other sound in the system and signalling a distinct difference in meaning in the morpheme in which it is used is a phoneme. A minimal contrastive difference, i.e., signalling a semantic difference, in any component of the grammar which is discrete in the system is a distinctive feature. Articulatory and acoustic features can immediately disclose distinction in the phonology. In order to extract the least distinction between sounds, minimal pairs, i.e., morphemes which contrast in but one sound are chosen;

such contrastive units are characterized as being in contrastive distribution. In addition, the targeted sounds of the two member set should ideally be characterized by a high degree of naturalness. Thus, OS *lið* 'limb' and OS *līð* of 'drink' differ only in their respective vowels *i* and *ī*, the first articulatorily and acoustically [-tense], the second [+tense]. The phonemes /i/ and /ī/ alone signal two distinct meanings of these words in paradigm. Either OS *lið* 'limb' or OS *līð* could also be contrasted with, e.g., OS *lud* 'sexual potency' (cf. Rauch 1975). Both contrastive pairs with OS *lud* are only near minimal, since the final consonants differ. The pair OS *līð* : *lud* is still less minimal, since the vowels of the two members differ not only acoustically as [-grave:+grave] but also as [+tense:-tense], respectively. The [-tense] vowel pair OS *lið* : *lud* demonstrates satisfactorily, however, the acoustic [-grave:+grave] and [-flat:+flat] distinctive features of the two phonemes /i/ and /u/, articulatory front unrounded contrasting with back rounded, respectively. Consonantally, e.g., *p* and *b* form a stronger natural class, i.e., share more features than do, e.g., *p* and *s*, yet all four function to distinguish the morphemes that embody them by means of articulatory/acoustic distinctive features.

Phonetically the *p* of OS *pīna* 'pain' differs from the *p* of OS *sprēkan* 'speak.' The first is aspirated, symbolized [p^h], i.e., it is accompanied by a puff of air; the second is unreleased, symbolized [p^-], lacking a puff of air. The consonantal articulatory feature aspiration, acoustically [+tense], is not distinctive in the *p* of the pair OS *pīna:sprēkan*, since the pair is far from minimal. Indeed the two *p*'s differ in pronunciation because they occur in mutually exclusive environments, on the one hand syllable initial, on the other hand, after *s*. Accordingly, the two pronunciations [p^h] and [p^-] of the phoneme /p/

are in complementary distribution and thus allophones of /p/. Allophones are not accountable for differences in the meanings of a morpheme pair; they represent phonetic variants of the same phoneme. Where *p* occurs in final position in a morpheme, it may be aspirated or unreleased. The articulatory/acoustic manifestation of the phoneme /p/ in a word such as OS *gelp* 'scorn' is thus said to be in a state of free variation; it is a free variant of /p/.

17.1 Segmental Phonemes of Old Saxon

The phonological system of OS allows division into segmental and suprasegmental or prosodic phonemes, the latter superimposed, so to speak, upon the individual segmental phonemes as well as across series of phonemes and morphemes (cf. sect. 17.2). Seventeen consonants and thirteen vowels constitute the segmental phonemes of OS; see sect. 17.3.3 on the positing of OS /ə/. Geminate and other consonant clusters, as well as diphthongs, are considered sequences of two or more segmental phonemes.

17.2 Old Saxon Systematic Phonemes

The segmental phonemes of OS evince unpredictable features and hence are basic or fundamental to the phonological structure of OS; they represent the systematic phonemes of OS. Noncontrastive features evinced in all allophones can be derived by phonological rules, wherein the systematic phonemes serve as the underlying representation or the rule input, and the systematic

OLD SAXON SYSTEMATIC PHONEMES

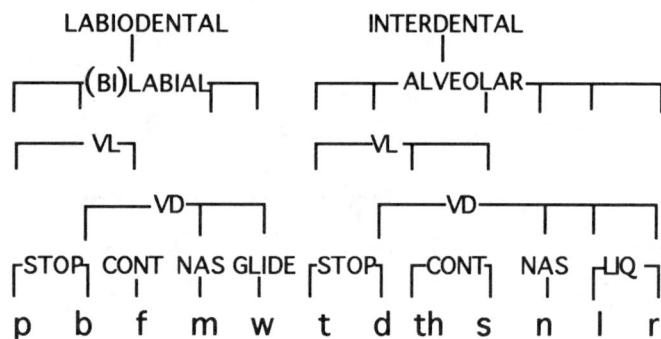

Systematic Phonemes (Chart): 17 - 17.2

(CONTINUED)

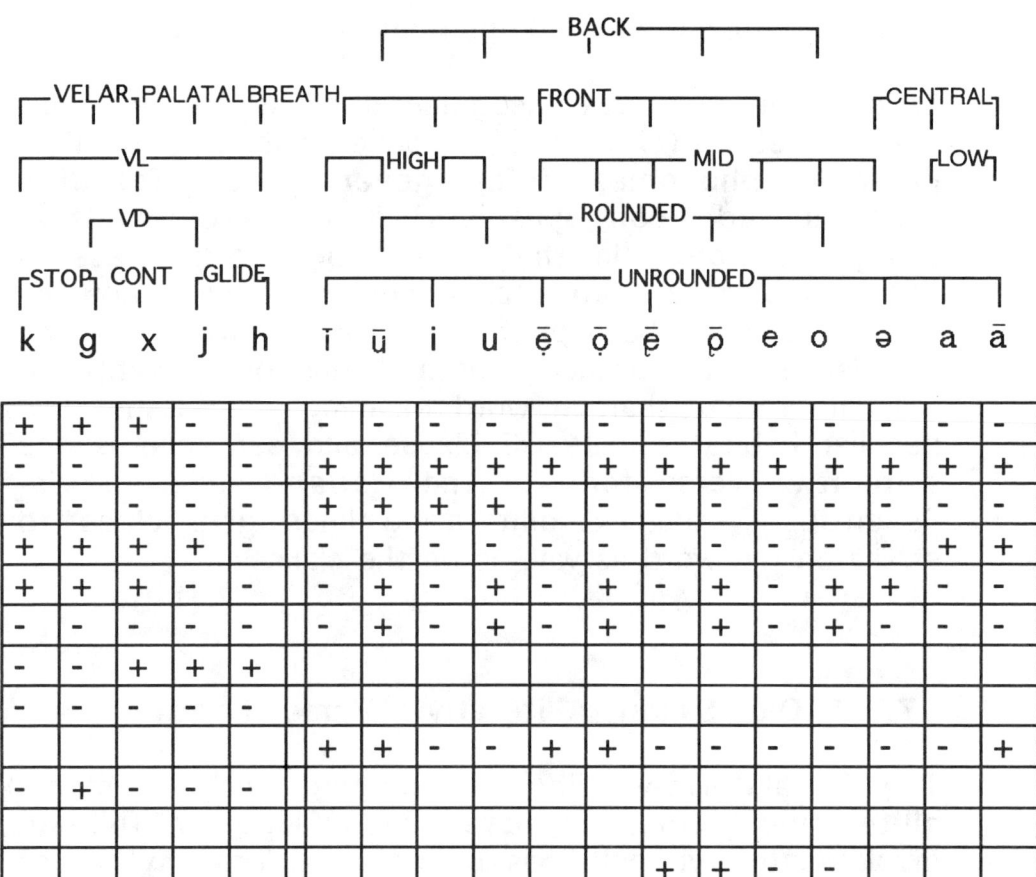

phones in phonetic representation serve as the output to the phonological rules. Thus, the aspiration of morpheme initial *p*, noted in sect. 17 above, could be accounted for by means of a phonological rule with /p/ as input and [p^h] as output (see further Chap. VI: 19.5). The systematic phonemes of OS are listed in the chart on pages 86-87.

17.3 Suprasegmental Phonemes of Old Saxon

Strictly speaking, every segmental sound has inherent pitch and stress (cf. sect. 16.2 above). Suprasegmental or prosodic phonemes refer generally to features superimposed upon syllable(s) in words or words in strings of words. In the latter, only word stress is considered, since word pitch is not characteristic of Old Saxon. However, both pitch and stress characterize the OS clause and sentence, where distinction in sentence meaning rather than in word meaning is at issue. The peculiar habitat of the OS clause and sentence is the alliterative verse form of the *Heliand* and *Genesis*. Felicitously, the OS alliterating lines give clues to stress on the word as well as on the clause.

17.3.1 Old Saxon Alliterative Verse Form

The OS alliterative line, in keeping with Germanic alliterative verse, consisted of a long or full-line divided into two half-lines by caesura. The rhythm of each half-line requires two beats, that is, main stressed syllables accompained by varying numbers of nonprimary stressed syllables. Alliteration chooses primary and at least secondary stressed syllables. The second half-line least secondary stressed syllables. The second half-line contains the principal alliterating sound or stave of the full-line, which thus contains the third main stress of the full-line or the first of the second half-line. The first half-line may contain one or two staves. The *Heliand* poet alliterated with the consonants *p, d, f, g, h, j, k, l, m, n, p, r, s, sp, st, sk, t, th, w*. Alliterating consonants required iconism in place and manner of articulation, but not in voice; the sibilant clusters did not alliterate with *s*. All OS vowels alliterate with one another. The alliteration also favors certain word classes. The broad set nominal, viz. nouns, adjectives, numerals, nonfinite verb forms, nominal adverbs, has priority for housing Germanic alliteration. The broad group verbal, i.e., finite verb forms and most adverbs, is less favored. Finally, the remaining set, consisting of function-type words such as pronouns, prepositions, and conjunctions, was avoided. These sets have a correlation in word stress (cf. sect. 17.3.2 below).

The verse form of the opening line of the *Heliand* can be marked as follows:

Mánega uuáron,   the sia iro mṓd gespṓn,
'There were many whose mood impelled them'

showing two primary stressed syllabes in each half-line and alliteration of two nominals in *m*, with the principal stave in the second half-line, viz. *mōd*. As is seen from line 1, the Old Saxon line allows for a great number of nonprimary stressed syllables. Indeed, the *Heliand* is characterized by the extended line, as, e.g., l. 605:

thana cuning an thesumu kēsurdōma. Saga ūs, undar
            huilicumu he sī thesaro cunneo afōdit.
'the king in this empire. Tell us into which of these
            clans he be born!'

In addition function words can on occasion bear a stave, e.g., l. 304:

*ō*dan *a*rbides. Ni uuelda sie *a*ftar thiu
'imparted hardship. He did not want (to accuse) her about that.'

The *Heliand* verse form thus evinces modifications of paradigm Germanic alliterative verse prompted by linguistic change, foremost the weakening of the intensity of Germanic stress, which led to proliferation of tertiary stressed syllables as is found, e.g., in vowel epenthesis and end syllable weakening (cf. Chap. VIII: 27); see further Lehmann 1956.

The OS alliterative verse form is extremely valuable for extracting features of the segmental phonology. So, e.g., the fricative nature of OS initial *g* can be inferred from its alliteration with *j* (<i>) as found in *Heliand* l. 198:

*g*eng thes *g*ēres gital. *I*ohannes quam
'The year ended. John came'

Graphemic evidence further supports continuant articulation for OS initial *g*. Thus where ms. M of the *Heliand* writes <gēres> ms. C writes <iares>. In turn, the ms. M <gēres> testifies to the palatal phoneme /j/ which induces palatal *e* (cf. Chap. VI: 19.4.16 and 19.4.30). Length of vowels, technically, a suprasegmental, is discussed in 17.3.2 below.

17.3.2 Word Stress Phonemes

OS has at least three suprasegmental phonemes of word stress: primary stress /´/, secondary stress /`/, and tertiary or weak stress, sometimes misnamed unstress and accordingly left overtly undesignated or signalled by /ˣ/. The distribution of the three degrees of stress may be formulated in a set of suprasegmental phonological rules (SuR). A phonological rule consists of an input (X), a process or equivalence arrow (⟶), and the constraint or environment (/) which determines the output. Thus, e.g., the rule X ⟶ Y/__ Z reads "X becomes Y in the environment before Z."

It is especially difficult to extract the stress phonemes of a historical language, such as OS, since accent marks which occur to one degree or another in all mss., PVCMS, do not yield complete or conclusive evidence (cf. Cordes 1973: 141; Taeger 1981: 141; Taeger 1981: 410-413). The suprasegmentals are thus extracted mainly from general Germanic stress and the particular metrical habits of OS. The three degrees of OS stress may be formulated as in the following set of suprasegmental rules (Brackets enclose various possibilities; α signals + and -). Suprasegmental (SuR) 1, 2, 3 are also ordered, as is observed immediately by the fact that SuR 1 and 2 apply before SuR3 which is best formulated as an "otherwise" rule. See also sect. 17.3.3.

SuR1: V ⟶ [ʹ] (a) initial syllable

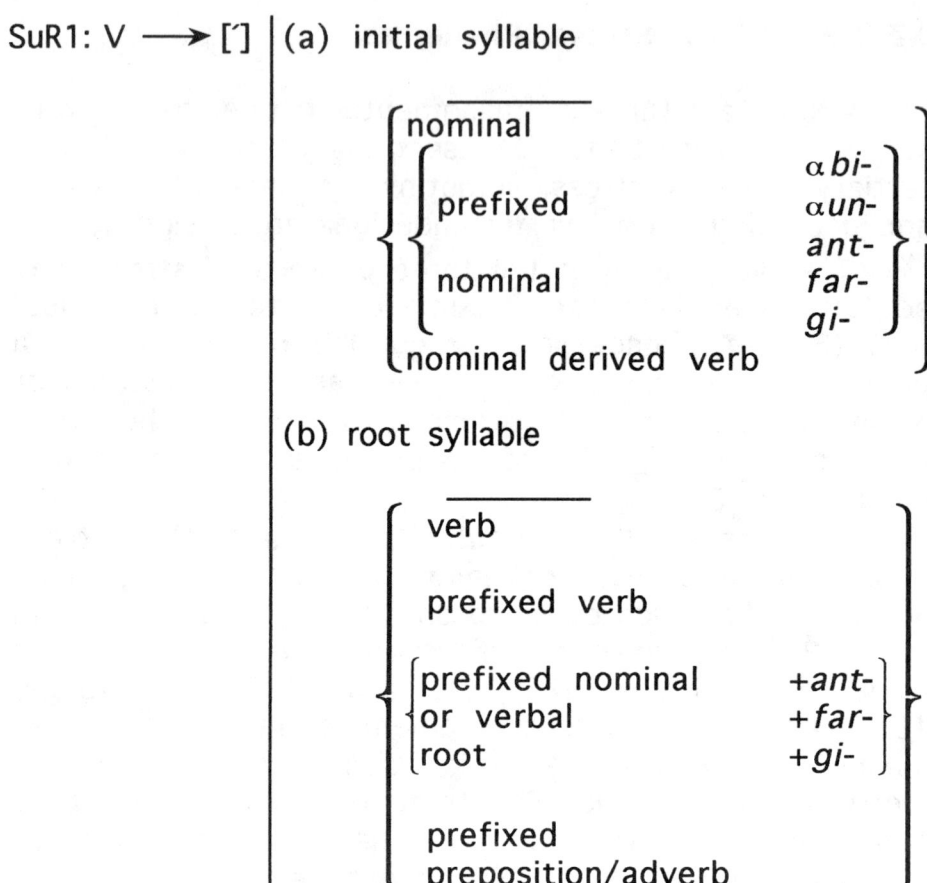

(b) root syllable

SuR1(a) yields, e.g., OS *técan* 'sign;' *bíhēt* 'scorn' but *biténgi* 'bound;' *únskuldig* 'innocent,' but *unspúod* 'evil;' *ándwordian* 'answer.' SuR1(b) yields, e.g., OS *stándan* 'stand' and *wiðarstándan* 'resist;' *antáhtoda* 'eighty,' *farwúrht* 'sin,' *gilőbo* 'faith;' *anéban* 'beside,' *tesámne* 'together.'

SuR2: V ⟶ [ˋ] | (a) last component

$$\begin{Bmatrix} \overline{\alpha 2 \text{ component compound}} \\ \alpha 3 \text{ component compound} \end{Bmatrix}$$

(b) second syllable

$$\begin{bmatrix} \alpha 3 \text{ or more syllable} \\ \text{word with heavy first} \\ \text{and second syllable} \end{bmatrix}$$

SuR2(a) can yield, e.g., OS *godspèll* 'gospel,' *orlaghwı̀la* 'fateful hour.' SuR2(b) can yield, e.g., OS *liobòsto* 'dearest.'

SuR3: V ⟶ [ˣ]   otherwise

SuR3 accounts thus, e.g., for OS *orlághwı̃lá* 'fateful hour' (cf. SuR2(a) above) or *fragodún* 'they asked.'

17.3.3 Syntactic Stress

The three suprasegmental phonological rules for OS paradigm word stress may be subverted by the syntagmatic syntactic stress, which is a metrical stress in the OS alliterative line. For example, by SuR1(a), SuR2(a) and SuR3 *ambahtman* 'servant(s)' is stressed, thus *ámbáhtmàn* in *Heliand* l. 2059:

> *thīne ambahtman   ērist brengean*
> '(you order) your servants first to bring'

ambahtman is syntactically (metrically) stressed *ámbàhtmán*. On the other hand, the linguistically induced

OS proliferation of weakly stressed syllables may already affect the word in paradigm, so that the teleology of the weakening of the primary and secondary stresses reamains speculative. The alpha (α) convention in rules SuR1 and SuR2 is thus in part accountable to the moveable syntactic stress of the metric line. Crucial evidence for the segmental phonemes derives from the phonological stress rules as well. Thus, by SuR3 the inflectional endings are affected, leading to the array of graphic variation, in particular <e,o> as <a>, <u,i> as <e,o> and the reverse (cf. Chap. III: 11.1; IV: 13.2), indicative of a so-called neutral vowel schwa [ə]. It is possible to posit an OS schwa phoneme /ə/ (cf. sect. 17.2 above) on, e.g., evidence from the behavior of the OS adverb-conjunction sō 'thus, so,' which is found graphically as <so, sio, suo, sa, se>. Unlike inflectional endings, however, OS sō also occurs under secondary, if not, primary stress, e.g., in *Heliand* line 163, where it houses the dominant stave:

selƀo giuuirkean, of he sō uueldi
'himself bring it about, if he so wished'

Syntactically induced secondary stress may be indicated by ms. C's <suo> in *Heliand* line 2508:

Sō duot thea meginsundeon an thes mannes hugi
'so do the mighty sins in the heart of man'

On the other hand, weak stress may be graphically indicated by ms. C's <sa> in *Heliand* line 3194:

mīnumu hērron, sō man it imu at his hoƀe kuðid
'my lord, as one informs him in his palace'

Certainly, syntactically induced weak stress is at issue in ms. C's <se> in *Heliand* line 14:

an buok scriƀan   endi sō manag gibod godes
'in book write   and so many a commandment of God'

The occurrence of OS *sō* outside of weak stress supports the phonemicization of /ə/ in OS.

Finally, a set of syntactic stress conventions may be formalized by the following SuR4, which generates the dominant stress in a phrasal or clausal syntagm:

SuR4: word ⟶ [dominant stress]

a) N̄n   Nn

b) FVb   non-F̄Vb

c) intensifying adv. $\left\{\begin{array}{c}\overline{\text{adj.}}\\ \text{adv.}\end{array}\right\}$

d) nominal adv.   ādj.

e) prēp.   FV

f) F̄V   prep.

g) F̄V   adv.

h) prēp.   pron

i) pron.   prēp.

SuR4(a) yields, e.g., OS *gódes weg* 'God's path;' (b) OS *hēt sie thō sámnon* 'he ordered them to gather there;' (c) OS *swīðo frúod* 'very wise;' (d) OS *bíttro gihugida* 'bitterly thought;' (e) OS *siu im áfter geng* 'she went after him;' (f) *woldon im hnīgan tuo* 'they wanted to adore him;' (g) OS *frāgoda níudlīko* 'he asked anxiously;' (h) OS *áftar mi* 'after me;' (i) OS *ina áno* 'without him.'

17.4 Old Saxon Syllable

A unit of sound which may or may not be larger than a single phoneme and which is not necessarily a morpheme is the syllable (σ). The syllable is composed of a vowel, which is the nucleus (Nu) and frequently one or more nonvowels. The fundamental universal syllable structure is CV (consonant vowel). The C is the onset (On) which may consist of more than one C. One or more C's following the Nu are the coda (Co). A syllable is heavy (cf. e.g., SuR2 of sect. 17.3.2 above) if it contains a V̄ or a V̆ followed by two consonants, the last of which may be the onset for the next syllable; a syllable is light if it contains V̆(C); (cf. further Vennemann 1988).

The syllable schemes for OS syllable division can be illustrated by the following words:

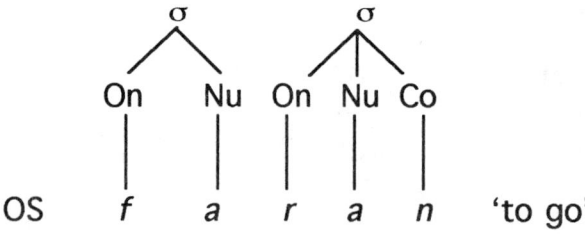

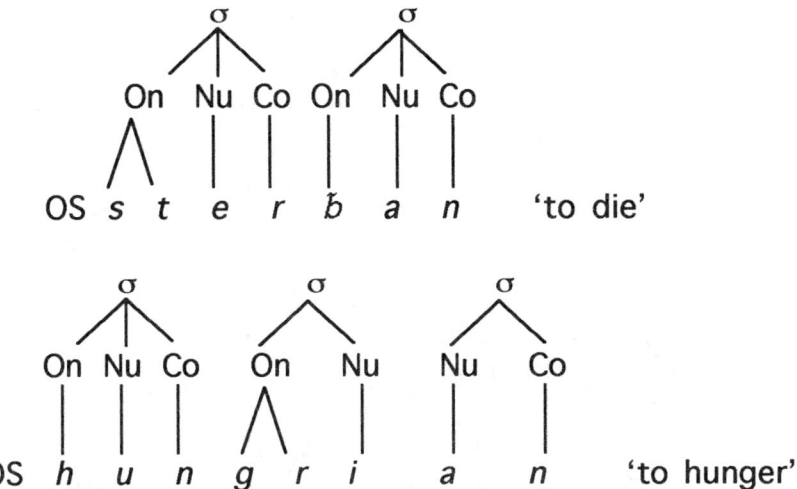

Nongeminate consonant clusters may form the coda of the preceding syllable or the onset of the following syllable, if constrained by the phonotactic rules of OS, that is the patterning of sound clusters or sequences in OS, which to a large extent are etymologically determined and thus natural to the language. Indeed, whether a single consonant is a syllable coda or a syllable offset is constrained by productive or perceived etymological morphemes. The following syllable schemas illustrate such phonotactic constraints:

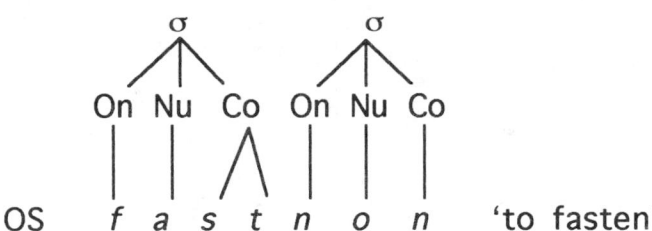

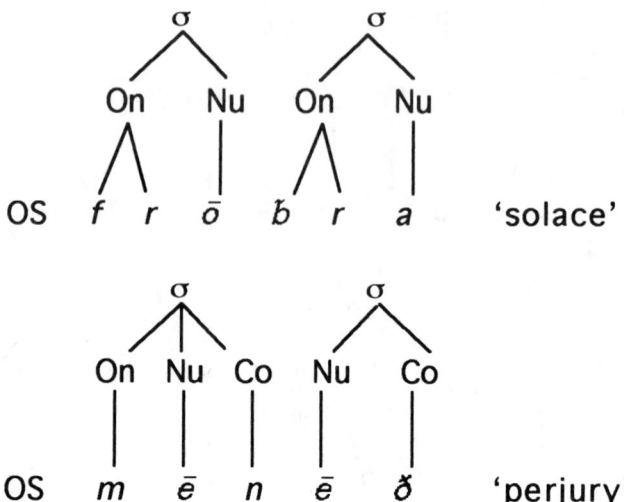

OS f r ō b̃ r a   'solace'

OS m ē n ē ð   'perjury'

An OS syllable structure rule may thus be formulated as follows:

    word ⟶ V(C-(C(-CV)))
               if not phonotactically
               otherwise constrained

Chapter Six

Sorting out the Graphemic Variation;
Heliand and *Genesis* Manuscripts;
Latin Prefaces; Old Saxon Speech Area,
Dialects and Megadialects;
Phonemic, Allophonic, Graphemic Fit

18. The Sound: Symbol Fit

The richness of the OS *Heliand* and *Genesis* data is such that the iconic principle of biuniqueness, which would establish a one-to-one fit between sound and symbol or grapheme, is seldom operable. This richness allows for naive spellings which are strongly iconic phonetically, such as <u> in ms. C *gaui* 3 p. sg. pret. subj. 'would give,' which indicates the voiced character of /f/ medially between vowels, while ms. M *gabi* reflects the genetic character of this medial /f/. Relative to ms. C *gaƀi*, ms. M *gabi* may also reflect orthographic lag. Considering the imp. sg. of the verb 'give,' ms. M yields *gef* compared with the ms. C *giƀ*; this evidence shows the ms. C <-ƀ> as orthographic lag in view of the phonological rule of final devoicing overtly indicated by ms. M in this instance (cf. Chap. VI: 19.5).

In the above discussion, we perceive the seeming inconsistencies and thus multiple choices facing the reader of OS. On the one hand, variant graphs may indicate dialects, in this case phonological differences between ms. C and ms. M (which may also indicate time differences in the same phonological change). On the other hand, variant graphs may indicate orthographic lag, paradigmatic connection (analogy, orthographic iconism) or occasionally scribal error. Beyond this, the reader contends with megadialect interference in the OS evidence, i.e., borrowings from contiguous Proto-West Germanic as well as from the neighboring Old English. Indeed, the OS graph <ƀ> is modeled on the borrowed OE graph <ð>, for example. In order to understand the nature of the primary OS evidence more fully, it is necessary to orient it in time and space.

19. Time/Space Setting of the Primary Old Saxon Data

19.1. The *Heliand* Manuscripts

The *Heliand* data are transmitted in two larger manuscripts, C and M, and three fragments P, V, and S. Ms. C, the so-called Cottonianus, housed in the British Library, London, consists of lines 1 through 5968 with a few small lacunas; it is the most complete *Heliand* document, numbering 165 manuscript leaves. The C ms. or Cotton Caligula AVII is dated tenth century (cf. plate I of ms. C, fit 1: lines 1-18a). The remaining four documents are dated in the ninth century. Ms. M, the Monacensis, is housed in the Bayrische Staatsbibliothek in Munich. More than one-sixth of the lines contained in ms. C are missing in ms. M. Labeled Cgm. 25, Ms. M contains 74 manuscript leaves and a half leaf which supplies the conclusion for the *Heliand* (cf. plate II of ms. M, fits 2-3: lines 117-179a). Fragment P, formerly housed in Prague, now found in the Museum für deutsche Geschichte in Berlin, is a single leaf fragment. Numbered R56/2537, the ms. P fragment contains lines 958 to 1006 of the *Heliand*. Lines 1279 to 1358 of the *Heliand* are recorded in one of four Vatican fragments, designated ms. V (Palat. Lat. 1447) and housed in the Vatican Library, Rome. The remaining three ms. V fragments comprise the OS *Genesis* fragments (cf. Chap. VI: 19.3.3 below). The most recently (1977) discovered *Heliand* fragment, ms. S, was uncovered in the Staatliche Bibliothek am Johannes-Turmeier-Gymnasium in Straubing. Ms. S contains discontinuous portions from *Heliand* fits V through IX. Now housed in the Bayrische Staatsbibliothek, Munich, the ms. S fragment consists of eight leaf sides, with only the top and the bottom third of the first two and the last two sides preserved (cf. Bischoff 1979; cf. plate III of ms. S, fit 7: lines 558b-582a and fit 8: lines 675-683a; lines 692-698).

19.2. The Role of the Latin *Heliand* and *Genesis* Prefaces

A prose preface, "Praefatio in librum antiquum lingua Saxonica conscriptum," consisting of two parts, referred to as A and B, and a verse preface, "Versus de poeta et interprete huius codicis," provide the rationale for the composition of the *Heliand* and *Genesis* narrative epics which account for approximately four-fifths of all extant OS documentation. Further, the prefaces give clues to such questions as the time of composition and to the personage of the author(s) of the *Heliand* and *Genesis*. For example, prose Preface A provides the relative timing for the composing of the OS epics in or shortly after the reign of Louis the Pious ("Ludouuicus piissimus Augustus"), who was emperor from 814 to 840. Preface A further reveals that the purpose of Louis in commissioning the Saxon poet ("de gente Saxonium") was to make the scriptures accessible to all his subjects, noneducated and educated alike ("non solum literatis, verum etiam illiteratis").

A labyrinth of linguistic and textual problems is associated with the Latin prefaces, not only with regard to their implications for the *Heliand* and *Genesis*, but also for the prefaces themselves. The time(s), place(s) and author(s) of the prefaces come into question. Indeed, the problem of the legitimacy of the prefaces relative to the *Heliand* and *Genesis* occupies a large portion of the *Heliand*'s textual history (cf., e.g., Hannemann 1939/1973, Krogmann 1947/1973, Haubrichs 1966/1973); the Introduction in Behaghel/Mitzka 1965, as well as in Behaghel/Taeger 1984).

Of the innumerable bits of evidence produced by the prefaces, preface A provides the word *vitteas* 'fits' by which the *Heliand* sections or chapters are designated. In fact ms. C confirms the existence of such running chapter heads. The word *vitteas* itself helps identify preface A as an early medieval piece rather than as a "Renaissance forgery" (Magoun 1984: 114) which, it is conjectured, accompanied yet another, now no longer extant, *Heliand* ms. in the sixteenth century (cf. Introductions in Behaghel/Mitzka 1965, Behaghel/Taeger 1984, Eichhoff/Rauch). *Vitteas* is a contamination of Gmc. root **fit* and Latin fem. acc. pl. suffix *-as*, the first deriving from IE **ped* 'foot.' Genetically related to ON *fitja* 'to tie the ends of yarn on a warp' and OHG *fizza* 'a tied set of wound yarns,' the metaphor of sectioning in weaving appears to fall within the semantic features of *vitteas*. The semantic trope extends to varying morphology such as ON *þāttr* which incorporates both the features "thread, strand" and "section" and relates genetically with Lat. *texere* 'weave.' For that matter, Eng. *rhapsody,* which can refer to a section of an epic poem, again derives from the weaving concept, Gk. *rhaptein* 'to sew.'

The poet, *vates* of preface A, reoccurs in preface B (*Vatem*) and in the verse preface (*Vates*). Both the latter two prefaces, in particular the verse preface (cf. plate IV), exploit the Caedmonian metaphor of a naive but divinely inspired poet. The quality of the poetry of the epics is profusely praised in preface B as surpassing all German poetry with its elegance ("cuncta Theudisca poëmata suo vincat decore") — a conviction recently reiterated by Sanders (1985: 1104). Finally, the gripping tensions of the Christian-Heathen intercultural milieu of the *Heliand* epic, strongly reflected in its linguistic and literary structures, has long stimulated scholarly discourse (cf. Belkin/Meier 1975; cf. especially Einhard 830/1960, Rathofer 1962, Murphy 1989).

19.3 Dialects and Megadialects

19.3.1 The Old Saxon Speech Area

The OS speech area is roughly, i.e., somewhat uncertainly, sketched both spatially and temporally. The eastern border neighboring on then Slavic territory ran in a line, the so-called *limes saxonicus*, roughly from Kiel in the north to Bardowieck, Lüneburg, Magdeburg, Halle, Merseburg, and perhaps as far south as Naumburg. The southern border of OS, neighboring on the Old High German speech area, cut across Germany approximately from Rossleben in a line Allstedt, Sangerhausen, Nordhausen, Duderstadt, to Hedemünden on the Werra, and thence from Münden to south of Olpe. The western border, contiguous to Old Low Franconian ran roughly in a line northward from south of Olpe to Elberfeld, Werden,

Essen, Dorsten, Bocholt, west of Doetinchen in the present Netherlands, north of Zutphen to Gorssel, and Apeldorn to Elburg on the Zuider Sea. The northern boundary, shared mainly with Old Frisian, ran roughly from the Zuider Sea east in a fairly straight line to Groningen, from where the boundary ran to south of Aschendorf to the Ems River and perhaps to the Weser River. The boundary continued, adjoining Frisian territory, somewhat inland from the mouth of the Weser River north to Cuxhaven. To the north-east, OS shared the Eider River as a boundary with Denmark (cf. plate V; cf. further Hartig 1985).

The term Old Low German is a latter-day misnomer (cf. otherwise Cordes 1980: 576) for Old Saxon which characterized the Saxons on the mainland in distinction to the Anglo-Saxons on the island. The Old Saxon language period is determined as circa 800 to 1150, separated from the following language period, appropriately called Middle Low German, by a lacuna in documentation of at least 100 years; Middle Low German documentation shows increasing interference from High German. Correspondingly, the south-east boundary with High German receded northward in the thirteenth century. Similarly the north-western and western boundaries receded toward the Ems River. On the other hand, the north-northwest boundary extended over some present day east Frisian areas. The northern boundary extended as well, but the great expansion was the twelfth century colonization of Slavic territory eastward across the Oder River to the Vistula River. The northward and eastward expansions were the prelude to the Hanseatic prestige of the Middle Low German language.

19.3.2 *Heliand* Dialects and Register

The OS speech area is sectioned grossly into four population groups: the Northalbingians or Northpeople, subdivided into Stormarn (around Hamburg), Holsten (to the North), and Dietmarschen (west coast). The remaining three groups are to the OS west: the Westphalians, the Engrians on both sides of the Weser River, and to the east, the Eastphalians (cf. plate V). These four groups, however, do not coincide diatopically with the known dialect divisions of OS, since the northern area lacks early documentation (although not necessarily language influence, cf. below), and evidence from the more southern areas (Westphalian, Engrian, Eastphalian) allow only an appoximate east:west division, i.e., roughly Hildesheim, Bad Gandersheim, Halberstadt, Merseburg as eastern dialects; and Essen, Werden, Freckenhorst, Corvey as western dialects. Indeed, Cordes (1973: 17) allocates the OS scriptoria to Westphalian (southwest Westphalian: Essen, Werden; north Westphalian: Freckenhorst, Münster, Osnabrück; east Westphalian: Herzebrock, Nerford, Corvey, Hameln, Fischbek, Paderborn, Minden) or to Eastphalian (Gandersheim, Lamspringe, Dorstadt, Wendhausen, Quedlinburg, Hildesheim, Halberstadt, Merseburg, Madgeburg). The bishoprics, with their attendant scriptoria, all date from the early OS period: Osnabrück (772/853), Bremen (787), Verden (788), Paderborn (795), Minden (803), Münster (805), Halberstadt (814), Hildesheim (814) (cf. plate V).

Yet the place and the time of the *Heliand* dialects are difficult to ascertain. The literature concerning the provenance of the *Heliand* mss. and their possible, i.e., hypothesized archetype or proto-manuscript, is labyrinthine and often contradictory. Thus, while

Krogmann (1947) places the writing of the *Heliand* protomanuscript at Werden on the Ruhr on the basis of such evidence as the <b>, or the *pāscha:ōstara* 'Easter' isoglosses, Haubrichs (1966) is able to finesse the Werden origin with a Fulda origin (the latter site more traditionally targeted, cf., e.g., König 1978: 57), by postulating both cities, whereby the poet in the course of his *Heliand* composition moved from Fulda to Werden. Similarly, while Cordes (1973: 16-17) rather hazily places ms. M "nach Westen, aber nicht in das südwestl. Westfälisch" and the ms. set PVC or their prototype "etwas weiter nach Osten, etwa in das Gebiet der oberen Weser," Bischoff (1979) considers Corvey, which certainly is not in the west of the OS speech area, but lies on the Weser River, as the provenance of ms. M. On the other hand, ms. C is widely held as having been written in (southern) England (Cordes 1973: 15, Behaghel/Taeger 1984: XVI), while the newly found ms. S fragments have been claimed for Werden, which is characterized as having a very Frisian monastery (Drögereit 1970, fon Wearinga 1986). Whereas for Krogmann (cf. 1947 above), <b> characterized Werden, for Drögereit (1950: 50-52, 102) <b> characterized Werden. In fact, these may not be contradictory pieces of evidence at all; they point to the inherent heterogeneity of OS.

Cordes (1973: 18-19) describes the dialect of ms. M as "Altnd. mit geringfügigen hd. Kriterien," and ms. C as "Altnd. mit einigen altfränk. und altengl. Kriterien." The ms. S fragments are considered as most proximate in language to that of ms. M, but also as displaying a great many more Frisianisms than ms. M (Behaghel/Taeger 1984: XVIII, fon Wearinga 1986: 25). OF, OE, OHG megadialect interference is discussed in section 19.3.3 below. As for isoglosses concerning the gross diatopic east:west division of the OS speech area, the *Heliand*

Speech Area; Interference: 19.3 - 19.3.3

mss., in distinction to the minor OS documents (cf. Sanders 1985b), show inconclusive evidence. So, e.g., the OS western end-syllable <a:o> isogloss correlating with OHG <e, a:o>, and the OS eastern end-syllable <e:a> isogloss correlating with OHG <e, a:o> turn out as a third set in *Heliand* ms. M, viz. <e:o>. The richness of variation is such that the ms. evidence simply defies conclusive standard dialect identification. Thus Scheuermann writes (1985: 1112): "Trotz der Divergenzen innerhalb einer Hs. und trotz der Differenzen der Hss. untereinander ist es nicht möglich, diese Erscheinungen derart diatopisch zu interpretieren, daß man sagen könnte, dem and. Dialekt A eigne die eine, B und vielleicht weiteren Dialekten die andere Form." This richness is amply displayed in all parts of the grammar of OS (cf., e.g., Rooth 1956/1973); it is widely visible, excruciatingly so for the reader, in the graphemics (cf. sect. 19.4 below).

The confusing nature of the *Heliand* data in contrast with the minor OS documents has led to the speculation that the language of the *Heliand* represents a quasi-pidgin language, used for the business of proselytizing. On the one hand, this is consonant with the conversion mission of the superstratum Franks (cf. sect. 19.2 above); on the other hand, it makes little sense if the ordinary OS native speaker had difficulties understanding a specialized level of usage. Alternately, the *Heliand* is viewed as a literary work representative of a more formal register which may have been the province of the more educated proselytizers (cf. further the Introduction in Eichhoff and Rauch 1973; Sanders 1985b; Scheuermann 1985). Transversing dialects and registers is, of course, time, so that a feature such as the notorious *cht* which correlates with *ft*, e.g., OS *craft*:*craht* 'power' has long been viewed as a later (tenth century) western change in progress from *f* to *h*, in addition to possibly being representative of a formal register. The newly found ms.

S (cf. Chap. VI: 19.1) dating from the ninth century evinces exclusively *ht*. On the other hand, this may also be accountable to yet another parameter in studying evidence, viz. the limited remains of ms. S.

19.3.3 Old Frisian, Old English, Old High German Megadialect Interference

Geographically situated as it is adjacent to the North Sea Coast with the confluence of various Germanic peoples, OS is by nature a heterogeneous dialect of West Germanic, i.e., recognizable by its seeming admixture of shared features, principally with OF, OE, and OHG. The affinity with OF and OS is understood, although not without controversy, as older by far; i.e., OS clearly belongs to the **Ingvaeonic** wing of the West Germanic dialects. One can hardly speak here of a stratal relationship and perhaps the term interference with regard to OF and OE is too strong; the relationship of these three dialects may have been one of ancient adstrata on the northwestern coast of the continent. Accordingly, OS was not monolithic by birth and one may view megadialect features, especially with OF and OE, as inherent to, or simply as, *Heliand* and *Genesis* manuscript dialect features. Indeed, the megadialect features help characterize the dialect features (cf. sect. 19.3.2 above).

The southern filiation of OS with OHG is generally held to be a later and/or gradually increasing phenomenon, i.e., more as an interference factor (cf. Rauch 1970/1973 and the pertinent literature discussed therein). Nevertheless, the shared isoglosses with either the North (Anglo-Frisian) or the South (High German) are similarly impressive. The Anglo-Frisian isoglosses include, e.g., the loss of nasal before *f*, *s*, *þ* with vowel length compensation (OS *fīf*:OHG *finf* 'five'); syncretism in the plural of the present and preterite, indicative and subjunctive verb suffix (OS *-ad, -en, -un, -in*); *r*-less pronominal morphology (OS *hē*:OHG *er* 'he'); syncretism of the first and second persons, singular and plural, accusative and dative personal pronouns (OS *mī*:OHG *mir, mih* 'me'); the *-s* masculine plural nominative/accusative noun morphology (OS *dagos*:OHG *tagă* 'days'); the tendency toward palatalization, vocalic and/or consonantal (OS *gīr*:OHG *jār* 'year'); lexical morphology (OS *-lūkan*:OHG *-sliozan* 'lock') (cf. further Simon 1965; Holthausen 1921: §§ 29, 30; Rooth 1956/1973: esp. 237).

Nowhere in the OS data is its filiation with OE, or, perhaps more felicitously stated in this instance, the shared features of OE with OS, more remarkable than in the contrastive *Geneses* evidence. The OS Vatican ms. (Palat. Lat. 1447) *Genesis* fragments consisting of Fragment I, ll. 1-26, Fragment II, ll. 27-107 and 112-150, and Fragment III, ll. 151-337, discovered by Karl Zangemeister in 1894 in the Vatican Library, confirmed the brilliant 1875 conjecture of Eduard Sievers that the so-called OE *Later Genesis* or *Genesis B* is a translation of a lost (at the time of the conjecture) OS poem (cf. Sievers 1878: XXXII). The source document represented by ms. V Fragment I, ll. 1-26 offers a superb line by line comparison with ll. 790-817 of the OE *Genesis B* target document. The native language of the *Genesis B* translator, nevertheless, remains widely disputed, i.e., whether OE or OS (cf. further Vickrey 1960; Rauch forthcoming b).

The High German interference in OS is repeatedly understood as such rather than as being autochtonous. Thus, the Anglo-Frisian nasal loss (cf. above) is countered by mixed evidence in the OS *Heliand* and *Genesis* mss.; compare ms. C *andran* with ms. M *ōdran* 'other.' In the case of the Ingvaeonic accusative/dative syncretism of the first and second person pronouns (cf. above), e.g., the accusative 1 p. sg. ms. M *mik* stands beside ms. C *mi* 'me.' On the lexical semantic level the janusean semantic features of OS *drōm* provide the key to both the OE gloss 'joy' and the OHG gloss 'dream,' for OE *drēam* and OHG *troum*, respectively, (cf. further Rauch 1992). Vocalic hallmarks of the period such as the monophthongization of Gmc. **ai* and **au*, which proceeded in English, Frisian, and Saxon practically unconstrained, but in High German strongly constrained by consonants (OHG *ē* < *Gmc. **ai/-h, r, w* and OHG *ō* < *Gmc. **au/-*dentals, Gmc. **h*) yielded an OS/OHG *ē* rather than an OE *ā*, and an OS/OHG *ō* rather than an OF *ā*. The weakness of the yield part of this observation is, of course, that OS obviously avoided a merger in the reflexes of the two Gmc. diphthongs. Rooth (1956/1973) characterizes the OS monophthongization as systemically Ingvaeonic, but orthographically High German.

Perhaps nowhere in OS phonology is graphemic interference from OHG so widely invoked as in the case of OS <ie, uo>, indicative of the OHG diphthongization of Gmc. $*\bar{e}_2$ and **ō*, although the teleology for the interference may differ. Thus, while Rooth, appealing to a prestige factor writes (1956/1973: 211-212): "Als Sachse sprach er [der Helianddichter] *ō*, und die *uo*-Schreibungen müssen als solche, Schreibungen, gedeutet werden, die unter dem modischen Einfluss des Fränkischen standen," Klein underscores a systematic or structural dynamic noting (1985: 1077): "Heute glaubt man zumeist, daß die 'fränkischen' Digraphen <ie>, <uo> nur dazu dienten, die geschlossenen asächs. *ẹ̄, ọ̄* von den offenen *ę̄* < *ai*, *ǭ* < *au* abzuheben."

The data are, typically for *Heliand* OS ambiguous. Concentrating, e.g., on the *ō* : *uo* set, one finds that ms. M exhibits approximately 1460 <ō> and 34 <uo>, while ms. C yields some 1750 <uo> and 119 <ō>; assorted scattered spellings include <ŏ, u, v̊, ó, oo ou>. The newly found ms. S exhibits (Taeger 1979: 183): "vollständige Umsetzung der ... vielerörteten Grapheme <uo, ie> zu <o, e>." Perhaps strategies operative within *Heliand* OS ought to be derived from more universal principles to shed light upon the <uo, ie> question. One can take as a point of departure the Van Ginneken/Jakobson (1956: 576) "tendency toward diphthongization of the main syllable and that towards apocope of the accompanying syllable." End-syllable weakening in the digraph-producing ms. C appears much less frequently than in the monograph-producing ms. M — a contradiction in view of the older age of ms. M. Thus, ms. C evinces glided vowels, if not full diphthongs compatible with end-syllable preservation and, accordingly, the converse of the Van Ginneken/Jakobson rule. The converse rule is possible if it is paralinguistically conditioned by the Trager (1958) vocal qualifier feature of extent, which opposes drawl to clipping. The drawl conditioner finds its substantiation not only in the relative preservation of end-syllable vowels and root diphthongs, but also in the cofeature of vowel epenthesis, e.g., *burug* 'city,' which abounds in ms. C as compared with ms. M. In fact, ms. C does not mimic OHG diphthongization orthography. Consider, e.g., ms. C *nuon* 'none, the ninth hour,' which reads *non* in ms. M as well as in OHG. Consider further that words such as OS *hie* 'he' and *thie* 'that, who,' characteristic of ms. C, are words unfamiliar to indigenous OHG. Interference from OHG is, therefore, impossible in OS words as these (cf. further Rauch 1980, 1986). The OS *Heliand* ms. data offer inherent dialect and megadialect ambiguities from the point of view of the modern reader; from the point of view of the native Old Saxons, they may well have represented their familiar mother tongue.

19.4 Phoneme, Allophone, Grapheme

The fit of each of the seventeen OS consonant and thirteen OS vowel phonemes relative to the graphemic representation as evidenced by the *Heliand* and *Genesis* mss. is displayed below. The phonemes are listed in the order of their sonority (cf. Chap. V: 16.1 and 17.2). Standard phonetic notation is employed; raised dash (e.g., k⁻) represents unreleased consonant, while raised tick (e.g., kⁱ) represents palatalizated consonant. An underline in a tabulation of graphs (e.g., initial [f] = <f, u̱, uu>) represents a relatively rare occurrence. Single occurrences of graphs or extremely rare graphemic occurrences are not schematized in the tabulation; they are listed in the immediately following discussion to each schema. Vocalically a subscript dot (e.g., ẹ) represents a close vowel, a subscript hook (e.g., ę) represents an open vowel. Careful distinction is observed between and among / /, [ ], < >. For consonants three **word** positions initial, medial, final signal the allophonic contexts in sections 19.4.1-19.4.17. These are not necessarily isostructural with **syllable** position, e.g., <d> of *niudlīco* 'carefully' is word medial but syllable final. The vowels are considered in root syllable under primary stress in sections 19.4.18-19.4.30; for vowels in medial or end syllable under weak stress see Chap. VIII: 27. OS before a given form represents use of a relatively shared graph, i.e., by at least two of the five manuscripts (MCPVS); use of a graph particularly germane to a ms. is identified by the particular ms. letter. Such data feed, of course, into the time, place, dialect, and megadialect considerations discussed above.

19.4.1 /p/

The phoneme /p/ has the allophones [pʰ, p, p⁻].

Initial:	[pʰ]	<p->	*pīna* 'pain'
	[p⁻]	<sp->	*sprekan* 'speak'
Medial:	[p]	<-p->	*dopean* 'baptize'

<-b-> for /p/ occurs in ms. C *galbo* imp. sg. 'boast.' Geminate /p/ occurs as <pp> in OS *uppan* 'above.'

Final:	[p⁻, p, pʰ]	<-p>	*diop* 'deep'

Geminate ,<-pp> occurs, e.g., in ms. C *upp* 'up.'

19.4.2 /b/

The phoneme /b/ has the allophones [b, pʰ, p, p⁻].

Initial:	[b]	<b->	*biscop* 'bishop'
Medial:	[b]	<-mb->	*umbi* 'around'

Geminate /b/ occurs as <-bb-> with one occurrence each of <-b̃b-> and <-ff-> in ms. C *lib̃biandes* pres. part. 'living' and ms. C *afheffian* 'lift up,' respectively.

Final:	[p⁻, p, pʰ]	<-mb>	*lamb* 'lamb'

19.4.3 /f/

The phoneme /f/ has the allophones [f, v]

Initial: [f] ⟨ f-, <u>u</u>-, uu- ⟩ ēnfald 'simple'

Medial: [f] <-f- + s, t, þ> eft 'again'

⟨ -f-, -b- + σ, -b- ⟩ efno 'even'

[v] ⟨ -b-, -ƀ-, -v-, -u-, -f- ⟩ geban 'give'

For [v] mss. P and V use <-ƀ-> exclusively and mss. C and S prefer <-ƀ->, while ms. M prefers <b>. Ms. S has frequent <-u->, which occurs seldom in mss. M and C. The geminate cluster <ff> is assigned to /b/ in the *OSL* (cf. 19.4.2).

Final: [f] ⟨ -f, -b, -<u>b</u>, -<u>u</u> ⟩ se*l*f 'self'

For the once occurring <ht> in mss. C, S *craft* 'power' see /X/ (cf. 19.4.15).

19.4.4 /m/

The phoneme /m/ has the phone [m]

    Initial: [m] <m->   *mīdan* 'avoid'

    Medial: [m] <-m->   *namo* 'name'

Geminate /m/ occurs as <-mm->, e.g., in OS *fremmian* 'do.'

    Final: [m] <-m>   *drōm* 'dream'

Geminate <-m> occurs, e.g., in ms. C *grimm* 'grim.'

19.4.5 /w/

The phoneme /w/ has the allophones [w, ə].

Initial: [w] ⟨ uu- / u- ⟩ +i, e, a, o   *uueg* 'path'

⟨ uu- / u- ⟩ + u   *uundar* 'wonder'

Initially after C and before V in, e.g., OS *quic* 'alive,' (cf. 19.4.13), or OS *tuuē* 'two.'

Medial: [w] ⟨ -uu- / -u- ⟩   *ēuuig* 'eternal'

<-h-> instead of <-uu-> as in ms. M *brāhon* dat. pl. 'brows,' <i> instead of <-uu-> as in ms. C *scadoian* 'shade,' <g> instead of <-uu-> in ms. M *nīgean* 'renew' may indicate the use of <-*uu*-> as a hiatus breaker; it may represent some sort of laryngeal friction or simply syllable juncture (cf. Rauch 1973). <-uu-> also alternates freely with zero grapheme, in particular before <u, o>, e.g., ms. C *fiori* 'four.'

Final: [ə] ⟨ -u / -o ⟩   *sēo* 'sea'

Because <-u, -o> alternate freely with zero grapheme as in *Heliand* l. 1152 *sē*, a [-ə] or [-ə]-like allophone of /w/ is assumed in final position.

19.4.6 /t/

The phoneme /t/ has the allophones [tʰ, t, t⁻].

Initial: [tʰ]   ⟨ t- / th- ⟩   *tīd* 'time'

[t⁻]   <st->   *stark* 'strong'

Medial: [t]   <-t->   *lātan* 'let'

<tt> for simpex /t/ occurs in ms. C *mohtta* 3 sg. pret. 'could;' <ht> for /t/ occurs in ms. M *gewiht* 'wisdom.'

Geminate /t/ occurs as <-tt->, e.g., in OS *luttil* 'little,' and as <t>, e.g., in ms. C *biteres* gen. sg. 'bitter.'

Final: [t̚ t, tʰ] ⟨ -t / -th ⟩ *eft* 'again'

Geminate <-tt> occurs, e.g., in ms. C *utt* 'out.' Affricate /ts/ occurs as <z, c>, e.g., OS *krūci* 'cross.'

19.4.7 /d/

The phoneme /d/ has the allophones [d, d̥, t̚, t, tʰ].

Initial: [d]   <d-> *dag* 'day'

An extremely rare <ð-> occurs in ms. C *ðōðes* gen. sg. 'death.'

Medial: [d] ⟨ -d- / -ð- / -th- ⟩ *alēdean* 'lead away'

[d̥ t] ⟨ -d- / -t- + σ⟩ *niudlīco* 'carefully'

The rare <-ð-, -th-> are considered scribal error (Holthausen 1921: 247), although <-rð-> occurs most, e.g., mss. C, *Genesis* dat. pl. *worðon* 'words.' That intervocalic <d, ð, th> was pronounced as [ð] (cf. sect.

19.4.8) is not out of the question, however. Yet a minimal pair such as *alēdean* 'lead away': *alēthian* 'disgust' argues for an intervocalic [d]. Extremely rare <-t-> in ms. M *giawāti* 'clothes' is considered either scribal error or megadialect (OHG) interference. Geminate /d/ occurs as <-dd->, e.g., in OS *biddian* 'request.'

Final: [t⁻, t, tʰ] ⟨ -d / -t / -ð / -th ⟩ *god* 'God'

The <-d> is most frequent; the *OSL* considers <-d> for [-t] orthographic lag. The <-rð> cluster as in ms. C *mēthomhorð* 'saved money' and the <-rth> in ms. C *horth* 'treasure' are noteworthy. The 3 sg. pres. and pres. pl. suffixes posited as (V)D (cf. Chap. II: 8.1) display dialect differences: ms. M prefers <-d>, while mss. C, *Genesis* prefer <-t>. Ms. C has frequent <ð>. The weak verb preterite participle has frequent <-t> in mss. V and C but also in ms. M. Class 2 weak has exclusive past participle <-t> in ms. V, frequent in mss. C and M. Geminate <-dd> occurs in *Genesis inwidd* 'sin.' That final <-d, t, ð, th> were pronounced [þ] (cf. sect. 19.4.8) is not out of the question.

19.4.8 /th/

The phoneme /th/ or /þ/ has the allophones [þ, ð].

Initial: [þ] ⟨ th-, ð-, t̠-, d̠- ⟩ *thīn* 'your'

Rare <t-> is considered scribal error; <d-> occurs in ms. M, <ð-> in mss. P, V, S. Ms. C prefers <th->.

Medial: [ð] ⟨ -ð-, -d-, -th- ⟩ *werðan* 'become'

Ms. P uses <-ð->; *Genesis* prefers <-ð->. Ms. M prefers <-d-> with seldom <-ð-, -th->. Ms. C prefers <-th-> beside <-ð->. <-d-> may result from megadialect (OHG) interference. The OS word *eftha* 'or' occurs as *efto* in *Genesis*. MS. M's *ettha, ettho, ohtho* spellings are interpreted as a geminate /þ/, while the <-f-> spellings are considered megadialect (OF) interference. Rare <-ht> occurs in ms. C *nihtscipies* gen. sg. 'hatred.'

Final: [þ] ⟨ -th, -ð, -d, -t, -ht̠ ⟩ *quath* 's/he said'

Ms. P, V prefer <-ð>. Ms. C prefers <-th>, while ms. M prefers <-d>, the latter possibly by megadialect (OHG) interference. Ms. C has several <-ht>, e.g., *wiht* 'against.'

19.4.9 /s/

The phoneme /s/ has the allophones [s, z].

    Initial: [s] <s->   *sīn* 'his

    Medial: [s] <-s- + σ> *lōsda* 'set free'
                [z] <-s->   *lōsien* 'to set free'

Geminate /-s-/ occurs, e.g., in OS *wissa* 3 sg. pret. 's/he knew.' Affricate /ts/ occurs as <z, c> (cf. Chap. VI: 19.4.6); ms. M writes *blidsea* and *blitzea* 'bliss' for ms. C *blizza* [ts]. Cf. Chap. VI: 19.4.13 for cluster <-sk->.

    Final: [s] <-s>   *hūs* 'house'

Geminate <-ss> occurs in ms. C *wirss* 'worse.'

19.4.10 /n/

The phoneme /n/ has the allophones [n, ŋ].

    Initial: [n] <n->   *nīð* 'hatred'

    Medial: [n] <-n->   *wintar* 'winter'
                [ŋ] <-n->   *engil* 'angel

Geminate /n/ occurs, e.g., in OS *sunna* 'sun.' <-n-> alternates freely with zero grapheme in, e.g., OS *jugaron* dat. pl. 'servants.' The co-existence of members of a set such as ms. C's *simnon, sinnon, simblon, simlon* 'always' represent assimilation and epenthesis phenomena.

Final: [n] <-n>   sk*ī̃n* 'visible'

Geminate <-nn> occurs, e.g., in mss. C, V, *Genesis mann* 'men.'

19.4.11 /l/

The phoneme /l/ has the phone [l].

Initial: [l] <l->   *līð* 'drink'

Medial: [l] <-l->   *quelan* 'die'

Geminate /l/ occurs as <-ll-> in, e.g., OS *quellianne* 'to kill.' Scribal error is attributed to ms. C *alldo* 'old' beside ms. M *aldo*.

Final: [l] <-l>   *dēl* 'deal, part'

Geminate <-ll> occurs, e.g., in OS *all* 'all.'

19.4.12 /r/

The phoneme /r/ has the phone [r].

Initial: [r] <r->   *rīki* 'rule, kingdom'

Medial: [r] <-r->   *erl* 'jarl, earl'

Geminate /r/ occurs as <-rr-> in, e.g., OS *sterro* 'star.'

Final: [r] <-r>   ēr 'before, earlier'

Geminate <-rr> occurs, e.g., in ms. C *hierr* 'here.'

19.4.13 /k/

The phoneme /k/ has the allophones [kʰ~k¹ʰ~k¹⁻~k~k¹ᵏ~k⁻~g].

Initial: [kʰ] ⟨ k-
              + a, o, u ⟩   *kuning* 'king'
              c-

         <ch->   *chananeo* 'Cana'
         <q- + w>   *quic* 'alive'

         [k¹ʰ] ⟨ k- + i,e
                            ⟩   *antkiennien* 'recognize'
                ki- + e

         [k¹⁻] ⟨ sc- + i,e
                            ⟩   *scīn* 'visible'
                sci- + e

Rare <ch> is considered OHG graphic interference. One occurrence of <x> is ms. M *xristes* 'Christ.' <c> before <i, e> is found in the cluster <sc>. <sc> is preferred by ms. C (cf. medial position below). ø for <k> occurs once in ms. V *salt* 2 sg. pres. 'you should.'

Medial: [k] $\left\langle \begin{array}{c} \text{-k-} \\ + a, o, u \\ \text{-c-} \end{array} \right\rangle$ *bōknian* 'illustrate'

 <-ch-> *wrāchi* 'revenge'

[k¹] $\left\langle \begin{array}{c} \text{-k-} + \text{i,e} \\ \text{-ki-} + \text{e} \\ \text{e} + \text{-ke-} \\ \text{i} + \text{-k-} \end{array} \right\rangle$ *tēkean* 'sign'

[g] $\left\langle \begin{array}{c} \text{-k-} \\ + n \\ \text{-g-} \end{array} \right\rangle$ *tēgno* gen. pl. 'sign'

Rare <ch> is considered OHG graphic interference. While <c> before <i, e> is found in the cluster <sc>, <c> alone before <i> is extremely rare since <ci> = affricate [tsi] as in OS *krūci* 'cross' through Latin interference. The cluster <sk> is found as <sch> in ms. C *hosche* 'scorn,' while <sch> in OS *pascha* 'Easter,' borrowed from Latin, is exclusive in both mss. M and C, but for one *pasca* in ms. M. Shibilation of <sk> to [ʃ] is not yet productive (cf. Lasch 1979); nonshibilant can also be deduced from alliteration, e.g., *Heliand* l. 4884: *skarp an skēðia: 'ef ik uuið thesa scola uueldi,' quað he*, "the sharp (sword) in its sheath: 'if I against this group would have wanted,' said he." Ms. C *scealt* 'you shall' is considered scribal interference from OE. Geminate /k/ occurs as <-kk, cc, ck, cch-> medially; scribal error is found in ms. C *rīkkian* 'powerful.'

Final: [k⁻, k, kʰ] ⟨ -k / -c ⟩ ōk 'also'

[k¹⁻, k¹, k¹ʰ] ⟨ -k / -c ⟩ ic 'I'

Ms. M *gelīch*, *gilīh*, and Genesis *gelīhc* 'same' are considered OHG graphic interference. A once occurring <-g> in ms. M *gehwilĭg* 'each' may be graphic confusion with the *-ig* suffix; cf. /j/ (19.4.16). <cc> is found in ms. C *quicc* 'alive.'

19.4.14 /g/

The phoneme /g/ has the phone [g].

Medial: [g] <-ng->   *engil* 'angel'

The positing of [k] for [g] in ms. C *githenkean* 'accomplish' on the basis of syllable final devoicing could lead to massive merger with roots in /-nk-/, e.g., OS *thenkean* 'think.' Indeed, Sehrt (1966: 594-5) lists ms. C *githenkean* both under *athengian* 'accomplish' and *thenkian* 'think.' There may be evidence for the phonemicization of [ŋ] in, e.g., ms. C *lansam-* 'long lasting' which could form a quasi-minimal pair with, e.g., *lofsam-* 'praiseworthy' (cf. further below). Geminate /g/ occurs, e.g., in OS *liggian* 'to lie, to prostrate.'

Final: [ŋg] <-ng> *bifeng* 3 p.sg. pret. 'caught'

As in medial position, there is evidence of [ŋg] toward [ŋ] phonemicization (cf. sect. 19.4.10). Mss. M and C metathesize genetic <-gn> to <-ng> in the 3 p. sg. pret. indic. *gifrang* 'perceived'; in fact, ms. C writes the ø alternate *gifran* even more frequently than expected *gifragn*. There is no evidence in the *Heliand* and *Genesis* fragments for syllable/word final devoicing of <ng>; on the other hand, final [g] after <n> would be the only OS voiced obstruent in final position.

19.4.15 /x/

The phoneme /x/ has the allophones [ɣ, x].

Initial: [ɣ] <g-+ a, o, u>   *gumo* 'man'

Medial: [ɣ] <-g- + a, o, u>   *niguni* 'nine'

$$[x] \left\langle \begin{matrix} a, o, u + -g- +s, t \\ -h- \\ a, o, u + -g- +\sigma \\ -h- \end{matrix} \right\rangle \begin{matrix} \textit{maht} \text{ 'can' 2 p. sg.} \\ \text{pres. indic.} \\ \textit{gihugda} \text{ 'memory'} \end{matrix}$$

Final: $[x] \left\langle \begin{matrix} a, o, u + -g \\ -h \\ -\underline{c} \\ \underline{-hg} \end{matrix} \right\rangle$ *dag* 'day'

19.4.16 /j/

The phoneme /j/ has the allophones [j, ç].

Initial: [j] <i-> *jungaro* 'disciple'
              <g- + i, e> *gehan* 'to say'
              <gi- + a, o, u> *giāmar* 'sad'

The rare 2 p. dat. pl. personal pronoun ms. M *giu* 'you' varies with frequent OS *iu* as well as less frequent *eu*. On the other hand, OS *gio* 'already' stands beside OS *io, eo* and also ms. C *iu*, perhaps two phonemes are involved, /j/ and /i/.

Medial: [j] ⟨ -V + -i- + V- ⟩ *lugina* 'lies'
              ⟨ -V + -g- + e, i ⟩

         [ç] ⟨ i, e + -h- + s, t
                i, e + -g- + s
                -h-   ⟩ *sehs* 'six'
                i, e + -g- +σ
                a = [ɛ, e] by umlaut ⟩

Rare <h + i> occurs in ms. M *tuhin* 3 p. pl. pret. subj. 'rear.' See Chap. VI: 19.4.5 for the use of <-ViV-> and <-VgeV-> as hiatus breakers. Nonprimary stressed <-ig-> varies freely with <-i-> in e.g., ms. C *mahtina* 'mighty' (ms. M *mahtigna*). The once occurring ms. M *suikle* 'bright' may point to syllable-final devoicing to [ç] (cf. Gallée 1910: §241 otherwise).

Final: [ç] <i, e + -g> *weg* 'path'

Nonprimary stressed <-ig> varies freely with <-i> in, e.g., ms. C *mahti* 'mighty' (ms. M *mahtig*).

19.4.17 /h/

The phoneme /h/ has the phone [h].

    Initial: [h] <h->   *hungar* 'hunger'

Variation occurs with zero grapheme, e.g., ms. C *ungres* gen. sg. 'hunger.' Nongenetic <h-> occurs, e.g., in *Genesis* ms. V *haband* 'evening.'

    Medial: [h] <-h->   *bifelhen* 'hand over'

Variation with zero grapheme is very frequent, especially intervocalically, e.g., ms. M *bifeleas* 2 p. sg. pres. subj. 'handed over.' Nongenetic <-h-> occurs, e.g., in ms. C *fēhmea* 'woman.' For the use of <-h-> intervocalically as a hiatus breaker; see Chap. VI: 19.4.5 above. There is no evidence for geminate /h/ in the *Heliand* and *Genesis* fragments.

    Final: [h] ⟨ -h / -ch ⟩   *hōh* 'high'

Variation with zero grapheme is frequent, e.g., OS *hō* 'high.' OS *thōh* 'yet' occurs as *thuoht* in the *Genesis*. Nongenetic <-h> occurs, e.g., in ms. C *giuuith* 'wisdom.' The evidence for the phoneme status of /h/ can be adduced from such pairs as OS *thurh* 'through':*thorn* 'thorn,' or ms. C *wīhes* gen. sg. 'temple':OS *wīges* 'war,' or OS *wīhdage* dat. sg. 'feast day':OS *wīgsaca* acc. sg. 'battle,' the first lexeme of each pair representing OS /h/.

19.4.18 /ī/

The phoneme /ī/ [i:] is represented graphically as <i or í> in, e.g., OS *īsarn* 'iron.' Except for ms. V *thíng* <í> occurs only in <í + C>. The once occurring <y> is found in ms. C *tyreas* gen. sg. 'honor,' as is the single occurrence of <ii>, viz. ms. C *siith* 'later.'

19.4.19 /ū/

The phoneme /ū/ [u:] is represented graphically as <u or ú> in, e.g., OS *ūt* 'out'. Quite seldom <ú> occurs in <ú + C> or word-final, e.g., ms. C *bú* 'house.' Ms. C offers rare <uu> in *uup* 'up.' No root graphic evidence for the palatal umlaut allophone [y] occurs.

19.4.20 /i/

The phoneme /i/ [ɪ] is represented graphically as <i or e> in, e.g., OS *fisk* 'fish.' Root <e> tends to be constrained, but not necessarily so, by a non-<i> in the following syllable, e.g., ms. C *melderon* 'more generous,' ms. M *gef* 2 p. sg. imp. 'give,' ms. C *be* 'by.' Phonetic iconism, paradigm iconism, or weak syntactic stress may account for the three <e>, respectively, which may actually have

Graph-/Phonemes/Allophones: 19.4 - 19.5   129

been pronounced [e or ɛ]. In the case of, e.g., *williad* pl. pres. indic., 2 p. pl. dual pres., 2 p. pl. imp. 'will', ms. M prefers <i> while ms. C prefers <e>. This may point to dialect differences, with phonological consequences, to be sure.

19.4.21 /u/

The phoneme /u/ [ʋ] is represented graphically as <u or o> in, e.g., OS *burg* 'city.' Root <o> occurs also constrained especially in <o + N> and <o + L(C)>, e.g., ms. M *fol* 'full.' Ms. C writes <o> beside preferred <u> in *gumo* 'man,' for which ms. C also shows two occurrences of <uo>, a spelling germane to the diphthongal counterpart of ms. M /ọ̄/ (cf. Chap. VI: 19.4.23). Root graphemic evidence of a palatal umlaut allophone [ʏ] or [i] occurs eleven times in the data. Ms. C offers <i> e.g., *andwirdi* 'answer,' *firiston* 'first' (first <i>), <iu>, *hiugiu* instr. sg. 'mood, heart;' ms. M offers two instances of <i> *barwirdig* 'very worthy.' <i> may represent OF interference.

19.4.22 /ẹ̄/

The phoneme /ẹ̄/ [e:] is represented graphically as <e or é> *lēt* 3 p. sg. pret. 'allowed.' <é> tends to occur in <é + C>. <i> occurs, e.g., in OS *hir* 'here;' it is interpreted as megadialect, viz. OF interference. <æ> occurs in ms. C *gængun* 3 p. pl. pret. indic 'go.' Ms. C often favors <ie>, e.g., *brief* 'letter;' <ie> represents diphthongal pronunciation [iə] of the phoneme sequence /i/ + /ə/ (cf. Chap. VI: 19.3.3 above). Ms. C has an instance of <eo> in *meoda* 'wage,' which is not totally surprising (cf. Chap. VI: 19.4.31 below). Ms. V writes <íe> and <ié> as well as *hier* 'here.' Ms. C writes a single <ei> in *thei* nom. sg. masc. 'the.' In addition to ms. preferences, which are reflective of ms. dialects, syntactic stress may be decisive in the choice of <e, ie>; <e> may represent [e] or even [ɛ] rather than [e:] especially in pronominal forms such as OS *hē* 'he' under weak syntactic stress.

19.4.23 /ǭ/

The phoneme /ǭ/ [o:] is represented graphically as <o or ó> in, e.g., OS *ōðar* 'other.' <ó> is found in <ó + C>. Ms. C offers a very rare <oo>, e.g., 3 p. pl. pret. subj. *gihoobin* 'lifted,' and ms. C yields an <a> in gen. sg. masc. *athres* 'other.' Ms. C is inclined to <uo>, e.g., *buok* 'book.' <ua> occurs, e.g., in ms. M *duat* 1 p. pl. pres. 'do;' <uæ> occurs in ms. M *duæ* 3 p. sg. pres. subj. 'do.' These diagraphs represent diphthongal pronunciation [uə] of the phoneme sequence /u/ + /ə/ (cf. Chap. VI: 19.3.3 above). <úo> and <uó> are found rarely in ms. V. Ms. C <ou> in *wrougdun* 3 p. pl. pret.indic. 'accused' is understood as scribal error for <uo>. Four occurrences, ms. C *freknean* acc. sg. masc. 'bold,' *temig* nom. sg. masc. 'free from' and ms. M *betien* 'to atone for' and *fegnien* 'evil' attest to a palatal umlaut allophone [ø:] in the root. The *Genesis atuemeas* 2 p. sg. pres. subj. 'might free' may point to palatal umlaut of <uo> or simply [uə]. The adverb OS *thŏh* 'yet' shows such variations as ms. C *theh, thuoh,* indicative of weaker and stronger syntactic stress, respectively.

19.4.24 /ẹ̄/

The phoneme /ẹ̄/ [ɛː] is represented graphically as <e or é or æ or a> in, e.g., OS lēð 'suffering.' <é> tends to occur in the sequence <é + C or st>. Very rare <i> occurs in ms. C, e.g., bithion dat. pl. 'both;' equally rare <ei> occurs in ms. M skreid 3 p. sg. pret. indic. 'walked.' Ms. M offers <ea> in nigiean 'no, not any' beside nigen. Ms. C yields an occurrence of <æ> in aræs 'arose.'

19.4.25 /ọ̄/

The phoneme /ọ̄/ [ɔ] is represented graphically as <o or ó> in, e.g., gihōrian 'to hear.' <ó> tends to occur in the sequence <ó + C>. Very rare <uo> is found in ms. C, e.g., guomono gen. pl. 'banquet.' Ms. V yields <oo> in gibood 3 p. sg. pret. indic. 'ordered,' while ms. C writes gibuod for the same word. One occurrence of <ou> is found in ms. C berouvoda 'robbed.' <a> occurs in ms. M bamo gen. pl. 'tree.' Palatal umlaut evidence for an allophone [œ] is very rare: ms. C thregian 'threaten' and ms. C herreon 'to hear.' Ms. C scoinosta 'most beautiful' may represent palatal umlaut or simply graphic metathesis, i.e., reversal of spelling.

19.4.26 /ẹ/

The phoneme /ẹ/ [ɛ] is represented graphemically as <e or i>, e.g., OS beran 'carry.' Megadialect (OF) influence may be seen in <i> as in ms. C fargibanne dat. inf. 'give.' Fairly rare <a> before non-<i> of a following syllable occurs in ms. C *barahtun* acc. pl. neut. wk. 'bright' and rare <æ> before non-<i> of a following syllable in ms. M *bærhtero* gen. pl. neut. str. 'bright.' Ms. M writes <o> in *ohtho* 'or,' perhaps OF interference. Ms. C also writes a substantial number of <o> in *wolda* 3 p. sg. pret. 'willed, wanted,' although *welda* prevails in ms. C, and occurs almost exclusively in ms. M. However, in the pl. pres. indic., 2 p. pl. dual pres., 2 p. pl. imp. *williad* 'will' ms. C displays its ms. dialect preference for <e> over ms. M's <i> (cf. Chap. VI: 19.4.20 above). The <eo> in ms. C *steorra* 'star,' *georno* 'gladly' are interpreted as OE megadialect interference. (See 19.4.22 concerning pronominal forms under weak syntactic stress.)

Evidence for phonemic merger of the palatal umlaut of *a* [ɛ] or perhaps [e] with OS /e/ is substantiated in particular by ms. C's weakening of the end syllable in, e.g., *gerwean* 'to prepare,' which it writes also as *giriwan* with the possible /i/ through OF megadialect interference. There are no data in the evidence to distinguish [ɛ] and [e]. The *garwian* of ms. M beside *gerwide* 3 p. sg. pret. 'prepared' suggests that the palatal umlaut of *a* should perhaps be considered an allophone of /a/ in ms. M's dialect. OHG megadialect interference is frequently invoked to justify OS *Heliand* and *Genesis* palatal umlaut data. In Classical Phonemic Theory secondary umlaut [æ] may be posited for <aht + i> in, e.g. OS *mahtig* 'powerful' which occurs without variation; note ms. M *garwian* may also indicate secondary umlaut for ms. M sequence <rw + i>.

That primary palatal umlaut of *a*, i.e., [e], is phonemically distinct from /e/, i.e., [ɛ], in *Heliand* Old Saxon is possible, yielding the contrast /ẹ/:/ę/. Umlaut evidence for the original filiation of Old Saxon with Old English and Old Frisian is certainly convincing (cf. Rauch 1970/73). Yet the weakening of the palatal umlaut conditioner to /ə/ (cf. Chap. VIII: 27) is not limited to syntagms with the umlauted *a*, e.g., dat. sg. ms. C *huge* 'mind' or ms. M *hugea*, beside *hugi* in both manuscripts. The umlaut conditioner is, moreover, maintained as <i> for semantic disambiguation, e.g., in the present subjunctive of modal verbs (cf. Chap. VIII: 29.2.1) and in the preterite subjunctive of all verbs (cf. Chap. VIII: 29.2.2). The fact that "The graphemic evidence for umlauted sounds of the *Heliand* ms. C outnumbers that of the older ms. M, yet the graphemic evidence for the loss of the umlaut conditioner is more frequent in ms. M than in ms. C" (Rauch 1970/1973: 465), should discourage simplistic correlation theories between umlauted vowel and conditioning vowel in seeking answers to all of the many challenging questions posed by the Old Saxon umlaut data. Finally, pragmatic discourse conditioning factors should also be considered in the understanding of umlaut phenomena (cf. Rauch 1991: 375).

19.4.27 /o/

The phoneme /o/ [ɔ] is represented graphically as <o or a>, e.g., OS *morgan* 'morning.' <a> occurs particularly in ms. C before the liquids <r, l>, e.g., *farahte* 'fear' with expected phonetic consequences [ɑ] or [ɒ]. Rare <uo> occurs in ms. C, e.g., *guod* 'God.' <u> occurs, e.g., in ms. C *fur* 'before.' Ms. C has two <o> in *andwordi* 'answer' as opposed to four <u>; accordingly /u/ is posited for the ms. C dialect in *andwurdi* with its one instance of palatal umlaut (cf. 19.4.2 above), while ms. M evinces without exception <o> in *andwordi* 'answer.' Palatal umlaut of <o> is but remotely possible in ms. C's single occurrence of *drihtnes* 'Lord' (ms. M writes *drohtines*), which never occurs as <u> in either ms.; it is considered reflective of megadialect (OE) interference.

19.4.28 /ə/

The phoneme /ə/, which plays a major role in weakly stressed syllables in OS (cf. Chap. VIII: 27 below), can be posited through its occurrence under syntactic stress in, e.g., *Heliand* line 163, where it houses the principal stave: *selƀo giuuirkean, of he sō uueldi* 'himself bring it about, if he so wished' (cf. Chap. V: 17.3.3 above). /ə/ has a range of allophones [ə, ʌ] perhaps also [ʉ], where it serves as an offglide.

19.4.29 /a/

The phoneme /a/ [a] is represented graphically as <a or o>, e.g., in OS *all* 'all.' Ms. C <á> in *mánon* 'admonish' as well as the <ua> in *huandmahal* 'home' are considered scribal error. <e> before non-<i> in following syllable occurs, e.g., in ms. C *restun* dat. sg. wk. 'death', which otherwise occurs as <a> in ms. C; ms. M uses only <e> in *restu* dat. sg. str. OF megadialect influence may be at issue with phonetic consequences, [ɛ], in dialect ms. M. Ms. C yields *mean* 'man,' as well as <ea> in *scealt* 2 p. sg. pres. 'shall' and in *weard* 'warden,' and <æ> in *æfter* 'after,' all of which can be viewed as OE megadialect interference at least graphemically. For that matter, <o> + N, e.g., in ms. C *on* 'on' can point to OE, OF interference, which, however, may more realistically simply be considered original Ingvaeonic filiation for OS; [ɔ]

Graph-/Phonemes/Allophones: 19.4 - 19.5   135

pronunciation is quite likely. *Heliand* OS yields prehistoric palatal umlaut instances in accord with OE, OF habits, e.g., ms. M *lengron* acc. sg. fem. 'longer' beside ms. C *langron*. Similarly, OS evinces Rückumlaut, unmutation, by lack of the umlaut conditioner on a short syllable class 1 weak verb, exactly as do OF and OE, e.g., OS *getalde* 3 p. sg. pret. indic. 'told' (cf. further Rauch 1970/1973). See Chap. VI: 19.4.26. above for discussion of palatal umlaut of <a>.

19.4.30 /ā/

The phoneme /ā/ [ɑː] is represented graphically as <a or á> as, e.g., in OS *frāgon* 'ask.' <á> occurs in <á + C>. Consistent <a> of *jār* 'year' in ms. C dialect is matched by <e> in ms. M dialect, thus *gēr* (cf. Chap. VI: 19.3.1); OE, OF megadialect interference is likely. Sufficient palatal umlaut evidence for allophone [ɛː] is seen, e.g., in ms. M *farlētid* 3 p. sg. pres. 'leave.'

19.4.31 Diphthongs

Vowel phoneme sequences which are diphthongal abound in the *Heliand* and *Genesis* graphemic data, in particular in the ms. C dialect. As with geminate consonant phonemes, the *OSL* considers diphthongs as a sequence of two phonemes rather than as unit phonemes. The richness of graphic variation is embodied in the following sets of graphs (cf. *OSL* Introduction):

136   *Chapter Six*

1. Graphemic set <io, ío, ió, ia, iá, ie, iu, i, eo, éo, ea, eu, e>, represented e.g., in OS *thiod* 'folk,' which employs six of these freely varying graphic sequences. Phonemically, the graphic sequence represents a diphthong somewhere in the range of the configurations /i/ or /e/ + /ə/, that is, with centralized offglide [ə] or slightly backed allophone of [ə], viz. [ʌ]. Probably the <ie> which varies with <e>, that is, /ẹ̄/ in all *Heliand* and *Genesis* mss. but ms. S, feeds or is in the process of feeding (merger) this graphemic set (cf. Chap. VI: 19.4.22 above).

2. Graphemic set <iu, io, ie, i, eo, eu, u>, represented e.g., in OS *liudi* 'people,' which evinces five of these freely varying graphic sequences. Phonemically a sequence of /i/ + fairly high central offglide allophone of /ə/, perhaps [ʉ]. A subset of graphemic set 2 may be the limited set <euw, iuw + non-i>, e.g., OS *treuwa* 'faithfulness.'

3. Graphemic set <ei, ai, ia>, represented e.g., *leia* 'rock.' Into this genetically small set feed such diphthongal sequences as those generated by root vowel + inflectional vowel, e.g., in OS *said* 3 p. sg. pres. 'sow.' Phonemically the set represents /e/ or /a/ with palatal offglide /i/.

4. Single member graphemic set <au> occurs, e.g., in OS *glau* 'wise.' Only mss. M and C yield graphemic evidence for <au>. Phonemically this small set represents /a/ with velar offglide /u/.

5. Graphemic set <uo, ua> is represented in all *Heliand* and *Genesis* mss. with the exception of ms. S. The <uo, ua> vary mostly with <o>, that is /ọ̄/. See Chap. VI:

19.4.23 above for additional scattered freely varying graphs of this set, which represent the phoneme sequence /u/ + centralized offglide /ə/.

Spurious diphthongs such as <oi> in OS *doit* 3 p. sg. pres. 'do,' <ea> in ms. C *hlea* 'rock' (which may join set 2), <ui> in OS *buide* 3 p. sg. pret. 'lived' are often generated by root vowel + stem and/or inflectional vowel. Similarly, it is possible that triphthongs may be signalled in such forms as, e.g., ms. V *duoan* 'do,' ms. M *bloiat* 3 p. pl. pres. 'bloom,' ms. C *duoian* 1 p. pl. pres. subj. 'do.' On the other hand, the graphic sequence ViV may represent /j/ (cf. Chap. VI: 19.4.16, Rauch 1973).

19.5 Old Saxon Systematic Phones

The OS systematic phones or allophones which have been explicitly extrapolated (sects. 19.4.1-19.4.31) from the *Heliand* and *Genesis* manuscript data are:

[ph, p, p⁻, b, f, v, m, w, tʰ, t, t⁻, d̥, d, p̥, ð, s, z, n, ŋ, l, r, kʰ, k¹ʰ, k¹⁻, k, k⁻, k¹, g, X, ɣ, j, ç, h, i:, u:, I, ʊ, e:, o:, ɛ:, ɔ:, e, ɛ, ɔ, ʉ, ə, ʌ, a, ɑ:]

Extrapolation of the derivation of the systematic phones from the systematic phonemes can also be demonstrated by phonological rules that generalize the predictability of these noncontrastive phoneme variants (cf. Voyles 1970/1971). Quite general synchronic phonological rules for the OS consonant evidence are word initial aspiration of stops, e.g., [pʰ], nonrelease of stops, e.g., [p⁻]. Less general are word medial syllable final devoicing coupled with word medial devoicing constrained by certain consonants, yielding [f, t, s, x, ç], and palatalization [k¹, k¹ʰ]. Very general are word final devoicing, yielding [p, f, t, p̬, k, x, ç] and intervocalic word medial voicing, yielding [b̥, ð, z, ɣ]. Vocalically, the more general phonological rules to be extrapolated include a strongly dialectally inclined diphthongization rule [iə, uə] and a palatal umlaut rule, e.g., [ɛ, e].

Chapter Seven

Configurating the Morphology;
Nonlinear Macro-syntax;
Subcategorization Rules in the Predicate,
Argument, Modality Constituents

20. Nonlinear Macro-syntax

The reader of the OS text, to be sure, cognizes some of the sentential or syntagmatic meaning of a word simply by its lexical category coupled with its inflectional morphology. Thus, e.g., *gōdon* of sample sentence (3) (cf. Chaps. II: 4, III: 9) *Hwat quiðis thu umbi gōdon?* 'What do you say about a Good One?' extracted and in isolation from the rest of the sentence in and of itself signals some sort of nonsubject pronoun argument. The lexical category (*gōdon* = substantive/adjective) together with the inflectional morphology (-*on* = acc. sg. masc. wk.) comprise the nonlinear micro-syntax (cf. Chap. II: 7). The more complete meaning of the word is cognized, however, relative to its semantic configurations with other words and, in turn, phrases in the sentence. Such configurations, in the form of phrase structures and subcategorization rules, comprise the nonlinear macro-syntax.

While *gōdon* 'Good One' combines with *umbi* 'about' in a prepositional phrase (PP) consisting of preposition (prep.) plus noun phrase (NP), the prepositional phrase derives from the complement (comp.) which, with the verb *quiðis* 'say,' is the rewrite of the verb phrase (VP). *Hwat* 'what' of sentence (3) is a noun phrase, specifically an *hw*-word or interrogative pronoun, which also derives from the complement. The remaining word of sentence (3), *thu* 'you,' represents the topmost noun phrase, i.e., that noun phrase which together with the verb phrase is the immediate rewrite of a sentence, thus:

sent.	→	NP *thu*	+ VP *quiðis hwat umbi gōdon*
VP	→	Vb *quiðis*	+ comp. *hwat umbi gōdon*
comp.	→	NP *hwat*	+ PP *umbi gōdon*
PP	→	prep. *umbi*	+ NP *gōdon*

The configuration of tense, mood, aspect, polarity, and diathesis semantic features is relegated to the modality constituent in the nonlinear macro-syntax of the *OSL*; accordingly the phrase structure rule for a sentence is properly written as: sent. → NP + M + VP.

21. Subcategorization rules

The nonlinear macro-syntax subcategorization rule (SScR) of the OS sentence centers in frames which derive the OS sentence as a predicate constituent, an argument constituent, and a modality constituent (cf. Chap. I: 2) in form, function and meaning.

22. Predicate Constituent

The predicate constituent syntactic subcategorization rules are assigned to eight sets of complements: simple or complex nominal (noun, pronoun, adjective, numeral), preposition, adverbial, infinitive, present participle, preterite participle, and sentence. This set division prevents excessive reduction, which can obscure the form, function, and/or semantic features. For example, an intransitive preterite participle complement of a verb (cf. SScR31), a present participle complement of a verb (cf. SScR2), and a nominal complement of a verb (cf. SScR2) are distinguished as separate inputs from one another. These three distinct complements rewrite as the same semantic feature [essive] relative to an intransitive verb. Similarly, e.g., SScR8, SScR9, SScR10, SScR11 could be conflated through their shared semantic output.

The predicate subcategorization frames further display grammatical cases: subject nominative ($noml_0$), predicate nominative ($noml_1$), accusative ($noml_2$), genitive ($noml_3$), dative ($noml_4$), instrumental ($noml_5$). The grammatical cases are rewritten as the semantic categories: agent (ag.), essive (ess., indicative of a state of being), object (O), patient (pat., indicative of a state of being affected). Specific verb valence is not indicated; however, general valence is expressed by the semantic features transitive (trans.) and intransitive (intrans.), the latter including the copula (cop.), and by the gross division into simple:complex nominal.

The SScRs are written for general set inclusion of the verbs. Thus, e.g., SScR4b does not specify the verb *brūkan* 'to enjoy,' e.g., in sentence (4) *siu iro barnes brūkan mōsti* 'She could enjoy her child,' as compulsorily restricted to cooccurrence with the genitive case, although *brūken* is subsumed by SScR4b. On the other hand, a verb such as *hōrian* has three sets of semantic features and accordingly is subsumed under three individual rules. SScR3 configurates the semantic features of the VP in a sentence such as (5) *thie ni weldun Cristes word hōrien* 'They did not want to hear the word(s) of Christ;' SScR4b configurates the semantic features of the VP in sentence (6): *Ne wolda thero Judeono gelpes hōrian* 'He did not want to listen to the mockery of the Jews;' SScR5 configurates the semantic features of the VP in sentence (7): *Ne williad iro drohtine hōrien* 'They did not want to obey their Lord.' While the differential inclusion of *hōrian* highlights the Vb of the VP, the inclusion of a verb such as *drinkan* 'to drink' highlights the NP of the Comp. in the VP. Thus, the semantic features of whole object (entire contents) in a sentence such as (8) *ik drinku ina* 'I drink it (the cup)' is configurated with the Vb by SScR3, whereas the semantic feature of a partial object (some) in a sentence as (9) *Lithes wīnes gedranc* 'He had drunk of the wine' is configurated with the same Vb by SScR4b.

In contrast to the semantic distinctions displayed by the VPs with *hōrian* and *drinkan* above, *alātan* 'forgive,' at least on the micro-discourse level, evinces variation, or neutralization of dependencies, of both comp. NPs in the following set of sentences: (10) *gi than williad alātan liudeo gehwilicun thero sacono* 'You are then willing to forgive all people their failings;' (SScR12), (11) *man ina alāte sacono* 'One might forgive him failings' (SScR8); (12) *he alātan mag liudeo gihwilicun saca* 'He may forgive all people failings' (SScR11).

The cost of rule generalization is, of course, the possible underspecification or adumbration of semantic features. So, e.g., the semantic configuration of *balg* with *ina* of sentence (13) *balg ina the biscop* 'The bishop became angry' could be subsumed by SScR3 if the coreferentiality, i.e., reflexivity of *ina* with *biscop* is ignored or left unstated. Similarly, the semantic frame of the reflexive *im* which is coreferential with the implicit subject of *fiscodun* in sentence (14) 'They fished' is not satisfied by the application of SScR5. An impersonal verb such as *brestan* 'to lack' in sentence (15) *im thes wīnes brast* 'They lacked wine,' i.e., 'Some wine was lacking to them,' 'It lacked to them of wine' requires a special rule. Only the most general syntactic subcategorization rules are formulated in the *OSL*.

Manuscript dialect differences in the application of the SScRs are not noted in the *OSL*, although they most frequently contribute valuable macro-discourse pragmatic distinctions and/or at least characterize the ms. dialect. Thus, ms. M writes sentence (16) *gi an thene sīð farad* 'you set out' with the Vb *farad* in the indicative present, but ms. C writes the same sentence *gi an thene sīð faran* with the Vb *faran* in the subjunctive present. Another case in point is sentence (17) of ms. M *wirðid tefallen an themu flōde* 'It is disintegrating in the deluge' with the auxiliary plus preterite participle *wirðid tefallen*, and the ms. C rendition of the same sentence with *tefallit*, the present active (cf. further Rauch 1981a).

22.1 Simple Nominal Complement

While the OS sentence (1) *Ic is engil bium* 'I am his angel' (cf. Chap. I: 2) is viewed as a proposition in which *engil* is in a relation of identity with the argument NP *ik*, as a syntactic sentence it is framed in the subcategorization rules as a simple nominal complement of the verb *bium*. Subject arguments whether analytic, i.e., expressed as a free morpheme, e.g., sentence (18) *erða biboda, hrisidun thia hōhun bergos, harda stēnos clubun* 'the earth quaked, the high mountains shook, the hard stones split,' or synthetic, i.e., expressed as part of a bound morpheme, e.g., sentence (19) *frāgoda niudlīco* 'he asked earnestly' are designated noml$_0$. The simple nominals of sentence (18), *erða, bergos, stēnos*, as well as the unexpressed *he* 'he' of sentence (5), extrapolated from the person desinence of *frāgoda*, viz. *-a*, and its anaphoric reference in the discourse, can be formalized in the following SScR1. Hereafter noml$_0$ will be assumed and, accordingly, no longer be indicated in the frame configurations:

SScR1: Vb + noml$_0$ → [Vb] + [α ag.]

Notice that verb valence is not at issue in SScR1; Vb is neutral relative to transitivity. Thus, SScR1 reads: the lexical category verb plus a subject nominal rewrites as the semantic/syntactic feature transitive or intransitive verb plus the semantic/syntactic feature agent.

SScR2: Vb + noml$_1$ → [intrans.] + [ess.]

SScR2 semantically configurates, e.g., *bium* with *engil* of sentence (1) *ik is engil bium* 'I am his angel (cf. above) and *lāgun* with *sāmquica* of sentence (20) *lāgun thia gisīðos sāmquica* 'the troops lay half-dead.' Notice [intrans.] includes the copula 'be,' 'become' and verbs with copulative semantic features, e.g., 'remain,' 'seem.' Observe as well that in the deep structure an adjective as *sāmquica* has sentence status (cf. SScR26, SScR29, SScR31).

SScR3: Vb + noml$_2$ → [trans.] + [O]

SScR3 semantically configurates, e.g., *drinku* with *inu* of sentence (8) *ik drinku inu* 'I drink it (the cup)'

$$\text{SScR4:} \quad \text{Vb + noml}_3 \rightarrow \begin{cases} \text{a. [cop.]} & + \text{[affiliation]} \\ \text{b. [trans.]} + \begin{cases} \text{[partitive O]} \\ \text{[whole O]} \end{cases} \end{cases}$$

SScR4a semantically configurates, e.g., *is* and *kunnies* of sentence (21) *hē is theses kunnies* 'He belongs to this sib.' SScR4b semantically configurates, e.g., *gedranc* with *wīnes* in sentence (9) *he thes wīnes gedranc* 'He had drunk of the wine.'

$$\text{SScR5:} \quad \text{Vb + noml}_4 \rightarrow \begin{cases} \text{a. [trans.]} & + \text{[pat.]} \\ \text{b. [intrans.]} & + \text{[goal]} \end{cases}$$

SScR5a semantically configurates, e.g., *theonoda* with *goda* of sentence (22) *hie simblon gerno gode theonoda* 'He always served God gladly.' SScR5b semantically configurates, e.g., the *quam* with the *im* of sentence (23) *im an drōme quam drohtines engil* 'In a dream the angel of the Lord came to them.'

22.2 Complex Nominal Complement

$$\text{SScR6:} \quad \text{Vb + noml}_4 \rightarrow \left\{ \begin{bmatrix} \text{wesan} \\ \text{werðan} \\ \text{thunkian} \end{bmatrix} \right\} + \text{[pat.]} + \text{[ess.]}$$

SScR6 semantically configurates *thunkid* with *thing*, which is coreferential with *thit* (a noml$_0$ and accordingly not framed, cf. SScR1 above) in sentence (24) *ni thunkid mi thit sōmi thing* 'It does not seem to me a fitting act.'

SScR7: Vb + noml$_2$ + noml$_2$ → [trans.] + [O] + [O]

SScR7 semantically configures *hētun* with *ina* and *Oliueti* in sentence (25) *hētun ina Judeo liudi Oliueti* 'The people of the Jews called it Oliveti.'

SScR8: Vb + noml$_2$ + noml$_3$ → [trans.] + [pat.] + [O]

SScR8 semantically configures *welda atuomian* with *barn morðes* in sentence (26) *welda manno barn morðes atuomian* 'He wanted to free the children of men from death.'

SScR9: Vb + noml$_2$ + noml$_4$ → [trans.] + [O] + [pat.]

SScR8 semantically configures *gaf* with *it* and *jungarun* in sentence (2) *gaf it is jungarun forð* 'He gave it to his disciples.' Notice that the lexical category inputs of SScR8 and SScR9 rewrite into the identical semantic features output. The next two rules, SScR10, SScR11 will also yield the output of SScR8 and SScR9.

SScR10: Vb + noml$_2$ + noml$_5$ → [trans.] + [pat.] + [O]

SScR10 semantically configures *weldun bilōsien* with *barn* and *liƀu* in sentence (27) *weldun that barn godes liƀu bilōsien* 'They wanted to deprive the child of God of life.'

SScR11: Vb + noml$_4$ + noml$_2$ → [trans.] + [pat.] + [O]

Predicate Constituent: 22 - 22.8   147

SScR11 semantically configurates *alātan mag* with *gihwilicun* and *saca* in sentence (12) *he alātan mag liudeo gihwilicun saca* 'He may forgive all people failings.'

SScR12: Vb + noml$_4$ + noml$_3$ →
[trans.] + [pat.] + $\begin{Bmatrix} \text{[partitive O]} \\ \text{[whole O]} \end{Bmatrix}$

SScR12 semantically configurates *williad alātan* with *gehwilicun* and *sacono* in sentence (10) *gi than williad alātan liudeo gehwilicun thero sacono* 'you are then willing to forgive all people their failings.'

22.3 Case Transformed to Prepositional Phrase

The semantic features of the grammatical cases noml$_1$, noml$_2$, noml$_3$, noml$_4$, noml$_5$, which serve as output to the rules in sections 22.1 and 22.2 above, can serve as input to rules in which the same semantic features are transformed into prepositional phrases. The output of these case transformation or substitution rules is prepositional phrases in which the case of the noun to the right side of the rule is constrained or governed by the preposition. Such transformation rules are integral to the syntactic subcategorization of the nonlinear macro-syntax.

SScR13: $_1$[ess.] → [te] + [Nn$_4$]

SScR13 reads: The semantic feature essive, which derives from a nominal$_1$ (predicate nominal), is transformed to the syntactic features preposition *te* plus noun₄ (dative). SScR13 yields *te kunige* of sentence (28) *Ērodes was gekoran te kunige* 'Herod was chosen as king' (cf. SScR2).

$$\text{SScR14:} \quad {}_3\begin{Bmatrix} \text{[partitive O]} \\ \text{[whole O]} \end{Bmatrix} \rightarrow \text{[fora]} + \text{[Nn}_4\text{]}$$

SScR14 results in the *fora thinge* of sentence (29) *scal allaro liudio gehwilic thinkean fora themu thinge* 'Each of all people must prepare for the judgment' (cf. SScR4b).

$$\text{SScR15:} \quad {}_2\text{[O]} \rightarrow \text{[for]} + \text{[Nn}_2\text{]}$$

SScR15 yields *for wārsagon* in sentence (30) *habdun ina for wārsagon* 'They considered him a prophet' (cf. SScR7).

$$\text{SScR16:} \quad {}_3\text{[O]} \rightarrow \text{[mid]} + \text{[Nn}_5\text{]}$$

SScR16 yields *mid ferahu* of sentence (31) *(dag) fulliad mid iro ferahu* 'They fill (the day) with their life' (cf. SScR8).

$$\text{SScR17:} \quad {}_4\text{[pat.]} \rightarrow \text{[an]} + \text{[Nn}_2\text{]}$$

SScR17 results in *an barn* of sentence (32) *swāroston an firiho barn fīund biwurpun* 'The enemies threw the worst (illnesses) to the children of men' (cf. SScR9).

$$\text{SScR18:} \quad {}_5\text{[O]} \rightarrow \text{[te]} + \text{[Nn}_4\text{]}$$

SScR18 results in *te dōðe* of sentence (33) *sunu drohtines adēldun te dōðe* 'They condemned the Son of Man to death' (cf. SScR10).

22.4 Adverbial Complement by Case or Case Transformed to Prepositional Phrase

An adverbial phrase complement of a verb rewrites as an adverb, e.g., *gerno* of sentence (34) *thigida ina gerno* 'He received him gladly,' as an adverb plus specifier, e.g., *swīðo* in sentence (35) *that wīf antfeng that godes ārundi gerno swīðo* 'The woman accepted God's errand very gladly,' and as a noun phrase constrained by compulsory case which itself may rewrite as a prepositional phrase. The adverbial subcategorization rules display some of the latter two possibilities. For simplification the Vb is unstated in these frames.

$$\text{SScR19:} \quad Nn_2 \rightarrow \begin{Bmatrix} \text{[definite time]} \\ \text{[space]} \\ \text{[goal]} \end{Bmatrix}$$

SScR19 semantically configurates the Vb with *allan dag, wegos, waldos* and *ōðil* of sentences (36), (37), (38), respectively. Sentence (36) reads: *bīdun allan dag that werod* 'The crowd waited all day.' Sentence (37) reads: *gengun wegos endi waldos* 'They went over paths and through forests.' Sentence (38) reads: *he scolde gifaran is fader ōðil* 'He should go to the home of his father.'

$$\text{SScR20:} \quad Nn_3 \rightarrow \begin{Bmatrix} \text{[indefinite time]} \\ \text{[manner]} \end{Bmatrix}$$

SScR20 semantically configurates the Vb with *gihwilīkes, forðwardes, willean* in sentences (39), (40), (41), respectively. Sentence (39) reads: *wī gisāhun morgno gihwilīkes blīkan thena sterron* 'Each morning we saw the star shine.' Sentence (40) reads: *bifellun forðwardes* 'They fell forward.' Sentence (41) reads: *Ērodeses thegan andward stod wrēðes willean* 'The thane of Herod stood angrily (with mean will).'

$$\text{SScR21: } Nn_4 \rightarrow \begin{Bmatrix} \text{[means]} \\ \text{[instrument]} \end{Bmatrix}$$

SScR21 semantically configurates the Vb with *wundron, wordun* in sentences (41), (42). Sentence (41) reads: *nu ligid hie wundron siok* 'Now he lies sick with wounds.' Sentence (42) reads: *god wordun lobodun* 'They praised God with words.'

$$\text{SScR22: } Nn_5 \rightarrow \begin{Bmatrix} \text{[singular means]} \\ \text{[singular circumstance]} \\ \text{[time]} \end{Bmatrix}$$

SScR22 semantically configurates *qualmu, werodu, hiudu* of sentences (43), (44), (45) respectively. Sentence (43) reads: *gisāhun iro barn biforan qualmu sweltan* 'They saw their child die by murder in their presence.' Sentence (44) reads: *habde ine thiu smale thiod werodu biworpen* 'The poor people had surrounded Him with a crowd.' Sentence (45) reads: *skīn was that hiudu* 'That became clear today.'

SScR23: [umbi] + $_2$[Nn] → [definite time]

SScR23 semantically configurates the Vb with the PP as a transform of SScR19 above, as found in sentence (46) *gewēt im thō umbi threa naht aftar thiu* 'He went then three nights later.'

SScR24: [mid] + $_5$[Nn] → [singular circumstance]

SScR24 semantically configurates the Vb with PP as a transform of SScR22 above. In close minimal pair relationship with sentence (44) above is sentence (47) *bewurpun ina thō mid werodu* 'They surrounded him with a crowd.' Sentence (48) *mid hwilicu arbēðiu thar thea erlos lebðin* 'With what toil the people lived there' provides another example of SScR24.

SScR25: [te] + $_4$[Nn] → [time]

SScR25 also semantically configurates the Vb with the PP as a transform of SScR22 above, as is seen in sentence (49) *tholodun hier manag te dage araƀiðwerco* 'They suffered much toil here today.'

22.5 Infinitive Complement

The infinitive complement of a verb assumes sentence status in deep structure as the embedded clause to the verb of the matrix clause.

SScR26: Vb + inf. → [intrans.] + [advbl. inf.]

SScR26 semantically configurates *quam* and *gangan* in sentence (50) *quam thar ēn wīf gangan* 'There came a woman walking.' Another example is sentence (51) *sīdodun idisi te them graƀe gangan* 'The woman went walking to the grave.' As a complement to an intransitive verb the infinitive is coreferentially related to the subject (cf. SScR2, especially S20, SScR29, SScR31); [advbl. inf.] underdetermines this semantic relation.

$$\text{SScR27:} \quad \text{Vb} + \alpha\, te + \text{inf.} + \begin{Bmatrix} \text{Nn}_2 \\ \text{Nn}_3 \\ \text{PP} \end{Bmatrix} \rightarrow \begin{Bmatrix} \text{[intrans.]} \\ \begin{bmatrix} \text{witan} \\ \text{egan} \\ \text{kunnan} \\ \text{willian} \end{bmatrix} \end{Bmatrix} +$$

$$\text{[equi-subject deletion]} + [\alpha te] + \text{[inf.]} + \begin{Bmatrix} [\text{O}] \\ [\text{goal}] \end{Bmatrix}$$

SScR27 semantically configurates *giwitun* with *sunu* and the unmarked, i.e., [-*te*], infinitive *sōkean* in sentence (52) *giwitun im tho eft te Hierusalem iro sunu sōkean* 'Thereafter they went to Jerusalem to seek their son.' Equi-subject deletion affects the subject of the embedded sentence whose verb appears as the surface infinitive. Sentence (53) displays SScR27 with the Nn$_3$ input *is*: *mīdan siu is ni wissa* 'She did not know to avoid it.' Notice sentence (53) employs *witan* which together with *ēgan* 'have,' *kunnan* 'know,' and the modal-like *willian* 'want,' are the only modal verbs (cf. chap II: 8. 2, 8, 2.3) which can occur in nonauxiliary function. Sentence (55) displays SScR27 with the PP input *furi is thiodan*: *geng furi is thiodan stān* 'He went to stand before his king.' The meaning of the PP is grossly subsumed by [O] and/or [goal]. Sentence (56) provides another example: *gē skuldige sind an that geld geban* 'You are guilty of giving to that payment.' The combined operation of SScR26 and SScR27 can be observed in sentence (57): *Thero giwēt im gangan tharod wið thia thiod sprecan* 'Then he went walking there to speak to the people.'

$$\text{SScR28:} \quad \text{Vb} + \begin{Bmatrix} \text{Nn}_2 \\ \text{Nn}_3 \end{Bmatrix} + \alpha\, te + \text{inf.} \rightarrow \text{[trans.]} +$$

$$\text{[O raising]} + [\alpha\, te] + \text{[inf.]}$$

SScR28 configurates semantically *gisah* with *ina kuman* of sentence (58): *hie ina kuman gisah* 'He saw him come.' The subject of the embedded sentence is raised to the object of the matrix sentence, the infinitive being the surface representation of the verb of the embedded sentence. Sentence (59) provides another example: *endi hēt sie ina haldan wel* 'And he commanded him to keep her well.' Observe the infinitive with case (inflected infinitive) in sentence (60) *ik iu sende tharod te gigaruwenne mīna gōma* 'I send you there to prepare my feast.'

22.6 Present Participle Complement

The present participle complement of a verb assumes sentence status in deep structure as the embedded clause to the matrix sentence verb.

SScR29: Vb + pres.part. →

[intrans.] + $\begin{cases} \text{[ess.]} \\ \text{[advbl. pres.part.]} \end{cases}$

SScR29 semantically configurates *wurðun* with *blīcandi* in sentence (61) *wurðun imu is wangun blīcandi* 'His cheeks became aglow.' Another example is sentence (62): *huī gangat gi sō gornondia?* 'Why do you go thus mourning?' (cf. SScR2, SScR27, SScR31). The intransitive *quam* plus adverbial present participle *gangandi* is found in sentence (63): *thuo quam im thar thie hēlago tuo gangandi godes suno* 'There the holy Son of God came walking toward them.' Equi-subject deletion affects the subject of the embedded sentence whose verb surfaces as the present participle.

$$\text{SScR30:} \quad \text{Vb} + \begin{Bmatrix} \text{Nn}_2 \\ \text{Nn}_3 \end{Bmatrix} + \text{pres.part.} \rightarrow$$

$$[\text{trans.}] + [\text{O raising}] + [\text{pres.part.}]$$

SScR30 semantically configurates *fand* with *sia slāpandia* in sentence (64) *fand sia slāpandia* 'He found them sleeping.' The subject of the embedded sentence is raised to the object of the matrix sentence; the present participle is the surface representation of the embedded verb (cf. SScR28).

22.7 Preterite Participle Complement

The preterite participle complement of a verb assumes sentence status in deep structure as the embedded clause to the matrix sentence verb.

$$\text{SScR31:} \quad \text{Vb} + \text{pret.part.} \rightarrow$$

$$[\text{intrans.}] + \begin{Bmatrix} [\text{ess.}] \\ [\text{advbl. pret.part.}] \end{Bmatrix}$$

SScR31 semantically configurates *wurðun* and *cumana* of sentence (65): *te Criste cumana wurðun bodan fan Bethaniu* 'Messengers were come to Christ from Bethany.' Observe that *wurðun* plus *cumana* yield a preterite intransitive plus an essive adjective (cf. SScR2, SScR29 sections 24.1, 24.3 below). *gengun* with the adverbial preterite participle *gebolgane* occurs in sentence (66):

gebolgane gengun nāhor mid nīðu 'Angrily they came closer with hatred.'

$$\text{SScR32: Vb} + \begin{Bmatrix} \text{Nn}_2 \\ \text{Nn}_3 \end{Bmatrix} + \text{pret.part.} \rightarrow$$

$$[\text{trans.}] + [\text{O raising}] + [\text{pret.part.}]$$

SScR32 semantically configurates *fundun* with *ina* and *gifaranan* of sentence (67) *fundun ina gifaranan thuo iu* 'Then they found him already gone (dead).' The subject of the embedded sentence is raised to the object of the matrix sentence, the preterite participle representing the deep structure verb of the embedded sentence. A second example is sentence (68) *er ina gicoranan habdi* 'He had him as a chosen one.' Observe *habdi* plus *gicoranan* yield a transitive preterite plus an adjective in coreferential essive relationship with the object *ina* (cf. SScR7 and sections 24.1, 24.3 below).

22.8 Sentence Complement

Participles, infinitives, adjectives can rewrite as deep structure sentences (cf. sections 22.5-22.7 above). Section 22.8 considers the sentence as a surface complement of the verb.

SScR33: Vb + sent. →

$$[\text{Vb}] + \begin{Bmatrix} [\text{conj.}] \\ [\text{hw-pron.}] \end{Bmatrix} \text{-sent.} + [\alpha\text{subj.}]$$

SScR33 semantically configurates *hiet* with the sentence introduced by the conjunction *that* followed by a verb in the subjunctive in sentence (69) *hiet that fruod gumo foroht ni wāri* 'He commanded that the old man not be afraid.' Sentence (70) displays optional *that*-deletion with *queðan: quað he gerno is geld gerewedi* 'He said that he gladly relinquished his money.' Further examples are sentence (71), which shows no subjunctive verb in the *untthat* clause: *that gēr furðor skrēd, untthat that friðubarn godes fiartig habda dago endi nahto* 'The year progressed, until the Peace Child of God counted forty days and nights,' and sentence (72) *warð ald gumo sprāca bilōsit, thoh he spahan hugi bāri* 'The old man was robbed of speech, although he bore wise thought.' An *hw*-pronoun occurs in sentence (73) *he gihugid, hwat hē selbo gifremida* 'He considered what he himself did.' The sentence as complement to the verb exhibits well the recursive characteristic of various phrase structure rules whereby sentences produce sentences which produce a potentially nonfinite series of sentences.

23. Argument Constituent

The argument constituent consists of a noun phrase which can be rewritten as determiner (D) plus noun, thus NP → D + Nn. The determiner can be an article (art.) (which subsumes deictic pronouns), a quantifier, or a possessive pronoun. The D + Nn phrase can be expanded by an adjective or a sentence. The syntactic subcategorization rules semantically configurate these several lexical categories with the noun.

Argument Constituent: 23 - 23.5

23.1 Article Determiner

The article determiner consists of a set of words which include the definite and indefinite article as well as the deictic pronouns *these, thit, thius

$$\text{SScR34:} \quad \alpha \text{ art.} + \text{Nn} \rightarrow \left\{ \begin{bmatrix} \text{thĕ} \\ \text{ein} \\ \text{these} \end{bmatrix} \right\} + [\text{Nn}]$$

SScR34 semantically configurates the NP head *wībe* with the article *themu* in sentence (74) *endi thō te themu wībe sprac* 'And then he spoke to the woman.' Sentence (75) gives another example: *thō quam thar ōk ēn widowa tō* 'Then a widow came there as well.' The optional article is displayed in the two outer clauses of sentence (18) *erða biboda, hrisdun thia hōhun bergos, harda stēnos clubon* '(The) earth quaked, the high mountains shook, (the) hard stones split.' Sentence (76) provides another example: *thanan scal thi kind ōdan werðan* 'Then shall (a) child be imparted to you.'

23.2 Quantifier Determiner

$$\text{SScR35:} \quad \text{quantifier} + \text{Nn} \rightarrow$$

$$\left\{ \begin{bmatrix} \text{sum, ēnig, ōðar, nigēn} \\ \text{gihwĕ, gihwilĭc} \\ \text{hwilĭc, manag, all} \\ \text{sulĭc, ful, middi} \\ \text{half, ginōg, faho} \\ \text{bēðie; numerals} \end{bmatrix} + \begin{matrix} [\text{Nn}] \\ [\text{partitive Nn}_3] \end{matrix} \right\}$$

SScR35 semantically configurates the NP head *wordu* with the quantifier *gehwilicu* in sentence (78) *nu he an abuh lērid wordu gehwilicu* 'Now he teaches in error with every word.' Another example is sentence (79) which employs two quantifiers: *thoh nam is mēda gehwe fulle* 'Then he took his complete, full salary.' Sentences (80), (81) display a partitive noun head. Sentence (80) reads *welde im thar wundres filu tēcno tōgean* 'He wanted to show them there many signs.' Sentence (81) with a numeral quantifier reads: *thu thar fīðis fīftig ferahtaro manno* 'You will find there fifty wise men.'

23.3 Possessive Pronoun Determiner, Intensifier Pronoun, Possessive Noun

SScR36: possessive pron. + Nn →

$$\left\{\begin{bmatrix} \text{mīn, thīn, sīn, is} \\ \text{unka, inka, ūsa, euwa} \end{bmatrix}\right\} + \text{Nn}$$

SScR36 semantically configurates *wordun* with *mīnun* in sentence (82) *wendeat aftar mīnum wordun* 'Turn to my words!'

The possessive pron. + Nn phrase can be expanded by a pronominal intensifier:

SScR37: possessive pron. + intensifier pron. + Nn

$$\rightarrow \left\{\begin{bmatrix} \text{selb} \\ \text{ēgan} \end{bmatrix}\right\} + [\text{Nn}]$$

SScR37 semantically configurates the possessive pron. *iru* and the intensifier pron. *selƀaru* with *dohter* in sentence (83) *quað that iru wāri harm gistandan, soroga at iru selƀaru dohter* 'She said that harm had been done to her, concern for her daughter herself.' Sentence (84) provides an example with *ēgan*: *ik bium thīn ēgan scalc* 'I am your own servant.'

Possession of a noun can be expressed by a second noun which acts attributively to the first noun.

SScR38: possessive Nn + Nn ⟶ [Nn₃] + [Nn]

SScR38 semantically configurates the possessive noun *waldandes* with the head noun *sunu* in sentence (85) *thō giwēt im the waldandes sunu mid them fiwariun forð* 'Then the Son of the Lord left with the four.'

23.4 NP Expansion by Adjective

The noun phrase can be expanded by an adjective in attributive function to the noun:

SScR39: adj. + Nn ⟶ [adj.] + [Nn]

SScR39 semantically configurates the two adjectives *hēlag* and *himilisc* with the noun *word* in sentence (86) *sie scoldun an buok scrīban hēlag himilisc word* 'They should write in a book the holy, heavenly word.'

The adjective, in turn, can be expanded by an intensifier:

SScR40: adj. intensifier + adj. + Nn →

$$\left\{\begin{bmatrix} so \\ su\overline{\imath}\eth o \end{bmatrix}\right\} + [adj.] + [Nn]$$

SScR40 semantically configurates the adjective intensifier *sō* with the adjective *rīkiumu* and the noun *drohtine* in sentence (87) *ic mōti an is giscuoha, an sō rīkiumu drohtine thea reomon antbindan* 'I could not loosen the straps of his shoes for such a powerful lord.' A second example is sentence (88) *sie an that ārundi tharod idisi sendin, Maria endi Martha, swīðo wunsama wīf* 'Mary and Martha, the very lovely women sent them there on an errand.'

23.5 NP Expansion by Sentence

The noun phrase can also be expanded by a sentence.

SScR41: noml + sent. →
[pron.] + [that-sent.] + [α subj.]

SScR41 semantically configurates the nominal, in this case pronoun, with the sentence introduced by the conjunction *that* and containing the verb in the subjunctive in sentence (89) *is ōðar betara that he ina fram werpa* 'Is the other, that he throw it away, better?' An example without the use of subjunctive in the verb of the *that*-sent. is found in sentence (90) *hē habad maht, that he ālātan mag* 'He has the power, that he may forgive.'

SScR42: noml + sent. →

[-referent] + $\left\{\begin{bmatrix}\text{thĕ-sent.}\\\text{sō-sent.}\end{bmatrix}\right\}$ + [α thār]

SScR42 semantically configurates the direct object noun or pronoun which is assumed by the verb *bōtta* and is therefore absent, i.e., minus referent with the anaphoric relative pronoun *them* and the relativizing particle *thar* in sentence (91) *bōtta, them thār blinde wārun* 'He healed (those), who were blind.' Sentence (92) provides another example: *sō ēgrohtful is, the thār alles geweldid* 'So merciful is (he), who rules over everything;' notice the subject referent for the anaphoric *the* is again assumed by the first verb. A final example is sentence (93): *ik selbo bium, that thār sāiu* 'I myself am (he), that sows.'

SScR43: noml + sent. →

[noml] + $\left\{\begin{matrix}\text{[hw-pron.-sent.]}\\\text{[th-pron.-sent.]}\end{matrix}\right\}$ + [α thār]

SScR43 semantically configurates the pronoun *them* with the anaphoric relative pronoun *the* in sentence (94) *sagde them, the he gecoran habda* 'He told them, whom he had chosen.' A second example is sentence (95): *endi gehuggean ni wili thana swāran balcon, the thu an thīnoro siuni habas* 'And you do not wish to consider the heavy beam, which you have in your sight.'

SScR44: noml + sent. →
        [noml] + [place advbl.-sent.]

SScR44 semantically configurates *cnōsla* with the place adverbial *thanan* in sentence (96): *quāmi te them cnōsla gihue thanan he cunneas was* 'Each should come to the sib, from which lineage he was.'

SScR45: noml + sent. →
[noml] + [sō-sent.] + [α pron.]

SScR45 semantically configurates the pronoun *gihwem* with the relative particle *sō* minus a relative pronoun in sentence (97): *thia sundiun sculun allaro erlo gihwem uƀilo githīhan, sō im fruocno tuo ferahes āhtið* 'The sins will bring evil to each of the men who boldly proscribed Him to death.'

24. Modality Constituent

The modality constituent proposes subcategorization rules for tense, mood, aspect, polarity, and diathesis (cf. Chap. II: 8)

24.1 Tense

OS has but two synthetic tenses, present and preterite. Present and preterite meaning, however, can also be conveyed by periphrasis with the verbs *werðan* 'become,' *wesan* 'be,' *hebbian* 'have' in present discourse settings. The present perfect and the preterite perfect are formed analytically with the auxiliaries *hebbian* 'have' or *wesan* 'be.' A future is formed analytically by the present stem with future adverb, or by the auxiliaries *skulan* 'shall,' werðan 'become' and wesan 'be' and to a lesser extent willian 'will' and mugan 'can' with given nonfinite forms.

The *Heliand* and *Genesis* mss. provide a vast richness of semantic/syntactic verb phrase evidence for the configuration of tense in OS. There is a high degree of polysemous verb phrases. Thus, e.g., sein and hebbian configurate with preterite participles both as aspectually marked (durative-perfective effective, hebbian also ingressive, cf. sect. 24.3 below) in the present and preterite tenses, and as aspectually unmarked in the present perfect and the preterite perfect tenses. As a rule of thumb, Lussky (1921) posits an inflected (noted in the syntactic subcategorization rules below as [plus case]) preterite participle in marked aspect occurrence. However, the OS preterite participle inflection is constrained exclusively by the masculine and feminine plural nominative with auxiliaries *wesan* and *werðan*. The auxiliary *hebbian* occurs in marked aspect occurrences with inflected participle constrained by the masculine and feminine accusative plural, but the singular as well. However, the macro-text discourse setting of the verb phrase frequently may be the arbiter of the modality semantics of the verb phrase. Similarly, *werðan* plus past participle can occur in an aspectually marked present or preterite verb phrase, or it can signal the unmarked future tense. Again the discourse setting may reveal the meaning of the verb phrase. Lussky (1921) rejects the use of *werðan* for the aspectually unmarked present perfect or past perfect. Not unlike other languages, this verb phrase evidence from OS bespeaks a diachronic synchrony undergoing strong semantic/ syntactic restructuring from primary aspect to primary tense (cf. section 24.3 below) in the verb phrase. And not unlike living languages in the midst of the restructuring, semantic ambiguity may characterize many such verb phrase occurrences. Still SScRs 46, 47 formulate an [α case] frame to allow for the nominative masculine/feminine plural preterite participle inflection, while SScR 49 posits a somewhat hypothetical [minus case] frame in a rule which also somewhat hypothetically excludes a *hebbian* frame.

SScR46: [pres.] →

$$\left\{\begin{array}{l}\text{a. [pres. stem]} \\ \text{b. [pres. }wer\eth an\text{]+[intrans.} \\ \quad\text{ perfective pret. part.]} \\ \quad\text{ +[}\alpha\text{ case]+[pres. context]} \\ \text{c. [pres. }wesan\text{]+[intrans.} \\ \quad\text{ perfective pret. part.]} \\ \quad\text{ +[}\alpha\text{ case]+[pres. context]} \\ \text{d. [pres. }hebbian\text{]+[}_2\text{trans. pret.} \\ \quad\text{ part.]+[}\alpha\text{ case]+[pres. context]}\end{array}\right\}$$

SScR46a yields present tense meaning through the present stem of the verb *sind* in sentence (98) *gī sind nū sō druobia* 'Now you are so depressed.' Another example is *is* in sentence (1) *ik is engil bium* 'I am His angel.' A third example is *nimad* in sentence (99): *Sulic lōn nimad weros waldādeo* 'The men take such reward for murder.'

SScR46b yields present tense meaning with durative-perfective ingressive aspectual features (cf. section 24.3 below) through semantically configurating *wirðid* with the intransitive perfective preterite participle *tefallen* in present tense discourse *wirðid teworpan* 'it is destroyed' in sentence 17´: *wirðid tefallen an themu flōde* 'It is destroyed; it is (beginning/in the process of) disintegrating in the deluge.'

SScR46c yields present tense meaning with durative-perfective effective aspectual features (cf. sect. 24.3 below) through semantically configurating *sint* with the intransitive perfective preterite participle plus case *cumana* in present tense discourse *sprikis* in sentence (99) *te hwī sprikis thu thes ... ne sint mīna noh tīdi cumana* 'Why do you speak of this ... My times are not yet come.'

SScR46d yields present tense meaning with durative-perfective effective aspectual features (cf. section 24.3 below) through semantically configurating *hebbias* with the transitive (configurated with noml$_2$ = *ina*) preterite participle *aslagan* in present tense discourse *sinkit* in sentence (100): *thu ina nu aslagan hebbias ... is drōr sinkit nu an erða* 'You have him now slain ... his blood is sinking into the earth.' Notice that the inherent or lexical aspect of the preterite participle verb is not significant in the SScR46d configuration.

SScR47: [pret.] →

$$\begin{Bmatrix} \text{a. [pret. stem]} \\ \text{b. [pret. }werðan\text{]+[intrans.} \\ \text{perfective pret. part.]} \\ \text{+[}\alpha\text{ case]+[pret. context]} \\ \text{c. [pret. }wesan\text{]+[intrans.} \\ \text{perfective pret. part.]} \\ \text{+[}\alpha\text{ case]+[pret. context]} \\ \text{d. [pret. }hebbian\text{]+[}_2\text{trans. pret.]} \\ \text{+[}\alpha\text{ case]+[pret. context]} \end{Bmatrix}$$

SScR47a yields preterite tense meaning through the preterite stem of the verb *giwēt* in sentence (101) *giwēt imu an Galileoland* 'He came to Galilee.' Another example is sentence (102) *sagdun thō lof goda* 'They then said praise to God.'

SScR47b yields preterite tense meaning with durative-perfective ingressive aspectual features (cf. section 24.3 below) through semantically configurating *warð* with the intransitive perfective preterite participle *giworðan* in preterite tense discourse *gilēstid, gisprak* in sentence (103): *warð it sān gilēstid, giwordan sō thar gisprak engil* 'It was accomplished immediately; it was happening as the angel said.'

SScR47c yields preterite tense meaning with durative-perfective effective aspectual features (cf. sect. 24.3 below) through semantically configurating *wārun* with the intransitive perfective preterite participle plus case *gifarana* in preterite discourse *sagda* in sentence (104): *slīðmōd cuning them wrekkiun sagda, thea thar en elilendi erlos wārun ferran gifarana* 'The sly king told the heroes who were each traveled abroad from afar.'

SScR47d yields preterite tense meaning with durative-perfective effective, possibly ingressive, aspectual features (cf. sect. 24.3 below) through semantically configurating *habda* with the transitive (configurated with noml$_2$ = *hēlagna gēst*) preterite participle *bifolhan* in preterite tense discourse *wārun* in sentence (105): *sia wārun gode lieba ... . habda im waldand god, them heliðon an iro hertan hēlagna gēst fasto bifolhan* 'They were dear to God ... the Lord God had the Holy Spirit firmly imbued in the hearts of the heroes.' The lexical aspect of the preterite participle verb is not significant in the SScR48d configuration.

SScR48: [fut.] →

$$\begin{Bmatrix} \text{a. [pres. stem]+[fut. advbl.]} \\ \text{b. } \begin{Bmatrix} \text{[pres. skulan]} \\ \text{[pres. willian]} \\ \text{[pres. mugan]} \end{Bmatrix} \text{+[inf.]} \\ \text{c. [pres. werðan]+[intrans. pret. part.]} \\ \text{d. [pres. sein]+[intrans. pret. part.]} \\ \text{+[}\alpha\text{ case]+[fut. context]} \end{Bmatrix}$$

SScR48a yields future tense meaning through the present stem *gangu* plus the future adverbial *at ērist* in sentence (105) *ik gangu imu at ērist tō* 'I will go to him first.'

SScR48b yields future tense meaning through the present stem *sculun* plus the infinitive *binden* in sentence (106) *mi sculun erlos binden* 'The earls will bind me.' Future tense meaning is conveyed by the present stem *williu* plus the infinitive *ōgean* in sentence (107) *sō hwilic sō manno barno ne wili wordun mīdan, ac gihit far gumskepi, that he mīn jungoro sī, thene williu ic eft ōgean far ōgun godes* 'Whoever of the children of men does not wish to deny (me) with his words, but acknowledges before the people, that he be my disciple, him will I often show before the eyes of God.' Notice the contrasting use of *wili* for present volition in the opening clause of sentence (107). Sentence (108) yields future tense meaning through *mugan* plus *fīðan*: *nu is Krist giboran an thera Davides burg ... thar gi ina fīðan mugan an Bethlemaburg* 'Now Christ is born in the city of David ... You will find him in Bethlehem.'

SScR48c yields future tense meaning through the present stem *wirðid* plus the intransitive preterite participle *cuman* in sentence (109) *nu wirðid sniumo herod cuman the mi farcōpot habad* 'He who sold me will quickly come here now.'

SScR48d yields future tense meaning through the present stem *sind* in semantic configuration with the intransitive preterite participle plus case *kumana* in the future discourse *nu oƀar tuā naht* in sentence (110) *gi witun alle that nu oƀar tuā naht sind tīdi kumana* 'You all know, that two nights from now, the time(s) will come.'

SScR49: [pres. perf.] →

$$\left\{\begin{array}{l} \text{a. [pres. hebbian]} + \left\{\begin{array}{l}\text{[intrans. imperfective}\\\text{pret. part. minus case]}\\+ \text{ [perf. context]}\\\text{[trans. pret. part.}\\\text{minus case]} + \text{[perf.}\\\text{context]}\end{array}\right\} \\ \text{b. [pres. wesan]} + \quad \begin{array}{l}\text{[intrans. pret. part.}\\\text{minus case]} +\\\text{[perf. context]}\end{array}\end{array}\right\}$$

SScR49a yields present perfect meaning through the present stem *hebbian* with the intransitive imperfective preterite participle in the context of prior action, backgrounding, (cf. Rauch 1981a) in sentence (111) *ef ik thar findo fīftig guodaro manno, thea te goda hebbian fasto gifangan, willi ik im iro ferah fargeƀan* 'If I find there fifty good men who have turned firmly to God, I will give them their life.' A transitive preterite participle *farwerkod* is seen with the present *haƀad* in the context of prior action, backgrounding in sentence

(112) *gi sculun lēdien undar thea liudi ... he is līƀes haƀad mid is wordun farwerkod* 'You will bring Him among the people ... He has forfeited His life with His words.'

SScR49b yields present perfect meaning through the present stem *sī* with the intransitive preterite participle *astandan* in the context of prior action, backgrounding in sentence (113) *thu hier wardon het that ina is jungron ne farstelan endi seggian that hie astantan sī fan raston* 'Stand watch here so that His disciples do not steal Him and say that He has arisen from the dead.'

SScR50: [pret. perf.] →

$$\left\{ \begin{array}{l} \text{a. [pret. hebbian]} + \left\{ \begin{array}{l} \text{[intrans. imperfective} \\ \text{pret. part. minus case]} \\ \text{+ [perf. context]} \\ \text{[trans. pret. part.} \\ \text{minus case] + [perf.} \\ \text{context]} \end{array} \right\} \\ \text{b. [pret. wesan] + [intrans. pret. part. minus} \\ \qquad\qquad\qquad \text{case] + [perf. context]} \end{array} \right\}$$

SScR50 yields preterite perfect meaning through the preterite stem *habdun* in semantic configuration with the intransitive imperfective preterite participle *gegangen* in the context of prior action, backgrounding in sentence (114) *thiu wīf soragodun, suma sprācun hwie im thema grōtan stēn fan themo graƀe scoldi gihwereƀian ... thiu frī habdun gegangan to them gardon, that sie te them graƀe mahtun gisehan selƀon* 'The women worried; some spoke, who should roll aside for them the great stone from the grave ... The women had gone to the garden, that they themselves could see to the grave.' A transitive preterite participle *githionod* stands in semantic configuration with the preterite *habde* in the context of prior action, backgrounding in sentence (50´) *quam thar ēn wīf gangan ald innan them alaha. Anna was siu hētan, siu habde ira drohtine wel githionod* 'There came an old woman walking in the temple. Anna was her name; she had served her Lord well.'

SScR50b yields preterite perfect meaning through configuration of the preterite *wārun* with the intransitive preterite participle *agangan* in the context of prior action, backgrounding in sentence (115) *ēn was iro thuo noh than firiho barnun biforan, endi thiu fībi wārun agangan* 'One (age) was still before the children of men, and the five (ages) had passed.'

24.2 Mood

Three moods are posited for OS, the indicative, generally considered the unmarked mood in statements and question; the subjunctive, a marked mood to convey an array of attitudes such as uncertainty, indirectness, possibility, irreality; and the imperative or hortative, a marked mood to convey a directive.

Modality Constituent: 24 - 24.5

SScR51: [indicative] →

{
a. [possibility]
   [reality]
b. [real conditional -sent.] → { [ef] / [of] } + [indic.]
c. [indirect question-sent.] →
   { [Vb { perception / knowing / communicating / concealing }] + [{ hw- / ef } -sent.] + [indic.] }
d. [factive-sent.] → [that] + [indic.]
e. [indirect speech] → [seggian] +
   { [pres.] + [factive-sent.] + [indic.]
     [pret.] + [factive-sent.] + [indic.] + [intention] }
f. [real advbl.-sent.] → [conj.] + [indic.]
}

SScR51a shows the unmarked indicative *bist* to convey semantic features of reality, possibility, in sentence (116) *thū bist lioht mikil allun elithiodun* 'You are a great light for all heathens.'

SScR51b displays the indicative *gōmid* in a real conditional sentence introduced by *ef* in sentence (117) *sō duot thea meginsundeon an thes mannes hugi thea godes lēra, ef he is ni gōmid wel* 'Thus act the capital sins in the mind of man against the teaching of God, if he does not heed well.' Another tense, as well as voice, is displayed by *warð afōdit* in the *ef* clause of sentence (118) *that ni mōsta forlātan negēn idis under Ebreon, ef iru at ērist warð sunu afōdit* 'No woman among the

Hebrews could neglect that if to her the first son was born.'

SScR51c displays the indicative *loƀodun* in a *hwō-* clause as a complement of the communicating/peceiving verb *hōrdun* in sentence (118) *hōrdun, hwō thiu engilo kraft loƀodun* 'They heard, how the group of angels praised God.'

SScR51d demonstrates the indicative *habða* in a factive complement clause introduced by *that* in sentence (119) *hi gecūŏde, that hi habda craft godes* 'He made known, that he had the power of God.'

SScR51e demonstrates the indicative *fargeƀan* in the indirect statement introduced by the present tense *seggiu* in sentence (120) *seggiu ik iu, that gī ne mugun fargeƀan* 'I say to you, that you can not forgive.' As an exception the subjunctive occurs in the *weldi* of the factive sentence introduced by the preterite *sagda* in sentence (121) *sagda, that hie weldi* 'He said that he wanted.'

SScR51f displays the indicative *habda* in a real adverbial clause complement introduced by the conjunction *und that* in sentence (122) *that gēr furðor skrēd, und that that barn fiartig habda dago* 'That year progressed, until the child was forty days old.' The conjunction *al sō* occurs in sentence (123) *habda hē gilēstid, al sō is gigengi was* 'He accomplished, as was his turn.' The conjunction *that* occurs in sentence (124) *gengun, that sie wið Krist sprākun* 'They went, (in order) that they might speak against Christ.' The adverb *nū* functions as a conjunction in sentence (125) *ik thī skal biddean, nū ik sus gigamalod bium* 'I want to beg you, since I am so aged.'

Modality Constituent: 24 - 24.5

SScR52: [subjunctive] →

$$\left\{\begin{array}{l}\text{a. [unreality]} \to \text{[subj.]} + \text{[pret.]} \\ \text{b. [unreal conditional-sent.]} \to \\ \quad \left\{\begin{array}{l}\text{[ef]}\\ \text{[of]}\end{array}\right\} + \text{[subj.]} + \text{[pret.]} \\ \text{c. [indirect question-sent.]} \to \\ \quad \text{[Vb}\left\{\begin{array}{l}\text{asking}\\ \text{seeking}\\ \text{learning}\\ \text{waiting}\\ \text{pondering}\\ \text{wanting}\\ \text{advising}\\ \text{emotion}\\ \text{determining}\end{array}\right\}\text{]} + \text{[}\left\{\begin{array}{l}\text{hw-}\\ \text{ef}\end{array}\right\}\text{-sent.]} + \text{[subj.]} \\ \text{d. [nonfactive-sent.]} \to \text{[that]} + \text{[subj.]} \\ \text{e. [indirect speech]} \to \\ \quad \text{[Vb}\left\{\begin{array}{l}\text{saying}\\ \text{communicating}\end{array}\right\}\text{]} + \text{[}\alpha\text{that]} + \text{[sent.]} + \text{[subj.]} \\ \text{f. [unreal advbl.-sent.]} \to \text{[conj.]} + \text{[pret.]}\end{array}\right\}$$

SScR52a demonstrates the subjunctive *wāri* to convey irreality in sentence (125) *ūs wāri thes firiwit mikil te witanne* 'Our curiosity to know was great.'

SScR52b displays the subjunctive *mahti* in an unreal conditional sentence introduced by *of* in sentence (126) *lībes weldi ina bilōsien, of he mahti gilēstien sō* 'He wanted to rob him of life, if he could achieve it.'

SScR52c displays the subjunctive *skoldīn* in a *hwō*-clause as a complement of a verb of determining in sentence (127) *talda, hwō sie skoldin iro selboro sundeo bōtean* 'He explained, how they should expiate their sins themselves.' Another example is sentence (128) *frāgodon, ef he wāri that barn godes* 'They asked, if He were the child of God.' Verbs of *saying, writing, thinking* are optionally constrained by the subjunctive; *seggian* inclines toward subjunctive constraint SScR51c).

SScR52d displays the subjunctive *bōttin* in a nonfactive complement clause introduced by *that* in sentence (129) *bōttin kuŏda that sie iro selboro sundia bōttin* 'He made known that they should expiate their sins themselves.'

SScR52e demonstrates the subjunctive *wissin* in the indirect statement, introduced by *that*, as a clause complement to the communicating verb *quādun* in sentence (130) *quādun, that sie wissin* 'They said, that they knew.' With minus conjunction *that*, the subjunctive occurs, e.g., in sentence (131) *quað, hē gerno is geld gerewedi* 'He said he gladly prepared his offering.' A sample with matrix verb *seggian* is sentence (131) *sagda, that kuman skoldi ēn kuning* 'He said, that a king should come.'

SScR52f displays the subjunctive in an unreal adverbial clause complement introduced by the conjunction *al sō* in sentence (132) *was im thō, al sō hē thrītig habdi wintro* 'It seemed to him as though he had thirty winters (was thirty years old).' The conjunction *that* occurs in sentence (133) *hwat scal ik duan, that ik heƀenrīki gehalan mōti* 'What shall I do, so that I may attain the kingdom of heaven.'

SScR53: [imperative/hortative] →

$$\begin{Bmatrix} \text{a. [directive]} \rightarrow [\alpha \text{ pron. noml}_0] + \\ \qquad [\text{imp}] + [2 \text{ p. sg.}] \\ \text{b. } [\alpha \text{ pron. noml}_0] + [\text{pres. indic.}] + \\ \qquad [\text{minus 2 p. sg.}] \\ \text{c. } \begin{Bmatrix} [\text{skulan}] \\ [\text{mugan}] \\ [\text{thurban}] \end{Bmatrix} + [\text{noml}_0] + [\text{pres. indic.}] + [\text{inf.}] \\ \text{d. [wita]} + [\text{inf.}] \\ \text{e. [pres. subj.]} \end{Bmatrix}$$

SScR53a yields the imperative through the 2 p. sg. *gehugi* with its pronominal subject *thu* in sentence (133) *gehugi thu an thinumu herton* 'Consider in your heart.' Another example is *gang* minus the subject pronoun, in sentence (134) *ef thu sīs Krist, godes suno, gang thi fan them krūce nidher* 'If you be Christ, God's son, descend from the cross.' Note that *thi* is dative reflexive and not the subject pronoun.

SScR53b yields the imperative through the present indicative *hebbiad* 2 p. pl. minus pronominal subject in sentence (135) *hebbiad ewan willion tharod* 'Direct your will there (to that).'

SScR53c yields the imperative through the present indicative *skulun* plus infinitive *sorgon* in sentence (136) *skulun gī sorgon, than gī an thene sīd farad* 'Worry (You should worry), when you set out on the journey.' An example with the present indicative *maht* plus infinitive is in sentence (137) *nu maht thu lēdien that kind undar ewa cunni* 'Now lead (you can bring) the child among your kin.'

SScR53d employs the interjection *wita* plus infinitive to yield the hortative in sentence (138) *wita kiasan im ōðrana niudsamna namon* 'Let us choose for him another desired name.' Still another example is in sentence (139) *wita is thana fadar frāgon* 'Let us ask then his father.'

SScR53e yields the hortative through the present subjunctive *sī* in sentence (139) *diurida sī drohtine* 'Honor be to the Lord.' Another example is the present subjunctive *folgon* in sentence (140) *folgon im te thero ferdi ... than lēbot ūs thoh duom after* 'Let us follow him on his journey ... Then fame remains after us.'

24.3 Aspect

Analogous to the suprasegmental phonological component, in which pitch and stress are coterminous, yet one or the other predominates to characterize a language, namely in OS stress, on the semantic/syntactic level the verb phrase, specifically the modality constituent, displays both tense and aspect. In OS tense is generally considered primary and hence aspect is assumed and largely left unstated. Indeed, the syntactic subcategorization rules for tense (sect. 24.1 above) leave the aspect unstated except where it occurs marked: SScR46b, c, SScR47b, c, SScR49a, b, SScR50a. The present section (24.3) speaks to both marked and unmarked major aspect sets of OS; aspectual subsets require further refinement

> SScR54: [imperfective] →
> [durative Vb] + α imperfective context]

SScR54 yields imperfective aspectual semantic features by configurating the lexically durative verb *standu* with imperfective discourse *gio* in sentence (141): *Gabriel bium ic hētan, the gio for goda standu* 'I, who always stand before God, am called Gabriel.' Lexically durative as well is *bium* in the sentence; Gabriel's name is an enduring fact.

SScR55: [perfective] →

$$\left\{\begin{array}{l}\text{a. [momentary Vb] + [}\alpha\text{ momentary context]}\\\text{b. [biginnan] + [durative infinitive]}\end{array}\right\}$$

SScR55a yields perfective aspectual semantic features by configurating the lexically momentary verb *quam* with perfective discourse *reht so* in sentence (142): *reht sō thuo āband quam, sō warth thar all gisamod siokoro manno* 'Just as evening came, all ill persons were gathering (beginning to gather) there.'

SScR55b yields perfective aspectual semantic features by configurating the lexically momentary verb *bigunnun* with the durative infinitive *seggean* in sentence (143): *thō bigunnun thea wīson man seggean iro swebanos* 'Then the wise men began to tell their dreams.'

SScR56: [durative-perfective] →

$$\left\{\begin{array}{l}\text{a. [effective]} \rightarrow \text{[wesan] +}\\\quad\text{[momentary pret. part.] + [}\alpha\text{ case]}\\\text{b. [ingressive]} \rightarrow \text{+ [werðan] +}\\\quad\text{[momentary pret. part.] + [}\alpha\text{ case]}\\\text{c. }\left\{\begin{bmatrix}\text{effective}\\\text{ingressive}\end{bmatrix}\right\} \rightarrow \text{[hebbian] +}\\\quad\text{[}_2\text{trans. pret. part.] + [}\alpha\text{ case]}\end{array}\right\}$$

SScR56a yields durative-perfective effective aspect by configuration of *sint* with the momentary preterite participle *cumana* plus case in sentence (99) *te hwī sprikis thu thes ... ne sint mīna noh tīdi cumana* 'Why do you speak of this ... My times are not yet come.' Durative-perfective includes the feature momentary, that is, *coming* has a beginning and an end, yet the end is long in coming. Lussky (1921:13) quotes Streitberg: "'Die durativ-perfektiven Verba ... heben den Moment der Vollendung hervor, setzen ihn in ausdrücklichen Gegensatz zu der vorausgehenden Dauer der Handlung.'" On the other hand, the added aspectual distinction between syntagm with *wesan* and syntagm with *werðan* is the lingering in an achieved state for the former and the ingression into a state for the latter (cf. Lussky op. cit: 27)

SScR56b yields durative-perfective ingressive aspect by configuration of *warth* with the momentary preterite participle *cuman* in sentence (144): *thuo warth āband cuman naht mid neflu* 'Then the evening was (in the process of) arriving.' Lussky (1921: 17) glosses sentence (144) "'Da machte der Abend die Bewegung des Kommens, bis er eintrat.'" He contrasts this semantically with the simplex form *quam* of sentence (142) which he (ibid) glosses "'Gerade als der Abend eintrat, da war.'" The ingressive semantic feature is corroborated through the co-occurrence of the ingressive *werðan* periphrasis with *biginnan* syntagms as the macro-discourse of sentence (143´) displays: *thō ward morgan cuman ... thō bigunnun thea wīson man seggean iro sweƀanos* 'Then the morning was (in the process of) setting in ... Then the wise men began to tell their dreams.'

As observed in section 24.1 above Lussky considers the inflected, [+case], participle with *werðan* as compulsorily marked aspect. Ms. M provides a minimal pair

Modality Constituent: 24 - 24.5

in sentence (145) *thar werðat mīna hendi gebundana, faðmos werðad mi thar gefastnod*. The subjects of both these passive clauses are plural, the first feminine, the second masculine. Only the first participle is [+case]. Accordingly, the glossing should read: 'There my hands are being bound, my hands and arms are fastened there,' distinguishing (Lussky 1921: 40) the "Zustand" from the "Abschluss der Tätigkeit," respectively. Perhaps of equal interest is the fact that ms. C does not inflect *gibundan*, indicative of the restructuring from primary aspect to primary tense in sentence (145).

SScR56c yields a durative-perfective aspect either effective or ingressive by configuration of *habad* with the transitive preterite participle *gicoranen* (with its noml$_2$ = *inan*) in sentence (146) *Kaiphas was he hēten; habdun ina gicoranen Judeo liudi* 'He was called Caiaphas; the people of the Jews had him as the elected one.' Lussky (1921: 30) fine-tunes the effective: ingressive features as "in Besitz haben" and "in Besitz bringen", respectively. Once again, it is noteworthy that ms. C displays primary tense in, e.g., sentence (147) *than habde ina craftag god ginerid wið iro nīðe* 'Then the powerful God had saved him from their hatred,' which ms. M with inflected, [+case], preterite participle *gineridan* still displays as primary aspect 'Then had the powerful God him saved from their hatred.'

24.4 Polarity

Polarity, that is, the universal feature of positive versus negative, is manifest in several components of the grammar. The negative member is generally considered the marked feature. The lexicon, e.g., yields such a word as *twiflian* 'doubt' with negative semantic features, i.e., nonbelief. Further the derivational morphology evinces negative variations, e.g., *ungilōbiga* 'unbelieving.' Negative semantic features discernible in the modality constituent of the nonlinear macro-syntax are formalized below.

SScR57: negative Vb →

$$[\alpha \text{ ne}] + \alpha \begin{Bmatrix} [\text{wiht}] \\ [\text{eowiht}] \end{Bmatrix} + [\text{ne}] + [\text{Vb}]$$

SScR57 shows the two optional intensifying negative morphemes *ne* and *wiht* combining in *neowiht* in semantic configuration with the negated verb in sentence (147) *imu nis biholan neowhiht ne wordo ne werko* 'Absolutely nothing of words or works is concealed from Him.' Less negative intensification is shown in sentence (148) *ne ik gio mannes ne warð wīs* 'Never did I know a man.' Sentence (149) displays still less negative morphology: *ni tharft thū stum wesan* 'You are not to be silent.' Notice in sentence (149) that *ni* displays more pronounced syntactic stress than *ne* (cf. Chap. VI: 19.4, 20).

SScR58: negative sentence →

$$\left\{\begin{array}{l} \text{a. } [ne] + [Vb \left\{\begin{array}{l}\text{attaining}\\ \text{effecting}\end{array}\right\} + that \text{-sent.}] + [\text{subj.}] \\[2ex] \text{b. } [ne] + \left\{\begin{array}{l} x[\text{pres.}] \\ y[\text{pret.}] \end{array}\right\} + \left\{\begin{array}{l} [ne] \\ [\text{nebu}] \end{array}\right\} + \left\{\begin{array}{l} x[\text{conj.}] \\ y[\text{indic.}] \end{array}\right\} \\[2ex] \text{c. } \left\{\begin{array}{l} x[\text{neg.-sent.}] \\ y[\text{posiv.-sent.}] \end{array}\right\} + \left\{\begin{array}{l} [\text{than}] \\ [\bar{e}r] \end{array}\right\} + \left\{\begin{array}{l} x[\text{indic.}] \\ y[\text{subj.}] \end{array}\right\} \\[2ex] \text{d. } \left\{\begin{array}{l} x[\text{neg.-sent.}] \\ y[\text{posiv.-sent.}] \end{array}\right\} + [\text{resultant}\left\{\begin{array}{l}\text{that}\\ \text{so}\end{array}\right\}] + \left\{\begin{array}{l} x[\text{subj.}] \\ y[\text{indic.}] \end{array}\right\} \\[2ex] \text{e. } [\text{neg. noml}] + \left\{\begin{array}{l} [\text{hw-sent.}] \\ [\text{th-sent.}] \end{array}\right\} + [\text{subj.}] \end{array}\right\}$$

SScR58a yields *ni gescōp* to negate the clause introduced by *that* and containing the subjunctive verb *bāri* in sentence (150) *nec it ōc god ni gescōp, that the gōdo bōm bāri gumano barnum bittres wiht* 'Neither did God create it, that the good tree would bear anything bitter for the children of men.'

SScR58b demonstrates a negative present tense verb *nis* followed by a negated present subjunctive verb *ni fargelden* in sentence (151) *nis thes tweho ēnig, ni sie ina fargelden sān* 'Not is there any doubt, that they pay him immediately.' Sentence (152) displays the negated preterite verb *ni was* followed by a negated preterite indicative *warð. thō ni was lang aftar thiu, ne it al sō gilēstid warð* 'It was not long thereafter, it all came about.' Notice the positive polarity of the second clause in sentences (151) and (152).

SScR58c displays the negated verb *ni mahtun* followed by the indicative verb *welda* introduced by *ēr* in sentence (153) *thes sie ni mahtun farstandan, ēr it im Krist seggean welda* 'They could not understand that, until Christ wanted to tell it to them.' The nonnegated *habad* is followed by the subjunctive *ēgin* introduced by *than* in sentence (154) *thiu habad friðu mēran, than thea man ēgin* 'She has more freedom, than the people have.'

SScR58d yields a negated verb *ni was* followed by a resultant *that*-clause with the verb in the subjunctive in sentence (153) *ni was gio fēmea sō gōd, that siu lang libbian mōsti* 'Never was there such a beautiful woman, that she could live long.' Sentence (154), on the other hand, displays a positive verb *habda* followed by a resultant *that*-clause with the verb in the indicative in sentence (154) *habda them heriskipie herta gisterkid that sia habdun bithwungana thiodo gihwilika* 'He had the hearts of the people strengthened, so that they had many people subjugated.'

SScR58e yields the negated nominal *ni wiht* followed in the next clause by the relative pronoun *that* as the object of the subjunctive verb *drōgin* in sentence (155) *ni was forlētid wiht, that skenkeon drōgin* 'None was left, which the cup-bearers could bring.'

24.5 Diathesis

Diathesis, or voice, is understood as a universal semantic feature wherein a relational syntactic change from object to subject is understood. Both the auxiliaries *werðan* and *wesan* enter into semantic configuration with preterite participles of transitive verbs; the inflection/noninflection of the participles (according to the constraints valid for the active voice) and/or the macro-discourse help determine the aspectual reading of the verb syntagms (cf. especially sect. 24.3 above).

SScR59: [passive] →

$\begin{Bmatrix} [\text{werðan}] \\ [\text{wesan}] \end{Bmatrix}$ + [trans. pret. part.] + [α case] + [α agent]

SScR59 semantically configurates *werðad* with the inflected, [+case], participle *gebundana* and with the minus case participle *gefastnod* in sentence (145) *thar werðat mīna hendi gebundana, faðmos werðad mi thar gefastnod* 'There my hands are being bound; my hands and arms are fastened there.' The *wesan* option is found in sentence (156) *wārun imu is faðmos gebundene* 'His hands and arms were bound.'

Chapter Eight

The Lexicon: Derivation and Compounding;
Nonnoun Nominal Inflection;
Weakly Stressed Vowels;
Inflection of the Verb Preterite Tense;
Inflection of the Imperative and Subjunctive

25. Noninflectional Morphology

The *Heliand* and *Genesis* lexicon of approximately 4000 words (Sanders 1985a: 1083) is strongly enhanced through the OS capacity for generating a vast and varied vocabulary by means of its derivational morphology and compounding capabilities. Ancient ABLAUT alternations represent a prehistoric source of vocabulary production as is witnessed, e.g., in the OS morphophonemic *i* : *u* alternation in *gebinden* inf. 'to bind': *gebunden* pret. part. 'bound' (cf. Chap. I: 3.3.1). Derivation and compounding is that branch of the nonlinear micro-syntax which is essentially paradigmatic in those components of a derived or compounded word which stay constant under inflection. Thus, the OS derivational adjective suffix *-sam* may be affixed to the OS noun *arƀed* 'toil' to yield *arƀetsam* 'arduous.' The derivational morphology remains constant, although the inflectional morphology changes are controlled by the syntagms. Thus, the OS derivational adjective *oƀarmuodig* 'haughty,' occurs as such, i.e., with zero inflection in the nom. sg. masc., but as *oƀarmuodiga* with the nom. pl. masc. inflection. The *-ig* derivation is suffixed to the compounded *oƀarmuod*, consisting of the free forms *oƀar*, prep. 'over,' and the noun *muod* 'sentiment.' In essence the difference between compounding and derivation is understood in the relative freedom of the component morphemes; while *oƀar* and *muoð* act as independent words in the OS lexicon, *-ig* does not, and it is accordingly a bound morpheme. Both the derivational suffix *-ig* as well as in particular the second component of the compound *oƀarmuod*, i.e., *muod*, appear relatively frequently in word formation; they may still have been productive morphemes in the *Heliand* and *Genesis* stages of OS. Free versus bound morpheme, however, is not the absolute distinguishing factor in determining a derived word from a compounded word. This is particularly the case with free prepositions combined with verb roots. The word-stress conditions differ for nouns and verbs (cf. Chap. V: 17.3.2), which may contribute to the fact that many free preposition plus verb syntagms are more accurately classified as prefixal derivations rather than as compounds. In addition, the semantic features of the preposition in syntagm with a verb may differ from the semantic features of the preposition in a prepositional phrase, e.g., *te-* of *tefallen* 'disintegrate' has among its semantic features [apart], while *te* in *te himile* 'to heaven' has among its semantic features [toward]. The criterion of separable or inseparable morpheme to distinguish prefixal derivation from compounding is also not conclusive in OS.

The change of lexical category, e.g., from participle to noun as in the word *hēliand* 'Savior' itself is another means of word production; it is a prehistorically restructured present participle of the verb *hēlian* 'to heal.' Similarly, a difference in gender or inflectional type or grammatical category may lead to a difference in meaning and hence be a form of word production, e.g., OS *man*, which is isomorphic for a noun 'man,' and a pronoun 'one,' or *hebbian* which is isomorphic for 'to have, possess' and 'to raise.'

25.1 Derivation

Derivation by prefix is very common with verbs, much less so with nouns. Adjectives, pronouns, numerals, adverbs, as well as prepositions, can be modified by prefixes. (A definitive distinction between prefixation and compounding is not absolute in all instances; cf. sect. 25 above). Prefixes include *for-, te-, bi-, umbi-, thurh-, at-, with-, af-, an-, un-, withar-, undar-, obar-, ant-, aftar-, a-, and-, mis-, gi-*. Thus, the root of the verb *hebbian* 'raise' occurs with the prefix *a-*, *ahebbian* 'raise up, begin;' the prefix *af-*, *afhebbian* 'raise up, away;' the prefix *gi-*, *gihebbian* '(perfective) raise up.' The prefix *for-* on the noun *gang* 'path' yields *forgang* 'death.' The adjective *wirðig* 'valuable,' is intensified by the prefix *gi-*, thus *giwirðig* 'precious.' The prefix *gi-* bears a high functional load, especially with nouns and with verbs; it is polysemous. Generic semantic features are lent to the pronoun *hwē* 'who' by the prefix *gi-* in *gihwē* 'whoever.' Although genetically a free morpheme in compounds, *ant-* with numerals is synchronically bound, e.g., in *antahtoda* 'eighty.' The adverb *tesamne* and the preposition *biforan* bear witness to *te-* and *bi-* prefixation, respectively.

Derivation by suffix has difficulties similar to those encountered in prefixal derivation, in that the distinction between affixation, i.e., derivation, and compounding is not always discernible. For example, OS *hēd* 'being' occurs but once as a free simplex in the *Heliand* and

Genesis data, but it is found several times in syntagm, e.g., *juguðhēd* 'youth,' *lēfhēd* 'sickness,' *magaðhēd* 'virginity.' The suffix *-skepi,* as in OS *friundskepi* 'friendship,' on the other hand, is not recorded at all as a free form in the data; accordingly it may qualify as suffixal. Still another criterion is synonymy of the free form with the bound form. Thus, OS-*ward* in syntagm with *forðward* 'forward' certainly does not share semantic features with the OS free form *ward* 'warden;' *-ward* is thus a suffix. Less certain is the degree of semantic overlap between the free form OS *haft* 'bound' and the occurrence of *haft* in, e.g., *treuhaft* 'faithful.'

On the basis of a synchronically free or bound form, then, the derivational suffixes of OS include *-skepi, -fald, -ōdi, -sam, -i, -nissi, -ið(a), -islo, -in(a), -unga, -inni, -(l)ing, -ar(i), -isk, -ig, -oni, -ward, -o, -tig, -(il)īn, -od, -ost* and variations thereof, e.g., *-ar, -or, -ir, -ur.*

To this list may be added the invariable stem suffixal elements to the verb root, e.g., *-i* of *nerian* 'save,' *-o* of *makon*, and a further suffix *-an* on *nerian*, as well as on *niman* 'take,' but a further suffix *-n* on *makon* (cf. Chap. II: 7). Similarly, a further *-d* suffix to the *-an* or *-n* suffix yields the present participle, thus *neriand, makond, nimand.*

Noun, adjective, adverb, and numerals are generated from many of the derivational suffixes, thus, *werod* 'people' derived by *-od* suffixed to *wer* 'man;' the adjective *arbetsam* (cf. sect. 25 above); the comparative *-er* and superlative *-ost* derivations, e.g., *sconiera* 'more beautiful,' *sconiost* 'most beautiful;' the adverbial derivation in *-o*, e.g., *diopo* 'deeply' beside the adjective *diop* 'deep'; and the numeral suffix *-tig*, e.g., *sibantig* 'seventy' to *sibun* 'seven.'

Words may be generated through combined derivations by suffix and prefix, thus, e.g., the above mentioned *antahtoda* 'eighty,' in which OS *ahto* 'eight' is embedded in a prefix and suffix frame. Similarly the past participle of the verb stems *nim-*, *neri-*, *mako-*(cf. Chap. II: 7), *ginuman* 'took,' *ginerid* 'saved,' and *gimacod* 'made' are embedded in a *gi-*prefix and an *-an* or *-d* suffix, the former characteristic of strong verbs, the latter of weak verbs. Notice the ablaut in the strong past participle (cf. Chap. I: 3.3).

25.2 Compounding

The *Heliand* and *Genesis* poet(s) is/are hardly surpassed in choice of relatively simple yet sublime words and phrases and their elegantly crafted interdigitation. Little wonder that all three Latin prefaces (cf. Chap. VI: 192) bear witness to the texts' sweet decor (Preface A: "sui decoris dulcedinem'), wealth of vocabulary, excellence of meaning (Preface B: "copia verborum ... excellentia sensuum"), and skillful diction (Versus "docta ... carmina"). The numerical-architectonic structuring of the *Heliand* (cf. Rathofer 1962) can only be compared with an awesome medieval stained glass architectural feat.

Compounding is effected by the union of two or more free forms into one word. The ability to enter into a compound relationship is shared by all lexical categories; compounding is, accordingly, a very productive method of word generation. In OS a wealth of nominals, especially nouns and adjectives, results from compounding. These compounds are rife with metaphor and they are studied in old Germanic verse, particularly Old Norse and Old English, as kennings (cf., e.g., Rankin 1910). Linguists since Panini (400 BC Indic grammarian) have classified compounds into three principal sets: copulative, determinative, and possessive. Set two is endocentric, i.e., one constituent serves as the head, which also determines the lexical category of the compound, while the other constituent serves as a dependent to modify the head. Thus, e.g., the compound noun *oƀarmuod* 'exuberance' (cf. sect. 25 above) consists of the noun head *muod* united with the dependent preposition *oƀar.* The third set is exocentric, i.e., there is no dependency relationship between the two constituents and the total sense of the compound refers to neither of the individual constituents. Thus, e.g., the two adjectives *gōd* 'good' and *willig* 'willing' unite in an adjective which means principally neither 'good' nor 'willing,' but 'devout.' Panini termed the copulative compounds dvandva, i.e., constituents united by 'and;' the determinative compounds karmadharaya, i.e., the dependent constituent describes the head constituent, and tatpurusha, i.e., the dependent constituent is affected by the head constituent; and the possessive compounds bahuvrihi, i.e., the two constituents reciprocally complement one another.

The sole copulative compound in OS is *gisunfader* 'son(s) and father,' referring to the disciples John and Jacob and their father (fit 14). This lone OS copulative compound, as matched by the *sunufaterungo* of the OHG "Lay of Hildebrand", attests to the astounding sophistication of the *Heliand* poet(s), who partook of the rich bequeathment of heroic Germanic lexicon.

The much studied nominal compounds have been subdivided (Carr 1939, Ilkow 1968, Cordes/Holthausen 1973, Zanni 1985) into seven major sets: (1) Nn + Nn, e.g., *brūdigomo* 'bridegroom,' (2) adj. + Nn, e.g., *aðalkuning* 'noble king,' (3) Vb + Nn, e.g., *swefresta* 'rest camp,' (4) Nn + adj., e.g., *wordwīs* 'articulate,' (5) adj. + adj., e.g., *elilandig* 'foreign,' (6) advbl. + Nn, e.g., *oƀarmuod* 'exuberance' (cf. above), and (7) advbl. + adj., e.g., *filuwīs* 'very wise.' The impressive OS epithet *aðalordfrumo* 'noble creator' of three constituents is composed more proximately of *aðal* + *ordfrumo*. On the other hand, the tripartite *erðlībigiskapu* 'earthly fate' has a superstructure *erðlībi* + *giskapu*.

26. The Inflection of Nonnoun Nominals

Nonnoun nominals include (1) personal pronouns, singular, plural, *dual* (two persons) of the first and second persons *ik* 'I,' *thū̆* 'you,' *wī̆* 'we,' *gī̆* 'you,' *wit* 'we two,' *git* 'you two,' (2) the third person singular and plural masculine, neuter, feminine anaphoric pronoun *hē̆* 'he,' *it* 'it,' *siu* 'she,' (3) the possessive pronoun *mīn* 'my,' *thīn* 'your,' *sīn* 'his, her, its,' *ūsa* 'our,' *euwa* 'your,' *unka* 'both our,' *inka* 'both your,' (4) the trigender deictic pronoun *thē̆*, *that*, *thiu* 'the,' singular and plural, which also serves as a relative pronoun, (5) the intensified trigender deictic pronoun *these 'this,' singular and plural, (6) trigender quantifiers such as *ēn* 'a, an,' *sum* 'some,' *ōðar* 'other,' *nigēn* 'not one,' *ēnag* 'one,' *ēnig* 'any,' *all* 'all,' *manag* 'many,' (this set can be expanded to include, e.g., *sulĭc* 'such,' cf. Chap. VII: 23.2), (7) *hw*-pronouns such as trigender *hwilĭc* 'which,' trigender *hwē̆* 'who,' trigender *hweðar* 'which of two,' (8) the reflexive pronoun, isomorphic with the dative and accusative of sets (1) and (2) above. The lack of independent reflexive morphology is shared with OE and OF (cf. Chap. VI: 19.3.3). Adjectives and numerals, as well as nonfinite verb forms such as the infinitive and participles are also considered nominals.

As with the inflection of the noun (cf. Chap. II: 10.1) a so-called strong : weak dichotomy divides nonnoun nominals into two sets of suffixes. The weak set (cf. sect. 26.1.3) is the marked set. It includes the comparative and optionally the superlative (which may also inflect as strong, cf. sect. 26.1) of the adjective with derivational suffix -Vr, -Vst, respectively (cf. sect. 25.1 above); adjectives in syntagm with the simple deictic pronoun; the unaccompanied adjective used as noun for a known referent, e.g., *gramon* 'the devil' (cf. Rauch 1983b); the adjectives *giwono* 'accustomed,' *alowaldo* 'all powerful,' *skolo* 'guilty,' *formo* 'the first;' and most occurrences of ordinal numbers from 'three' onward (cf. sect. 26.1.2 below). A set of quantifier adjectives including *all* 'all,' *manag* 'many,' *middi* 'mid,' *faho* 'few,' *half* 'half,' *ful* 'full,' *ginōg* 'enough,' *bēðie* 'both' occurs in the *Heliand* and *Genesis* data as strong. All other nonnoun nominal occurrences are unconstrained weak and strong.

26.1 Trigender Strong Nonnoun Nominal Suffix

The strong nonnoun nominal desinences overlap quite extensively with the masculine, neuter, feminine desinences of the strong noun (cf. Chap. II: 11.1, 12.1, Chap. III: 14.1). However, the masculine dative and accusative singular, the neuter dative singular, the feminine dative and genitive singular, as well as the trigender genitive plural, differ and are characteristic of the inflection of the pronoun.

Nonnoun Nominal Inflection: 26 - 26.1.4 193

The FIF of the pronoun is indeed the trigender nominative singular. Yet to capture the essence of the pronoun, i.e., to extrapolate the generalized shape of the nominative singular for the mnemonic convenience of the reader of the OS texts, the nominative singular will be segmented. Such segmentation reveals just how much of the pronoun inflection exerts itself in the strong nonnoun nominal paradigm. This generalization is at the cost of a nominative singular ø-suffix which occurs in multisyllable *hw*-pronouns and in adjectives; it is shown as a ø option. A further cost of the special nominative singular pronominal suffix generalization is that the ø-suffix alone is posited for all other nominal paradigms in the *OSL*. Set (1) pronouns are treated in part suppletively (cf. sect. 26.1.1)

	Feminine	Masculine	Neuter
Sg. Nom.	-iu(s)/-ø	-e/-ø	-Vt/-ø
Acc.	-(i)a	-(V)n(V)	↓ ↓
Gen.	-Vra	-Vs	←
Dat.	-Vru	-Vmu	←
Instr.		-(i)u(s)	←
Pl. Nom.Acc.	-ia/-e	←	←/-iu(s)/ø
Gen.	-Vro	←	←
Dat.	-Vm	←	←

26.1.1 Trigender Pronoun

	Set (2): Anaphoric Pronoun				Set (4): Deictic Pronoun		
	Fem.	Masc.		Neut.	Fem.	Masc.	Neut.
Sg.Nom.	s|iu 'she'	h|ĕ		i t	th|iu 'the'	th|ĕ	th|at
Acc.	s|ia	ina		i t	th|ia	th|ena	↓↓
Gen.	i r a	is		←	th|era	th|es	←
Dat.	i r u	imu		←	th|eru	th|emu	←
Instr.							th|iu
Pl.Nom.	s|ia	←	←/s|iu		th|ia	←	←/th|iu
Acc.	↓↓	←	↓↓↓		↓↓	←	↓↓↓
Gen.	i r u	←	←		th|ero	←	←
Dat.	i m	←	←		th|em	←	←

The segmentation of the anaphoric pronoun reveals that it is virtually isomorphic with the trigender strong nonnoun nominal suffix (cf. sect. 26.1 above), and that it has but two "root" alternates: *s-* in the fem. nom. acc. sg. and the trigender nom. acc. pl. and *h-* in the nom. sg. masc. The immediate advantage of this segmentation can be viewed in the deictic pronoun, which has the identical suffixes as the anaphoric pronoun plus a uniform *th-* "root."

The variations in the anaphoric pronoun are quite predictable from the now familiar graphemic variation so characteristic of the *Heliand* and *Genesis* data (cf. especially Chap. VI). Because the pronoun is susceptible to varying syntactic stress, occurrences such as *he* instead of *hē* or *hie, et* and *es* instead of *it* and *is, im* and *in* instead of *imu* and *ina* are reflective of weak syntactic stress and/or ms. dialect preference. The end syllable variation <i, u> varying with lower <e, o>; <e, o> varying with lower <a>; <a> varying with raised <e, o>; and <m> with <n> (cf. Chap. III: 11.1, 12.1, Chap. IV: 14.1 and Chap. VI) prevails in the anaphoric pronoun paradigm, thus, e.g., acc. sg. masc. *ina* ~ *ine*; dat. sg. masc. neut. *imu* ~ *imo* (but also rare *imi*); rare *in* instead of *im* in the pl. dat. The gen. sg. fem. *ira* ~ *iro* ~ *iro* ~ *ire*; nom. sg. fem. *siu* ~ *sie* ~ *sea* ~ *sia* evince, to be sure, the known end-syllable variation, but also the ongoing merger of the feminine dative and genitive singular, and the feminine nominative and accusative singular, which, in turn, may be phonetically stimulated, i.e., end-syllable drift toward /ə/ (cf. sect. 30 below) and merger in set 1 diphthongs (cf. Chap. VI: 19.4.31), respectively. The feminine nominative accusative singular and the nominative accusative plural all genders are in the process of merging; similarly the feminine dative genitive singular and the genitive of all genders are merging. Paradigm iconism or perhaps megadialect (OE) interference is further visible in inorganic *h*-forms of vowel initial pronouns, e.g., *him, hina*. Ms. M *hī* may be megadialect interference.

The variation in the deictic pronoun is very similar to that witnessed in the anaphoric pronoun. Megadialect (OE) interference is seen in the nom. sg. masc. *se* of ms. C. Striking in the deictic pronoun are the digraph spellings where they are not parallel in the anaphoric pronoun, e.g., acc. sg. masc. *thiena* ~ *thaene*, beside *thane, thena* ~ *thana* ~ *thene* ~ *than* ~ *then* ~ *thenne*, and the greater variety of digraphs, e.g., in the masc. sg. nom. *thea* ~ *thia* ~ *thei* beside *thie*. Note, of course, the basic inclination of the deictic toward a lower stem suffix, e.g., -*at* instead of anaphoric *it*, -*ena* instead of anaphoric *ina*, -*era* instead of anaphoric *ira*, -*em* instead of anaphoric *im*.

Set (5): Intensified Deictic Pronoun

	Feminine	Masculine	Neuter
Sg. Nom.	thius 'this'	*thes|e	thit
Acc.	thes|a	thes|an	thit
Gen.	thes|ara	thes|es	←
Dat.	thes|aru	thes|umu	←
Instr.			thius
Pl. Nom.Acc.	thes|e	←	←/thius
Gen.	thes|aro	←	←
Dat.	thes|um	←	←

The segmentation of the intensified deictic pronoun is in accord with the generalized trigender strong nonnoun nominal suffix of section 26.1 above. The nom. acc. sg. fem, instr. sg. neut. and nom. acc. pl. neut. *thius* reveals well the compound nature of the intensified deixis. A segmentation such as *th-iu-s* would show this deictic pronoun to consist of root *th* plus inner inflection *iu*, plus noncontiguous or second root *s*, which are actually the genetic facts. Notice the *th* and *s* in all forms but the neut. nom. acc. sg. *thit*, which is distinct from the simple deixis purely by vowel quality, thus *that*. Indeed, graphic variation of the sort *thet* would obscure either or both the deictic or the intensified deictic pronoun of the neut. nom. acc. sg. We find occurrences of *thet* and *thit* in ms. C where ms. M has *that*; contrariwise an occurrence of ms. C *that* is matched by ms. M *thit*. *thitt* also occurs as a nom. sg. f. *thus*. The variations noted for the anaphoric and the deictic pronouns are prevalent in the intensified deixis. If the *thius* and *thit* forms are understood as having ø-suffix, then they, as well as the trigender *-e* plural of the intensified deictic pronoun, show this

Nonnoun Nominal Inflection: 26 - 26.1.4

paradigm to be isomorphic with the strong adjective suffix, excluding the instrumental.

Set (7): *hw-* Pronoun

	Masc.	Neut.	Fem.	Masc.	Neut.
Sg. Nom.	hw|ĕ 'who'	hw|at	hwilĭc 'which'	hwilĭc	←
Acc.	hw|ena	↓	hwilĭc|a	hwilĭc|an	↓
Gen.	hw|es	←		hwilĭc|es	←
Dat.	hw|em	←	hwilĭc|aru	hwilĭc|umu	←
Instr.		hw|iu		hwilĭc|u	←
Pl. Nom.Acc				hwilĭc|e	←
Gen.					
Dat.					hwilĭc|un

The simple interrogative pronoun *hwĕ* 'who' also shows some variation of the types found in the anaphoric and deictic pronouns. The instr. sg. neut. is most commonly *hwī* although *hwō* also occurs.

The compounded interrogative *hwilĭc* 'which,' by its ø-suffix nom. sg. all genders, acc. sg. neut. and its nom. acc. pl. *-e* suffix and nom. acc. pl. neut. ø-suffix, bespeaks the strong adjective suffix including the instrumental.

Set (1) personal pronouns of the first and second persons, singular *ik* 'I,' *thū* 'you,' plural *wī* 'we,' *gī* 'you,' and dual *wit* 'we two,' *git* 'you two' allow some generalizations, but they also display suppletion, i.e., noniconic forms, e.g., the nom. dual *wit* and the dat. acc. dual *unk*. Generalizations which can be derived are: (a) The acc. suffix is *-k*, thus *mik* 'me,' *thik* 'you;' in the dual *unk* 'we two,' *ink* 'you two' it serves as both the acc. and dative. (b) The dative suffix is ø, thus *mĭ* 'me,' *thĭ* 'you,' which are also alternate forms for the accusative singular; in the plural *ūs* and *eu* serve as both dat. and acc. (c) The gen. sg. suffix is -*n*, thus *mīn* 'my,' *thīn* 'your,' while the gen. pl. and dual show a -*Vr(V)* suffix, thus *ūser* 'our,' *euwar* 'your,' *unkero* 'our two' and **inkero* 'your two.' Notice that the personal pronoun evinces a nominative, an objective (combined dat. acc.), and possessive (cf. set 3 below) form. OS customary graphic variations occur.

Set (3) possessive pronoun *mīn* 'my,' *thīn* 'your,' *sīn* 'his, her, its,' *ūsa* 'our,' *euwa* 'your,' *unka* 'both our,' *inka* 'both your,' with the exception of *sīn* are isomorphic or near isomorphic with the genitive of the personal pronoun (cf. sets (1) and (3) below). Near isomorphy is seen in the plural and dual possessive pronoun with the -*rV* which terminates the plural and dual genitive personal pronoun. Since the possessive pronouns are adjectives, they inflect as the strong adjective (cf. sect. 26.1.2 below). Set (6) quantifying pronouns are also inflected as the strong adjective.

26.1.2 Trigender Strong Adjective

	Feminine	Masculine	Neuter
Sg. Nom.	gōd|'good'	gōd|	gōd
Acc.	gōd|a	gōd|an	↓
Gen.	gōd|era	gōd|es	←
Dat.	gōd|eru	gōd|umu	←
Instr.		gōd|u	←
Pl. Nom.Acc.	gōd|e	←	←/gōd
Gen.	gōd|aro	←	←
Dat.	gōd|um	←	←

Note the ø-suffix nominative singular FIF for the strong adjective desinence. Because of the end syllable variation, which most frequently confuses <i ~ e>, <u ~ o>, <e ~ a ~ o>, <m ~ n> (cf. sect. 25.1.1 above) and the possible loss of final vowels, particularly in third syllable, the trigender strong adjective paradigm as given above is fairly abstract. Most striking are the following syncretisms:

(a) The acc. sg. masc. neut. -an occurs also in ms. M as -an with frequent -en, less so -on; in ms. C it occurs as -an, less so -on, rare -en. The dat. sg. masc. neut. occurs in ms. M as un- and -umu, less so -um, seldom -on, rare -om; in ms. C it occurs as -on, seldom -an, rare -om, -un, -en. The dat. pl. occurs in ms. M as -un, less -on, seldom -om, -um; ms. C shows -on, some -an and -un. Clearly ms. C's -on suffix in the dat. sg. masc. neut., acc. sg. masc., and dat. pl. gives strong evidence of merger of the three cases. Very obvious is ms. M's -un evidence for the syncretism of the dat. sg. masc. neut. with the dat. pl. suffix.

(b) The gen. sg. fem. -*era* is but a rare (ms. C) occurrence; most common is -*aro* in both mss. M and C. Ms. M evinces also -*ero*, -*ara*, -*aro*, -*aru*; ms. C -*era*, -*ero*. The dat. sg. fem. -*eru* is also only a rare (ms. M) occurrence; most common is -*aro* in mss. M and C. Ms. M also employs -*oro*, -*ero* and rare -*uru*, -*oru*, -*era*, -*eru*; ms. C uses also, but less so, -*ero*, rare -*era*, -*oro*. The genitive pl. -*aro* is prevalent in both mss. M and C. Less frequent in ms. M is -*oro*, much less -*ero*, and rarely -*era*. Ms. C employs quite frequently -*ero*, seldom -*oro*, rarely -*ara*, -*era*, -*ora*. Without doubt, the gen. dat. sg. fem. and the gen. pl. are syncretized in -*aro*.

(c) The nom. acc. pl. -*e* is strongly represented only in ms. M beside -*a*, while ms. C, but for two exceptions, evinces -*a*. The nom. acc. pl. -*a*, in turn, shows syncretism with the acc. sg. fem. -*a* suffix. The only case that is spared any degree of syncretism is the gen. sg. masc. neut., certainly predictive of modern West Germanic languages such as English and German. The instrumental singular is, of course, of very low functional load.

The most important suffix alternate dependent upon the adjectival root is an acc. sg. masc. -*na* suffix which is constrained in bisyllabic adjectives by heavy ($\bar{V}$ or $\check{V}CC$, cf. Chap. V: 17.4) root syllable followed by light ($\check{V}(C)$ cf. V: 17.4) derivational suffix syllable, and in polysyllabic adjectives by light derivational suffix syllable, e.g., acc. sg. masc. *hēlagna* 'holy,' *silubrinna* 'silver.' Exceptions occur, e.g., *ēnna* 'one,' but also *ēnan*; contrariwise, e.g., *hēlagan*.

The adjective root/stem itself is susceptible to the systemwide phonological rules of medial voicing and final devoicing of consonants (cf. Chap. VI: 19.5). Vowel syncope occurs in the inflectional suffix, e.g., gen. pl. *mahtigro* 'mightier;' *lungro* 'stronger;' and in the derivational suffix, e.g., acc. sg. neut. *hluttar* 'clear, light' beside gen. sg. neut. *hluttres*, nom. sg. fem. *oðar* 'other' beside acc. sg. fem. *oðra*. Finally, adjectives whose roots are extended genetically by an *i* or whose roots end in -*u* may be treated as FIFs with stems in *i*, e.g., *rīki* 'powerful; or *u* e.g. *glau* 'wise,' respectively (cf., e.g., Chap. III: 11.2, 11.2.1). The cardinal numbers *ēn* 'one,' *twēne* 'two,' *thria* 'three' are inflected as strong adjectives.

The cardinal numbers *fiori* 'four,' *fīui* 'five,' *sehsi* 'six,' *sibuni 'seven,' *ahti 'eight,' *niguni* 'nine,' *tehani* 'ten,' *twelifi* 'twelve' are inflected as strong adjective stems extended with *i* when the numbers are pronominal, i.e., not attributive adjectives, or when they are in Nn + adj. linear order; otherwise these cardinal numbers are uninflected. The ordinal numbers *ērist*, *furist* 'first,' *thriddi 'third,' *niguð show strong and weak (cf. sect. 26.1.3 below) adjective inflection. Strong inflection only is found in the ordinal number *ōðar* 'second,' while the remaining ordinal numbers inflect according to the weak adjective declension (below).

26.1.3 Trigender Weak Adjective

The trigender weak adjective desinences are, in effect, isomorphic with the trigender weak noun suffix (cf. Chap. IV: 15.1).

	Masculine	Neuter	Feminine
Sg. Nom.	-ø	-ø	-ø
Acc.	-n	↓	∀-un
Gen. Dat.	│	←---- ∀-on	│
Pl. Nom. Acc.	│	————→	↓
Dat.	↓	←---- ∀-on	←
Gen.	-no	←---- ∀-ono	←

The FIF or base form is the nominative singular, masc. *gōdo* 'good,' neut. *gōda*, fem. *gōda*. The subtractive feature ∀ signals that the final vowel of the FIF syncopates before the weak adjective inflectional suffix. The now familiar graphic variations are in effect. Mss. M and C show ms. dialect features. Noteworthy is ms. C's near merger of the nom. sg. all genders into an *-a* suffix and ms. C's merger of the pl. nom. acc. all genders into a *-un* suffix. On the other hand ms. C slightly prefers *-en* in the masc. neut. genitive. Ms. M dialect is moving toward merger of the masc. and fem. sg. acc. dat. and masc. neut. fem. pl. nom. acc. into an *-on* suffix. Indeed, OS evidence points strongly toward a uniform weak adjective suffix inclining toward /-ən/ (cf. sect. 27 below).

	Masculine	Neuter	Feminine
Sg. Nom.	gōdo	gōda	gōda
Acc.	gōdon	↓	gōdun
Gen./Dat.	│	gōdon	│
Pl. Nom.Acc.	│	gōdun	↓
Dat.	↓	gōdon	gōdon
Gen.	gōdono	gōdono	gōdono

Adjective stems in *-i* have a FIF accordingly, so, e.g., *rīkio* 'powerful.' For the distribution of the weak adjective see section 26 above. Comparative and superlative adjectives that are not derivable simply by *-Vr*, *-Vst* suffix (cf. sects. 25.1, 26 above), i.e., suppletive morphology, require reader memorization, e.g., *gōd* 'good,' *bētara, bezta*; *ūbil* 'bad,' *wirsa, wirsista*; *luttil* 'little,' *minnera, minnista*; *mikil* 'large,' *mēra, mēsta*.

26.1.4 Nonfinite Verb

The verb infinitive, inflected infinitive (so-called gerund), and the present and preterite participles are nominal forms. The customary OS vocalic and dental graphic variations are in effect (cf. Chap. II: 8.1, Chap. VI: 19.4.7).

The infinitive of the strong verb, which provides the root for itself, the present tense indicative and subjunctive, the imperative, and the present participle (cf. Chap. I: 3.3), is thus considered the FIF of the verb in the lexicon. With the exception of anomalous verbs (cf. Chap. II: 8.2.3) and infinitives with *-on* suffix, the stems of all OS strong and weak verbs liable to inflection are the FIF infinitive less *-an* or *-en* (e.g., *niman* 'take,' *nerian* 'save'); in the case of *-on* verbs (e.g. *makon* 'make'), the inflectible stem is simply less *-n* (cf. Chap. II: 8.1). The anomalous verb *d(u)ŏn* 'do' similarly shows an *-n* infinitive suffix; **stān* 'stand' occurs in ms. C as the infinitive *stann*. The anomalous infinitive *wesan* 'be' is suppletive relative to its present tense inflection. Notice, then, that the paradigm weak verbs have but one fundament, in distinction to four possible fundaments for strong verbs (cf. Chap. I: 3.2, 3.3). The infinitive, of course, has a high functional yield in the verb complement (cf. Chap. VII).

The inflected infinitive or gerund occurs in the *Heliand* and *Genesis* data only in the dative sg. masc. neut. strong, thus, e.g., *githenkeanne* of sentence (157): *nio hie sō wīdo ni can te githenkeanne* 'Never may he think so widely,' or *gigaruwenne* of sentence (158) *ik iu sende tharod te gigaruwenne mīna gōma* 'I send you there to prepare my feast(s).'

The present participle consists of the participial suffix *-andi* affixed to the verb stem of the infinitive; in the case of a verb stem final *-o*, *-ndi* is suffixed. The title name of the largest corpus of OS data, *hēliand* 'saviour,' displays well present participle formation built on the infinitive stem *hēli-* 'to save' (cf. Chap. IV: 13.2). The present participle plays a major role in the verb phrase (cf. Chap. VII). It inflects according to both the weak and the strong adjective inflection.

The preterite participle, which in the case of the strong verb represents one of four possible alternating vowel forms or ABLAUTS (fundament d, cf. Chap. I: 3.3) consists of verb stem embedded in a *gi*-prefix and an *-an* suffix, e.g., *ginuman* 'took' (cf. sect. 25.1 above). The weak preterite participle is characterized by a dental suffix, thus, e.g., *ginerid* 'saved,' *gimacod* 'made' (cf. sect. 25.1 above). Prefixed verbs forego the pret. part. *gi-* prefix, thus, e.g., *farlāten* 'relinquished,' or *gifrumid* 'accomplished,' pret. parts. to *farlātan* and *gifrummian*, respectively. Preterite participles inflect as both the weak and the strong adjective inflection. Of the eleven modal auxiliary verbs, only the infinitives of *ēgan* 'own' and *witan* 'know' are attested in the *Heliand* and *Genesis* data; this is indicated by the nonasterisk. Neither

Schwa; Preterite Indicative: 27 - 28.2.3

present participle nor preterite participle forms of any of the eleven modal auxiliary verbs occur in the data.

Rare infinitives, gerunds, and present participles show an extended suffix on verbs whose infinitive stem ends in *-on*, thus, e.g., *haloian* 'fetch' beside *halon*, *wacogeandi* and *wacoiande* 'watching' beside expected **wacondi* (cf. Chap. II: 8.1, Chap. VIII). OHG, OE and OF show similarly extended verb forms, attesting to this megadialect verb isogloss (cf. Sehrt 1940/1973).

27. Weakly Stressed Vowels

Throughout the *OSL*, in particular with regard to the study of inflectional morphology (cf. e.g. Chap. III: 11.1, 12.1, Chap. IV: 14.1, Chap. VIII: 26.1.1, 26.1.2), the leitmotif of vocalic graphic confusion has been formulated as <i, u> varying with lower <e, o>; <e, o> varying with lower <a>; and <a> varying with raised <e, o>. The obdurate question of the phonetic reflex of graphic variation under weak stress has vexed OS research to such an extent (cf., e.g., Klein 1977) that it may be allocated to one of the notorious moot questions of Germanic linguistics.

The *Heliand* manuscripts yield four weakly stressed ms. dialect sets: ms. P, V <i, a, o, u>; ms. S <i, e, a ~ o, u>; ms. M <i, a ~ e, o, u>; ms. C <i, e, a, o, u>. A few references to the literature give an indication of the tenuousness, indeed timidity, enveloping the OS weak stress graphemics. Sanders (1973: 40-41) writes: "Für die Erscheinungsweise der Vokale nebentoniger Silben (Vor-, Mittel- und Endsilben) im As. läßt sich als Faustregel formulieren: Ursprüngliche Längen sind meist in die entsprechenden Kürzen übergegangen, ursprüngliche Kürzen verfallen der Abschwächung zu [ə]. Dieser Vorgang ist allerdings wenigstens in der Schrift erst gegen Ende der as. Periode, um 1100, vollzogen; selbst unter der Annahme, daß es sich bei vielen noch volltonig erscheinenden kurzen Nebensilbenvokalen nur um traditionell beibehaltene Schreibungen handelte, nachdem die Abschwächung bereits eingetreten war, gestattet das Gesamtbild der as. Überlieferung nicht, all diese *a, o, u* usw. schon als Allophone des einen Phonems /ə/ zu betrachten."

Cordes (1973: 214) explains: "Die Festlegung des Hauptakzents auf die erste Wk-Silbe ... mußte notwendig zur Folge haben, daß die Vokale der untergeordneten Akzentstellen ihre extremen Artikulationskomponenten verloren. Es trat zunächst eine 'Indifferenz' ein, die (1) in der Vertauschung der V sichtbar werden kann, (2) zu immer größerer Unsicherheit der Schreiber und schließlich (3) zu völliger 'Reduzierung' auf eine mittlere Stelle und Lage der Artikulation führte, die meistens als /ə/, in Verbindung mit einem vokalisierten /r/ auch als /ɒ/ auftritt. Abgesehen von der durch das Übergewicht der 'Endungen' hervorgerufenen Synkope ... zeigt sich die altnd. Graphie von diesem Vorgang noch nicht berührt, doch macht sich in der späteren Periode seit etwa Beginn des 11. Jh. die Unsicherheit zunehmend bemerkbar."

In spite of an instinctual understanding of the OS weakly stressed vowel inclination or drift toward /ə/, researchers still find it necessary to stop short of positing a /ə/ for OS *Heliand* and *Genesis* data. The *OSL* demonstrates, indeed, the phonemic status of /ə/ (cf. Chap. V: 17.3.3). Instead of being mired or deadlocked in retracing old arguments, the focus could be shifted somewhat to other parts of the system to ascertain whether, in fact, *Heliand* and *Genesis* OS did not already support /ə/ and its allophones (cf. Chap. VI: 19.4.28) in weakly stressed syllables. After all, *Heliand* ms. C is but a century removed from the Sanders/Cordes eleventh century birth of /ə/. In fact, ms. C displays better preserved end syllables than does the century older ms. M, which is certainly incongruous with the chronological drift of end-syllable decay. Another part of the system strongly coordinated with end-syllable decay is umlaut of root syllable, which in general umlaut theory reacts positively to loss or weakening of the end syllable conditioner. Yet, the evidence for umlaut graphemes in ms. C outnumbers that in ms. M (cf. Chap. V: 19.4.26).

On the one hand, syncope phenomena (cf. Cordes above), e.g., ms. M *dopte* 'baptized' (ms. C *dopida*), and apocope phenomena ms. C *guodon* dat. sg. masc. 'good' (ms. M *godumu*), on the other hand, epenthesis phenomena, e.g., ms. C *burug* 'city' (ms. M *burg*), are vital systemic strategies which feed the OS inclination toward /ə/. Epenthetic vowels are constrained by the liquids *l, r* and are frequently iconic with the root syllable vowel, less so with the end syllable (cf. Chap. IV: 13.1), although <a> is fairly common with root syllable <e> and <o>, the latter when not before <w>. In the OS epenthesis habits we witness again the intermingling tendencies especially of weakly stressed <e, a, o>. In turn, regard the remarkable <u ~ o ~ i> epenthetic variation, *wuruhteon, wurohtion* 'workers,' *warihtio* 'worker,' all in ms. C. The OS native speaker as well as the modern reader of OS hardly cognizes a stem such as *wur V ht-* as composed of three distinct epenthetic vowels.

28. Inflection of the Verb
Preterite Tense Indicative

The traditional bifurcation of the OS verb into strong and weak (cf. Chap. I: 3.2) is actually based on the formation of the preterite tense. Strong verbs are those which do not use a dental suffix adjoining the preterite tense inflections to form their preterite tense; weak verbs are those which employ a dental suffix, to which the preterite tense inflections are affixed.

28.1 Preterite Tense Indicative Suffix

The preterite tense indicative inflections of the strong and weak verbs fall into one of two sets, one without dental, the other with dental. All verb types which form their preterite by dental suffix are dental preterites; these include part of both the *-(a)d* present tense plural types and the *-un* present tense plural types, as well as the anomalous verbs *d(u)ŏn* 'do' and *willian* 'will' (cf. Chap. II: 8). All other verbs, i.e., a large subset of the *-(a)d* present tense plural verbs and the anomalous verb *wesan* 'be' (which has strong verb set V ABLAUT) have a nondental preterite tense. The anomalous *stān* 'stand' exhibits no preterite forms in the *Heliand* and *Genesis* data; a possible OS *gān* is not documented in the data.

	Nondental Preterite	Dental Preterite
Sg. 1.3	-ø	-da
2	-i	-des
Pl.	-un	-dun

The preterite indicative desinences are distinct from the present indicative endings (cf. Chap. II: 8.1), yet it is to be observed that the isomorphism of the 1 p. sg. and 3 p. sg. as well as the plural *-dun*, albeit minus the dental, show some commonality with the *-un* present plural suffix paradigm. The preterite tense suffixes are added to the preterite singular and preterite plural alternating vowel fundaments (forms b and c, cf. Chap. I: 3.3 and 3.3.1) in the case of the nondental preterites. It is to be noted that the singular preterite fundament (form b) provides the root for the 1 p. and 3 p. only; the root of the 2 p. sg. is provided by the plural preterite fundament (cf. sect. 28.2 below). In the case of the dental preterites, the preterite tense suffixes are generally (cf. sect. 28.2.2 below) affixed to the stem of the infinitive, i.e., the FIF, minus -*an*, -*en*; infinitive final -*on* minus -*n* only.

The familiar graphic variations occur. The vowels occur as -*(d)on*, -*(d)an*, -*(d)e*, -*(d)as*, -*(d)os*. The dental may occur as <th, ð> (cf. Chap. VI: 19.4.7). The suffix variation <t> is root-determined (cf. sect. 28.2.2 below).

28.2 Preterite Tense Plural Types

Nondental Preterite	Dental Preterite		
Sg.1.3. gaf 'gave'	nerida 'saved'	makoda 'made'	skolda 'should'
2 gābi	nerides	makodes	skoldes
Pl. gābun	neridun	makodun	skoldun

Genetically strong verbs (so indicated in the lexicon, cf. Chap. I: 3.2) consisting of seven subsets, and the verb *wesan* 'be' (which has strong verb set V ABLAUT) form their preterite by nondental suffix. All other verbs: the genetically weak verbs with three subsets, the modal auxiliary verbs, as well as the anomalous verbs *d(u)ŏn* 'do' and *willian* 'will' form their preterite by dental suffix. A rare instance of both weak and strong inflection is seen in 3 p. sg. pret. *saida* 'sowed' beside strong subclass VII *(obar)seu* 'oversowed.'

28.2.1 The Nondental Preterite

The nondental preterites form their preterite by nondental desinences which are accompanied by vowel alternations (ABLAUT) as given in the b and c fundaments (cf. Chap. I: 3.3). If the verb ending and the syntax suggest a preterite form to the reader of the OS text, it can be confirmed by the ABLAUT of the verb root. The FIF necessary for achieving lexical meaning can be identified by reference to the seven ABLAUT alternations.

Pret. 1.3. sg. root vowel		ABLAUT set
ē	=	I, VII
a	=	III, IV, V
ō	=	II, VI
e	=	VII
io	=	VII

Pret. pl. & 2p.sg. root vowel		ABLAUT set
i	=	I
u	=	II, III
ā	=	IV, V
ō	=	VI
ĕ̄	=	VII
io	=	VII

If the reader is familiar with the verb root shape in each of the seven ABLAUT classes, immediate disambiguation is possible. For example, the *a* of the 3 p. sg. pret. *warð* indicates a possible ABLAUT set III, IV, or

V. The salient characteristics outlined for the root shapes of the seven sets (Chap. I: 3.3.1) firmly place *warð* into set III, whose tell-tale shape is root vowel followed by resonant (r, l, m, n) plus C (consonant). Once the set membership is identified, the reader looks to the (a) fundament, the infinitive of the set, which is the FIF, for the purpose of ascertaining the lexical meaning *werðan* 'become' (cf. Chap. I: 3.3). Memorization of the characteristic root shapes of the seven ABLAUT sets or reference to the strong verb dictionary finder chart (cf. Chap. I: 3.3.1) acts as a servo-mechanism for cognizing the entire strong verb corpus in the OS data.

The preterite indicative of the anomalous verb *wesan* 'be' is 1.3 sg. *was*, 2 sg. *wāri*, pl. *wārun*; a 2 p. sg. *wart* also occurs.

28.2.2 The Dental Preterite

Dental preterites with stem ending in *-i* evince rare stem ending variation with *-e*, thus ms. C *andwordeda* 'answered.' Ms. C shows an *-ia* twice in *andwordiade*. Ms. M writes *githigedi* 'accepted' and ms. V writes *gerewedi* 'prepared.' A case of stem ending in *-o* varying with *-e* is found in ms. C *forohtedin* 'feared.'

Although the paradigm weak verb is characterized by invariable root and/or stem throughout its inflection possibilities (present and past tenses, participles), weak verb subsets exist which exhibit variable stems; the variable stem may be accompanied by variable root vowel or variable root consonantism. Dental preterite suffix *-t* synchronically induced by the contiguous root consonant is also possible.

A subset of dental preterites whose infinitive stems end in -*i* does not admit the preterite stem that ends in -*i*. These fall into three further sets: (a) those whose preterite root is isomorphic with the root of their infinitive, e.g., *hōrian* 'hear,' *hōrda* 3.p. sg. 'heard;' (b) those with simplex root consonant in the preterite compared with geminate root consonant in the infinitive, e.g., *antkennian* 'perceive.' *antkenda* 3.p. sg. 'perceived;' (c) those whose preterite root differs from the root of their infinitive, e.g., *gisellian* 'hand over,' *gisaldun* 3.p. pl. 'handed over.'

While preterites from sets (a) and (b) pose no lexical problem to the reader of the OS texts, preterites from set (c), because of their variable root vowel and/or consonant, require special observation. Set (3) *gisellian* includes *tellian* 'recount,' with compulsory *e*-infinitive ~ *a*-preterite alternation; the *a* is understood as genetically unumlauted (Rückumlaut) relative to the *e* (cf. Chap. VI: 19.4.29). Such *e* ~ *a* alternation is optional in *queddian* 'greet,' *leggian* 'lay' (*ledda* occurs beside *legda*), *sendian* 'send,' which evince both *e* and *a* in the preterite, e.g., *senda, sanda*. The verb *huggian* 'think' has a preterite both as *hugdun* and *hogdun*.

A number of set (3) dental preterites without preterite stem suffix -*i*, whose infinitive final root consonant is *k*, have *h* instead of *k* in their preterite root. Notice the dental itself is *t* instead of *d*, iconically induced by the voiceless verb root final consonant from the point of view of synchrony. Most of these preterites are also accompanied by a root vowel alternation and three occur without the root nasal of the infinitive: with no vowel alternation *sōkian* 'seek,' *sōhta*; with vowel alternation *wekkian* 'awaken,' *wahta*; *wirkian* 'work,' *warhta*; with vowel alternation and *n*- drop *thenkian* 'think,' *thāhta*; *thunkian* 'seem,' *thūhta*; *brengian* 'bring,' *brāhta*.

Presence or absence of stem vowel *i* in the preterite hardly distinguishes these verbs as preterites; however, the compulsory vowel and/or consonant differences associated with the *i-* less preterite stems do make the lexical identification of these verbs a challenge relative to their infinitive stems. Thus witness, e.g., verbs which evince both an *i*-preterite stem and an *i*-less preterite stem *dopida* 'baptized' beside *dopta*; clearly the dental signals the preterite, not the *i* or lack of it. Note as well, that the *o*-stem vowel of verbs such as *makoda* 'made' plays no role in distinguishing such forms as preterites; only the dental and the endings signal tense and person.

As observed in Chap. I: 8.2.2 the eleven so-called modal auxiliary verbs, which carry high functional load, must be memorized because of the variable root vowel of nine of these verbs (**mōtan* 'must' and *ēgan* 'own' excepted), coupled with root consonant and dental suffix variations in the preterite of ten of them (**mōtan*, **ēgan* included); **dugan* 'be of use' has no attested preterite in the OS data. The verbs *ēgan* 'own,' **thurban* 'need,' **mugan* 'be able' show their root consonants devoiced followed by the iconically suited *t* dental suffix, thus *ehta*, *thorfta*, *mahta*. The preterite indicative of *witan* 'know' is *wissa*. A preterite root consonant *s* joined by an iconic preterite *t*-suffix occurs in *mōsta, farmonsta, (gi)onsta, consta* and *(gi)dorsta*, which are preterites to *mōtan* 'must, may,' **farmunan* 'disdain,' **(gi)unnan* 'grant,' *kunnan* 'can,' and *(gi)durran* 'dare,' respectively. *mohta* shows geminate *t* in ms. C *mohtta*. Usual OS graphemic variations in the root vowels and the end syllable occur (cf. Chap. VI: 19.4 and Chap. VIII: 27). The generalization can be drawn that the -*t* suffix helps characterize the preterite of the modal auxiliary verbs; indeed only *scolda* pret. to **skulan* 'should' employs the weak preterite paradigm *d*-suffix.

28.2.3 Anomalous Verbs

The anomalous verb *d(u)ŏn* 'do' has a dental preterite with root vowel variation, thus: 1.3 p. sg. *deda* (*Genesis fordæda* 'ruined'), 2 p. sg. *dedos* and *dadi*; plural *dedun* and *dadun*. The anomalous verb *willian/wellian* 'will' has a dental preterite both with and without root vowel alternation, thus *walda*, and *wolda*. For the dental preterites generally, the usual OS graphemic variations are possible (cf. Chap. VI: 19.4, Chap. VIII: 27).

29. The Inflection of the Nonindicative Verb Moods

29.1 The Imperative

The 2 p. sg. imperative is formed with the bare infinitive stem of the verb, i.e., the infinitive (cf. sect. 26.1.4 above) less *-an* or *-en* in the case of strong, most weak verbs and the anomalous verb *wesan* 'be;' in the case of weak *-on* verbs and the anomalous verb *d(u)ŏn* 'do' the bare stem is simply less *-n*: *nim* 'take,' *neri* 'save,' *wes* 'be,' *folgo* 'follow,' *d(u)o* 'do.' The imperative root vowel of the strong verb ABLAUT sets II, III, IV, V and the anomalous verb *wesan* can evince root vowel *e* or *i*, thus, e.g., ms. C *hilp*, ms. M *help* 'help.' The 2 p. pl. imperative is isomorphic with the 2 p. pl. indicative (cf. Chap. II: 8.1); *wesat* 'be' is an exception. The anomalous verb *willian* 'will' occurs only in the plural imperative in the *Heliand* and *Genesis* data. The final vowels are also subject to usual OS graphic variation.

29.2 The Subjunctive

29.2.1 Present

With the exception primarily of the modal auxiliary verbs, the present subjunctive suffix for OS strong and weak verbs can be generalized as an *e*, thus 1.3 p. sg. -*e*, 2 p. sg. -*es*; pl. -*en*. In the case of strong verbs, most weak verbs, and the anomalous verb *willian* 'will,' the present subjunctive suffix is affixed to the infinitive stem, i.e., the verb FIF less -*en* or -*an*, yielding, e.g., *gebe* 1.3 p. sg. 'would give,' *gihorie* 3 p. sg. 'would hear,' *willie* 1.3 sg. 'would want.' The anomalous verb *wesan* evinces two occurrences of 3 p. sg. *wese*, one *wesa* 'would be' beside usual suppletive present subjunctive *sī* 1.3 p. sg., *sīs* 2 p. sg., *sīn* 2 p. pl.

Weak verbs with infinitive final -*on*, e.g., *makon* 'make' employ their stem vowel *o* with and without the present subjunctive *e*-suffix, thus, e.g., *maco* 3 p. sg. 'would make' and *thiono* 3 p. sg. 'would serve' beside the extended (by *e* with further phonetic matter, cf. sect. 26.1.4) forms such as ms. C *ahtoie*, ms. M *hatogea* 3 p. sg. 'would consider' and ms. M *gethologian*, ms. C *githoloian* 2 p. pl. 'would endure.' The anomalous verb *d(u)ŏn* 'do' evinces present subjunctive *duoas* 2 p. sg.; *doe, duo, dua, duæ* 3 p. sg.; *duoian, doan, duan* 1 p. pl.; *duan* 2 p. pl.; *duon, duan, doen* 3 p. pl. The explanation of the extended forms for the purpose of disambiguation from the indicative (Sehrt 1940/1973) appears reasonable.

The modal auxiliary verbs (cf. Chap. I: 8.2.2) remarkably (cf. sect. 29.2.2 below) form their present subjunctive with an *i*-suffix, thus, e.g., *witi* 'would know,' *ēgi* 'would own,' *mugi, moti* 'would have to,' *thurƀin* 'would need,' *sculi* 'should,' *farmuni* 'would disdain.' The modal auxiliaries *dugan* and *(af)unnan* or *(gi)unnan* yield no subjunctive forms in the data, whether present or preterite; *gidurran* 'dare,' *kunnan* 'can,' yield no present subjunctives. Several indicatives occur, thus 2 p. pl. *witun* (ms. M), 3 p. pl. *muotun* (ms. C), 1.2.3 p. pl. *sculun* (ms. C) which is actually a nonlinear syntactic subcategorization problem. The modal auxiliary *mōtan* 'must, have to' shows an occurrence of *muotig* 1 p. sg. (ms. C; cf. Chap. VI: 19.4.16).

29.2.2 Preterite

The preterite subjunctive suffix for the OS strong and weak verbs can be generalized as an *-i* which occurs as *-di* in the case of the latter, thus 1.3 p. sg. *-(d)i*, 2 p. sg. *-(d)is*, pl. *(d)in*. In the case of strong verbs and the anomalous verb *wesan* 'be' (with strong verb set V ABLAUT) the preterite subjunctive suffix is affixed to the (c) fundament (the so-identified preterite plural ABLAUT; cf. Chap. I: 3.3), thus, e.g., *nāmi* 3 p. sg. 'would have taken,' *wārin* 3 p. pl. 'would have been.' In the case of the weak verbs the preterite dental plus the preterite subjunctive suffix is affixed to the infinitive stem (the FIF less *-an* or *-en*; with infinitives ending in *-on*, minus *-n* only), thus, e.g., *gineridi* 3 p. sg. 'would have saved,' *thianodin* 3 p. pl. 'would have served.' The preterite subjunctive of the anomalous verbs *willian* 'will' and *d(u)ŏn* 'do' is with dental, thus 1.3 p. sg. *weldi, woldi*, 1.3 p. pl. *weldin*; 3.p. sg. *dādi, dĕdi*, 3 p. pl. *dādin, dĕdin*. The forms cited above do not evince variation with the subjunctive <i> suffix, which could lead to obscuring of the subjunctive mood. Parsimonious though language may be on the expression level, and contrary to the inclination of OS toward /ə/ in weakly stressed syllable, (cf. sect. 27 above) the maintained <i> subjunctive forms display the inherent strategies of language for semantic (content level) disambiguation.

The preterite subjunctive of the modal auxiliary verbs exhibits the generalized preterite subjunctive *i*-suffix along with the variable root vowel of the modal auxiliary verbs (with the exception of *mōtan* 'must' and *ēgan* 'own'), coupled with root consonant and preterite dental suffix variation (cf. sect. 28.2.2 above). The verbs **dugan* 'be of use.' *(far)munan* 'disdain,' **gi-* or **af-unnan* yield no preterite subjunctive forms in the *Heliand* and *Genesis* data. The verbs **ēgan* 'own,' **thurban* 'need,' **mūgan* 'be able' show their root consonant devoiced, followed by the phonologically iconically suited *t* dental suffix, thus, e.g., *ēhti* 'would have owned,' *thorfti* 'would have needed,' *mahti* 'would have been able.' The preterite subjunctive of *witan* 'know' is *wissi*. A preterite root consonant *s* joined by an iconic preterite *t*-suffix occurs in *mosti, consti, (gi)dorsti*, which are preterite subjunctives to *mōtan* 'must,' **kunnan* 'can,' and **(gi)durran* 'dare,' respectively. Indeed, the generali-zation can be drawn that the *ti*-suffix characterizes the preterite subjunctive of the modal auxiliary verb. All persons and numbers attested for the preterite subjunctive of *skulan*, e.g., *scoldi* 'should have,' employ a *d*-preterite suffix, which is phonetically iconic with its root final consonant *l*. The well-maintained subjunctive *i* suffix (cf. above) appears as *e* four times in the preterite subjunctive of modal verbs, some of which, to be sure, have a relatively high functional load in the subjunctive: 3 p. sg. *wisse* 'would have known' (*Genesis*), 3 p. sg. *mahte* 'would have been able' (ms. C), 3 p. sg. *scolde* 'should have' (ms. M), *(gi)dorste* 'would have dared' (ms. C). Indicative forms occur, thus 3 p. sg. *mahta* (mss. M,

C), 3 p. sg. *muosta* (ms. C), *scolda* (ms. C). The modal auxiliaries *mugan 'be able' and *thurban 'need' show 3 p. sg. *mohtig, mahtig* (both ms. C) and 1 p. sg. pret. *thorftig* (ms. C), respectively; certainly supported by the OS adjectives *mahtig* 'mighty' and *thurftig* 'needy' as well as by phonetic considerations (cf. Chap. VI: 19.4.16).

30. Further Linear and Nonlinear Syntax Rules

30.1 Linear Order

The OS independent declarative, interrogative, and imperative unmarked and marked word orders are found in Chap. II: 6. Much of the phrase structure linear order is demonstrated in the syntactic subcategorization rules of Chap. VII. In sect. 30.1.1 the dependent sentence order will be displayed; sect. 30.1.2 displays the basic linear order of lexical category phrases.

30.1.1 The Dependent Sentence

The unmarked word order of the OS dependent clause is SOVb; the marked orders are SVbO and VbSO:

SOVb: *Habdun ina gicoranen, that **he thes godes hūses gōmien scoldi**.*
'They have chosen him, that he could guard the house of God.'

SVbO: *Sō mag im thes gōdon giwirkean, huldi hebencuninges, — **sō hwe sō habad** hluttra **trewa** up the them alomahtigon gode.*

'Thus can he acquire the favor of the Good-One, the heavenly King, whoever has pure fidelity to the Almighty God.'

VbS(O): *Hwanda wit habdun aldres ēr, efno twēntig wintro an uncro weroldi, ēr than **quāmi** thit **wīf** te mi.*
'For we two had of age earlier, equally twenty winters in our world, ere this woman/wife came to me.'

30.1.2 Lexical Category Phrases

The unmarked word order of the OS nonfinite verb is [FVb] + [-FVb], thus finite Vb *mag* followed by the nonfinite Vb *faran* of sentence (159): *ni mag thār faran ēnig thegno thurh that thiustri* 'Not can any of the thanes go there through the darkness.' The marked order of the nonfinite verb, [-FVb] + [FVb], is exemplified by the nonfinite Vb *bedrogan* preceding the finite Vb *habbiad* in sentence (160) *bedrogan habbiad sie dernea wihti* 'Evil spirits have deceived them.'

The order of the OS noun as the head, relative to an adjective, possessive noun, or relative clause within its domain is as follows: Unmarked are the orders [adj.] + [Nn] and [possessive Nn] + [Nn]. Thus, the adjective *faho* precedes the noun *folcskepi* in sentence (161): *ferid ina werodes lūt, fāho folcskepi* 'Few people, take it (that path), a small group,' and the possessive noun *godes* precedes the noun *sunu* in sentence (162) *thō sprak imu angegin the gōdo godes sunu* 'Then the good Son of God answered him.' The unmarked order of the relative clause is [Nn] + [relative sent.]; thus the noun *bezta* is followed by the relative sentence *thero the io giboran wurði* in sentence (163) *habdun im te gisīdea sunu drohtines, allaro barno bezta, thero the io giboran wurði* 'They had as their traveling companion the Son of the Lord, the best of all children, who was ever born.' Marked orders are the orders [Nn] + [adj.] and [Nn] + [possessive Nn]. Thus, e.g., the noun *wallos* is followed by the adjective *hōha* in sentence (164) *wallos hōha felliad te foldum* 'High walls crash to earth,' and the noun *craft* is followed by the possessive noun *godes* in sentence (165) *scolda thuo that sehsta sāliglīco cuman thuru craft godes endi Cristas giburd* 'The sixth (age) should happily arrive, through the power of God and Christ's birth.' (Notice the unmarked order of 'Christ's birth'). The marked order for the relative clause within the domain of the noun is [relative sent.] + [Nn]; thus the (pro)noun *themu* is preceded by the relative clause *hwene thu hēr an erðu eldebarno gebindan willies* in sentence (166): *hwene thu hēr an erðu eldebarno gebindan willies: themu is bēðiu giduan, himilrīki biloken, endi hellie sind imu opana* 'Whom of humankind you may want to bind, to him both is done, heaven locked, and the hells are open to him.'

The preposition occurs in pre-position in the unmarked order of the OS prepositional phrase, [prep.] + [Nn], as evidenced by the preposition *umbi* preceding the noun *hūs* in sentence (167) *thea liudi stōdun umbi that hēlaga hūs* 'The people stood around the temple.' The preposition in postposition represents marked order for the PP, thus, e.g., the (pro)noun *ina* is followed by the preposition *umbi* in sentence (168) *hwurbun ina umbi mōdag manno folc* 'The hostile people surrounded Him.'

Adverb placement relative to the verb head in the verb phrase is both [Vb] + [adv.] and [adv.] + [Vb] as seen in the

Further Syntax Rules: 30 - 30.2

intensified adverb *swĭðo hardlĭco* following *gibōd* in sentence (169) *the cuning gibōd swĭðo hardlĭko* 'The king commanded very sternly,' and as seen in the adverb *hlūdo* preceding the verb *kumid* in sentence (170) *hlūdo he sie mid hofnu kūmid* 'Loudly does he bewail them (his deeds) with lamentation.' Compulsory [adv.] + [Vb] occurs in all verb phrases with the negative adverb *ni* 'not,' as, e.g., *ni* directly before *mōstun* in sentence (170) *was im thoh an sorgun hugi, that sie erbiward ēgan ni mōstun* 'Their heart was in sorrow, that they could not have an heir.'

30.2 Occasional Optional Congruence Rules

OS *Heliand* data reveal occasional optional congruence rules affecting number (sent.171), gender (sent.172), case (sent.173), person (sent.174), mood (sent.175), and the weak/strong adjective option (sent.176, sent.161): Thus, [compound subject] + [singular verb] occurs in sentence (171) *wann wind endi water* 'Wind and water fought,' with compound subject *wind, water* congruent with verb singular *wann*. [α gender coreference] is demonstrated by the neuter deixis *that* coreferent with the masculine adjective *enna* in sentence (172) *gisāhun that barn godes enna standan* 'They saw the Child of God stand alone.' The case of the relative pronoun is iconic with the case of the anaphoric referent, thus [referent case x] + [relative pronoun case x], instead of with the case the relative pronoun should take from its own clause in, e.g., sentence (173) *gi sculun is geld niman alles thes unrehtes, thes gi ōðrun hĭr gilēstead an thesumu liohte* 'You shall take his recompense for all the injustice, which you do to others here in this world.'

Accusative *that* is to be expected instead of the lower clause relative pronoun genitive *thes*, which is congruent with genitive *thes* of the higher clause (cf. also sentence (91), Chap. VII: 23.5). On the other hand, in sentence (174) the relative pronoun is incongruent with its verb: *Gabriel bium ik hētan, the gio for goda standu* 'Gabriel am I called, who stands ever before God.' The 1 p. *standu* of the lower clause is congruent with the *ik* of the higher clause, rather than with the relative pronoun *the* of its own clause, thus [referent x] + [relative pronoun x] + [finite verb x]. Sentence (175) displays an indicative *scal* in the complement clause of an imperative/hortative *lata*, thus [imperative hortative -sent.] + [sent. α subjunctive]: *sō lāta imu thit an innan sorga, huō he scal an themu māreon dage wið thene rīkeon god an reðiu standen* 'So let it be for him a concern within, how he shall stand to give account on that famous day before the powerful God.' Finally, strong and weak adjective distribution (cf. sect. 26 above) is shown as optional in sentences (176) and (177). Thus, contrary to rule, [deixis] + [strong adjective] occurs in the deictic pronoun *thes* plus the strong adjective *mahtiges* in sentence (176): *mōste thar thō an thes mahtiges Kristes barme restien* 'He could then rest there in the lap of the mighty Christ.' Again, contrary to rule, unpreceded weak adjective [minus deixis] + [weak adjective] occurs in *faho* in sentence (161): *ferid ina werodes lūt, fāho folcskepi* 'Few people take it (that path), (a) small group.'

Selected Readings

Old Saxon

    Heliand: Fits I, II, VII, VIII, XXXII, XXXVII, XXXVIII, XXXIX, LII, LIII
    Genesis Fragment
    Minor Documents: Charms, *Psalm V.9.* Explication

Latin

    Prose Preface(s)
    Verse Preface

Old High German

    Charm Against Worms
    Notker: Psalm V.9. Explication
    Tatian: Luke 1.5-25
    Otfrid: 1, 17
    Muspilli

Old English

    Genesis Passages
    Cædmon

Old Saxon

Heliand

Fit I

    Manega uuāron,   the sia iro mōd gespōn,
2.3 that sia bigunnun reckean that girūni,   that thie rīceo Crist
    undar mancunnea   māriða gifrumida
5   mid uuordun endi mid uuercun. That uuolda thō uuīsara filo
    liudo barno loƀon,   lēra Cristes,
    hēlag uuord godas,   endi mid iro handon scrīƀan
    berehtlīco an buok,   huō sia is gibodscip scoldin
    frummian, firiho barn.   Than uuārun thoh sia fiori te thiu
10 under thera menigo,   thia habdon maht godes,
    helpa fan himila,   hēlagna gēst,
    craft fan Criste, —   sia uurðun gicorana te thio,
    that sie than ēuangelium   ēnan scoldun
    an buok scrīƀan   endi sō manag gibod godes,
15 hēlag himilisc uuord: sia ne muosta heliðo than mēr,
    firiho barno frummian,   neuan that sia fiori te thio
    thuru craft godas   gecorana uurðun,
    Matheus endi Marcus, —   sō uuārun thia man hētana —
    Lucas endi Iohannes;   sia uuārun gode lieƀa,
20 uuirðiga ti them giuuirkie.   Habda im uualdand god,
    them heliðon an iro hertan   hēlagna gēst
    fasto bifolhan   endi ferahtan hugi,
    sō manag uuīslīk uuord   endi giuuit mikil,
    that sea scoldin ahebbean   hēlagaro stemnun
25 godspell that guoda,   that ni haƀit ēnigan gigadon huergin,
    thiu uuord an thesaro uueroldi,   that io uualdand mēr,
    drohtin diurie   eftho derƀi thing,

```
       firinuuerc fellie    eftho fīundo nīð,
       strīd uuiðerstande —,   huand hie habda starkan hugi,
30     mildean endi guodan,   thie thes mēster uuas,
       aðalordfrumo      alomahtig.
       That scoldun sea fiori thuo    fingron scrīban,
       settian endi singan    endi seggian forð,
       that sea fan Cristes    crafte them mikilon
35     gisāhun endi gihōrdun,   thes hie selbo gisprac,
       giuuīsda endi giuuarahta,   uundarlīcas filo,
       sō manag mid mannon    mahtig drohtin,
       all so hie it fan them anginne    thuru is ēnes craht,
       uualdand gisprak,    thuo hie ērist thesa uuerold giscuop
40     endi thuo all befieng    mid ēnu uuordo,
       himil endi erða    endi al that sea bihlidan ēgun
       giuuarahtes endi giuuahsanes:    that uuarð thuo all mid
                                                      uuordon godas
       fasto bifangan,    endi gifrumid after thiu,
       huilic than liudscepi    landes scoldi
45     uuīdost giuualdan,    eftho huar thiu uueroldaldar
       endon scoldin.    Ēn uuas iro thuo noh than
       firio barnun biforan,    endi thiu fībi uuārun agangan:
       scolda thuo that sehsta    sāliglīco
       cuman thuru craft godes    endi Cristas giburd,
50     hēlandero bestan,    hēlagas gēstes,
       an thesan middilgard    managon te helpun,
       firio barnon ti frumon    uuið fīundo nīð,
       uuið dernero duualm.    Than habda thuo drohtin god
       Rōmanoliudeon farliuuan    rīkeo mēsta,
55     habda them heriscipie    herta gisterkid,
       that sia habdon bithuungana    thiedo gihuilica,
       habdun fan Rūmuburg    rīki giuunnan
       helmgitrōsteon,    sāton iro heritogon
       an lando gihuem,    habdun liudeo giuuald,
```

Old Saxon

60 allon elitheodon.   Erodes uuas
   an Hierusalem   oƀer that Iudeono folc
   gicoran te kuninge,   sō ina thie kēser tharod,
   fon Rūmuburg   rīki thiodan
   satta undar that gisīði.   Hie ni uuas thoh mid sibbeon
                                                        bilang
65 aƀaron Israheles,   eðilgiburdi,
   cuman fon iro cnuosle,   neuan that hie thuru thes kēsures
                                                        thanc
   fan Rūmuburg   rīki habda,
   that im uuārun sō gihōriga   hildiscalcos,
   aƀaron Israheles   elleanruoƀa:
70 suīðo unuuanda uuini,   than lang hie giuuald ēhta,
   Erodes thes rīkeas   endi rādburdeon held
   Iudeo liudi.   Than uuas thar ēn gigamalod mann,
   that uuas fruod gomo,   habda ferehtan hugi,
   uuas fan them liudeon   Levias cunnes,
75 Iacobas suneas,   guodero thiedo:
   Zacharias uuas hie hētan.   That uuas sō sālig man,
   huand hie simblon gerno   gode theonoda,
   uuarahta after is uuilleon;   deda is uuīf sō self
   — uuas iru gialdrod idis: ni muosta im erƀiuuard
80 an iro iuguðhēdi   giƀiðig uuerðan —
   libdun im farūter laster,   uuaruhtun lof goda,
   uuārun sō gihōriga   heƀancuninge,
   diuridon ūsan drohtin: ni uueldun derƀeas uuiht
   under mancunnie,   mēnes gifrummean,
85 ne saca ne sundea.   Uuas im thoh an sorgun hugi,
   that sie erƀiuuard   ēgan ni mōstun,
   ac uuārun im barno lōs.   Than scolda he gibod godes
   thar an Hierusalem,   sō oft sō gigengi gistōd,
   that ina torhtlīco   tīdi gimanodun,
90 sō scolda he at them uuīha   uualdandes geld

hēlag bihuuerban,   hebancuninges,
godes iungarskepi: gern uuas he suīðo,
that he it thurh ferhtan hugi   frummean mōsti.

Fit II

Thō uuarð thiu tīd cuman, —   that thar gitald habdun
95 uuīsa man mid uuordun, —   that scolda thana uuīh godes
Zacharias bisehan.   Thō uuarð thar gisamnod filu
thar te Hierusalem   Iudeo liudio,
uuerodes te them uuīha,   thar sie uualdand god
suuīðo theolīco   thiggean scoldun,
100 hērron is huldi,   that sie hebancuning
lēðes alēti.   Thea liudi stōdun
umbi that hēlaga hūs,   endi geng im the gihērodo man
an thana uuīh innan.   That uuerod ōðar bēd
umbi thana alah ūtan,   Ebreo liudi,
105 huuan ēr the frōdo man   gifrumid habdi
uualdandes uuilleon.   Sō he thō thana uuīrōc drōg,
ald aftar them alaha,   endi umbi thana altari geng
mid is rōcfatun   rīkiun thionon,
— fremida ferhtlīco   frāon sīnes,
110 godes iungarskepi   gerno suuīðo
mit hluttru hugi,   sō man hērren scal
gerno fulgangan —,   grurios quāmun im,
egison an them alaha: he gisah thar aftar thiu ēnna engil
                                                                godes
an them uuīha innan,   the sprac im mid is uuordun tō,
115 hēt that frōd gumo   forht ni uuāri,
hēt that he im ni andrēdi: 'thīna dādi sind', quað he,
'uualdanda uuerðe   endi thīn uuord sō self,
thīn thionost is im an thanke,   that thu sulica githāht habes
an is ēnes craft.   Ic is engil bium,

120 Gabriel bium ic hētan,   the gio for goda standu,
    anduuard for them alouualdon,   ne sī that he me an is
                                        ārunði huarod
    sendean uuillea.   Nu hiet he me an thesan sīð faran,
    hiet that ic thi thoh gicūdði,   that thi kind giboran,
    fon thīnera alderu idis   ōdan scoldi
125 uuerðan an thesero uueroldi,   uuordun spāhi.
    That ni scal an is lība gio   līðes anbītan,
    uuīnes an is uueroldi: sō habed im uurdgiscapu,
    metod gimarcod   endi maht godes.
    Hēt that ic thi thoh sagdi,   that it scoldi gisīð uuesan
130 hebancuninges,   hēt that git it heldin uuel,
    tuhin thurh treuua,   quað that he im tīras sō filu
    an godes rīkea   forgeban uueldi.
    He quað that the gōdo gumo   Iohannes te namon
    hebbean scoldi,   gibōd that git it hētin sō,
135 that kind, than it quāmi,   quað that it Kristes gisīð
    an thesaro uuīdun uuerold   uuerðan scoldi,
    is selbes sunies,   endi quað that sie sliumo herod
    an is bodskepi   bēðe quāmin'.
    Zacharias thō gimahalda   endi uuið selban sprac
140 drohtines engil,   endi im thero dādeo bigan,
    uundron thero uuordo: 'huuō mag that giuuerðan sō', quað
                                                            he,
    'aftar an aldre?   it is unc al te lat
    sō te giuuinnanne,   sō thu mid thīnun uuordun gisprikis.
    Huuanda uuit habdun aldres ēr   efno tuēntig
145 uuintro an uncro uueroldi,   ēr than quāmi thit uuīf te mi;
    than uuārun uuit nu atsamna   antsibunta uuintro
    gibenkeon endi gibeddeon,   siðor ic sie mi te brūdi gecōs.
    Sō uuit thes an uncro iuguði   gigirnan ni mohtun,
    that uuit erbiuuard   ēgan mōstin,
150 fōdean an uncun flettea, — nu uuit sus gifrōdod sint,
    habad unc eldi binoman   elleandādi,

that uuit sint an uncro siuni gislekit   endi an uncan sīdun lat;
flēsk is unc antfallan,   fel unscōni,
is unca lud geliðen,   līk gidrusnod,
155 sind unca andbāri   ōðarlīcaron,
mōd endi megincraft, —   sō uuit giu sō managan dag
uuārun an thesero uueroldi,   sō mi thes uundar thunkit,
huuō it sō giuuerðan mugi,   sō thu mid thīnun uuordun gisprikis'.

Fit VII

Thoh thar than gihuilic hēlag man
Krist antkendi,   thoh ni uuarð it gio te thes kuninges hoƀe
them mannun gimārid,   thea im an iro mōdseƀon
540 holde ni uuārun,   ac uuas im sō bihalden forð
mid uuordun endi mid uuerkun,   antthat thar uueros ōstan,
suīðo glauua gumon   gangan quāmun
threa te thero thiodu,   thegnos snelle,
an langan uueg   oƀar that land tharod:
545 folgodun ēnun berhtun bōkne   endi sōhtun that barn godes
mid hluttru hugi: uueldun im hnīgan tō,
gean im te iungrun: driƀun im godes giscapu.
Thō si Erodesan thar   rīkean fundun
an is seli sittien,   slīðuurdean kuning,
550 mōdagna mid is mannun: — simbla uuas he morðes gern —
thō quaddun sie ina cūsco   an cuninguuīsun,
fagaro an is flettie,   endi he frāgoda sān,
huilic sie ārundi   ūta gibrāhti,
uueros an thana uuracsīð: 'huueðer lēdiad gi uundan gold
555 te geƀu huilicun gumuno?   te huī gi thus an ganga kumad,
gifaran an fōðiu.   Huat, gi nētuuanan ferran sind
erlos fon ōðrun thiodun.   Ic gisiu that gi sind eðiligiburdiun

Old Saxon

cunnies fon cnōsle gōdun: nio hēr ēr sulica cumana ni
                                                                                        uurðun
ēri fon ōðrun thiodun,   sīðor ik mōsta thesas erlo folkes,
560 giuualdan thesas uuīdon rīkeas.   Gi sculun mi te uuārun
                                                                                        seggean
for thesun liudio folke,   bihuuī gi sīn te thesun lande cumana'.
Thō sprācun im eft tegegnes   gumon ōstronea,
uuordspāhe uueros: 'uui thi te uuārun mugun', quāðun sie,
'ūse ārundi   ōðo gitellien,
565 giseggean sōðlīco,   biuhuuī uui quāmun an thesan sīð
                                                                                        herod
fon ōstan thesaro erðu.   Giu uu ārun thar aðalies man,
gōdsprākea gumon,   thea ūs gōdes sō filu,
helpa gihētun   fon hebencuninge
uuārum uuordun.   Than uuas thar ēn uuittig man,
570 frōd endi filuuuīs   — forn uuas that giu —,
ūse aldiro ōstar hinan, —   thar ni uuarð sīðor ēnig man
sprākono sō spāhi; —   mahte rekkien spel godes,
huuand im habde forliuuan   liudio hērro,
that he mahte fon erðu   up gihōrean
575 uualdandes uuord: bithiu uuas is giuuit mikil,
thes thegnes githāhti.   Thō he thanan scolda,
afgeben gardos,   gadulingo gimang,
forlāten liudio drōm,   sōkien lioht ōðar,
thō he im is iungron hēt   gangan nāhor,
580 erbiuuardos,   endi is erlun thō
sagde sōðlīco: — that al sīðor quam,
giuuard an thesaro uueroldi — :   thō sagda hē that hēr
                                                                                        scoldi cuman ēn uuīscuning
māri endi mahtig   an thesan middilgard
thes bezton giburdies;   quað that it scoldi uuesan barn
                                                                                        godes,
585 quað that he thesero uueroldes   uualdan scoldi

gio te ēuuandaga,   erðun endi himiles.
He quað that an them selbon daga,   the ina sāligna
an thesan middilgard   mōdar gidrōgi,
sō quað he that ostana   ēn scoldi skīnan
590 himiltungal huīt,   sulic sō uui hēr ne habdin ēr
undartuisc erða endi himil   ōðar huerigin,
ne sulic barn ne sulic bōcan.   Hēt that thar te bedu fōrin
threa man fon thero thiudu,   hēt sie thenkean uuel,
huan ēr sie gisāuuin ōstana   up sīðogean,
595 that godes bōcan gangan,   hēt sie garuuuian sān,
hēt that uui im folgodin,   sō it furi uurði,
uuestar obar thesa uueroldi.   Nu ist it al giuuārod sō,
cuman thurh craft godes: the cuning is gifōdit,
giboran bald endi strang: uui gisāhun is bōcan skīnan
600 hēdro fon himiles tunglun,   sō ic uuēt, that it hēlag drohtin,
marcoda mahtig selbo.   Uui gisāhun morgno gihuilikes
blīcan thana berhton sterron,   endi uui gengun aftar them
                                                                            bōcna herod
uuegas endi uualdas huuīlon.   That uuāri ūs allaro uuilleono
                                                                                    mēsta,
that uui ina selbon gisehan mōstin,   uuissin, huar uui ina
                                                                                sōkean scoldin,
605 thana cuning an thesumu kēsurdōma.   Saga ūs, undar
                                                    huilicumu he sī thesaro cunneo afōdit.'
Thō uuarð Erodesa   innan briostun
harm wið herta,   bigan im is hugi uuallan,
sebo mid sorgun: gihōrde seggean thō,
that he thar obarhobdon   ēgan scoldi,
610 craftagoron cuning   cunnies gōdes,
sāligoron undar them gisīðea.   Thō he samnon hēt,
sō huuat sō an Hierusalem   gōdaro manno
allaro spāhoston   sprācono uuārun
endi an iro brioston   bōkcraftes mēst

Old Saxon

615 uuissun te uuārun,   endi he sie mid uuordun fragn,
suīðo niudlīco   nīðhugdig man,
cuning thero liudio,   huar Krist giboran
an uueroldrīkea   uuerðan scoldi,
frīðugumono bezt.   Thō sprak im eft that folc angegin,
620 that uuerod uuārlīco,   quāðun that sie uuissin garo,
that he scoldi an Bethleem giboran uuerðan: 'sō is an ūsan
bōkun giscrīban,
uuīslīco giuuritan,   sō it uuārsagon,
suuīðo glauua gumon   bi godes crafta
filuuuīse man   furn gisprācun,
625 that scoldi fon Bethleem   burgo hirdi,
liof landes uuard   an thit lioht cuman,
rīki rādgebo,   the rihtien scal
ludeono gumskepi   endi is geba uuesan
mildi obar middilgard   managun thiodun.'

Fit VIII

630 Thō gifragn ic that sān aftar thiu   slīðmōd cuning
thero unārsagono uuord   them uurekkiun sagda,
thea thar an elilendi   erlos uuārun
ferran gifarana,   endi he frāgoda aftar thiu,
huan sie an ōstaruuegun   ērist gisāhin
635 thana cuningsterron cuman,   cumbal liuhtien
hēdro fon himile.   Sie ni uueldun is im thō helen eouuiht,
ac sagdun it im sōðlīco.   Thō hēt he sie an thana sīð faran,
hēt that sie ira ārundi   al undarfundin
umbi thes kindes cumi,   endi the cuning selbo gibōd
640 suīðo hardlico,   hērro ludeono,
them uuīsun mannun,   ēr than sie fōrin uuestan forð,
that sie im eft gicūðdin,   huar he thana cuning scoldi

sōkean at is selðon;   quað that he thar uueldi mið is
                                          gisīðun tō,
bedon te them barne.   Than hogda he im te banon uuerðan
645 uuāpnes eggiun.   Than eft uualdand god
thāhte uuid them thinga: he mahta athengean mēr,
gilēstean an thesum liohte: that is noh lango skīn,
gicūðid craft godes.   Thō gengun eft thiu cumbl forð
uuānum undar uuolcnun.   Thō uuārun thea uuīson man
650 fūsa te faranne: giuuitun im forð thanan
balda an bodskepi: uueldun that barn godes
selbon sōkean.   Sie ni habdun thanan gisīðeas mēr,
būtan that sie thrie uuārun: uuissun im thingo giskēd,
uuārun im glauue gumon,   the thea geba lēddun,
655 Than sāhun sie sō uuīslīco   undar thana uuolcnes skion,
up te them hōhon himile,   huō fōrun thea huuīton sterron
— antkendun sie that cumbal godes —,   thiu uuārun thurh
                                          Krista herod
giuuarht te thesero uueroldi.   Thea uueros aftar gengun,
folgodun ferahtlīco   — sie frumide the mahte —
660 antthat sie gisāhun,   sīðuuōrige man,
berht bōcan godes,   blēc an himile
stillo gestanden.   The sterro liohto skēn
huuīt obar them hūse,   thar that hēlage barn
uuonode an uuilleon   endi ina that uuīf biheld,
665 thiu thiorne githiodo.   Thō uuarð thero thegno hugi
blīði an iro briostun: bi them bōcna forstōdun,
that sie that friðubarn godes   funden habdun,
hēlagna hebencuning.   Thō sie an that hūs innan
mid iro gebun gengun,   gumon ōstronea,
670 sīðuuōrige man: sān antkendun
thea uueros uualdand Krist.   Thea uurekkion fellun
te them kinde an kneobeda   endi ina an cuninguuīsa
gōdan grōttun   endi im thea geba drōgun,
gold endi uuīhrōg   bi godes tēcnun

Old Saxon

675   endi myrra thar mid.   Thea man stōdun garouua,
        holde for iro hērron,   thea it mid iro handun sān
        fagaro antfengun.   Thō giuuitun im thea ferahton man,
        seggi te selðon   sīðuuōrige,
        gumon an gastseli.   Thar im godes engil
680   slāpandiun an naht   suueban gitōgde,
        gidrog im an drōme,   al so it drohtin self,
        uualdand uuelde,   that im thūhte that man im mid uuordun
                                                             gibudi,
        that sie im thanan ōðran uueg,   erlos fōrin,
        liðodin sie te lande   endi thana lēðan man,
685   Erodesan   eft ni sōhtin,
        mōdagna cuning.   Thō uuarð morgan cuman
        uuānum te thesero uueroldi. Thō bigunnun thea uuīson man
        seggean iro suebanos;   selbon antkendun
        uualdandes uuord,   huuand sie giuuit mikil
690   bārun an iro briostun: bādun alouualdon,
        hēron hebencuning,   that sie mōstin is huldi forð,
        giuuirkean is uuilleon,   quāðun that sea ti im habdin
                                                            giuuendit hugi,
        iro mōd morgan gihuuem.   Thō fōrun eft thie man thanan,
        erlos ōstronie,   al sō im the engil godes
695   uuordun giuuīsde: nāmun im uueg ōðran,
        fulgengun godes lērun: ni uueldun themu ludeo cuninge
        umbi thes barnes giburd   bodon ōstronie,
        sīðuuōrige man   seggian giouuiht,
        ac uuendun im eft an iro uuillion.

Fit XXXII

        Sō gifragn ik that thō selbo   sunu drohtines,
        allaro barno bezt   biliðeo sagda,
        huilic thero uuāri   an uueroldrīkea

undar heliðcunnie   himilrīkie gelīch;
2625 quað that of luttiles huat   liohtora urði,
sō hōho afhuobi,   'sō duot himilrīki:
that is simla mēra,   than is man ēnig
uuāme an thesaro uueroldi.   Ōk is imu that uuerk gelīch,
that man an sēo innan   segina uuirpit,
2630 fisknet an flōd   endi fāhit bēðiu,
ubile endi gōde,   tiuhid up te staðe,
liðod sie te lande,   lisit aftar thiu
thea gōdun an greote   endi lātid thea ōðra eft an grund
                                         faran,
an uuīdan uuāg.   Sō duod uualdand god
2635 an themu māreon dage   menniscono barn:
brengid irminthiod,   alle tesamne,
lisit imu than thea hluttron   an hebenrīki,
lātid thea fargriponon   an grund faren
hellie fiures.   Ni uuēt heliðo man
2640 thes uuīties uuiðarlāga,   thes thar uueros thiggeat,
an themu inferne   irminthioda.
Than hald ni mag thera mēdan man   gimacon fīðen,
ni thes uuelon ni thes uuilleon,   thes thar uualdand skerid,
gildid god selbo   gumono sō huilicumu,
2645 sō ina hēr gihaldid,   that he an hebenrīki,
an that langsame lioht   līðan mōti.'
Sō lērda he thō mid listiun.   Than fōrun thar thea liudi tō
obar al Galilǣo land   that godes barn sehan:
dādun it bi themu uundre,   huanen imu mahti sulic uuord
                                         cumen,
2650 sō spāhlīco gisprokan,   that he spel godes
gio sō sōðlīco   eggean consti,
sō craftiglīco giqueðen: 'he is theses kunnies hinen',
                                         quāðun sie,
'the man thurh māgskepi: hēr is is mōder mid ūs,
uuīf undar thesumu uuerode.   Huat, uui the hēr uuitun alle,

Old Saxon

2655 sō kūð is ūs is kuniburd   endi is knōsles gehuat;
auuōhs al undar thesumu uuerode: huanen scolde imu sulic
                                                                           geuuit cuman,
mēron mahti,   than hēr ōðra man ēgin?'
Sō farmunste ina that manno folc   endi sprākun im
                                                                           gimēdlic uuord,
farhogdun ina sō hēlagna,   hōrien ni uueldun
2660 is gibodskepies.   Ni he thar ōk biliðeo filu
thurh iro ungilōbon   ōgean ni uuelde,
torhtero tēcno,   huand he uuisse iro tuīflean hugi,
iro uurēðan uuillean,   that ni uuārun uueros ōðra
sō grimme under ludeon,   sō uuārun umbi Galilæo land,
2665 sō hardo gehugide: sō thar uuas the hēlago Krist,
giboren that barn godes,   si ni uueldun is gibodskepi thoh
antfāhan ferhtlīco,   ac bigan that folc undar im,
rincos rādan,   huō sie thene rīkeon Krist
uuēgdin te uundron.   Hētun thō iro uuerod cumen,
2670 gesīði tesamne: sundea uueldun
an thene godes sunu   gerno gitellien
uurēðes uuilleon;   ni uuas im is uuordo niud,
spāharo spello,   ac sie bigunnun sprekan undar im,
huō sie sō craftagne   fan ēnumu clibe uurpin,
2675 oƀar ēnna berges uual: uueldun that barn godes
līƀu bilōsien.   Thō he imu them liudiun samad
frōlīco fōr: ni uuas imu foraht hugi,
— uuisse that imu ni mahtun   mennsicono barn,
bi theru godcundi   ludeo liudi
2680 ēr is tīdiun uuiht   teonon gifrummien,
lēðaro gilēsto —,   ac he imu mid them liudiun samad
stēg uppen thene stēnholm,   antthat sie te theru stedi
                                                                           quāmun,
thar sie ine fan themu uualle niðer   uuerpen hugdun,
fellien te foldu,   that he uurði is ferhes lōs,
2685 is aldres at endie.   Thō uuarð thero erlo hugi,

```
           an themu berge uppen    bittra githāhti
           luðeono tegangen,   that iro ēnig ni habde sō grimmon
                                                              seƀon
           ni sō uurēðen uuilleon,   that sie mahtin thene uualdandes
                                                              sunu,
           Krist antkennien;   he ni uuas iro cūð ēnigumu,
     2690  that sie ina thō undaruuissin.   Sō mahte he undar iro
                                                              uuerode standen
           endi an iro gimange   middiumu gangen,
           faren undar iro folke.   He dede imu thene friðu selƀo,
           mundburd uuið theru menegi   endi giuuēt imu thurh middi
                                                              thanan
           thes fīundo folkes,   fōr imu thō, thar he uuelde,
     2695  an ēne uuōstunnie   uualdandes sunu,
           cuningo craftigost:   habde thero custes giuuald,
           huar imu an themu lande   leoƀost uuāri
           te uuesanne an thesaru uueroldi.
```

Fit XXXVII

```
           'thu bist the uuāro   uualdandes sunu,
           libbiendes godes,   the thit lioht giscōp,
           Crist cuning ēuuig:   sō uuiliad uui queðen alle,
     3060  iungaron thīne,   that thu sīs god selƀo,
           hēleandero bezt.'   Thō sprac imu eft is hērro angegin:
           'sālig bist thu Sīmon', quað he, 'sunu Ionases;   ni mahtes
                                                              thu that selƀo gehuggean,
           gimarcon an thīnun mōdgithāhtiun,   ne it ni mahte thi
                                                              mannes tunge
           uuordun geuuīsien,   ac dede it thi uualdand selƀo,
     3065  fader allaro firiho barno,   that thu sō forð gisprāki,
           sō diapo bi drohtin thīnen.   Diurlīco scalt thu thes ōn
                                                              antfāhen,
```

hluttro habas thu an thīnan hērron gilōbon, hugiskefti sind
    thīne stēne gelīca,
sō fast bist thu sō felis the hardo; hēten sculun thi firiho
    barn
sancte Pēter: obar themu stēne scal man mīnen seli
    uuirkean,
3070 hēlag hūs godes; thar scal is hīuuiski tō
sālig samnon: ni mugun uuið them thīnun suīðeun crafte
anthebbien hellie portun. Ik fargibu thi himilrīceas slutilas,
that thu mōst aftar mi allun giuualdon
kristinum folke; kumad alle te thi
3075 gumono gēstos; thu habe grōte giuuald,
huene thu hēr an erðu eldibarno
gebinden uuillies: themu is bēðiu giduan,
himilrīki biloken, endi hellie sind imu opana,
brinnandi fiur; sō huene sō thu eft antbinden uuili,
3080 antheftien is hendi, themu is himilrīki,
antloken liohto mēst endi līf ēuuig,
grōni godes uuang. Mid sulicaru ik thi gebu uuilliu
lōnon thīnen gilōbon. Ni uuilliu ik, that gi thesun liudiun noh,
mārien thesaru menigi, that ik bium mahtig Crist,
3085 godes ēgan barn. Mi sculun ludeon noh,
unsculdigna erlos binden,
uuēgean mi te uuundrun — dōt mi uuīties filo —
innan Hierusalem gēres ordun,
āhtien mīnes aldres eggiun scarpun,
3090 bilōsien mi lību. Ik an thesumu liohte scal
thurh ūses drohtines craft fan dōde astanden
an thriddiumu dage'. Thō uuarð thegno bezt
suīðo an sorgun, Sīmon Petrus,
uuarð imu hugi hriuuig, endi te is hērron sprak
3095 rink an rūnun: 'ni scal that rīki god', quað he,
'uualdand uuillien, that thu eo sulic uuīti mikil
githolos undar thesaru thiod: nis thes tharf nigiean,

```
                hēlag drohtin.'    Thō sprak imu eft is hērro angegin,
                māri mahtig Crist    — uuas imu an is mōde hold —:
     3100  'huat, thu nu uuiðeruuard bist', quað he,    'uuilleon mīnes,
                thegno bezto!    Huat, thu thesaro thiodo canst
                menniscan sidu:    thu ni uuēst the maht godes,
                the ik gifrummien scal.    Ik mag thi filu seggean
                uuārun uuordun,    that hēr undar thesumu uuerode standad
     3105  gesīðos mine,    thea ni mōtun suelten ēr,
                huerƀen an hinenfard    ēr sie himiles lioht,
                godes rīki sehat.'    Cōs imu iungarono thō
                sān aftar thiu    Sīmon Petrus,
                Iacob endi Iohannes,    thea gumon tuēne,
     3110  bēðea thea gibrōðer,    endi imu thō uppen thene berg giuuēt
                sunder mid them gesīðun,    sālig barn godes,
                mid them thegnun thrim,    thiodo drohtin,
                uualdand thesaro uueroldes:    uuelde im thar uundres filu,
                tēcno tōgean,    that sie gitrūodin thiu bet,
     3115  that he selƀo uuas    sunu drohtines,
                hēlag heƀencuning.    Thō sie an hōhan uuall
                stigun stēn endi berg,    antat sie te theru stedi quāmun,
                uueros uuiðer uuolcan,    thar uualdand Krist,
                cuningo craftigost    gicoren habde,
     3120  that he is godkundi    iungarun sīnun
                thurh is ēnes craft    ōgean uuelde,
                berhtlīc biliði.
```

Fit XXXVIII

```
                                         Thō imu thar te bedu gihnēg,
                thō uuarð imu thar uppe    oðarlīcora
                uuliti endi giuuādi:    uurðun imu is uuangun liohte,
     3125  blīcandi sō thiu berhte sunne:    sō skēn that barn godes,
                liuhte is līchamo:    liomon stōdun
```

uuānamo fan themu uualdandes barne;   uuarð is geuuādi
                                                          sō huīt
sō snēu te sehanne.   Thō uuarð thar seldlīc thing
giōgid aftar thiu: Elias endi Moyses
3130 quāmun thar te Criste   uuið sō craftagne
uuordun uuehslean.   Thar uuarð sō uunsam sprāka,
sō gōd uuord undar gumun,   thar the godes sunu
uuið thea mārean man   mahlien uuelde,
sō blīði uuarð uppan themu berge: skēn that berhte lioht,
3135 uuas thar gard gōdlic   endi grōni uuang,
paradise gelīc.   Petrus thō gimahalde,
helið hardmōdig   endi te is hērron sprac,
grōtte thene godes sunu: 'gōd is it hēr te uuesanne,
ef thu it gikiosan uuili,   Crist alouualdo,
3140 that man thi hēr an thesaru hōhe   ēn hūs geuuirkea,
mārlīco gemaco   endi Moysese ōðer
endi Eliase thriddea: thit is ōdas hēm,
uuelono uunsamost.'   Reht sō he thō that uuord gesprak,
sō tilēt thiu luft an tuē: lioht uuolcan skēn,
3145 glītandi glīmo,   endi thea gōdun man
uulitscōni beuuarp.   Thō fan themu uuolcne quam
hēlag stemne godes   endi them helidun thar
selbo sagde,   that that is sunu uuāri,
libbiendero liobost: 'an themu mi līcod uuel
3150 an mīnun hugiskeftiun.   Themu gi hōrien sculun,
fulgangad imu gerno.'   Thō ni mahtun the iungaron Cristes
thes uuolcnes uuliti   endi uuord godes,
thea is mikilon maht   thea man antstanden,
ac sie bifellun thō forðuuardes: ferhes ni uuāndun,
3155 lengiron lībes.   Thō geng im tō the landes uuard,
behrēn sie mid is handun   hēleandero bezt,
hēt that sie im ni andrēdin: 'ni scal iu hēr derien eouuiht,
thes gi hēr seldlīkes   giseen habbiad,
mēriaro thingo.'   Thō eft them mannun uuarð

3160 hugi at iro herton   endi gihēlid mōd,
     gibade an iro breostun: gisāhun that barn godes
     ēnna standen,   uuas that ōðer thō,
     behliden himiles lioht.   Thō giuuēt imu the hēlago Crist
     fan themu berge niðer;   gibōd aftar thiu
3165 iungarun sīnun,   that sie oƀar ludeono folc
     ni sagdin thea gisioni: 'er than ik selƀo hēr
     suīðo diurlīco   fan dōðe astande,
     arīse fan theru restu: sīðor mugun gi it rekkien forð,
     mārien oƀar middilgard   managun thiodun
3170 uuīdo aftar thesaru uueroldi.'

Fit XXXIX

                     Thō giuuēt imu uualdand Crist
     eft an Galileo land,   sōhte is gadulingos,
     mahtig is māgo hēm,   sagde thar manages huat
     berhtero biliðeo,   endi that barn godes
     them is sāligun gesīðun   sorgspell ni forhal,
3175 ac he im openlīco   allun sagde,
     them is gōdun iungarun,   huō ine scolde that ludeono folc
     uuēgean te uundrun.   Thes uurðun thar uuīse man
     suuīðo an sorgun,   uuarð im sēr hugi,
     hriuuig umbi iro herte: gihōrdun iro hērron thō
3180 uualdandes sunu   uuordun tellien,
     huat he undar theru thiodu   tholoian scolde,
     uuilliendi undar themu uuerode.   Thō giuuēt imu uualdand
                                                              Crist,
     gumo fan Galilea,   sōhte imu ludeono burg,
     quāmun im te Cafarnaum.   Thar fundun sie ēnan kuninges
                                                              thegan
3185 uulankan undar themu uuerode: quāð that he uuāri
                                                       giuueldig bodo

Old Saxon

  aðalkēsures; he grōtte aftar thiu
  Sīmon Petrusen, quād that he uuāri gisendid tharod,
  that he thar gimanodi manno gehuiliken
  thero hōbidscatto, the sie te themu hobe scoldin
3190 tinsi gelden: 'nis thes tueho ēnig
  gumono nigiēnumu, ne sie ina fargelden sān
  mēðmo kusteon, biūten iuuue mēster ēno
  habad it farlāten. Ni scal that līcon uuel
  mīnumu hērron, sō man it imu at is hobe kūðid,
3195 aðalkēsure.' Thō geng aftar thiu
  Sīmon Petrus, uuelde it seggian thō
  hērron sīnumu: he uuas is an is hugi iu than,
  giuuaro uualdand Crist: — imu ni mahte uuord ēnig
  biholen uuerðen, he uuisse hugiskefti
3200 manno gehuuilikes —: hēt thō thene is mārean thegan,
  Sīmon Petrus an thene sēo innen
  angul uuerpen: 'suliken sō thu thar ērist mugis
  fisk gifāhen', quað he, 'sō teoh thu thene fan themu flōde te thi,
  antklemmi imu thea kinni: thar maht thu undar them kaflon nimen
3205 guldine scattos, that thu fargelden maht
  themu manne te gimōdea mīnen endi thīnen
  tinseo sō huilican, sō he ūs tō sōkid.'
  He ni thorfte imu thō aftar thiu ōðaru uuordu
  furður gibioden: geng fiscari gōd,
3210 Sīmon Petrus, uuarp an thene sēo innen
  angul an ūðeon endi up gitōh
  fisk an flōde mid is folmun tuēm,
  teklōf imu thea kinni endi undar them kaflun nam
  guldine scattos: dede al, sō imu the godes sunu
3215 uuordun geuuīsde. Thar uuas thō uualdandes
  megincraft gimārid, huō scal allaro manno gehuilic
  suīðo uuilliendi is uueroldhērron

        sculdi endi scattos,   thea imu giskeride sind,
        gerno gelden: ni scal ine fargūmon eouuiht,
3220 ni farmuni ine an is mōde,   ac uuese imu mildi an is hugi,
        thiono imu thiolīco: an thiu mag he thiodgodes
        uuillean geuuirkean   endi ōk is uueroldhērron
        huldi habbien.

Fit LII

        Thō im anduuordi   alouualdo Krist
4295 gōdlīc fargaf   them gumun selbo:
        'that habað sō bidernid', quað he, 'drohtin the gōdo
        iac sō hardo farholen   himilrīkies fader,
        uualdand thesaro uueroldes,   sō that uuiten ni mag
        ēnig mannisc barn,   huan thiu mārie tīd
4300 giuuirðid an thesaro uueroldi,   ne it ōk uuāran ni kunnun
        godes engilos,   thie for imu geginuuarde
        simlun sindun: sie it ōk giseggian ni mugun
        te uuārun mid iro uuordun,   huan that giuuerðen sculi,
        that he uuillie an thesan middilgard,   mahtig drohtin,
4305 firiho fandon.   Fader uuēt it ēno
        hēlag fan himile: elcur is it biholen allun,
        quikun endi dōdun,   huan is kumi uuerðad.
        Ik mag iu thoh gitellien,   huilic hēr tēcan biforan
        giuuerðad uunderlīc,   ēr than he an these uuerold kume
4310 an themu māreon daga: that uuirðid hēr ēr an themu
                                          mānon skīn
        iac an theru sunnun sō same;   gisuerkad siu bēðiu,
        mid finistre uuerðad bifangan;   fallad sterron,
        huīt hebentungal,   endi hrisid erðe,
        bibod thius brēde uuerold   — uuirðid sulicaro bōkno filu —:
4315 grimmid the grōto sēo,   uuirkid thie gebenes strōm
        egison mid is ūðiun   erðbūandiun.

Old Saxon

     Than thorrot thiu thiod   thurh that gethuing mikil,
     folc thurh thea forhta: than nis friðu huergin,
     ac uuirðid uuīg sō maneg   oƀar these uuerold alla
4320 hetelīc afhaben,   endi heri lēdid
     kunni oƀar ōðar: uuirðid kuningo giuuin,
     meginfard mikil: uuirðid managoro qualm,
     open urlagi   — that is egislīc thing,
     that io sulik morð sculun   man afhebbien —,
4325 uuirðid uuōl sō mikil   oƀar these uuerold alle,
     mansterƀono mēst,   thero the gio an thesaru middilgard
     suulti thurh suhti: liggiad seoka man,
     driosat endi dōiat   endi iro dag endiad,
     fulliad mid iro ferahu;   ferid unmet grōt
4330 hungar hetigrim   oƀar heliðo barn,
     metigēdeono mēst: nis that minniste
     thero uuīteo an thesaru uueroldi,   the hēr giuuerðen sculun
     ēr dōmes dage.   Sō huan sō gi thea dādi gisean
     giuuerðen an thesaru uueroldi,   sō mugun gi than te uuāran farstanden,
4335 that than the lazto dag   liudiun nāhid
     māri te mannun   endi maht godes,
     himilcraftes hrōri   endi thes hēlagon kumi,
     drohtines mid is diuriðun.   Huat, gi thesaro dādeo mugun
     bi thesun bōmun   biliði antkennien:
4340 than sie brustiad endi blōiat   endi bladu tōgeat,
     lōf antlūkad,   than uuitun liudio barn,
     that than is sān after thiu   sumer gināhid
     uuarm endi uunsam   endi uueder scōni.
     Sō uuitin gi ōk bi thesun tēknun,   the ik iu talde hēr,
4345 huan the lazto dag   liudiun nāhid.
     Than seggio ik iu te uuāran,   that ēr thit uuerod ni mōt,
     tefaran thit folcscepi,   ēr than uuerðe gefullid sō,
     mīnu uuord giuuārod.   Noh giuuand kumid
     himiles endi erðun,   endi steid mīn hēlag uuord

4350 fast forðuuardes   endi uuirðid al gefullod sō,
     gilēstid an thesumu liohte,   sō ik for thesun liudiun gespriku.
     Uuacot gi uuarlīco: iu is uuiscumo
     duomdag the māreo   endi iuues drohtines craft,
     thiu mikilo meginstrengi   endi thiu mārie tīd,
4355 giuuand thesaro uueroldes.   Fora thiu gi uuardon sculun,
     that he iu slāpandie   an suefrestu
     fārungo ni bifāhe   an firinuuercun,
     mēnes fulle.   Mūtspelli cumit
     an thiustrea naht,   al sō thiof ferid
4360 darno mid is dādiun,   sō kumid the dag mannun,
     the lazto theses liohtes,   sō it ēr these liudi ni uuitun,
     sō samo sō thiu flōd deda   an furndagun,
     the thar mid lagustrōmun   liudi farteride
     bi Nōeas tīdiun,   biūtan that ina neride god
4365 mid is hīuuiskea,   hēlag drohtin,
     uuið thes flōdes farm: sō uuarð ōk that fiur kuman
     hēt fan himile,   that thea hōhon burgi
     umbi Sodomo land   suart logna bifeng
     grim endi grādag,   that thar nēnig gumono ni ginas
4370 biūtun Loth ēno: ina antlēddun thanen
     drohtines engilos   endi is dohter tuā
     an ēnan berg uppen: that ōðar al brinnandi fiur
     ia land ia liudi   logna farteride:
     sō fārungo uuarð that fiur kumen,   sō uuarð ēr the flōd sō
                                                                 samo:
4375 sō uuirðid the lazto dag.   For thiu scal allaro liudio gehuilic
     thenkean fora themu thinge;   thes is tharf mikil
     manno gehuilicumu: bethiu lātad iu an iuuuan mōd sorga.

Fit LIII

Huand sō huan sō that geuuirðid,   that uualdand Krist,
māri mannes sunu   mid theru maht godes,
4380 kumit mid thiu craftu   kuningo rīkeost
sittean an is selbes maht   endi samod mid imu
alle thea engilos,   the thar uppa sind
hēlaga an himile,   than sculun tharod heliðo barn,
elitheoda kuman   alla tesamne
4385 libbeandero liudio,   sō huat sō io an thesemu liohte uuarð
firiho afōdid.   Thar he themu folke scal,
allumu mankunnie   māri drohtin
adēlien aftar iro dādiun.   Than skēðid he thea farduanan man,
thea faruuarhton uueros   an thea uuinistron hand:
4390 sō duot he ōk thea sāligon   an thea suīðeron half;
grōtid he than thea gōdun   endi im tegegnes sprikid:
'kumad gi', quiðid he, 'the thar gikorene sindun,   endi antfāhad thit craftiga rīki,
that gōde, that thar gigereuuid stendid,   that thar uuarð gumono barnun
giuuarht fan thesaro uueroldes endie: iu habad gehuuīhid selbo
4395 fader allaro firiho barno: gi mōtun thesaro frumono neotan,
geuualdon theses uuīdon rīkeas,   huand gi oft mīnan uuilleon frumidun,
fulgengun mi gerno   endi uuārun mi iuuuaro gebo mildie,
than ik bithuungan uuas   thurstu endi hungru,
frosto bifangan   eftho an feteron lag,

```
4400  biklemmid an karkare:    oft uurðun mi kumana tharod
      helpa fan iuuun handun:    gi uuārun mi an iuuuomu hugi mildie,
      uuīsodun mīn uuerðlico.'    Than sprikid imu eft that uuerod
                                                                 angegin:
      'frō mīn the gōdo', queðat sie,    'huan uuāri thu bifangan sō,
      bethuungan an sulicun tharabun,    sō thu fora thesaru thiod
                                                                    telis,
4405  mahtig mēnis?    Huan gisah thi man ēnig
      bethuungen an sulicon tharabun?    Huat, thu habes allaro
                                                          thiodo giuuald
      iac sō samo thero mēðmo,    thero the io manno barn
      geuunnun an thesaro uueroldi.'    Than sprikid im eft uualdand
                                                                    god:
      'sō huat sō gi dādun', quiðit he,    'an iuuues drohtines namon,
4410  gōdes fargābun    an godes ēra
      them mannun, the hēr minniston sindun    thero nu undar
                                                     thesaru menegi standad,
      endi thurh ōdmōdi    arme uuārun
      uueros, huand sie mīnan    uuilleon fremidun — sō huat sō gi
                                                      im iuuuaro uuelono fargābun,
      gidādun thurh diuriða,    that antfeng iuuua drohtin selbo,
4415  thiu helpe quam te hebencuninge.    Bethiu uuili iu the hēlago
                                                                  drohtin
      lōnon iuuuan gilōbon:    gibid iu līf ēuuig.'
      Uuendid ina than uualdand    an thea uuinistron hand,
      drohtin te them farduanun mannun,    sagad im that sie
                                                     sculun the dād antgelden,
      thea man iro mēngiuuerk:    'nu gi fan mi sculun', quiðit he,
4420  'faran sō forflōcane    an that fiur ēuuig,
      that thar gigareuuid uuarð    godes andsacun,
      fīundo folke    be firinuuerkun,
      huand gi mi ni hulpun,    than mi hunger endi thurst
      uuēgde te uundrun    eftha ik geuuādies lōs
4425  geng iāmermōd,    uuas mi grōtun tharf,
```

Old Saxon

     than ni habde ik thar ēnige helpe,   than ik geheftid uuas,
     an liðokospun bilokan,   eftha mi legar bifeng,
     suāra suhti: than ni uueldun gi mīn siokes thar
     uuīson mid uuihti: ni uuas iu uuerð eouuiht,
4430 that gi mīn gehugdin.   Bethiu gi an hellie sculun
     tholon an thiustre.'   Than sprikid imu eft thiu thiod angegin:
     'uuola uualdand god', queðad sie,   'huī uuilt thu sō uuið thit
                                                             uuerod sprekan,
     mahlien uuið these menegi?   Huan uuas thi io manno tharf,
     gumono gōdes?   Huat, sie it al bi thīnun gebun ēgun,
4435 uuelon an thesaro uueroldi'.   Than sprikid eft uualdand god:
     'than gi thea armostun', quiðid he,   'eldibarno,
     manno thea minnoston   an iuuuomu mōdsēbon
     heliðos farhugdun,   lētun sea iu an iuuuomu hugi lēðe,
     bedēldun sie iuuuaro diurða,   than dādun gi iuuuana drohtin
                                                             sō sama,
4440 giuuernidun imu iuuuaro uuelono: bethiu ni uuili iu uualdand
                                                             god,
     antfāhen fader iuuua,   ac gi an that fiur sculun,
     an thene diopun dōd,   diublun thionon,
     uurēðun uuiðersakun,   huand gi sō uuarhtun biforan.'
     Than aftar them uuordun   skēðit that uuerod an tuē,
4445 thea gōdun endi thea ubilon: farad thea fargriponon man
     an thea hētan hel   hriuuigmōde,
     thea faruuarhton uueros,   uuīti antfāhat,
     ubil endilōs.   Lēdid up thanen
     hēr hebencuning   thea hluttaron theoda
4450 an that langsame lioht: thar is līf ēuuig,
     gigareuuid godes rīki   gōdaro thiado.'

Genesis Fragment

„Uuela, that thu nu, Ēua, habas," quað Adam, „ubilo
                                                      gimarakot
unkaro selbaro sīð. Nu maht thu sehan thia suarton hell
ginon grādaga; nu thu sia grimman maht
hinana gihōrean, nis hebanrīki
5   gelīhc sulīcaro lōgnun: thit uuas alloro lando scōniust,
that uuit hier thuruh unkas hērran thank hebbian muostun,
thar thu them ni hōrdis thie unk thesan haram giried,
that uuit uualdandas uuord farbrākun,
hebankuningas. Nu uuit hriuuig mugun
10 sorogon for them sīða, uuand he hunk selbo gibōd,
that uuit unk sulic uuīti uuardon scoldin,
haramo mēstan. nu thuingit mi giu hungar endi thrust,
bitter balouuerek, thero uuāron uuit ēr bēðero tuom.
Hū sculun uuit nu libbian, efto hū sculun uuit an thesum
                                                          liahta uuesan,
15 nu hier huuīlum uuind kumit uuestan efto ōstan,
sūðan efto norðan? gisuuerek upp dribit
— kumit haglas skion himile bitengi —,
ferid forð an gimang (that is firinum kald):
huīlum thanne fan himile hēto skīnit,
20 blīkit thiu berahto sunna: uuit hier thus bara standat,
unuuerid mid giuuādi: nis unk hier uuiht biuoran
ni te skadoua ni te scūra, unk nis hier scattas uuiht
te meti gimarcot: uuit hebbiat unk giduan mahtigna god,
uualdand uurēðan. Te huī sculun uuit uuerðan nu?
25 Nu mag mi that hreuuan, that ik is io bad hebanrīkean god,
uualdand th . . . .

Minor Documents: Charms, *Psalm V.9*. Explication

Against Sprain

Primum pater noster. Visc flōt aftar themo uuatare, verbrustun sīna vetherun: thō gihēlida ina ūse druhtin. Thē selvo druhtin, thie thena visc gihēlda, thie gihēle that hers theru spurihelti! Amen.

Against Worms

Gang ūt, nesso, mid nigun nessiklīnon, ūt fana themo marge an that bēn, fan themo bēne an that flēsg, ūt fan themo flēsgke an thia hūd, ūt fan thera hūd an thesa strāla! Drohtin, uuerthe sō!

Against Catarrh

Crist uuarth giuund,
thō uuarth hē hēl gi ōk gisund,
that bluod forstuond:
sō duo thū bluod!
Amen ter, pater noster ter.

Against Sprain

Quam Krist endi sce. Stephan ti thero burg ti Saloniun. Thar uuarth sce. Stephanes hros entphangan. Sō sō Krist gibuotta themo sce. Stephanes hrosse that entphangana, sō gibuotiu ic it mid Kristes fullēsti thessemo hrosse. Paternoster. Uuala Krist, thū geuuertho gibuotian thuruch thīna ginātha thessemo hrosse that

antphangana atha that spurihalta, sōse thū themo sce.
Stephanes hrosse gibuottos tī thero burg Saloniun! amen.

Psalm V, 9. Explication

Domine, deduc me in justitia tua; propter inimicos meos dirige in conspectu tuo viam meam. Uuola thū, drohtin, ūt lēdi mik an thīnemo rehte thuru mīna fīanda, endi gereko mīnan uueg an thīnero gesihti! Uuola thū, drohtin, gereko mīn līf tuote thīneru hēderun gesihti, thuru thīn emnista reht tōte thēn ēuuigon mendislon: thuru mīna fīanda endi thia heretikere endi thia hēthinun. That is mīn te duonne, that ik mīna fuoti sette an thīnan uueg, endi that is thīn te duonne, that thū mīnan gang girekos. Quoniam non est in ore eorum veritas; cor eorum vanum est. Thiu uuārhēd nis an themo mūthe thero heretikero: uuan thiu īdalnussi beuualdid iro hertono. Uuan thiu tunga folgod thena selfkuri thes muodes. Uuan sia ne hebbed sia an iro herton. Uuan alla thia besuīkid the fīand, the hē īdeles herton findid.

Latin

Prose Preface(s)

Praefatio in librum antiquum lingua Saxonica conscriptum

Cum plurimas Reipublicæ utilitates Ludouuicus piissimus Augustus summo atque præclaro ingenio prudenter statuere atque ordinare contendat, maxime tamen quod ad sacrosanctam religionem æternamque animarum salubritatem at-
5   tinet, studiosus ac devotus esse comprobatur hoc quotidie solicite tractans, ut populum sibi a Deo subiectum sapienter instruendo ad potiora atque excellentiora semper accendat, et nociva quæque atque superstitiosa comprimendo compescat. In talibus ergo studiis suus iugiter benevolus ver-
10 satur animus, talibus delectamentis pascitur, ut meliora semper augendo multiplicet et deteriora vetando extinguat. Verum sicut in aliis innumerabilibus infirmiorbusque rebus, eius comprobari potest affectus, ita quoque in hoc magno opusculo sua non mediocriter commendatur benevolentia. Nam
15 cum divinorum librorum solummodo literati atque eruditi prius notitiam haberent, eius studio atque imperii tempore, sed Dei omnipotentia atque inchoantia mirabiliter actum est nuper, ut cunctus populus suae ditioni subditus, Theudisca loquens lingua, eiusdem divinæ lectionis nihilominus notionem acceperit.
20 Præcepit namque cuidam viro de gente Saxonum, qui apud suos non ignobilis vates habebatur, ut vetus ac novum Testamentum in Germanicam linguam poetice transferre studeret, quatenus non solum literatis, verum etiam illiteratis, sacra divinorum præceptorum lectio panderetur. Qui iussis
25 Imperialibus libenter obtemperans nimirum eo facilius, quo desuper admonitus est prius, ad tam difficile tanque arduum se statim contulit opus, potius tamen confidens de adiutorio

obtemperantiæ, quam de suæ ingenio parvitatis. Igitur a mundi creatione initium capiens, iuxta historiæ veritatem quæque excellentiora summatim decerpens, interdum quædam ubi commodum duxit, mystico sensu depingens, ad finem totius veteris ac novi Testamenti interpretando more poetico satis faceta eloquentia perduxit. Quod opus tam lucide tamque eleganter iuxta idioma illius linguæ composuit, ut audientibus ac intelligentibus non minimam sui decoris dulcedinem præstet. Iuxta morem vero illius poëmatis omne opus per vitteas distinxit, quas nos lectiones vel sententias possumus appellare.

Ferunt eundem Vatem dum adhuc artis penitus esset ignarus, in somnis esse admonitum, ut Sacræ legis præcepta ad cantilenam propriæ linguæ congrua modulatione coaptaret. Quam admonitionen nemo veram esse ambigit, qui huius carminis notitiam studiumque eius compositoris atque desiderii anhelationem habuerit. Tanta namque copia verborum, tantaque excellentia sensum resplendet, ut cuncta Theudisca poëmata suo vincat decore. Clare quidem pronunciatione, sed clarius intellectu lucet. Sic nimirum omnis divina agit scriptura, ut quanto quis eam ardentius appetat, tanto magis cor inquirentis quadam dulcedinis suavitate demulceat. Ut uero studiosi lectoris intentio facilius quæque ut gesta sunt possit invenire, singulis sententiis, iuxta quod ratio huius operis postularat, capitula annotata sunt.

Verse Preface

Versus de poeta et interprete huius codicis

Fortunam studiumque viri lætosque labores,
carmine privatum delectat promere vitam,
qui dudum impresso terram vertebat aratro,
intentus modico et victum quærebat in agro,
5 contentus casula fuerat; cui culmina testa,
postesque acclives; sonipes sua lumina nunquam
obtrivit, tantum armentis sua cura studebat.
o fœlix nimium proprio qui vivere censu
prævaluit fomitemque ardentem extinguere diræ
10 invidiæ, pacemque animi gestare quietam.
gloria non illum, non alta palatia regum,
divitiæ mundi, non dira cupido movebat.
invidiosus erat nulli nec invidus illi.
securus latam scindebat vomere terram
15 spemque suam in modico totam statuebat agello.
cum sol per quadrum cœpisset spargere mundum
luce sua radios, atris cedentibus umbris,
egerat exiguo paucos menando iuvencos
depellens tecto vasti per pascua saltus.
20 lætus et attonitus larga pascebat in herba,
cumque fatigatus patulo sub tegmine, fessa
convictus somno tradidisset membra quieto,
mox divina polo resonans vox labitur alto,
,, O quid agis Vates, cur cantus tempora perdis?
25 incipe divinas recitare ex ordine leges,
transferre in propriam clarissima dogmata linguam".
nec mora post tanti fuerat miracula dicti.
qui prius agricola, mox et fuit ille poeta:
tunc cantus nimio Vates perfusus amore,
30 metrica post docta dictavit carmina lingua.
cœperat a prima nascentis origine mundi,
quinque relabentis percurrens tempora secli,

venit ad adventum Christi, qui sanguine mundum
faucibus eripuit tetri miseratus Averni.

Old High German

Charm Against Worms

Gang uz, Nesso,   mit niun nessinchilinon,
uz fonna marge in deo adra,   vonna den adrun in daz fleisk,
fonna demu fleiske in daz fel,   fonna demo velle in diz tulli.
                            Ter pater noster.

Notker : Psalm V, 9. Explication

    Domine deduc me in iustitia tua propter inimicos meos. Leite mih trúhten in dinemo rehte umbe mina fíenda die mih ilent daraba cheren. Leite mih in dinemo rechte nals in ménnischon dién ioh reht tunchet úbelis mit ubele lonon. Dirige in conspectu tuo viam meam. Keríhte minen uueg in dínero gesíhte. Daz herza geríhte daz ist in dinero gesíhte nals in ménnischon. Quoniam non est in ore eorum veritas. Uuarheit neist in iro munde. In déro ménnischon munde minero fíendo neist si. Cor eorum vanum est. Iro herza ist uppig. Uuie mag ténne uuar íro múnde sin?

Tatian: Luke 1.5-25

    Uuas in tagun Herodes thes cuninges Judeno sumēr biscof namen Zacharias fon themo uuehsale Abiases inti quena imo fon Aarones tohterun inti ira namo uuas Elisabeth. Siu uuārun rehtiu beidu fora gote, gangenti in allēm bibotun inti in gotes rehtfestīn ūzzan lastar, inti ni uuard in sun, bithiu uuanta Elisabeth uuas unberenti inti beidu framgigiengun in iro tagun. Uuard thō, mit thiu her in biscofheite giordinōt uuas in antreitu sīnes uuehsales fora gote, after giuuonu thes biscofheites, in lōzze framgieng, thaz her uuīhrouh branti ingangenti in gotes tempal, inti al thiu menigī uuas thes folkes ūzze, betōnti in thero zīti thes rouhennes. Araugta sih imo gotes engil, stantenti in zeso thes altares thero uuīhrouhbrunsti. Thanān thō Zacharias uuard gitruobit thaz sehenti, inti forhta anafiel ubar inan. Quad thō zi imo thie engil: 'ni forhti thū thir, Zacharias, uuanta gihōrit ist thīn gibet, inti thīn quena Elysabeth gibirit thir sun, inti nemnis thū sīnan namon Johannem. Inti her ist thir gifeho inti blīdida, inti manage in sīnero giburti mendent. Her ist uuārlīhho mihhil fora truhtīne inti uuīn noh līd ni trinkit inti heilages geistes uuirdit gifullit fon hinān fon reve sīnero muoter, inti manage Israheles barno giuuerbit zi truhtīne gote iro. Inti her ferit fora inan in geiste inti in megine Heliases, thaz her giuuente herzun fatero in kind, inti ungiloubfolle zi uuīstuome rehtero, garuuen truhtīne thuruhthigan folc'.

   Inti quad Zacharias zi themo engile: 'uuanān uueiz ih thaz? ih bim alt, inti mīn quena fram ist gigangan in ira tagun'. Thō antlingōnti thie engil quad imo: 'ih bim Gabriel, thie azstantu fora gote, inti bim gisentit zi thir thisu thir sagēn. Inti nū uuirdist thū suīgēnti inti ni maht sprehhan unzan then tag, in themo thisu uuerdent, bithiu uuanta thū ni giloubtus mīnen uuortun, thiu thār gifultu uuerdent in iro zīti'. Inti uuas thaz folc beitōnti Zachariam, inti vvuntorōtun thaz her lazzēta in templo. Her uzgangenti ni mohte sprehhan zi in, inti forstuontun thaz her gisiht gisah in templo, her thaz bouhnenti in thuruhuuonēta stum. Inti gifulte uurdun thō taga sīnes ambahtes, gieng in sīn hūs; after thēn tagon intfieng Elisabeth sīn quena inti tougilta sih fimf mānōda quedenti: 'uuanta sus teta mir trohtīn in tagon, in thēn her giscouuuōta arfirran mīnan itiuuīz untar mannon'.

Otfrid: I, 17

Nist mán nihein in uuórolti,	thaz sáman al irságeti,
uuio manag vuúntar vuurti	zi theru drúhtines gibúrti.
Bi thíu thaz ih irduálta,	thar fórna ni gizálta,

scál ih iz mit uuíllen   nu súmaz hiar irzéllen. —
5 Tho drúhtin Krist gibóran uuard   (thes méra ih ságen nu ni thárf),
   thaz blidi uuórolt uuurti,   theru sáligun gibúrti,
   Thaz ouh gidán uuurti,   si in éuuon ni firvuúrti
      (iz uuás iru anan hénti,   tho dét es druhtin énti):
   Tho quamun óstana in thaz lánt   thie irkantun súnnun fart,
10   stérrono girústi: thaz uuárun iro lísti.
   Sie éiscotun thes kíndes   sario thés sinthes,
      ioh kúndtun ouh tho mári,   thaz er ther kúning uuari;
   Uuarun frágenti,   uuar er gibóran uuurti,
      ioh bátun io zi nóti,   man in iz zéigoti.
15 Sie zaltun séltsani   ioh zéichan filu uuáhi,
      uuúntar filu hébigaz   (uuanta er ni hórta man thaz,
   Thaz io fon mágadbúrti   man gibóran vuurti)
      inti ouh zéichan sin scónaz   in hímile so scínaz;
   Ságetun, thaz sie gáhun   stérron einan sáhun,
20   ioh dátun filu mári,   thaz er sín uuari:
   'Uuir sáhun sinan stérron,   thoh uuir thera búrgi irron,
      ioh quámun, thaz uuir bétotin,   gináda sino thígitin.
   O'star filu férro   so scéin uns ouh ther stérro;
      ist íaman hiar in lánte,   es íauuiht thoh firstánte?
25 Gistirri záltun uuir io,   ni sáhun uuir nan ér io:
      bithiu bírun uuir nu giéinot,   er niuuan kúning zeinot.
   So scríbun uns in lánte   man in uuórolti alte;
      thaz ír uns ouh gizéllet,   uuio iz íuuo buah singent'.
   So thísu uuort tho gáhun   then kúning ana quámun,
30   híntarquam er hárto   thero sélbero uuorto,
   Ioh mánniliches hóubit   uuárd es thar gidrúabit:
      gihórtun úngerno   thaz uuír nu niazen gérno.
   Thie búachara ouh tho tháre   gisámanota er sare,
      sie uuas er frágenti,   uuar Kríst giboran uurti;
35 Er sprach zen éuuarton   sélben thesen uuórton.
      gab ármer ioh ther rícho   ántuurti gilícho,
   Thia burg nántun se sár,   in féstiz datun álauuar
      mit uuórtun then ér thie áltun   fórsagon záltun.

So er giuuísso thar bifánd, uuar drúhtin Krist gibóran
                    uuard,
40 tháht er sar in fésti mihilo únkusti.
 Zi ímo er ouh tho ládota thie uuísun man theih ságeta,
  mit ín gistuant er thíngon ioh filu hálingon.
 Thia zít éiscota er fon ín, so ther stérro giuuon uuas
                    quéman zi in,
  bat síe iz ouh birúahtin, bi thaz selba kínd irsúahtin.
45 'Gidúet mih', quad er, 'ánauuart bi thes stérren fart,
  so fáret, eiscot tháre bi thaz kínd sáre.
 Sin éiscot iolícho ioh filu giuuárlicho,
  slíumo duet ouh thánne iz mir zi uuízzanne.
 Ih uuíllu faran béton nan (so ríet mir filu mánag man),
50 thaz íh tharzúa githinge ioh imo ouh géba bringe',
 Lóug ther uuénego mán: er uuánkota thar filu frám;
  er uuólta nan irthúesben ioh uns thia frúma irlesgen. —
 Thaz ímbot sie gihórtun ioh iro férti íltun;
  yrscéin in sar tho férro ther séltsano sterro.
55 Sie blídtun sih es gáhun, sár sie nan gisáhun,
  ioh filu fráuualicho sin uuártetun gilicho.
 Léit er sie tho scóno thar uuas thaz kínd frono,
  mit síneru ferti uuas er iz zéigonti.
 Thaz hús sie tho gisáhun, ioh sar thara ín quamun,
60 thar uuas ther sún guater mit síneru muater.
 Fíalun sie tho frámhald (thes guates uuárun sie báld),
  thaz kind sie thar tho bétotun, ioh húldi sino thígitun.
 Indátun si tho tháre thaz iro dréso sare,
  réhtes sie githáhtun, thaz sie imo géba brahtun:
65 Mýrrun inti uuírouh ioh gold scínantaz ouh,
  géba filu mára: sie súahtun sine uuára.
 Ih págen thir thaz in uuára, sie móhtun bringan méra:
  thiz uuás sus gibari, theiz géistlichaz uuári.
 Kúndtun sie uns thánne, so uuir firnémen alle,
70 gilóuba in giríhti in theru uuúntarlichun gífti:
 Thaz er úrmari uns éuuarto uuari,
  ouh kúning in gibúrti, ioh bi unsih dót uuurti. —

Sie uuurtun sláfente   fon éngilon gimánote,
  in dróume sie in zélitun   then uueg sie fáran scoltun;
75 Thaz síe ouh thes ni tháhtin,   themo kúninge sih náhtin,
  noh gikúndtin thanne   thia frúma themo mánne.
Tho fúarun thia ginóza   ándara stráza
  hárto ílente   zi éiginemo lánte.

   Mánot unsih thisu fárt,   thaz uuír es uuesen ánauuart,
     uuir únsih ouh birúachen   inti eigan lánt suachen.
   Thu ni bíst es uuan ih uuís: thaz lánt thaz heizit páradis.
     ih meg iz lóbon harto,   ni girínnit mih thero uuórto
5 Thóh mir megi lídolih   sprechan uuórto gilíh
     ni mag ih thóh mit uuorte   thes lóbes queman zi énte.
   Ni bist es ío giloubo;   sélbo thu iz ni scóuuo,
     ni mahtu iz óuh noh thanne   yrzellen íomanne.
   Thar ist líb ana tód,   líoth ana fínstri,
10   éngilichaz kúnni   ioh éuuingo uuúnni.
   Uuir éigun iz firlázan: thaz mugun uuir ío riazan,
     ioh zen ínheimon   io émmizigen uuéinon.
   Vuir fúarun thanana nóti   thuruh úbarmuati;
     yrspúan unsih so stíllo   ther unser múatuuillo.
15 Ni uuóltun uuir gilós sin   (harto uuégen uuir es scin):
     nu riazen élilente   in frémidemo lante.
   Nu ligit uns úmbitherbi   thaz unser ádalerbi,
     ni níazen sino gúati: so duat uns úbarmuati.
   Thárben uuir nu léuues   líebes filu mánages
20   ioh thúlten híar nu nóti   bíttero ziti.
   Nu birun uuir mórnente   mit séru hiar in lánte,
     in mánagfalten uuúnton   bi únseren sunton;
   A´rabeiti mánego   sint uns híar io gárauuo,
     ni uuollen héim uuison   uuir uuénegon uuéison.
25 Vuolaga élilenti!   hárto bistu hérti,
     thu bist hárto filu suár,   thaz ságen ih thir in álauuar.
   Mit árabeitin uuérbent   thie héiminges thárbent;
     ih haben iz fúntan in mír: ni fand ih líebes uuiht in thír;
   Ni fand in thír ih ander gúat   suntar rózagaz muat,

30   séragaz herza   ioh mánagfalta smérza.
        Ob uns in múat gigange,   thaz unsih héim lange,
          zi thémo lante in gáhe   ouh iámer giháhe:
        Farames so thíe ginoza   ouh ándara straza,
          then uuég ther unsih uuénte   zi éiginemo lánte.
35   Thes selben pádes suazi   suachit réine fuazi;
          si thérer situ in mánne   ther tharána gange:
        Thu scalt haben gúati   ioh mihilo ótmuati,
          in hérzen io zi nóti   uuaro káritati.
        Dua thir zi giuuúrti   scono fúriburti;
40   uuis hórsam io zi gúate,   ni hóri themo muate
        I´nnan thines hérzen kust   ni láz thir thesa uuóroltlust;
          fliuh thia géginuuerti: so quimit thir frúma in henti.
        Húgi, uuio ih thar fóra quad: thiz ist ther ánder pad:
          gang thésan uueg, ih sagen thir éin: er giléitit thih héim.
45   So thú thera héimuuisti   níuzist mit gilústi,
          so bistu góte liober,   ni intratist scádon niamer.

Muspilli

        ... sin tac piqueme,   daz er touuan scal.
        uuanta sar so sih diu sela   in den sind arhevit,
        enti si den lihhamun   likkan lazzit,
        so quimit ein heri   fona himilzungalon,
5   daz andar fona pehhe: dar pagant siu umpi.
        sorgen mac diu sela,   unzi diu suona arget,
        za uuederemo herie   si gihalot uuerde.
        uuanta ipu sia daz Satanazses   kisindi kiuuinnit,
        daz leitit sia sar   dar iru leid uuirdit,
10   in fuir enti in finstri: daz ist rehto virinlih ding.
        upi sia avar kihalont die   die dar fona himile quemant,
        enti si dero engilo   eigan uuirdit,
        die pringent sia sar uf in himilo rihi:
        dar ist lip ano tod,   lioht ano finstri,
15   selida ano sorgun: dar nist neoman siuh.

Old High German

```
        denne der man in pardisu      pu kiuuinnit,
        hus in himile,       dar quimit imo hilfa kinuok
        pidiu ist durft mihhil
        allero manno uuelihemo,       daz in es sin muot kispane,
20      daz er kotes uuillun      kerno tuo
        enti hella fuir      harto uuise,
        pehhes pina:       dar piutit der Satanasz altist
        heizzan lauc.      so mac huckan za diu,
        sorgen drato,       der sih suntigen uueiz.
25      uue demo in vinstri scal       sino virina stuen,
        prinnan in pehhe:      daz ist rehto paluuic dink,
        daz der man haret ze gote      enti imo hilfa ni quimit.
        uuanit sih kinada      diu uuenaga sela:
        ni ist in kihuctin      himiliskin gote,
30      uuanta hiar in uuerolti       after ni uuerkota.
           So denne der mahtigo khuninc       daz mahal kipannit,
        dara scal queman       chunno kilihaz:
        denne ni kitar parno nohhein      den pan furisizzan,
        ni allero manno uuelih      ze demo mahale sculi.
35      dar scal er vora demo rihhe      az rahhu stantan,
        pi daz er in uuerolti eo      kiuuerkot hapeta.
           Daz hortih rahhon       dia uueroltrehtuuison,
        daz sculi der antichristo       mit Eliase pagan.
        der uuarch ist kiuuafanit,      denne uuirdit untar in uuic
                                                            arhapan.
40      khenfun sint so kreftic,      diu kosa ist so mihhil.
        Elias stritit       pi den euuigon lip,
        uuili den rehtkernon      daz rihhi kistarkan:
        pidiu scal imo helfan      der himiles kiuualtit.
        der antichristo      stet pi demo altfiante,
45      stet pi demo Satanase,      der inan varsenkan scal:
        pidiu scal er in deru uuicsteti      uunt pivallan
        enti in demo sinde      sigalos uuerdan.
        doh uuanit des vilo ... gotmanno,
        daz Elias in demo uuige      aruuartit uuerde.
50      so daz Eliases pluot      in erda kitriufit,
```

so inprinnant die perga, poum ni kistentit
enihc in erdu, aha artruknent,
muor varsuuilhit sih, suilizot lougiu der himil,
mano vallit, prinnit mittilagart,
55 sten ni kistentit, verit denne stuatago in lant,
verit mit diu vuiru viriho uuison:
dar ni mac denne mak andremo helfan vora demo
                                                              muspille.
denne daz preita uuasal allaz varprinnit,
enti vuir enti luft iz allaz arfurpit,
60 uuar ist denne diu marha, dar man dar eo mit sinen
                                                              magon piehc?
diu marha ist farprunnan, diu sela stet pidungan,
ni uueiz mit uuiu puaze: so verit si za uuize.
    Pidiu ist demo manne so guot, denner ze demo
                                                              mahale quimit,
daz er rahono uueliha rehto arteile.
65 denne ni darf er sorgen, denne er ze deru suonu quimit.
ni uueiz der uuenago man, uuielihan uuartil er habet,
denner mit den miaton marrit daz rehta,
daz der tuival dar pi kitarnit stentit.
der hapet in ruovu rahono uueliha,
70 daz der man er enti sid upiles kifrumita,
daz er iz allaz kisaget, denne er ze deru suono quimit;
ni scolta sid manno nohhein miatun intfahan.
    So daz himilisca horn kilutit uuirdit,
enti sih der suanari ana den sind arhevit
74 [der dar suannan scal toten enti lepenten],
75 denne hevit sih mit imo herio meista,
daz ist allaz so pald, daz imo nioman kipagan ni mak.
denne verit er ze deru mahalsteti, deru dar kimarchot ist:
dar uuirdit diu suona, die man dar io sageta.
denne varant engila uper dio marha,
80 uuechant deota, uuissant ze dinge.
denne scal manno gilih fona deru moltu arsten.

Old High German

```
         lossan sih ar dero leuuo vazzon:         scal imo avar sin lip
                                                                  piqueman,
         daz er sin reht allaz         kirahhon muozzi,
         enti imo after sinen tatin         arteilit uuerde.
 85      denne der gisizzit,         der dar suonnan scal
         enti arteillan scal         toten enti quekkhen,
         denne stet dar umpi         engilo menigi,
         guotero gomono:         gart ist so mihhil:
         dara quimit ze deru rihtungu so vilo         dia dar ar resti
                                                                  arstent.
 90      so dar manno nohhein         uuiht pimidan ni mak,
         dar scal denne hant sprehhan,         houpit sagen,
         alero lido uuelihc         unzi in den luzigun vinger,
         uuaz er untar desen mannun         mordes kifrumita.
         dar ni ist eo so listic man         der dar iouuiht arliugan megi,
 95      daz er kitarnan megi         tato dehheina,
         niz al fora demo khuninge         kichundit uuerde,
         uzzan er iz mit alamusanu furimegi
         enti mit fastun         dio virina kipuazti.
         denne der paldet         der gipuazzit hapet,
 99      denner ze deru suonu quimit.
100      uuirdit denne furi kitragan         daz frono chruci,
         dar der heligo Christ         ana arhangan uuard.
         denne augit er dio masun,         dio er in deru menniski anfenc,
         dio er duruh desse mancunnes         minna far^doleta.
```

Old English

Genesis Passages

235 'ac niótað inc þæs ōðres ealles.   forlætað þone ǣnne beám,
  wariað inc wið þone wæstm: ne wyrð inc wilna gæd.'
  Hnigon þā mid heáfdum   heofoncyninge
  georne tōgēnes   and sædon ealles þanc,
  lista and þāra lāra: hē lēt heó þæt land būan.
240 Hwærf him þā tō heofenum   hālig drihten,
  stīðferhð cyning.   Stōd his handgeweorc
  somod on sande,   nyston sorga wiht
  tō begrornianne,   būtan þæt heó godes willan
  lengest læsten: heó wæron leóf gode,
245 þenden heó his hālige word   healdan woldon.
    Hæfde se alwalda   engelcynna,
  þurh handmægen   hālig drihten
  tēne getrymede,   þæm hē getruwode wel,
  þæt hie his giongorscipe   fulgangan wolden,
250 wyrcean his willan: forþon hē him gewit forgeaf
  and mid his handum gescēop,   hālig drihten.
  Gesett hæfde hē hie swā gesæliglīce,   ǣnne hæfde hē swā
      swīðne geworhtne,
  swā mihtigne on his mōdgeþōhte: hē lēt hine swā micles
      wealdan,
  hēhstne tō him on heofona rīce.   Hæfde hē hine swā hwītne
      geworhtne;
255 swā wynlic wæs his wœstm on heofonum,   þæt him cōm
      from weroda drihtne:
  gelīc wæs hē þam leóhtum steorrum;   lof sceolde hē
      drihtnes wyrcean,

dȳran sceolde hē his dreámas on heofonum   and sceolde his
                                               drihtne þancian
þæs leánes þe hē him on þām leóhte gescerede;   þonne lēte
                                               hē his hine lange wealdan:
ac hē awende hit him tō wyrsan þinge,   ongan him winn up
                                               ahebban
260 wið þone hēhstan heofnes waldend,   þe siteð on þām
                                               hālgan stōle;
deóre wæs he drihtne ūrum: ne mihte him bedyrned
                                               weorðan,
þæt his engyl ongan   ofermōd wesan,
ahōf hine wið his hērran,   sōhte hetesprǣce,
gylpword ongeán,   nolde gode þeówian,
265 cwæð þæt his līc wǣre   leóht and scēne,
hwīt and hiówbeorht: ne meahte hē æt his hige findan,
þæt hē gode wolde   geongerdōme,
þeódne þeówian;   þūhte him sylfum,
þæt hē mægyn and cræft   māran hæfde,
270 þonne se hālga god   habban mihte,
folcgestælna.   Feala worda gespræc
se engel ofermōdes: þōhte þurh his ānes cræft,
hū hē him strenglīcran   stōl geworhte,
heáhran on heofonum,   cwæð þæt hine his hige speone,
275 þæt hē west and norð   wyrcean ongunne,
trymede getimbro,   cwæð him tweó þūhte,
þæt hē gode wolde   geongra weorðan:
'Hwæt sceal ic winnan?' cwæð hē,   'nis mī wihtæ þearf
hearran tō habbanne: ic mæg mid handum swā fela
280 wundra gewyrcean;   ic hæbbe geweald micel
tō gyrwanne   gōdlecran stōl
heárran on heofne.   Hwȳ sceal ic æfter his hyldo þeówian,
būgan him swilces geongordōmes?   Ic mæg wesan god
                                               swā hē.

Old English

      Bigstandað mē strange geneátas,   þā ne willað me æt
                                                           þām strīðe geswīcan,
285 hæleðas heardmōde: hie habbað mē tō hearran gecorene,
      rōfe rincas: mid swilcum mæg man rǣd geþencean,
      fōn mid swilcum folcgesteallan: frȳnd synd hie mīne georne,
      holde on hyra hygesceaftum.   Ic mæg hyra hearra wesan,
      rǣdan on þis rīce;   swā mē þæt riht ne þinceð,
290 þat ic ōleccan   āwiht þurfe
      gode æfter gōde ǣnegum: ne wille ic leng his geongra
                                                                         wurðan.'
      þā hit se allwalda   eall gehȳrde,
      þæt his engyl ongan   ofermēde micel
      ahebban wið his hearran   and spræc heálīc word
295 dollīce wið drihten sīnne: sceolde hē þā dǣd ongyldan,
      worc þæs gewinnes gedǣlan   and sceolde his wīte habban,
      ealra morðra mǣst: swā dēð monna gehwilc,
      þe wið his waldend   winnan ongynneð
      mid māne wið þone mǣran drihten.   þā wearð se mihtiga
                                                                            gebolgen,
300 hēhsta heofones waldend,   wearp hine of than heán stōle.
      Hete hæfde hē æt his hearran gewunnen,   hyldo hœfde his
                                                                            ferlorene,
      gram wearð him se gōda on his mōde: forþon he sceolde
                                                                         grund gesēcean
      heardes hellewītes,   þæs þe hē wann wið heofnes waldend.
      Acwæð hine þā fram his hyldo   and hine on helle wearp,
305 on þā deópan dala,   þǣr hē tō deófle wearð,
      se feónd mid his gefērum eallum: feóllon þā ufon of
                                                                                 heofnum
      þurh longe þrāge,   swā þreó niht and dagas
      þā englas on helle,   and heó ealle forsceóp
      drihten tō deóflum,   forþon heó his dǣd and word
310 noldon weorðian: forþon hē heó on wyrse leóht

under eorðan neoðan,   ællmihtig god,
sette sigeleáse   on þā sweartan helle
— þær hæbbað heó on ǣfyn   ungemet lange,
ealra feónda gehwilc   fȳr edneówe;
315 þonne cymð on ūhtan   eásterne wind,
forst fyrnum cald —;   symble fȳr oððe gār,
sum heard geswinc   habban sceoldon:
worhte hit him tō wīte —   hyra woruld wæs gehwyrfed
forman sīðe —,   fylde helle
320 mid þām andsacum.   Heóldon englas forð
heofonrīces hēhðe,   þa ǣr hyldo godes,
lāre gelǣston: lāgon þā ōðre,
fȳnd on þām fȳre,   þe ǣr swā feala hæfdon
gewinnes wið heora waldend: wīte þoliað,
hātne heaðowelm   helle tōmiddes,
325 brand and brāde līgas,   swilce eác þā biteran rēcas,
þrosm and þȳstro,   forþon hie þegnscipe
godes forgȳmdon: hie hyra gāl beswāc,
engles oferhygd: noldon alwaldan
word weorðian,   hæfdon wīte micel:
330 wǣron þā befeallene   fȳre tō botme
on þā hātan hell   þurh hygeleáste
and þurh ofermētto,   sōhton ōðer land:
þæt wæs leóhtes leás   aud wæs līges full,
fȳres fǣr micel.   Fȳnd ongeáton,
335 þæt hie hæfdon gewrixled   wīta unrīm
þurh heora miclan mōd   and þurh miht godes
and þurh ofermētto   ealra swīðost.

Thā spræc se ofermōda cyning,   þe ǣr wæs engla
                                              scȳnost,
hwītost on heofne   and his hearran leóf,
340 drihtne dȳre,   oð hie tō dole wurdon,

Old English

```
         þæt him for gālscipe    god sylfa wearð,
         mihtig on mōde yrre:    wearp hine on þæt morðer innan,
         niðer on þæt nióbedd    and sceóp him naman siððan,
         cwæð þœt se hēhsta      hātan sceolde
345      Sātan siððan.  Hēt hine þære sweartan helle,
         grundes gȳman,   nalles wið god winnan.
         Sātan maðelode,    sorgiende spræc,
         se þe helle forð    healdan sceolde,
         giēman þæs grundes —   wæs ǣr godes engel
350      hwīt on heofne,   oð hine his hyge forspeón
         and his ofermetto     ealra swīðost,
         þæt hē ne wolde    wereda drihtnes
         word wurðian —:    weoll him on innan
         hyge ymb his heortan,   hāt wæs him ūtan
355      wrāðlīc wīte.   Hē þā worde cwæð:
         'Is þes œnga stede    ungelīc swīðe
         þām ōðrum hām,     þe wē ǣr cūðon,
         heán on heofonrīce,   þe mē mīn hearra onlāg,
         þeáh wē hine for þām alwaldan    āgan ne mōston,
360      rōmigan ūres rīces.  Næfð hē þeáh riht gedōn,
         þæt hē ūs hæfð befœlled    fȳre tō botme,
         helle þǣre hātan,   heofonrīce benumen:
         hafað hit gemearcod    mid moncynne
         tō gesettanne.   þæt mē is sorga mǣst,
365      þæt Ādam sceal,    þe wæs of eorðan geworht,
         minne stronglīcan    stōl behealdan,
         wesan him on wynne    and wē þis wīte þolien,
         hearm on þisse helle.  Wālā āhte ic mīnra handa geweald
         and mōste āne tīd    ūte weorðan,
370      wesan āne winterstunde!
```

* * * *

```
790  Ādam gemǣlde    and tō Ēvan spræc:
     'Hwæt, þū Ēve hæfst    yfele gemearcod
     uncer sylfra sīð.   Gesyhst þū nū þā sweartan helle
     grǣdige and gīfre?    Nū þū hie grimman meaht
     heonane gehȳran:    nis heofonrīce
795  gelīc þām līge,    ac þis is landa betst,
     þæt wit þurh uncres hearran þanc    habban mōston,
     þǣr þū þām ne hiérde,    þe unc þisne hearm geræd,
     þæt wit waldendes    word forbrǣcon,
     heofoncyninges.    Nū wit hreōwige magon
800  sorgian for þīs sīðe:    forþon hē unc self bebeád,
     þæt wit unc wīte    warian sceolden,
     hearma mǣstne.    Nū slīt mē hunger and þurst
     bitre on breóstum,    þæs wit bēgra ǣr
     wǣron orsorge    on ealle tīd.
805  Hū sculon wit nū libban    oððe on þȳs lande wesan,
     gif hēr wind cymð    westan oððe eástan,
     sūðan oððe norðan,    gesweorc up færeð:
     cymeð hægles scūr    hefone getenge,
     færeð forst on gemang    — se byð fyrnum ceald —:
810  hwīlum of heofnum    hāte scīneð,
     blīcð þeós beorhte sunne,    and wit hēr baru standað
     unwered wœdo:    nys unc wuht beforan
     tō scūrsceade    ne sceattes wiht
     tō mete gemearcod,    ac unc is mihtig god,
815  waldend wrāðmōd.    Tō hwon sculon wit weorðan nū?
     Nū mē mæg hreówan,    þæt ic bæd heofnes god,
     waldend þone gōdan,    þæt hē þē hēr worhte tō mē
     of liðum mīnum,    nū þū mē forlǣred hæfst
     on mīnes herran hete,    swā mē nu hreówan mæg
820  ǣfre tō aldre,    þæt ic þē mīnum eágum geseah.'
```

Cædmon

In ðeosse abbudissan mynstre wæs sum brōðor syndriglīce mid godcundre gife gemǣred ond geweorðad, for þon hē gewunade gerisenlīce lēoð wyrcan, þā ðe tō ǣfestnisse ond tō ārfæstnisse belumpen, swā ðætte, swā hwæt swā hē of godcundum stafum þurh bōceras geleornode, þæt hē æfter medmiclum fæce in scopgereorde mid þā mǣstan swētnisse ond inbryrdnisse geglengde, ond in Engliscgereorde wel geworht forþ brōhte. Ond for his lēoþsongum monigra monna mōd oft tō worulde forhogdnisse ond tō geþēodnisse þæs heofonlīcan līfes onbærnde wǣron. Ond ēac swelce monige ōðre æfter him in Ongelþēode ongunnon ǣfeste lēoð wyrcan, ac nǣnig hwæðre him þæt gelīce dōn meahte: for þon hē nalæs from monnum nē þurh mon gelǣred wæs þæt hē þone lēoðcræft leornode, ac hē wæs godcundlīce gefultumed ond þurh Godes gife þone songcræft onfēng; ond hē for ðon nǣfre nōht lēasunge nē īdles lēoþes wyrcan meahte, ac efne þā ān þā ðe tō ǣfestnisse belumpon, ond his þā ǣfestan tungan gedeofanade singan.

Wæs hē, sē mon, in weoruldhāde geseted oð þā tīde þe hē wæs gelȳfdre ylde, ond nǣfre nǣnig lēoð geleornade. Ond hē for þon oft in gebēorscipe, þonne þǣr wæs blisse intinga gedēmed þæt hēo ealle sceolden þurh endebyrdnesse be hearpan singan, þonne hē geseah þā hearpan him nēalēcan, þonne ārās hē for scome from þǣm symble ond hām ēode tō his hūse.

Þā hē þæt þā sumre tīde dyde, þæt hē forlēt þæt hūs þæs gebēorscipes ond ūt wæs gongende tō nēata scipene, þāra heord him wæs þǣre neahte beboden, þā hē ðā þǣr in gelimplīce tīde his leomu on reste gesette ond onslēpte, þā stōd him sum mon æt þurh swefn ond hine hālette ond grētte ond hine be his noman nemnde: "Cædmon, sing mē hwæthwugu." Þā ondswarede hē, ond cwæð, "Ne con ic nōht singan; ond ic for þon of þeossum

gebēorscipe ūt ēode ond hider gewāt, for þon ic nāht singan ne
cūðe." Eft hē cwæð, sē ðe wið hine sprecende wæs, "Hwæðre þū
mē meaht singan." Þā cwæð hē, "Hwæt sceal ic singan?" Cwæð
hē, "Sing mē frumsceaft." Þā hē ðā þās andsware onfēng, þā
ongon hē sōna singan in herenesse Godes Scyppendes þā fers ond
þā word þe hē næfre gehȳrde, þǣre endebyrdnesse þis is:

"Nū sculon herigean   heofonrīces Weard,
Meotodes meahte   ond his mōdgeþanc,
weorc Wuldorfæder,   swā hē wundra gehwæs,
ēce Drihten,   ōr onstealde.
Hē ǣrest sceōp   eorðan bearnum
heofon tō hrōfe,   hālig Scyppend;
þā middangeard   monncynnes Weard,
ēce Drihten,   æfter tēode,
fīrum foldan,   Frēa ælmihtig."

Þā ārās hē from þǣm slǣpe ond eal þā þe hē slǣpende song
fæste in gemynde hæfde; ond þǣm wordum sōna monig word in
þæt ilce gemet Gode wyrðes songes tōgeþēodde. Þā cōm hē on
morgenne tō þǣm tūngerēfan, sē þe his ealdormon wæs; sægde
him hwylc gife hē onfēng; ond hē hine sōna tō þǣre abbudissan
gelǣdde, ond hire þæt cȳðde ond sægde.

Þā heht hēo gesomnian ealle þā gelǣredestan men ond þā
leorneras, ond him ondweardum hēt secgan þæt swefn, ond þæt
lēoð singan, þæt ealra heora dōme gecoren wǣre, hwæt oððe
hwonan þæt cumen wǣre. Þā wæs him eallum gesegen — swā
swā hit wæs — þæt hit wǣre from Drihtne sylfum heofonlīc gifu
forgifen. Þā rehton hēo him ond sægdon sum hālig spell ond
godcundre lāre word; bebudon him þā, gif hē meahte, þæt hē in
swinsunge lēoþsonges þæt gehwyrfde. Þā hē ðā hæfde þā wīsan
onfongne, þā ēode hē hām tō his hūse ond cwōm eft on morgenne,

ond þȳ betstan lēoðe geglenged, him āsong ond āgeaf þæt him beboden wæs.

Ðā ongan sēo abbudisse clyppan ond lufigean þā Godes gife in þǣm men, ond hēo hine þā monade ond lǣrde þæt hē woruldhād forlēte ond munuchād onfēnge; ond hē þæt wel þafode. Ond hēo hine in þæt mynster onfēng mid his gōdum, ond hine geþēodde tō gesomnunge þāra Godes þēowa, ond heht hine lǣran þæt getæl þæs hālgan stǣres ond spelles. Ond hē eal þā hē in gehȳrnesse geleornian meahte, mid hine gemyndgade, ond swā swā clǣne nēten eodorcende, in þæt swēteste lēoð gehwerfde. Ond his song ond his lēoð wǣron swā wynsumu tō gehȳranne, þætte þā seolfan his lārēowas æt his mūðe wreoton ond leornodon.

Song hē ǣrest be middangeardes gesceape, ond bī fruman moncynnes, ond eal þæt stǣr Genesis, þæt is sēo ǣreste Moyses bōoc; ond eft bī ūtgonge Israhela folces of Ægypta londe, ond bī ingonge þæs gehātlandes; ond bī ōðrum monegum spellum þæs hālgan gewrites canones bōca; ond bi Cristes menniscnesse, ond bi his þrōwunge, ond bi his ūpāstīgnesse in heofonas; ond bi þæs Hālgan Gāstes cyme, ond þāra apostola lāre; ond eft bi þǣm ege þæs tōweardan dōmes, ond bi fyrhtu þæs tintreglīcan wiites, ond bi swētnesse þæs heofonlīcan rīces, hē monig lēoð geworhte; ond swelce ēac ōðer monig be þǣm godcundan fremsumnessum ond dōmum hē geworhte. In eallum þǣm hē geornlīce gēmde þæt hē men ātuge from synna lufan ond māndǣda, ond tō lufan ond tō geornfulnesse āwehte gōdra dǣda; for þon hē wæs, sē mon, swīþe ǣfest ond regollecum þēodscipum ēaðmōdlīce underþēoded; ond wið þǣm þā ðe in ōðre wīsan dōn woldon, hē wæs mid welme micelre ellenwōdnisse onbærned. Ond hē for þon fægre ende his līf betȳnde ond geendade.

Old Saxon Glossary

āband noun, masc. str., evening
abaro noun, masc. wk. (always without article, only pl.), children (refers always to the Jews)
Ā(Ă)dam prop. noun, Adam
adēlian vb., wk. 1, to sort out, judge
aðali noun, neut. str., nobility (collective)
aðalkēsur noun, masc. str., noble emperor
aðalordfrumo noun, masc. wk., noble creator
af prep., from, out of
afgeban vb., str. V, (+acc.), to relinquish, depart
afhebbian vb., str. VI, to raise, begin
afōdian vb., wk. 1, (+acc.), to bear, give birth
aftar adv., after, afterwards
aftar, after prep. (+dat., instr.), after, behind, along, according to
agangan vb., str. VII, to elapse, slip by, pass
ahebbian vb., str. VI, to begin, start, raise up
āhtian vb., wk. 1, to proscribe, ambush
ak conj., but rather, but, however
alah noun, masc. str., temple
alātan vb., str. VII, to release, deliver
ald adj., old, aged
aldar noun, neut. str., life, age
aldiro noun, masc. wk., ancestor, forefather, elder
aldron vb., wk., age
all adj., all
all, al adv., all, completely
allaro adv. (gen. pl. of "all"), very (+a superl.) of all, the very best

alomahtig   adj., almighty
alōsian   vb., wk. 1, to take away, remove
alowaldo   adj., almighty
alowaldo   noun, wk., almighty
altari   noun, masc. str., altar
ambahtman   noun, masc. str., servant
an   prep. (+dat., acc.), in, near, on, upon
anagin, anginni   noun, masc. str., beginning
anbītan, an(t)bītan   vb., str. I, to enjoy, consume, partake
andbāri   noun, neut. str., appearance
andsako   noun, masc. wk., adversary, enemy
andward   adj., present
andwordi   noun, neut. str., answer, reply
angegin   adv., towards, in reply
angegin   prep. (dat., acc.), towards, against
angul   noun, masc. str., hook
antbindan   vb., str. III, to unbind, loose
antdrādan, andrēdan   vb., str. VII, to fear, dread
antfāhan   vb., str. VII, to receive
antfallan   vb., str. VII, to fall away, fall down
antgeldan   vb., str. III, to recompense, atone for, make good
anthebbian   vb., wk. 3, to withstand
antheftian   vb., wk. 1, to unbind, free
antkennian, ankennian   vb., wk. 1, to recognize
antklemmian   vb., wk. 1, to force upon
antlēdian   vb., wk. 1, to lead forth
antlūkan   vb., str. II, to open, unlock, disclose
antsibunta   card. num. (+gen. part.), seventy
antstandan   vb., str. III, to bear, withstand
antthat   conj., until
arīsan   vb., str. I, to arise
arm   adj., poor, needy
ārundi   noun, neut. str., errand
astandan   vb., str. III, to arise
at   adv., at, in, on

Old Saxon

at   prep. (+dat.),   at, in, on
athengian, anthengian   vb., wk. 1,   to do, carry out
atsamne   adv.,   together, united, joined
awahsan   vb., str. VI,   to grow up

bald   adj.,   bold
baluwerk   noun, neut. str.,   evil deed
bank   noun, fem. str.,   bench, seat
bano   noun, masc. wk.,   murderer
bar   adj.,   bare
barn   noun, neut. str.,   child, son, person
bed   noun, neut. str.,   bed
beda   noun, fem. str.,   prayer, request
bedon   vb., wk. 2,   to pray
bēðie, bēðea, bēde   pron.,   both
beran   vb., str. IV,   to bear, carry
berg   noun, masc. str.,   mountain
berht, beraht   adj.,   shining
berhtlīk   adj.,   shining, bright
berhtlīko, berehtlīko   adv.,   brightly, shiningly
bet   comp. adj.,   better
Bethleem   prop. noun,   Bethlehem
betst, bezt, best   adj. (superl. of god),   best
bi, be   prep.,   with, at, by
bibon   vb., wk. 2,   to quake, tremble
biddian   vb., str. V,   to ask, request
bidēlian   vb., wk. 1, to rob, take
bidernian   vb., wk. 1,   to hide, conceal
bifāhan   vb., red. 1,   to surround, encompass, grasp
bifallan   vb., str. VII,   to fall, fall down
bifelhan   vb., str. III,   to commit oneself, to order, bury
biforan   adv.,   before
biginnan   vb., str. III,   to begin
bigraban   vb., str. VI,   to bury

bihaldan	vb., str. VII, to hold, possess, hide
bihauwan	vb., str. VII, to hew off
bihelan	vb., str. IV, to hide, conceal
bihlīdan	vb., str. I, to enclose, cover, hold
bihrīnan	vb., str. I, to calm
bihuuī	pron., because of what, which, wherefore, how
	bi + hwat (instr.)
bihwerban	vb., str. III, (+acc.), to do, carry out
bilang	adj., kin, related
biliði	noun, neut. str., picture, sign, likeness
bilōsian	vb., wk. 1, to rob
bilūkan	vb., str. II, to close, lock
bindan	vb., str. III, to bind
biniman	vb., str. IV, to take away, rob
biodan	vb., str. II, to offer
bisehan	vb., str. V, to see, watch
bist	vb., 2nd sg. pres. of "wesan" (to be), are
bitengi	adj., pressing, binding
bithiu	pron., because of that, therefore
	bi-that (instr.)
bithwingan	vb., str. III, to compel, force, oppress
bittar	adj., bitter, evil, hostile
bittro	adv., bitter, hostile, angry
bium	vb., 1st sg. pres. of "wesan" (to be), am
biūtan, būtan	conj., unless, except, only
biwerpan	vb., str. III, to wrap, surround
blad	noun, neut. str., leaf
blēk	adj., shining, bright; pale
blīði	adj., bright, shining, joyful, happy
blīðsean	vb., wk. 1, to make happy
blīkan	vb., str. I, to shine
blind	adj. blind
blōian	vb., wk. 1, to bloom
bodo	noun, masc. wk., messenger
bodskepi	noun, masc. str., message, commandment

Old Saxon

bōggebo, bāggebo   noun, masc. wk., giver of rings, lord
bōgwini, bāgwini   noun, masc. str., servant who has been given rings
bōk   noun, fem.-neut. str., book, writing tablet
bōkan   noun, neut. str., beacon, sign
bōkkraft   noun, masc. str., knowledge, learnedness
bōm   noun, masc. str., tree
brēd   adj., broad, wide
brengian   vb., wk. 1, to bring
brinnan   vb., str. III, to burn
briost, breost   noun, neut. str. (pl. only), breast, bosom
brōðar; pl. gibrōðar   noun, masc. const., brother
brūd   noun, fem. str., bride, wife, woman
brustian   vb., wk. 1, to break open, burst
būan   vb., wk. 1, to live, remain
burg   noun, fem. str., city, fortress, area

dād   noun, fem. str., deed
dag   noun, masc. str., day
darno   adv., secretly
derbi, derabi   adj., powerful, evil, hostile
derian   vb., wk. 1, to damage, injure
derni   adj., hidden, secret, evil
diop   adj., deep
diopo   adv., deeply
diubal   noun, masc. str., devil
diurian   vb., wk. 1, to praise, glorify
diuriða, diurða   noun, fem. str., glory, honor
diurlīko   adv., dearly, gloriously
dōd   adj., dead
dōð   noun, masc. str., death
dohtar   noun, fem., daughter
dōian   vb., wk. 1, to die

dōm	noun, masc. str.,	judgment
dōmdag	noun, masc. str.,	doomsday
dragan	vb., str. VI,	to bear, carry, bring
drīban	vb., str. I,	to drive, impell
drinkan	vb., str. III,	to drink
driosan	vb., str. II,	to fall, drop
drohtin	noun, masc. str.,	lord
drōm	noun, masc. str.,	revelry, life, dream
drus(i)non	vb., wk. 2,	to become faded, shriveled, withered
d(u)ŏn	vb., athematic,	to do
dwalm	noun, masc. str.,	confusion, error, stupidity

Ebreo	noun, masc. wk.,	Hebrew
eðiligiburd	noun, fem., str.,	noble birth
ef	conj.,	if
efno	adv.,	even, like
eft	adv.,	after, again, back, afterward
eftha, eftho	conj.,	or, either ... or
ēgan	vb., pret.-pres.,	to have, own
ēgan	participial adj.,	own
eggia	noun, fem. str.,	edge, sword
egislīk	adj.,	dreadful, horrible
egiso	noun, masc. wk.,	fright, terror, fear
ēht	noun, fem. str.,	possession
eldi	noun, fem.,	age
eldibarn	noun, neut. str.,	man, mankind
Ē(Ĕ)lias	prop. noun,	Elijah
elilendi	noun, neut. str.,	foreign country, foreign parts
elithioda	noun, fem. str.,	foreign people, heathen
elithiodig	adj.,	foreign, from various peoples
elkor	adv.,	otherwise, else
elliandād	noun, fem. str.,	physical strength, vigor
ellianrōf	adj.,	famous for might

Old Saxon

ellior	adv.,	somewhere else
ēn	adj.,	single, alone, only, a, an
ēn	num.	'one'
ēn	indef. art.	'a, an'
ēndago	noun, masc. wk.,	day of death
endi	conj.,	and
endi	noun, masc. str.,	end, purpose, content, beginning
endilōs	adj.,	endless, eternal
endion	vb., wk. 2,	to end
engil	noun, masc. str.,	angel
ēnig	indef. pron.,	any
eowiht	pron.,	something, anything
ēr	adv.,	earlier, before
ēr	conj.,	before
ēr	noun, masc. str.,	messenger
ēr	prep. (+dat.),	before
ēra	noun, fem. str.,	honor, respect
erbiward	noun, masc. str.,	heir, inheritance protector, son
erða	noun, fem. str.,	earth, world, inhabitants of the earth
erðbūandi	participial noun,	land-dwellers
ērist	adj. (superl. of comp. ēr),	first
ērist	adv. (superl. of comp. ēr),	first, at first
erl	noun, masc. str.,	earl, nobleman
erlskepi	noun, masc. str.,	people, folk
Erodes	prop. noun,	Herod
ēron	vb., wk. 2,	to give, support
eu, iu, giū	pers. pron., 2nd pl., acc.-dat.,	you
euwa, euwe, iuwa, iuwe, giuwa	adj., poss. adj., 2nd pl.,	your
euwar, iuwar, iuwer; iuwaro, iuworo, iuwera	pers. pron., 2nd pl. gen.,	yours
Ēva	prop. noun,	Eve
ēvangēlium	noun, masc. str.,	gospel
ēwandag	noun, masc. str.,	eternity
ēwig	adj.,	eternal

fadar	noun, masc., father
fāðï	noun, neut. str., (on) foot
fagar	adj., beautiful, peaceful
fagaro	adv., beautifully
fāhan	vb., str. VII, to catch, take
fallan	vb., str. VII, to fall
fan, fon	prep. (+dat., instr.), from, of
fandon	vb., wk. 2, to seek, try, waylay, punish
faran	vb., str. VI, to move, go, travel, fare
farbrekan	vb., str. V, to break, overstep
fard	noun, fem., str., journey
fardōn	vb., athematic, to do wrong, sin
farflōkan	vb., str. VII, to curse, damn
fargeban, forgeban	vb., str. V, to forgive; loan; give
fargeldan, forgeldan	vb., str. III, to pay, reward
fargripan	participial adj., damned
fargūmon	vb., wk. 2, to neglect
farhelan	vb., str. IV, to hide, conceal
farhuggian	vb., wk. 1, to despise, scorn
farlātan, forlātan	vb., str. VII, (+acc.), to avoid, leave, relinquish
farlīhan, forlīhan	vb., str. I, to grant, bestow, give
farm	noun, masc. str., rush, storm
farmunan	vb., pret.-pres., to despise, scorn
farstandan	vb., str. III, to protect, defend; to hinder; to understand, recognize
farterian	vb., wk. 1, to destroy
fārungo	adv., suddenly
farūtar	prep. (+acc.), without
farwirkian	vb., wk. 1, to sin, ruin
fast	adj., fast, solid
fasto	adv., firmly
fel	noun, neut. str., skin
felis	noun, masc. str., rock
fellian	vb., wk. 1, to fell, cause to fall

Old Saxon

fer	adv.,	far
ferah, ferh, fera	noun, neut. str.,	life, soul, spirit
fergon	vb., wk. 2,	to ask for, request
ferht	adj.,	wise, understanding, pious
ferhtlīko	adv.,	wisely
ferran, ferrana	adv.,	from afar
feteros	noun, masc. str. (pl.),	fetters
fīf	adj.,	five
filo, filu	subst. neut.,	much
filu, filo	adv.,	much, very
filuwīs	adj.,	very wise, experienced
findan, fīðan	vb., str. III,	to find, meet, encounter
fingar	noun, masc. str.,	finger
finistar	noun, neut. str.,	darkness
firihos	noun, masc., pl. only,	people
firina	noun, fem. str.,	sin, evil
firina	adv.,	evilly, very
firinwerk	noun, neut. str.,	sin
firiwit	noun, neut. str.,	curiosity
firiwitlīko	adv.,	inquisitively; eager to know
fisk	noun, masc. str.,	fish
fiskari	noun, masc. str.,	fisherman
fisknet	noun, neut. str.,	fish net
fīund	noun, masc. str.,	fiend, devil, evil man, enemy
fiur	noun, neut. str.,	fire
fiwar, fiuwar, fior	adj.,	four
fiwar, fiuwar, fior	noun, str.,	four
flēsk	noun, neut. str.,	flesh, body
fletti	noun, neut. str.,	house, hall, chamber
flōd	noun, masc.-fem. str.,	flood, river, water
fōdian	vb., wk.,	to produce, bear, raise, feed
folda	noun, fem. str.-wk.,	earth
folgon	vb., wk. 2,	to follow, follow after
folk, folc	noun, neut. str.,	people, folk
folkskepi	noun, neut. str.,	people, tribe
folkweros	noun, masc. str. (pl.),	men of the folk

folmos   noun, masc. str. (pl.),   the hands
for, far, fur, fora   prep.,   before, because, for
forð   adv.,   forth, out, forward
forðward, forðwerd   adv.,   forward
forðwardes, -werdes, forwardes, -werdes   adv.,   forwards
forgang   noun, masc. str.,   death, passing away
forht, foraht   adj.,   fearful, afraid
forhta   noun, fem. str.,   fear
forn   adv.,   earlier, a long time ago
forndagos, furndagos   noun, masc. str. (pl.),   former days, earlier times only in the idiom 'an forndagun'
frāgon, frāgoian   vb., wk. 2,   to ask
fregnan   vb., str. III,   to ask, question
fremmian   vb., wk. 1,   to accomplish, do, carry out
friðu   noun, masc. str.,   peace, security
friðubarn   noun, neut. str.,   child of peace
friðugumo   noun, masc. wk.,   peace-bringer
friund   noun, masc. str.,   friend, relative
frōd, fruod   adj.,   old, wise
frōdon   vb., wk.,   to age, be wise
frōio, frōho, frāho   noun, masc. wk.,   Lord, Master
frōlīko   adv.,   happily, confidently
frost   noun, masc. str.,   frost, cold
fruma   noun, fem. str.,   good
frummian   vb., wk. 1,   to carry out, do, accomplish
ful   adj.,   full
fulgangan   vb., str. VII,   to follow, obey, do
fullian   vb., wk. 1,   to fill, fulfill
furðor   adv. (comp. of 'forð'),   farther, further
furi   adv.,   before, ahead
fūs   adj.,   ready

Old Saxon

Gabriel   prop. noun,   Gabriel
gaduling   noun, masc. str.,   close relative, landsman, clan member
Galilea (land)   prop. noun,   Galilee
gaman   noun, neut. str.,   joy, gladness; desire
gang   noun, masc. str.,   path, way, course
gangan   vb., str. VII,   to go
gard   noun, masc. str.,   field, earth; (pl.): home, house, this world
garo   adv.,   fully, completely, well
garu   adj.,   ready, armed, decorated
gar(u)wian, ger-, gir-   vb., wk. 1,   to prepare, arm
gast   noun, masc. str.,   guest
gastseli, gestseli   noun, masc. str.,   guest room
ge, gi, gie, gia   conj.,   and, both ... and
geba   noun, fem. str.,   gift, present, favor
geban   noun, masc. str.,   sea
geban   vb., str. V,   to give
geginward, -werd, -wardi   adj.,   present, face-to-face
gehan   vb., str. V,   to declare, confess
gēl   adj.,   happy; haughty, arrogant
geld   noun, neut. str.,   payment, repayment
geldan   vb., str. 3,   to pay, reward
genower   adv.,   there
gēr   noun, masc. str.,   spear
gern   adj.,   yearning
gerno   adv.,   gladly, willingly, joyfully
geron   vb., wk. 2,   to desire; request, demand
gērtal   noun, neut. str.,   year
gēst   noun, masc. str.,   spirit
geth   conj.,   also
gethwing   noun, neut. str.,   distress, affliction, trouble
gī(i), ge   pers. pron., 2nd pl. nom.,   you

gialdrod	adj., aged (past part. of 'aldron')
gibāda	noun, fem. str., comfort, solace, consolation
gibeddeo	noun, masc. wk., bed companion
gibenkeo	noun, masc. wk., table companion
giberan	vb., str. IV, to bear, give birth
gibiðig	adj., given, granted
gibindan	vb., str. III, to bind
gibiodan	vb., str. II, to order, command
gibod	noun, neut. str., commandment
gibodscip	noun, neut. str., bidding, tidings, message, commandment
gibrengian	vb., wk. 1, to bring, lead
gibrōðar	noun, masc. pl., brothers
giburd	noun, fem. str., birth
gidōn	vb., athematic, to do, make
gidragan	vb., str. VI, to bear, carry, bring, give birth
gidrog	noun, neut. str., vision, illusion
gidurran	vb., pret.-pres., to dare, have courage
gifāhan	vb., str. VII, to catch, capture
gifrāgi	adj., famous, well-known
gifregnan	vb., str. III, to hear
gifremmian	vb., wk. 1, to go
gifrummian	vb., wk. 1, to do, accomplish, carry out
gifullian	vb., wk. 1, to fill, satiate, fulfill
gigado	noun, masc. wk., like, equal
gigamalod	participial adj., aged
gigarwian, gigerwian	vb., wk. 1, to prepare, decorate
gigengi	noun, neut. str., turn
gigirnan	vb., wk. 1, to succeed, achieve
gihaldan	vb., str. VII, to own, possess, hold; save, protect, hold
giheftian	vb., wk. 1, to bind, manacle, chain
gihēlian	vb., wk. 1, to heal, cure, save
gihērod	participial adj., holy, noble, distinguished
gihētan	vb., str. VII, to promise

Old Saxon

gihnīgan	vb., str. I,	to nod, bow
gihōrian	vb., wk. 1,	to hear, obey
gihōrig	adj.,	obedient
gihug(i)d	adj.,	minded
gihuggian	vb., wk. 1,	to think, conceive
gihwe, gihwē, gihwat	indef. pron.,	every, all, each
gihwerbian	vb., wk. 1,	to turn over
gihwilik	indef. pron.,	each
gikiosan	vb., str. II,	to choose, select
gikūðian	vb., wk.,	to announce, make known
gilēsti	noun, neut. str.,	deed, accomplishment
gilēstian	vb., wk. 1,	to do, carry out, accomplish
gilīk	adj.,	like, of the same kind
gilōbian	vb., wk.,	to believe
gilōbo	noun, masc. wk.,	faith, belief
gimahlian	vb., wk. 1,	to speak, talk
gimako	noun, masc. wk.,	the like, the equal
gimakon	vb., wk. 2,	to make
gimang	noun, neut. str.,	crowd, company
an gimang - among		
gimanon	vb., wk. 2,	to warn, remind
gimarkon	vb., wk. 2,	to mark, determine, be aware
gimēdlīk	adj.,	silly, foolish
gimōdi	noun, neut. str.,	agreement
ginesan	vb., str. V,	to be saved
giniman	vb., str. IV,	to take
ginon	vb., wk. 2,	to yawn, gape
giqueðan	vb., str. V,	to speak, announce
girādan	vb., str. VII,	to cause
girūni	noun, neut. str.,	secret, mystery
giseggian	vb., wk. 3,	to report, make known
gisehan	vb., str. V,	to see
gisīð	noun, masc. str.,	companion, follower, servant
gisīði	noun, neut. str.,	band, crowd, host; band, company, following

gisiun, gisiuni	noun, neut. str.,	visage; vision
giskapu	noun, neut. str. (pl.),	fate
giskēd, giskēð	noun, neut. str.,	information, instruction(s), direction(s); knowledge
giskeppian	vb., str. VI,	to create
giskerian	vb., wk.,	to grant
gispanan	vb., str. VI,	to drive, compel; persuade
gisprekan	vb., str. IV,	to speak
gistandan	vb., str. III,	to stand, stay, remain
gisterkid	past part. of 'sterkian',	strengthened
giswerk	noun, neut. str.,	darkness, dark clouds
giswerkan	vb., str. III,	to darken, become overcast
git	pers. pron., 2nd dual, nom.,	you (two)
gitellian	vb., wk. 1,	to count, reckon, determine, accuse, say, recount, tell
githāht	noun, fem. str.,	thought, belief, faith
githionon	vb., wk. 2,	to serve
githiudo	adv.,	properly, correctly, rightly
githolon, githolian, githoloian	vb., wk. 2,	to endure, suffer, bear
gitiohan	vb., str. II,	to pull
gitōgian	vb., wk. 1,	to show
gitrūon	vb., wk. 2,	to believe, trust
giu, iu	adv.,	already, before, earlier
giwādi	noun, neut. str.,	clothing, garment
giwahsan	past part. of 'wahsan',	grown
giwald	noun, masc.-fem. str.,	power, rule
giwaldan	vb., str. VII,	to rule, have power
giwand	noun, neut. str.,	end, turning point
giwar	adj.,	aware
giwāron	vb., wk. 2,	to come true
giweldig	adj.,	empowered, trusted
giwendian	vb., wk. 1,	to turn away
giwerðan	vb., str. III,	to become, happen, come to pass
giwernian	vb., wk. 1,	to refuse, deny (someone something)
giwīhian	vb., wk. 1,	to bless, hallow

Old Saxon

giwin	noun, neut. str., battle, fight
giwinnan	vb., str. III, to bring about, cause, gain, win
giwirki	noun, neut. str., work, task
giwirkian	vb., wk. 1, to do, make, bring about, wreak, prepare
giwīsian	vb., wk. 1, to show, proclaim, announce
giwit	noun, neut. str., wisdom, understanding
giwītan	vb., str. I, to go, depart
giwrītan	vb., str. I, to write
gladmōd, gladmōdi	adj., happy, joyful
glau	adj., wise
glīmo	noun, masc. wk., gleam
glītan	vb., str. I, to shine
god	noun, masc. str., God
gōd, guod	adj., good
gōd	noun, neut. str., good; goods, property
godkundi	noun, fem., divinity
gōdlīk	adj., good, glorious
godspell	noun, neut. str., Gospel, good news
gōdsprāki	adj., well-spoken
gold	noun, neut. str., gold
goldfat	noun, neut. str., gold vessel, cup
gōma	noun, fem. str., feast
grādag	adj., greedy
graf	noun, neut., str., grave
grim	adj., grim, evil, hostile
grimman	vb., str. III, to rage
griot	noun, neut. str., sand, grit, shore, earth
grīpan	vb., str. I, to grasp
grōni	adj., green
grōt	adj., great, heavy, large
grōtian	vb., wk. 1, to greet
grund	noun, masc. str., ground, earth
gruri	noun, masc. str., terror, fear
guldin	adj., golden

gumo   noun, masc. wk.,   man, human being
gumskepi   noun, neut. str.,   horde, people, folk

hagal   noun, masc. str.,   hail
halba   noun, fem. str.,   side
hald   adv.,   more
haldan   vb., str. VII,   to hold
half   adj.,   half
halla   noun, fem. str.,   hall, room
hand   noun, fem. str.,   hand
hard   adj.,   bold, brave, strong; hard, sharp, heavy
hardlīko   adv.,   strongly, sternly
hardmōdig   adj.,   courageous, bold
hardo   adv.,   sternly, very
harm   noun, masc.-neut. str.,   harm, pain
hē(ĕ), hie; hī(ì)   pers. pron., masc. sg., nom.,   he
hebankuning   noun, masc. str.,   king of heaven
hebanrīki   adj.,   heavenly
hebanrīki   noun, neut. str.,   kingdom of heaven
hebantungal   noun, neut. str.,   star
hebanwang   noun, masc. str.,   heaven's meadow
hebbian   vb., wk. 3,   to have
hēdro   adv.,   brightly, clearly
hēlag   adj.,   holy
hēlagferah   adj.,   of holy mind
helan   vb., str. IV,   to hide, conceal
hēlian   vb., wk. 1,   to heal, save
hēliand, hēleand, hēland   noun,   Heliand, Savior, Healer
helið   noun, masc. str.,   hero, man, person
heliðkunni   noun, neut. str.,   man, mankind
hellia   noun, fem. str.-wk.,   hell
helmgitrōsteo   noun, masc. wk.,   warrior, armed man
helpa   noun, fem. str.,   help, salvation

Old Saxon

helpan   vb., str. III,   to help
hēm   noun, neut. str.,   home
hēr   adj., high, exalted
hēr, hier, hīr   adv.,   here; hither
heri   noun, masc.-fem. str.,   crowd, people, army
heridōm   noun, masc. str.,   kingdom
heriskepi, heriskipi   noun, neut. str.,   host, crowd, people
heritogo   noun, masc. wk.,   leader
herod   adv.,   here, hence
Herodes   prop. noun, masc. str.,   Herod
hērro   noun, masc. wk.,   master, lord
herta   noun, neut. wk.,   heart
hēt   adj., hot, burning
hētan   vb., str. VII,   to call, name, command
hetigrim   adj.,   hostile, grim, hate-filled
hetilīk   adj.,   hostile
hēto   adv.,   hotly
hettiand, hetteand   noun (pres. part.),   persecutor, enemy
Hierusalem   prop. noun,   Jerusalem
hildiskalk   noun, masc. str.,   warrior
himil   noun, masc. str.,   heaven
himilisc, himilisk   adj.,   heavenly
himilkraft   noun, fem. str.,   heavenly host
himilrīki   noun, neut. str.,   heaven, heavenly kingdom
himiltungal   noun, neut. str.,   star
hinan   adv.,   from here, hence, henceforth
hinana   adv.,   from here
hinfard, hinenfard   noun, fem. str.,   death, departure
hirdi   noun, masc. str.,   shepherd, protector
hiudu   adv.,   today
hīwa   noun, fem. wk.,   wife, spouse
hīwiski   noun, neut. str.,   household, family
hlūd   adj., loud
hlū(ŭ)ttar   adj.,   bright, clear, pure
hluttro   adv.,   sincerely, openly

hnīgan   vb., str. I, to bow, bend, lean
hōbid   noun, neut. str., head
hōbidskat   noun, masc. str., head tax
hof   noun, masc. str., court, enclosed area
hōh   adj., high
hōhi   noun, fem., height
hōho   adv., highly, widely
hold   adj., friendly, gracious, generous, bound
hōrian   vb., wk. 1, to hear
hreuwan   vb., str. II, to rue
hris(s)ian   vb., wk. 1, to shiver, quake, shake
hriuwig   adj., sad, troubled
hriuwigmōd   adj., sad, sorrowful
hrōpan   vb., str. VII, to call
hrōrian   vb., wk. 1, to move
huggian   vb., wk. 1, to think, remember, consider
hugi   noun, masc. str., thought, feeling, heart, opinion, mind
hugiskefti   noun, fem. str. (pl.), spirit, attitude, mind
huldi   noun, fem. str., grace, favor
hungar   noun, masc. str., hunger
hūs   noun, neut. str., house
hwan   adv., when
hwanan   adv., from where, whence
hwand, hwanda   conj., for, because
hwār, hwar   adv., where, when
hwargin   adv., somewhere
hwarod   adv., whither
hwē, hwat   indef. pron., who, what; (+gen.) what kind of, how many; sō hwē sō - whatever
hweðar   conj., if, whether
hweðar   indef. pron., who, which, what
hwerban   vb., str. III, to go, wander, turn
hwergin   adv., anywhere, somewhere
hwīla, hwīl   noun, fem. str., time, a while

Old Saxon

hwilīk, hwelīk   inter. pron., which
hwīt   adj., white, shining
hwō, hu, huō   inter. pron., how

Iā(ă)kob, Iā(ă)kobus   prop. noun, Jacob (patriarch or apostle)
idis   noun, fem. str., woman
ik   pers. pron., 1st sg., nom., I
im   pers. pron., masc.-fem.-neut., pl. dat., them
imu, imo, im   pers. pron., masc. sg. dat., him
imu, imo, im   pers. pron., neut. sg. dat., it
ina, ine   pers. pron., masc. sg. acc., him
infern   noun, neut. str., hell
ink   pers. pron., 2nd dual acc.-dat., you (two)
inka   adj., poss. pron., 2nd dual, your (two)
inker(o)   pers. pron., 2nd dual gen., your (two)
innan   adv., inside, within
io, eo, gio   adv., ever
Iohannes   prop. noun, Jonas (father of the apostle Peter)
irminthiod   noun, fem. str., people, men
irminthioda   noun, fem. str., people, men
ira, ire, iru, iro   pers. pron., fem. sg. gen., her
iro, iru, ira, ire   pers. pron., fem. sg. dat., her
iro, ira, era   pers. pron., masc.-fem.-neut. pl. gen., their
iru, iro, ira   pers. pron., fem. sg. dat., her
is, es   pers. pron., neut. sg. gen., its
is, es   pers. pron., masc. sg. gen., his
Israhel   prop. noun, Israel
ist, is   vb. (cf. 'wesan'), 3rd sg. pres., is
it, et   pers. pron., neut. sg. nom.-acc., it
iu   pers. pron., 2nd pl. acc.-dat., you
Iudeo   prop. noun, masc. wk., Jew
īwa, iuwa, ewa   poss. pron., 2nd pl., your

ja, gia   conj., and, both ... and
jak   conj., and, and also
jāmarmōd   adj., sad, distressed
juguð   noun, fem. str., youth
juguðhēd   noun, fem str., youth
jungaro   noun, masc. wk., servant
jungarskepi   noun, masc. str., service

kaflos   noun, masc. str. pl., jaws
kald   adj., cold
Kapharnaum   prop. noun, Capernaum
karkari   noun, masc. str., prison
kēsur, kēser   noun, masc. str., emperor
kēsurdōm   noun, masc. str., kingdom, empire
kind   noun, neut. str., child, young man
kinni   noun, neut. str., cheek, chin
kiosan   vb., str. II, to choose, select
klif   noun, neut. str., cliff
klūstarbendi   noun, fem. str. (pl.), fetters, chains
kniobeda   noun, fem. str., kneeling prayer
knōsal   noun, neut. str., family, birth
kraft   noun, masc.-fem. str., strength, power
kraftag, kraftig   adj., mighty, powerful
kraftiglīko   adv., powerfully, mightily
Krist, Christ   prop. noun, masc. str., Christ
kristin   adj., Christian
kūð   adj., known
kuman   vb., str. IV, to come
kumbal, kumbl   noun, neut. str., shimmering sign
kumi   noun, masc. str. pl., coming, advent, arrival
kuniburd   noun, fem. str., family, kin
kuning   noun, masc. str., king

Old Saxon

kuningsterro	noun, masc. wk.,	king's star (star of Bethelehem)
kuningstōl	noun, masc. str.,	throne
kuningwīsa	noun, fem. str.-wk.,	a manner befitting a king
kunnan	vb., pret.-pres.,	to know, understand, be able
kunni	noun, neut. str.,	origin, birth, kin, tribe
kūsko	adv.,	honorably
kust	noun, fem. str.,	choice, decision, the best

laðoian	vb., wk. 2,	to invite; call, summon
lagustrōm	noun, masc. str.,	waves, waters
lahan	vb., str. VI,	to find fault with, reprove, rebuke
land	noun, neut. str.,	land, earth
landskepi	noun, neut. str.,	land, country
landwīsa	noun, fem. str.,	custom of the country
lang	adj.,	long
lango	adv.,	long, a long time
langsam	adj.,	long-lasting, eternal
lastar	noun, neut. str.,	fault, sin, guilt
lat	adj.,	late
lātan	vb., str. VII,	to let, release, leave, permit
lēdian	vb., wk. 1,	to lead, bring, bear
lēð	adj.,	hostile, hated, evil
lēð	noun, neut. str.,	evil
legar	noun, neut. str.,	sickness
lēra	noun, fem. str.,	instruction, dogma, tenet
lērian	vb., wk. 1,	to teach
lēriand	noun, masc. str.,	teacher
lesan	vb., str. V,	to collect, sort, read
Lē(ĕ)vi	prop. noun,	Levi
libbian	vb., wk. 3,	to live
lið	noun, masc. str.,	limb
līð	noun, neut. str.,	friut wine, drink

līðan vb., str. I, to go, depart, pass
liðokospos noun, masc. str. pl., bonds, chains
liðon vb., wk. 2, to bring, lead
līf noun, neut. str., life, body
liggian vb., str. V, to lie
līk noun, neut. str., body, flesh
līkhamo noun, masc. wk., body
līkon vb., wk. 3, to please
līnon vb., wk. 2, to learn
liof adj., dear, beloved, valued
liogan vb., str. II, to lie
    is quidi liagan - to be untrue to his word
lioht noun, neut. str., light; world; life
lioht adj., light, bright, clear
liohtian, liuhtian vb., wk. 1, to shine
liohto adv., openly, sincerely, frankly; brightly, clearly
liomo noun, masc. wk., shine, ray
list noun, fem. str., wisdom
liudi noun, fem. str. pl., people
liudskepi noun, neut. str., people
loƀon vb., wk. 2, to praise
lof noun, neut. str., praise
lōf noun, neut. str., leaf
lō(ŏ)gna noun, fem. str.-wk., flame, hellfire
lōn noun, neut. str., reward, pay
lōnon vb., wk. 2, to reward, pay
lōs adj., free, without
Lōth prop. noun, Lot
Lucas prop. noun, Lucas
lud noun, masc.-fem. str., sexual potency
luft noun, masc.-fem. str., air
lūkan vb., str. II, to close
lust noun, fem. str., desire, joy
luttil adj., small, little

Old Saxon

māg	noun, masc. str., relative, family member
magað	noun, fem. str., maiden
māgskepi	noun, masc. str., relationship
mahlian	vb., wk. 1, to speak, talk
maht	noun, fem. str., power, strength
mahtig	adj., mighty
māki	noun, masc.-neut. str., sword
makon	vb., wk. 2, to make
man(n)	noun, masc. str., man; servant, vassal, knight; man, (pl.) people; one (indef. pron.)
manag	adj., much, many
mankunni	noun, neut. str., mankind, humanity
māno	noun, masc. wk., moon
mansterbo	noun, masc. wk., dying
Marcus	prop. noun, Mark
māri	adj., glorious, famous, known
mārian	vb., wk. 1, to announce, make known
māriða	noun, fem. str., famous deed
markon	vb., wk. 2, to mark, determine
mārlīko	adv., marvelously
Matheus	prop. noun, Matthew
mēda	noun, fem. str.-wk., reward, pay
mēðom	noun, masc. str., treasure
meginfard	noun, fem. str., campaign
meginkraft	noun, fem.-masc. str., force, strength
meginstrengi	noun, fem., strength, power
mēn	noun, neut. str., sin, crime, misdeed
mēngiwerk	noun, neut. str., evil deed, sin
mēnian	vb., wk. 1, to mean, intend
menigi	noun, fem. str., people, multitude, crowd, troop
mennisk, mannisk	adj., human
mennisko	noun, masc. wk., man, human
mēr	adv. (comp.), more
mēr	noun, subst. comp., indecl., more
mēro	adj. (comp.), more, greater, stronger, higher

mēst adj. (superl.), most, greatest
mēster noun, masc. str., master
meti noun, masc. str., food, sustenance
metigēdia noun, fem. str. (?), famine
metod noun, masc. str., God, Fate
mī(ì), me pers. pron., 1st sg. dat., me
mid adv., with
miδ, mið, midi, mit, met prep. (dat.), with
middi adj., mid
middilgard noun, masc.-fem. str., earth
mik (cf. mī(ì), me) pers. pron. 1st sg. acc., me
mikil adj., great, much
mildi adj., friendly, gentle, generous
mīn adj., poss. pron., my, mine
mīn pers. pron., 1st sg. gen., of me, mine
minnia noun, fem. str., love
minnisto adj. (superl.), least, slightest
mōd noun, masc.-neut. str., mind, sense
mōdag, mōdig, mōdeg adj., angry, hostile, enraged
mōdar noun, fem., mother
mōdgithāht noun, fem. str., thoughts, fellings, emotion
mōdsebo noun, masc. wk., heart, mind, thought
morð noun, neut. str., murder
morðwerk noun, neut. str., murder
morgan noun, masc. str., morning
mōtan vb., pret.-pres., may, be permitted to
Moyses prop. noun, Moses
mugan vb., pret.-pres., can, may, might
mundburd noun, fem. str., protection, help
mūtspelli, mūdspelli noun, neut. str., end of the world
myrra noun, fem. str., myrrh

nāh adj., near
nāhian vb., wk. 1, to near, approach

Old Saxon

nāhor	adv. (comp. to 'n ah'),	nearer, closer
naht	noun, fem. str.,	night
namo	noun, masc. wk.,	name
ne, ni	particle, negation	

    ne ... ne ... - neither ... nor ...

nerian	vb., wk. 1,	to save, free
nēthwanan	adv.	

    ni wet hwanan - I know not from where

newan	conj.,	unless, except
nīð	noun, masc. str.,	hate
niðar	adv.,	downwards
nīðhugdig	adj.,	hostile, inimical
nigēn	adj.,	no, none
nigēn	indef. pron.,	no, none
niman	vb., str. IV,	to take, choose, receive
nio, nia, neo	adv.,	never
niotan	vb., str. II,	to enjoy, use
niowiht, neowiht, niewiht	adv.,	absolutely not
niowiht, neowiht, niewiht	indef. pron.,	nothing
niud	noun, masc. str.,	desire, longing
niudlīko	adj.,	carefully, eagerly
Nōe	prop. noun,	Noah
noh	adv.,	until now, yet, still
noh	conj.,	nor
norðan	adv.,	from the north
nū(ŭ)	adv.,	now, already
nū(ŭ)	conj.,	therefore, since, now

oƀar, oƀer, ofer	prep. (+dat., acc.),	over, across, above
oƀarhōƀdio	noun, masc. wk.,	overlord, ruler
oƀarmōdig	adj.,	proud, haughty, arrogant
ōƀian	vb., wk. 1,	to celebrate

ōd	noun, neut. str., property, prosperity, happiness
ōdan	adj., (participle), given out, presented, bestowed on
ōðar	adj., other, second, another
ōðarlīk	adj., changed
ōdmōdi	noun, neut. str., humility
oft	adv., often
ōgian	vb., wk. 1, to show, make known
ōk	conj., also, and
opan	adj., open
opanlīko	adv., openly, clearly, plainly
ord	noun, masc. str., point, tip (of a weapon)
ōstan	adv., from the east
ōstana	adv., from the east
ōstar	adv., toward the east, eastwards
ōstarweg	noun, masc. str., way to the east
ōstrōni	adj., eastern, coming from the east

paradīs	noun, neut. str., paradise
Pē(ĕ)trus	prop. noun, St. Peter
porta	noun, fem. wk., gate, door

qualm	noun, neut. str., death
queðan	vb., str. V, to speak, say
queddian	vb., wk. 1, to greet, address
quena	noun, fem. wk., woman, wife
quidi	noun, masc. str., speech, word
quik	adj., alive, living

rād	noun, masc. str., advice; profit; remedy, relief
rādan	vb., str. VII, to advise, plan

Old Saxon

rādburd noun, fem. str., sovereign authority
rādgebo noun, masc. wk., counselor; ruler
rasta, resta noun, fem. str.-wk., rest, grave, death
reht adv., as soon as
rehto adv., properly, lawfully
rekkian, reckean vb., wk. 1, to tell, explain
rihtian vb., wk. 1, to rule, direct
rīki, rīc- adj., powerful, mighty
rīki noun, neut. str., dominion, kingdom, realm, rule; ruler
rink noun, masc. str., man, young warrior
rōkfat noun, neut. str., censer
Rōmanoliudi noun, masc. str., Roman people
Rūmuburg prop. noun, fem. str., Rome
rūna noun, fem. str., secret discussion

saka noun, fem. str., fault, matter, dispute, quarrel
sālig adj., good, pious, blessed
sāliglīko adv., blessedly
sama, samo adv., same
samad, samod adv., together
samnon, samnoian vb., wk. 2, to gather, assemble
sān adv., immediately, already
sancte adj., sainted
sand noun, masc. str., sand; bank, shore
sebo noun, masc. wk., spirit, heart
sedal, seðal noun, masc. str., peace
seg noun, masc. str., man
seggian vb., wk. 3, to say
segina noun, fem. str., fishnet, seine
sehan vb., str. V, to see, see to
sehsto adj., ordinal number, sixth
seldlīk adj., wonderful
self, selbo dem. pron., str.-wk. adj. inflection, self

seli   noun, masc. str.,   hall, main room; house
seliða   noun, fem. str.,   house, residence
sendian   vb., wk. 1,   to send
sēo, sēu   noun, masc. str.,   sea
seola   noun, fem. str.,   soul, life
sēr   adj.,   pained, sorrowful, sad
settian   vb., wk. 1,   to set, lay, set down
sia, sie, sea, se   pers. pron., masc.-fem. pl. nom.-acc.,   they, them
sia, sie, sea   pers. pron., fem. sg. acc.,   her
sibbia   noun, fem. str.,   tribe, clan, kinship group
sīda   noun, fem. str.,   side
sidu   noun, masc. str.,   custom, usage
sīð   noun, masc. str.,   way, journey, fate, time
sīðon, sīðogean   vb., wk. 2,   to go
sīðor   adv.,   after, later, since
sīðor   conj.,   after, since, later
sīðwōrig   adj.,   travel-weary
sīgan   vb., str. I,   to sink, set
simbla, simla   adv.,   always, ever
simblon, simlun   adv.,   always, ever; nonetheless
Sīmon   prop. noun,   Simon Peter (the apostle)
sīn   poss. adj.,   his, its
sind   vb. (cf. 'wesan'), 3rd pl. pres.,   [they] are
singan   vb., str. III,   to sing
siok   adj.,   sick
sittian   vb., str. V,   to sit, remain
siu, sie, sea   pers. pron., neut. pl. nom.-acc.,   they, them
siu, sia, sie, sea   pers. pron., fem. sg. nom.,   she
siun   noun, fem. str.,   vision, sight, eye
skakan   vb., str. VI,   to go, hurry
skāla   noun, fem. wk.,   drinking cup
skarp   adj.,   sharp
skat   noun, masc. str.,   coin, money
skēdan, skēðan   vb., str.,   to part, separate

Old Saxon

skenkio	noun, masc. wk.,	cup-bearer
skerian	vb., wk. 1,	to grant, distribute, share out
skīn	adj.,	visible
skīnan	vb., str. I,	to shine
skio(n)	noun, masc. str.,	overcast, cloudy sky
skīr(i)	adj.,	nothing but, pure
skōni	adj.,	fair, beautiful
skrīban, scrīban	vb., str. 1,	to write
skulan	vb., pret.-pres.,	should, have to
skuld	noun, fem. str.,	obligation, debt
slāpan	vb., str. VII,	to sleep
slekkian	vb., wk.,	to weaken
slīðmōd	adj.,	evil-souled
slīðwurdi	adj.,	evil, angry-word speaking
slutil	noun, masc. str.,	key
snel	adj.,	rash, swift, bold
snēo	noun, masc. str.,	snow
sniumo, sliumo	adv.,	swiftly, quickly
sē, se, so	adv., conj.,	so, thus

    sō ... sō - indefinite
    al sō - even as

Sodomaland	prop. noun,	the land of Sodom
sōðlīko	adv.,	truly, rightly
sōkian	vb., wk. 1,	to seek
sorga, soraga	noun, fem. str.,	care, attention, sorrow
sorgon	vb., wk. 2,	to sorrow
sorgspell	noun, neut. str.,	sad, painful news
spāh(i)	adj.,	wise, clever
spāhlīko	adv.,	wisely, sagely
spanan	vb., str. VI,	to incite, entice
spel	noun, neut. str.,	word, speech
spilon	vb., wk. 2,	to move in a spritely manner, dance
sprāka	noun, fem. str.-wk.,	language, speech; instruction; discussion
sprekan	vb., str. IV,	to speak

stað	noun, masc. str.,	edge, bank, shore
stān	vb., anom.,	to stand, be present
standan	vb., str. III,	to stand, be present
stark	adj.,	strong; angry, hostile
stedi	noun, fem. str.,	place
stemna, stemnia	noun, fem. str.-wk.,	voice
stēn	noun, masc. str.,	stone
stēnholm	noun, masc. str.,	mountain
sterkian	vb., wk. 1,	to strengthen
sterro	noun, masc. wk.,	star
stīgan	vb., str. I,	to climb
stillo	adv.,	still
strang	adj.,	strong
strīd	noun, masc. str.,	strife, dispute, quarrel
strōm	noun, masc. str.,	stream, current, tide
sūðan	adv.,	from the south
suht	noun, fem. str.,	sickness, pestilence
sulik	pron.,	such
sumar	noun, masc. str.,	summer
sundar	adv.,	especially, particularly
sundea	noun, fem. str.-wk.,	sin, evil deed
sundion	vb., wk. 2,	to do wrong, sin, offend
sunna	noun, fem.-masc. str.-wk.,	sun
sunu	noun, masc. str.,	son
sus	adv.,	so, thus, in this way
swār	adj.,	heavy
swāro	adv.,	heavily, oppressively
swart	adj.,	black, dark
sweban	noun, masc. str.,	sleep, dream
swefresta	noun, fem. str.,	bed
sweltan	vb., str. III,	to die
swīð, swīði	adj.,	strong, great
swīðo	adv.,	very

te, ti, tō	adv., too
te, ti	prep. (+dat., instr.), to
tefaran	vb., str. VI, to pass away
tegangan	vb., str. VII, to dwindle away, vanish
tegegnes	adv., toward, before
tēkan	noun, neut. str., sign
teklioban	vb., str. II, to cleave
telātan	vb., str. VII, to part
tellian	vb., wk. 1, to say, tell, recount, explain
tesamne	adv., together
tīd	noun, fem. str., time, hour
tins	noun, masc. str., tribute
tiohan	vb., str. II, to raise, take
tiono	noun, masc. wk., evil deed, crime, sin
tīr	noun, masc. str., honor, fame
tō	adv., to
tōgian	vb., wk. 1, to show, prove, demonstrate
tōm, tōmi	adj. (+gen.), free of
torht	adj., bright, shining
torhtlīko	adv., shiningly
treuwa	noun, fem. str., faith, trust
tugiðon	vb., wk. 2, to grant
tunga	noun, fem. wk., tongue
tungal	noun, neut. str., star
tweho	noun, masc. wk., doubt
twelif	cardinal number, twelve
twēne, twa, twō, twē	cardinal number, two
twēntig	adj., cardinal number (+gen.), twenty
twīfli	adj., doubtful, faithless
than, thanna, thanne	adv., then
than, thanna, thenne	conj., then, as, while, during; with comp. X than Y
thanan	adv., thence, from that

thank, thanc	noun, masc. str., favor, thanks, reward
thar	adv., there, then; where, when, whither; since
tharf	noun, fem. str., need, necessity, lack
tharod	adv., thither
that	dem. pron., neut. sg. nom.-acc., the, that
that	conj., that
thau	noun, masc. str., custom
the	particle, indeclinable rel. pron. (with 3rd pers.), who, that
the, thie	dem. pron., masc. nom. sg., the
the, thie	dem. pron., art., the
thea, thia, thie, the	dem. pron., masc.-fem. pl. nom., the, who
thea, thia, thie, the	dem. pron., masc.-fem. pl. acc., the, whom
thegan	noun, masc. str., boy, vassal, man, follower
thē(ĕ)m, thē(ĕ)n	dem. pron., masc.-fem.-neut. pl. dat., the
them, themo. themu	dem. pron., neut. sg. dat., the
themu, themo, them	dem. pron., masc. sg. dat., the, this
thena, thene, thana, thane	dem. pron., masc. sg. acc., the
thenkian	vb., wk. 1, to think
thera, theru, thero	dem. pron., fem. sg. gen., the
thero, thera	dem. pron., masc.-fem.-neut. pl. gen., the
theru, thero, thera	dem. pron., fem. sg. dat., the
thes	dem. pron., masc. sg. gen., the
thes, thas	dem. pron., neut. sg. gen., the
thesa, these	dem. pron., fem. sg. acc., this
thesa, these	dem. pron., fem. pl. nom.-acc., these
thesan, thesen, theson	dem. pron., masc. sg. acc., this
thesara, thesaro, thesoro	dem. pron., fem. sg. gen., this
thesaro, thesoro	dem. pron., masc.-fem.-neut. pl. gen., these
thesaru, thesaro, thesoro, thesero, thesara	dem. pron., fem. sg. dat., this
these	dem. pron., masc. sg. nom., this

Old Saxon

these, thesa   dem. pron., masc.-neut. pl. nom.-acc., (cf. 'thius' neut.), these
theses, thesas   dem. pron., masc.-neut. sg. gen., this
thesum, thesun, theson   dem. pron., masc.-fem.-neut. pl. dat., these
thesumu, thesamo, thesum, thesun, theson   dem. pron., masc.-neut., sg. dat., this
thī(i)   pers. pron., 2nd sg. acc.-dat., you
thia, thie, thea   dem. pron., fem. sg. acc., the
thiggian   vb., wk. 1, to receive, beg
thik, thī(i)   pers. pron., 2nd sg. acc., you
thīn   poss. adj., your
thīn   pers. pron., 2nd sg. gen., your
thing   noun, neut. str., thing, court, situation, matter
thioda   noun, fem. str., people, folk; multitude
thiodan   noun, masc. str., ruler
thiodgod   noun, masc. str., almighty God
thiodgumo   noun, masc. wk., admirable man; man of the people
thiodkuning   noun, masc. str., king of the people
thiof   noun, masc. str., thief
thiolīko   adv., humbly
thionon   vb., wk. 2, to serve
thionost   noun, neut. str., service
thiorna   noun, fem. wk., maiden, maid, virgin
thit   dem. pron., neut. sg. nom.-acc., this
thiu   dem. pron., masc.-neut. sg. instr., the
thiu   dem. pron., neut. pl nom.-acc. (cf. 'thea'), the
thiu, thia   dem. pron., fem. sg. nom., the
thius   dem. pron., neut. sg. instr.; fem. sg. nom., this
thius   dem. pron., neut. pl., nom.-acc., these
thiustri   adj., dark
thiustria   noun, fem. str., darkness
thō, thuo   adv., conj., then, now
thoh   adv., yet, however

thoh conj., although, though, however
tholon, tholian, tholoian vb., wk. 2, to suffer, endure, bear
thorron vb., wk. 2, to perish, pass away
thria, thrie, threa adj., cardinal number, three
thriddio ordinal number, third
thū(ŭ), tu pers. pron., 2nd sg. nom., you
thunkian vb., wk. 1, to seem, appear
thurban vb., pret.-pres., to have cause, have need
thurh, thuru(c) prep. (+acc.), through, by means of
thurst noun, masc. str., thirst
thus adv., thus, in this manner
thwingan vb., str. III, to oppress

ubil adj., evil, bad
ubil noun, neut. str., evil
ubilo adv., evilly
ūðia noun, fem. wk., wave
umbi adv., around
umbi prep. (+acc.), around, about
undar, under prep. (+dat., instr., acc.), under, among
undarfindan vb., str. III, to report, give an account
undartwisk prep. (+acc.), between
undarwitan vb., pret.-pres., to recognize
ungilōbo noun, masc. wk., unbelief
unk pers. pron., 1st dual acc.-dat., us (two)
unka adj., poss. pron., 1st dual, our (two)
unkero, unkaro pers. pron., 1st dual gen., our (two)
unmet adv., immeasurably, very
unskōni adj., not beautiful
unskuldig adj., innocent
unsundig adj., innocent
unwand adj., unchanging, true
unwerid participial adj., unclothed
ŭp adv., up

Old Saxon

upōd	noun, masc. str.,	heavenly glory
uppa	adv.,	above
uppan	adv.,	above, upwards
uppan	prep. (+dat., acc.),	upon, on, up
urlagi	noun, neut. str.,	battle, war
us	pers. pron., 1st pl. dat.,	us
ūsa, ūse	adj., poss. pron., 1st pl.,	our
ūser	pers. pron., 1st pl. gen.,	ours
ūta	adv.,	outside, abroad
ūtan	adv.,	outside

wāg, wēg	noun, masc. str.,	wave, sea
wahsan	vb., str. VI,	to grow, wax
wakon	vb., wk. 2,	to watch, be awake, be on guard
wal	noun, masc. str.,	wall
wald, uuald	noun, masc. str.,	forest
waldan	vb., str. VII,	to rule, have power over
waldand	noun, masc. str. (pres. part. of 'waldan'),	ruler, Lord
wallan	vb., str. VII,	to burn, flare, waver
wānam, wānum	adj.,	beautiful, shining, bright
wānamo	adv.,	brightly, beautifully
wang	noun, masc. str.,	field, meadow pasture
wanga	noun, fem. str.,	cheek
wānian	vb., wk. 1,	to believe, hope
wāpan	noun, neut. str.,	weapon
wāpanberand	noun + pres. part., masc.,	weapon-bearer, warrior
wār	adj.,	true
wār	noun, fem.-neut. str.,	truth
	te uuārun - in truth	
ward	noun, masc. str.,	warder, protector, guardian
wardon	vb., wk. 2,	to guard, protect, be watchful
wārlīko	adv.,	truly

warm adj., warm
wārsago noun, masc. wk., soothsayer, prophet
wedar noun, neut. str., weather
weg, uueg noun, masc. str., way, street, path
wēgian vb., wk. 1, to torment
wehslon, wehslan, wehslean vb., wk. 2, to change, exchange
wel adv., well, good
wela, wala, wola interj., hail, joy; woe
welo noun, masc. wk., goods, possessions, riches
wendian vb., wk., to turn, change, depart
wennian vb., wk. 1, to lead, draw to oneself
wer noun, masc. str., man, human being
werð adj., worthy, valuable, acceptable, dear
werðan vb., str. III, to become, happen
werðlīko adv., properly, worthily
werk noun, neut. str., work, deed, act
werod noun, neut. str., horde, crowd, people
werold noun, masc.-fem. str., world, earth, people, life, existence
weroldaldar noun, neut. str., age of the world
weroldcuning noun, masc. str., world-king
weroldhērro noun, masc. wk., master, ruler of the world
weroldrīki noun, neut. str., world
werpan vb., str. III, to throw, cast
wesan vb., anom. (cf. 'sind', 'bium'), to be
westan adv., from the west
westar adv., westwards
wī(ì), we pers. pron., 1st pl. nom., we
wīd adj., wide, broad, far
wið prep. (+dat., acc., instr.), against, towards, with
wiðar adv., back
wiðar prep. (+dat., acc., instr.), against
wiðarlāga noun, fem. str., the same, the like, counterpart
wiðarsako noun, masc. wk., enemy, fiend
wiðarstandan vb., str. VI, to withstand

Old Saxon

wiðarward   adj., opposed, hostile
wiðarward   adv., backwards
wiðermōd   adj., hostile, offensive, repugnant
wīdo   adv., wide, far
wīf   noun, neut. str., wife
wīg   noun, masc. str., war, battle
wīh   noun, masc. str., temple
wīhrōk   noun, masc. str., incense
wiht   noun, masc. str., a thing, something
willian   vb., anom., to want to
willio   noun, masc. wk., will, intention, grace, favor, wish, attitude, thought, advantage
wīn   noun, masc.-neut. str., wine
wind   noun, masc. str., wind
windan   vb., str. III, to turn, wind, twist
wini   noun, masc. str., friend, blood-friend, comrade
winistar   adj., left
wintar   noun, masc. str., winter, year
wirðig   adj., worthy
wirkian   vb., wk. 1, to do, work, prepare, carry out
wīs   adj., learned, clever, wise
wīsian   vb., wk. 1, to show, tell
wiskumo   adj., masc. wk., certainly coming
wīskuning   noun, masc. str., wise king
wīslīk   adj., wise
wīslīko   adv., wisely, with wisdom
wīson   vb., wk. 2, to visit
wit   pers. pron., 1st dual nom., we (two)
witan   vb., pret.-pres., to know, understand
wīti   noun, neut. str., punishment, pain, suffering; punishable evil
witig   adj., wise
wlank   adj., bold, proud
wlenkian   vb., wk. 1, to make bold, empower
wliti   noun, masc. str., brilliance, shine, appearance, form, face

wlitiskōni   noun, fem.,   shining beauty
wōl   noun, masc. str.,   sickness, plague
wolkan   noun, neut. str.,   cloud
wonon, wunon   vb., wk. 2,   to stay, dwell, live
word   noun, neut. str.,   word
wordspāh   adj.,   word-wise
wōstunnia   noun, fem. str.,   waste, desert
wraksīð   noun, masc. str.,   path to a foreign land
wrēð   adj.,   sorrowful, angry, hostile
wrekkio   noun, masc. wk.,   hero from abroad
wundar   noun, neut. str.,   wonder, miracle
wundarlīk   adj.,   wonderful, miraculous
wundron   vb., wk. 2,   to wonder
wunnia   noun, fem. str.,   joy
wunsam   adj.,   ecstatic, delightful
wurð(i)giscapu   noun, neut. str. pl.,   the Fates

Zacharias   prop. noun,   Zacharias (priest and father of John the Baptist)

Latin Glossary

a, ab   prep. (abl.),   from, away from; by
ac, atque   conj.,   and
accendō, -ere   vb. 3,   to kindle; inflame, excite
accipiō, accipere   vb. 3,   to take, receive, accept
acclīvis, -e   adj. 3,   inclined, upwards
ad   prep. (acc.),   to, towards
adhūc   adv.,   thus far, hitherto, up to this time, even, still
adiūtorium, -ī   noun, neut. 2,   help, aid, assistance, support
admoneō, -ēre   vb. 2,   to admonish, remind; advise; urge, incite
admonitiō, -ōnis   noun, fem. 3,   a reminding, a friendly admonition
adventus, -ūs   noun, masc. 4,   arrival, advent
aeternus, -a, -um   adj.,   eternal, everlasting
affectus/adfectus   past part. adficio, -ere (vb. 3),   affected, influenced
agellus, -ī   noun, masc. 2,   a little field
ager, agrī   noun, masc. 2,   land, field, open country
agō, agere, ēgi, actus   vb. 3,   to drive, do, discuss, live, spend
       actum est - it has come to pass, it has been brought about
agricola, -ae   noun, masc. 1,   a tiller of the fields, farmer
alius, -a, -ud   adj. & pro.,   another, other, different
altus, -a, -um   adj.,   grown, great; high, noble; deep, lofty
ambīgō, -ere   vb. 3,   to go about or round; to doubt, hesitate, be uncertain
amor, -ōris   noun, masc. 3,   love, longing, desire
anhēlātiō, -ōnis   noun, fem. 3,   panting
anima   noun, fem. 1,   soul, spirit
animus   noun, masc. 2,   soul, mind

(an)notō, -āre   vb. 1, to mark, distinguish, denote, write
antiquus, -a, -um   adj., old, ancient
appellō, -āre   vb. 1, to address; name, call
appetō, -ere   vb. 3, to make for, to grasp; to seek, desire
apud   prep. (acc.), at, near, by, with, among
arātrum, -ī   noun, neut. 2, the plow
ardens, -entis   adj. 3, hot, glowing, burning
ardentius   adv. comparative, more ardently, more eagerly
arduus, -a, -um   adj., steep, towering, lofty, difficult
armentum, -ī   noun, neut. 2, cattle for plowing; herd
ars, artis   noun, fem. 3, skill, way, method, art, knowledge
āter, atra, atrum   adj., black, dark, gloomy; sad, unfortunate
attineō, attinēre   vb. 2, hold, keep; pertain to, concern
attonitus, -a, -um   adj. (p. part. of attonō, -ere), struck by thunder; stunned, terrified; inspired, frantic
audiō, -īre   vb. 4, to hear, listen to; to learn by hearing
augeō, augēre   vb. 2, to increase, make grow, augment
Avernus, -i   noun, masc. 2, the infernal regions, hell

benevolentia, -ae   noun, fem. 1, good-will, friendly disposition, kindness
benevolus, -a, -um   adj., kind, obliging, well-disposed

cantilēna, -ae   noun, fem. 1, an old song, twaddle, chatter
cantus, -ūs   noun, masc. 4, song, melody, poetry
capiō, capere, cēpī, captus   vb. 3, to take, seize
capitulum, -ī   noun, neut. 2, a little head, chapter
carmen, -inis   noun, neut. 3, a song, tune; poetry, a poem
casula, -ae   noun, fem. 1, a little hut, cottage
cēdō, -ere   vb. 3, to go, proceed; withdraw, depart, yield

Latin

census, -ūs — noun, masc. 4, census; property, wealth
Christus, -ī — proper noun, masc. 2, Christ
clarē — adv., clearly, brightly, distinctly, illustriously
clarus, -a, -um — adj., clear, distinct, evident, plain; loud
coaptō, -āre — vb. 1, to fit together
cōdex, -dicis — noun, masc. 3, the trunk of a tree; a book
coepiō, coepere, coepī, coeptus — vb. defective, to begin, commence
commendō, -āre — vb. 1, to commit to the care, keeping, or protection of anyone, to recommend, to set off, to render agreeable
commōdum, -ī — noun, neut. 2, a suitable time, opportunity, convenience
compescō, -ere — vb. 3, to hold in, restrain, check, curb
compōnō, -ere — vb. 3, to put, place, lay, bring together; to collect; to compose
compositor, -ōris — noun, masc. 3, an arranger, adjuster; composer, author
comprimō, -ere — vb. 3, to press together, to compress; to restrain, stop, suppress
comprobō, -āre — vb. 1, to approve fully; to confirm, prove, establish
conferō, -ferre — vb. irreg., to bring or put together, collect; reflex., to devote, apply oneself
confīdō, -ere — vb. semi-deponent (3), to have complete trust; to be assured; to believe firmly
congruus, -a, -um — adj., agreeing, fit, suitable
conscrībō, -ere — vb. 3, to write together; compose
conspectus, -ūs — noun, masc. 4, look, sight, view
contendō, -ere — vb. 3, to strain, exert, strive
contentus, -a, -um — adj., past part. contineō, -ēre, contented
convīvō, -ere, -vixī, victus — vb. 3, to live with, feast with
copia, -ae — noun, fem. 1, plenty, abundance
cor, cordis — noun, neut. 3, the heart

creātiō, -ōnis   noun, fem. 3,   choice, election; creation
culmeus, -a, -um   adj.,   thatched
cum   conj.,   when; (also prep.,   with)
cunctus, -a, -um   adj.,   all, all collectively, the whole
cupīdō, -inis   noun, fem. 3,   eager desire, passionate longing
cur   interrog. adv.,   why, wherefore
cura, -ae   noun, fem. 1,   care, carefulness, concern; pains, trouble, attention

de   prep. (abl.),   from, away from; of
decerpō, -ere   vb. 3,   to pluck off, pluck away; to gather; to derive
decor, -oris   noun, masc. 3,   grace, comeliness, beauty
dēdūcō, -ere   vb. 3,   to lead, bring down
dēlectāmentum, -ī   noun, neut. 2,   delight, pleasure, amusement
delectō, -āre   vb. 1,   to divert, attract, delight; to take delight in
dēmulceō, -ēre   vb. 2,   to stroke down, caress by stroking
dēpellō, -ere   vb. 3,   to drive down, away, out; expel, remove, dislodge
dēpingō, -ere   vb. 3,   to paint, to repesent in painting, to depict
dēsīderium, -ī   noun, neut. 2,   desire, longing, grief for the absence or loss of a person or thing
dēsuper   adv.,   from above
deterior, -ius   adj. comparative,   lower, inferior, poorer, worse
Deus   noun, masc. 2,   God
devōtus, -a, -um   past part. dēvoveō,   consecrated, devoted
dictō, -āre   vb. 1,   to say often, repeat; dictate; to get written down
dictum, -ī   noun, neut. 2,   a word, saying, speech
difficilis, -e   adj. 3,   difficult
dīrigō, -ere   vb. 3,   to arrange, direct

Latin

dīrus, -a, -um   adj.,   fearful, horrible, dire
distinguō, -ere   vb. 3,   to mark off, distinguish, divide, set off
ditiō, -ōnis (diciō, -ōnis)   noun, fem. 3,   power, sovereignty, authority
divinus, -a, -um   adj.,   divine, godly
divitiae, -ārum   noun, fem. 1,   riches, wealth
doctus, -a, -um   adj., past part. doceō, -ēre,   taught, learned, instructed; experienced, clever, shrewd
dogma, -atis   noun, neut. 3,   philosophical doctrine
Dominus, -ī   noun, masc. 2,   lord
dūcō, -ere   vb. 3,   to draw, lead
dūdum   adv.,   some time ago, a little while ago, not long since
dulcēdō, -inis   noun, fem. 3,   sweetness, pleasantness, charm
dum   adv. and conj.,   yet; now, for a moment; while, during the time that, until

ego   pers. pron., 1st sg.,   I
ēleganter   adv.,   tastefully, choicely, neatly
ēloquentia, -ae   noun, fem. 1,   eloquence
eō   adv., eō ... quo with comparatives,   the ... the ...
ergo   adv.,   consequently, therefore, accordingly
eripiō, -ripere, -ripuī, -reptus   vb. 3,   to snatch away, tear out
ēruditus, -a, -um   adj.,   instructed, educated, trained
esse   vb. infin. (sum, esse, fui, futurus),   to be
et   conj.,   and
etiam   conj.,   as yet, still
      nōn sōlum ... sed (or verum) etiam - not only ... but also
excellentia, -ae   noun, fem. 1,   eminence, distinction
excellentior   adj., comparative of excellens, -entis,   more excellent
exiguum, -ī   noun, neut. 2,   small extent
ex(s)tinguō, -ere   vb. 3,   to put out, extinguish; abolish, destroy

facētus, -a, -um   adj., fine, elegant; witty
facilior, facilius   adj., comparative of facilis, -e, easy to do, easy
fatīgō, -āre   vb. 1, to weary, tire, fatigue
fauces, -ium   noun, fem. 3, jaws
fēlix -icis   adj. 3, fortunate, lucky, successful, happy
ferō, ferre, tulī, lātus   vb. irreg., to bear, bring, carry; to report to others, to spread abroad, speak of
fessus, -a, -um   adj., weary, tired, exhausted
fīnis, -is   noun, masc. 3, end, boundary, limit, border
fōmes, -itis   noun, masc. 3, touchwood, tinder
fortuna, -ae   noun, fem. 1, chance, fate, lot, luck, fortune

gens, gentis   noun, fem. 3, clan; people, tribe, nation
Germanicus, -a, -um   adj., Germanic
gerō, gerere, gessī, gestum   vb. 3, to carry about, bear; conduct oneself; do, wage
gestō, -āre   vb. 1, to carry, bear about
glōria, -ae   noun, fem. 1, fame, renown, glory

habeō, -ēre   vb. 2, to have, to hold; passive: to be considered, to be held to be
herba, -ae   noun, fem. 1, a blade, stalk; grass
hic, haec, hōc   pron. or pron. adj., this
historia, -ae   noun, fem. 1, story, narrative, history

Latin

īdem, eadem, idem   adj. and pron., the same
idioma, -ae   noun, fem. 1, idiom
igitur   adv., then, so, therefore, accordingly
ignarus, -a, -um   adj., ignorant of, unacquainted with
ignōbilis, -e   adj. 3, unknown, obscure, inglorious; of humble birth
ille, illa, illud   demon. pron., that
illiteratus, -a, -um   adj., unlettered, illiterate
imperialis, -e   adj. 3, imperial, of the empire or state
imperium, -ī   noun, neut. 2, command, order; power; an area governed, an empire
imprimō, -primere, -pressī, -pressus   vb. 3, to press into, upon
in   prep. (acc. or abl.), in, into
inchoantia, -ae   noun, fem. 1, beginning, commencement, inception
incipiō, -cipere, -cēpī, -ceptus   vb. 3, to take in hand, begin, commence
infirmior   adj., comparative of infirmus, -a, -um, more feeble, weaker
ingenium, -i   noun, neut. 2, nature; ability, talent, genius
inimīcus, -ī   noun, masc. 2, enemy, foe
initium, -ī   noun, neut. 2, an entering upon, beginning
inumerābilis, -e   adj., that cannot be counted, innumerable
inquīrō, -ere   vb. 3, to seek, search for
instruō, -struere   vb. 3, to set up, build; prepare, provide, train
intellectus, -ūs   noun, masc. 4, a perceiving, sensation; understanding, comprehension; intellect
intellegō, -ere   vb. 3, to distinguish, discriminate, perceive, understand
intentiō, -ōnis   noun, fem. 3, a stretching, straining; attention
intentus, -a, -um   adj., past part. intendo, -ere, stretched, tense, taut; anxious; (dat.) intent upon

interdum   adv., sometimes, occasionally, now and then
interpres, -pretis   noun, masc. (c.) 3, a negotiator, mediator, messenger; expounder, explainer, interpreter
interpretor, -ārī   vb. deponent, to put an interpretation upon, to understand in a certain sense, to translate
inveniō, -īre   vb. 4, to come upon, find, meet with; discover
invidia, -ae   noun, fem. 1, envy, grudging, jealousy, ill-will; odium
invidiosus, -a, -um   adj., envious; hateful, causing hate or ill-feeling (dat.)
invidus, -a, -um   adj., envious, unfavorable to
is, ea, id   demon. pron., he, she, it; this or that person or thing
ita   adv., so, thus, in this fashion
iugiter   adv., continuously, perpetually
issum, -ī   noun, neut. 2, an order, command
iustitia, -ae   noun, fem. 1, justice, fairness, equity
iuvencus, -a, -um   adj., young; as noun: a young bullock
iuxtā   adv., close by, near; in like manner, equally

lābor, lābī, lapsus sum   vb. deponent, to glide, slide, fall down, slip
labor, -ōris   noun, masc. 3, work, labor, toil, effort
laetus, -a, -um   adj., fat, rich; copious; bright, pleasant, fortunate, propitious
largus, -a, -um   adj., abundant, plentiful, numerous, copious
lātus, -a, -um   adj., broad, wide; rich, full; extensive
lectiō, -ōnis   noun, fem. 3, a picking out, selecting; a reading
lector, -ōris   noun, masc. 3, reader
lēx, lēgis   noun, fem. 3, law, ordinance, rule, precept; contract, covenant, agreement
libenter   adv., willingly, with pleasure
liber, -rī   noun, masc. 2, the inner bark of a tree; a book
līmen, -inis   noun, neut. 3, threshold, doorway, entrance; home, house, dwelling

Latin

lingua, -ae   noun, fem. 1,   tongue, language
lit(t)erātus, -a, -um   adj.,   lettered, inscribed with letters; learned, liberally educated
loquor, loquī   vb. deponent,   to speak
lūceō, -ēre   vb. 2,   to be bright, shine, glitter
lūcidē   adv.,   clearly, plainly, lucidly
lūx, lūcis   noun, fem. 3,   light, daylight

magis   adv. comparative,   more, to a greater extent, rather
magnus, -a, -um   adj.,   great, large
maximē   adv., superlative of magis,   in the highest degree, most of all, especially, very
mediocriter   adv.,   moderately, ordinarily
melior   adj., comparative of bonus, -a, -um,   better, more fortunate
membrum, -ī   noun, neut. 2,   limb, member of the body
menandō   gerund (from mīnor, -ārī),   by threatening, menacing, exciting
metricus, -a, -um   adj.,   of measuring, metrical
meus, -a, -um   poss. adj., 1st sg.,   my
minimus, -a, -um   adj., superlative of parvus, -a, -um,   smallest, least; very little
mirabiliter   adv.,   wonderfully, marvelously
mīrāculum, -ī   noun, neut. 2,   a wonderful thing, prodigy, miracle
miserātus, -a, -um   adj., past part. of misereor, -ērī   having pitied, had compassion on, commiserated
modicus, -a, -um   adj.,   moderate, temperate; ordinary, undistinguished
modulātiō, -ōnis   noun, fem. 3,   a rhythmical measure
mora, -ae   noun, fem. 1,   delay, space of time, hindrance
mōs, mōris   noun, masc. 3,   will, humor, inclination; custom, wont, usage; manner

moveō, -ēre, mōvī, mōtus   vb. 2,   to move, set in motion, stir
mox   adv.,   soon, presently; then, thereupon
multiplicō, -āre   vb. 1,   to increase many times, multiply
mundus, -ī   noun, masc. 2,   the world, the universe
mysticus, -a, -um   adj.,   secret, mystic

nam   conj.,   for
namque   conj., emphatic,   for
nascor, -ī, nātus sum   vb. deponent,   to be born, to come into existence, arise, be produced
nec, neque   adv., negative particles,   not, and not; neither ... nor
nēmō   pron.,   no one
nihilominus   adv.,   no less, nevertheless, notwithstanding
nīmīrum   adv.,   undoubtedly, truly, certainly
nimium   adv.,   particularly, excessively
nimius, -a, -um   adj.,   very great, very much
nocivus, -a, -um   adj.,   hurtful, injurious
nōn   adv.,   not
nos   pron., 1st pl. nom.,   we
nōtiō, -ōnis   noun, fem. 3,   a making oneself acquainted; an examination, investigation; an idea, notion, conception
nōtitia, -ae   noun, fem. 1,   a being known; fame, celebrity; knowledge, acquaintance; idea, notion, conception
novus, -a, -um   adj.,   new, fresh, young
nūllus, -a, -um   adj. and pron.,   no, none, not any
numquam   adv.,   never, by no means
nūper   adv.,   lately, not long ago, in recent times

obtemperantia, -ae   noun, fem. 1,   obedience
obtemperō, -āre   vb. 1,   to comply with, conform to, submit to

Latin

obterō, -terere, -trīvī, trītum   vb. 3,   to trample, crush, destroy
omnipotentia, -ae   noun, fem. 1,   omnipotence; great power
omnis, omne   adj. 3,   all, every, whole
opus, -eris   noun, neut. 3,   work, labor
opusculum, -ī   noun, neut. 2,   a little work
ordinō, -āre   vb. 1,   to set in order, to govern, arrange
ordō, -inis   noun, masc. 3,   a series, line, row, order, arrangement ex ordine - in regular succession
orīgō, -inis   noun, fem. 3,   origin, source, beginning
ōs, ōris   noun, neut. 3,   mouth; face, countenance

palatium, -ī   noun, neut. 2,   palace
pandō, -ere   vb. 3,   to stretch out, extend; lay open, reveal, disclose
parvitās, -ātis   noun, fem. 3,   littleness, smallness
pascō, -ere   vb. 3,   to feed, nourish, make grow; to feast, gratify
pascua, -ōrum   noun, neut. 2,   pastures
Pater noster   Our Father, the Lord's Prayer
     pater   noun, masc. 2
     noster   poss. adj.
patulus, -a, -um   adj.,   open, standing open; spreading, extended
paucus, -a, -um   adj.,   a few
pāx, pācis   noun, fem. 3,   peace, calm, serenity, quiet
penitus   adv.,   internally, inwardly; in the inmost part, deep inside
per   prep. (acc.),   through, along, over; by means of, with, by way of
percurrō, -currere   vb. 3,   to run through, pass through; mention in passing
perdō, -ere, -didī, -ditus   vb. 3,   to destroy, ruin, do away with; waste, squander

perdūcō, -ere   vb. 3,   to lead through, bring along; to continue, prolong

perfundō, -ere, -fūdī, -fūsus   vb. 3,   to pour over, to steep (in), fill with

piissimus   adj., superlative of pius, -a, -um,   most/very pious, devout

plūrimus   adj., superlative of multus, -a, -um,   very many

poēma, -atis   noun, neut. 3,   poem

poēta, -ae   noun, masc. 1,   poet, maker

poēticē   adv.,   poetically, after the manner of a poet

poēticus, -a, -um   adj.,   poetical

polus, -ī   noun, masc. 2,   a pole (south or north); the sky, heavens

populus, -ī   noun, masc. 2,   people, public, nation

possum, posse   vb. irreg.,   to be able; I (you, he) can

post   adv. and prep. (acc.),   behind, after; according to

postis, -is   noun, masc. 3,   a doorpost, door, doorway

postulō, -āre   vb. 1,   to claim, demand, request

potior   adj., comparative of potis, pote,   preferable, better

praeceptor, -ōris   noun, masc. 3,   teacher, instructor, preceptor

praeceptum, -ī   noun, neut. 2,   a command, rule, injunction

praecipiō, -cipere   vb. 3,   to take before, receive in advance; to instruct, advise, warn, admonish, teach

praeclarus, -a, -um   adj.,   very bright/clear, excellent, admirable

Praefatiō, -ōnis   noun, fem. 3,   preface, introduction

praestō, -stāre   vb. irreg.,   to stand before; to perform, fulfil; to show, manifest, exhibit

praevaleō, -valēre, -valuī   vb. 2,   to be very strong or powerful, to be stronger than others, to prevail, to get the upper hand

prīmus, -a, -um   adj., superlative of prior, prius,   first, foremost, the very first

prius   adv.,   before, previously; sooner, rather; formerly, in former times

Latin

privātus, -a, -um   adj., private
prōmō, -ere   vb. 3, to bring forth, bring out, produce; disclose, express
prōnuntiātiō, -ōnis   noun, fem. 3, a public declaration; judgement; proposition; delivery
proprius, -a, -um   adj., one's own, special, particular, peculiar
propter   prep. (acc.) and adv., prep.: near, close to, next to; on account of, by reason of, because of; adv.: near, near at hand
prūdenter   adv., prudently, discreetly

quadrum, -ī   noun, neut. 2, square; proper order
quaerō, -ere   vb. 3, to seek, search for
quam   adv. with comparative, than
quantō ... tantō   adv., relat., the ... the
quatenus   conj. and adv., how far, to what extent; in so far as, since; that, so that
-que   conj. (always enclitic), and
quī, quae, quod   rel. pron., who, which, what
quīdam, quaedam, quoddam   adj. and pron., a certain person or thing
quidem   adv., indeed, even
quiētus, -a, -um   adj., resting, quiet, peaceful, calm
quinque   indeclin. adj., five
quis, quid   interrog. and indef. pron., who, what; anyone, anybody, anything
quisque, quaeque, quidque   adj., each, every
quō   adv.
      quō ... eō + comparatives - the ... the ... (see: eō)
quoniam   conj., since, seeing that, whereas, because
quoque   adv. of emphasis, postpositive, also, too
quotidie   adv., daily, every day

radius, -ī   noun, masc. 2,   staff, rod, stake; ray, beam of light
ratiō, -ōnis   noun, fem. 3,   a reckoning, account, computation,
                         calculation
recitō, -āre   vb. 1,   to read aloud, read publicly
relābor, -ābī, -lapsus sum   vb. deponent,   to slide, glide, flow,
                         fall back
religiō, -ōnis   noun, fem. 3,   scrupulousness, respect for what
                         is sacred, religious;   later: religion
rēs, reī   noun, fem. 5,   thing, object, matter, affair,
                         circumstance
resonō, -āre   vb. 1,   to sound back, give back an echo;
                         resound, echo
resplendeō, -ēre   vb. 2,   to glitter back, gleam again
Rēspūblica   compound noun, fem. 5,   the state
    rēs, reī   noun, fem. 5,   thing, object, matter, affair
    pūblicus, -a, -um   adj.,   belonging to the people, public
rēx, rēgis   noun, masc. 3,   ruler, king, prince

sacer, sacra, sacrum   adj.,   sacred, holy, consecrated
sacrosanctus, -a, -um   adj.,   consecrated with religious
                         ceremonies; holy, sacred, inviolable
saeculum, -ī   noun, neut. 2,   a generation, a century; the
                         spirit of the age, the times
saltus, -ūs   noun, masc. 4,   a forest or mountain pasture; a
                         pass, dale, revine, glade
salūbritās, -ātis   noun, fem. 3,   wholesomeness, soundness,
                         health
sanguis, -inis   noun, masc. 3,   blood
sapienter   adv.,   more wisely
satis   indecl. adj.,   enough
Saxōnicus, -a, -um   adj.,   Saxon

Latin

Saxōnis   noun, masc. 3,   Saxon
scindō, -ere, scidī, scissus   vb. 3,   to cut, rend, tear asunder, split
scriptūra, -ae   noun, fem. 1,   a writing, composition
sē   reflex. pron.,   oneself
sēcūrus, -a, -um   adj.,   free from care, tranquil; unconcerned
sed   conj.,   but
semper   adv.,   always, ever
sēnsus, -ūs   noun, masc. 4,   sense, feeling; judgment, perception
sententia, -ae   noun, fem. 1,   opinion, thought, meaning; a thought expressed in words, a sentence, period
sibi   reflex. pron.,   to oneself
     suī   gen.
     sibi   dat.
     sē, sēsē   acc.
     sē, sēsē   abl.
sīc   adv.,   so, thus, in this way
sīcut   adv.,   as, just as
singulus, -a, -um   adj.,   single, separate, one at a time, one alone
sōl, sōlis   noun, masc. 3,   the sun
sollicite/solicite   adv.,   anxiously, carefully
     sollicitāre   to incite, rouse, instigate
sōlum   adv.,   only, merely
sōlummodo   adv., emphatic,   alone, only, merely, barely
     sōlum   alone, only, merely
     modo   by measure, according to a limit
somnus, -ī   noun, masc. 2,   sleep, slumber
sonipēs, -pedis   noun, masc. 3,   sounding with the feet; a horse
spargō, -ere   vb. 3,   to scatter, strew, sprinkle, pour forth, throw about
spēs, -eī   noun, fem. 5,   expectation, hope
statim   adv.,   without yielding, firmly, steadfastly
statuō, -ere   vb. 3,   to put, place, set up, establish
studeō, -ere   vb. 2,   to be eager, be earnest, take pains,

strive after
studiōsus, -a, -um   adj., eager, zealous, diligent, studious
studium, -ī   noun, neut. 2, zeal, eagerness, enthusiasm; study
suāvitās, -ātis   noun, fem. 3, sweetness, pleasantness
sub   prep. (abl. or acc.), underneath, under
subdō, -ere   vb. 3, to put, place, lay, set under; to subject, subdue
subiciō, -icere   vb. 3, to throw, place, set under; to subject
sum, esse, fuī, futūrus   vb. irreg., to be
summātim   adv., slightly, summarily, briefly
summus, -a, -um   adj., superlative of superus, -a, -um, very high, very great
superstitiōsus, -a, -um   adj., superstitious, superstitiously believed in
suus, -a, -um   reflex. or poss. pron., his, her, its, their (own)

taeter, -tra, -trum   adj., foul, noisome, hideous, offensive
tālis, -e   adj. 3, of such a kind, such
tam   adv., so, so far, to such a degree
tamen   conj., however, yet, nevertheless
tanque/tantumque   adj., such, so great
tantum   adv., so much, so far; only
tantus, -a, -um   adj., of such a size, so great, much
tegmen, -inis   noun, neut. 3, a cover, covering
tempus, -oris   noun, neut. 3, a division, section; a portion of time, a period of time
ter   adv., three times, thrice
terra, -ae   noun, fem. 1, earth, land, ground, soil
testa, -ae   noun, fem. 1, a piece of clay, shell, a covering
Testāmentum, -ī   noun, neut. 2, testament
Theudiscus, -a, -um   adj., German
tōtus, -a, -um   adj., the whole, complete, entire
tractō, -āre   vb. 1, to drag along, pull about; handle, treat,

Latin

trādō, -ere, tradidī, -ditus   vb. 3, to hand over, give up, surrender, deal with
transferō, -ferre   vb. irreg., to carry over or across; to copy, to translate
tunc   adv., then, at that time; next, then
tuus, -a, -um   poss. adj., 2nd sg., your

ubi   adv., where, wherever; when
ūllus, -a, -um   adj., any; as noun: anyone, anything
umbra, -ae   noun, fem. 1, a shade, shadow
ut   conj., that, so that, as
ūtilitās, -ātis   noun, fem. 3, usefulness, profit, advantage

vānus, -a, -um   adj., empty, void; vain, idle, worthless
vastus, -a, -um   adj., empty, waste, deserted, desolate
vātes, -is   noun, masc. 3, a prophet, soothsayer, seer, poet
vel   conj. or adv., or, or rather; even, actually
veniō, -īre, vēnī, ventus   vb. 4, to come, arrive
verbum, -ī   noun, neut. 2, word
vēritās, -ātis   noun, fem. 3, truth, reality
vērō   adv., in truth, truly
versō, -āre   vb. 1, to turn, ply; (pass. in middle sense: to be engaged in, to be employed in)
versus, -ūs   noun, masc. 4, a row, line; verse
vertō, vertere, vertī, versum   vb. 3, to turn, turn round
vērum   adv., in truth, truly
verus, -a, -um   adj., true, real, genuine
vetō, -āre   vb. 1, to forbid, prohibit
vetus, -eris   adj., old, ancient, of long standing
via, -ae   noun, fem. 1, way, road, street, path

vīctus, -ūs   noun, masc. 4,   manner of life, way of living; support, nourishment, food
vincō, vincere, vīcī, victum   vb. 3,   to conquer, overcome, defeat, subdue, vanquish
vir, virī   noun, masc. 2,   a man, male person
vīta, -ae   noun, fem. 1,   life
vittea, -ae   noun, fem. 1,   fit
vīvō, -ere, vixī, victum   vb. 3,   to live, to be alive
vōmer, -eris   noun, masc. 3,   plowshare
vox, vōcis   noun, fem. 3,   a voice, cry, call

Old High German Glossary

Aaron   prop. noun, masc. str.,   Aaron
Abias   prop. noun, masc. str.,   Abia
ādra   noun, fem., str.-wk.,   blood vessel, vein
(h)after   prep. (dat.),   along, on, through, after, according to, in consequence of
aha   noun, fem. str.,   water, river, flood
(h)al, all   adj.,   all, whole, complete
alamuosa   noun, fem. str.,   alms
alawār   adj./adv.,   completely true, certain, right; in accordance with the truth, facts
alt   adj.,   old, wasted, bygone   (superl.: altist - ancient)
altāri   noun, masc. str.,   altar
altfīant   noun, masc. str.,   age old foe, Satan
ambaht   noun, neut. str.,   service, ministration, office
ana   prep. (dat., acc., instr.) and adv.,   in, on, at, with, against, to, toward
anafallan (anafallen)   vb., str. VII,   to fall, fall on, befall, overcome
anaqueman   vb., str. IV/V (past part.),   to come to, befall someone, press upon
anawart   adj.,   aware, knowing
      anawart giduan - make aware, make known to, reveal to
andar   num., pron., adj.,   the second; another
anfāhan   vb., VII,   to get, receive
āno   prep. (dat., acc., gen.), adv., conj.,   without, except for, next to; if not; after; besides
antichristo   noun, masc. wk.,   anti-Christ
antlingōn   vb., wk. 2,   to answer
antreita   noun, fem. str.,   order, series, succession

antwurti   noun, neut. str.,   answer, promise, oracle
ar   prep. (dat., instr.),   out of, from, outside of
araugen (irougen)   vb., wk. 1,   to make visible, to show, reveal
arfirran   vb., wk. 1,   to take away, remove
arfurpan (irfurben)   vb., wk. 1,   to sweep away, clean, clear away
argēn   vb., irreg.,   to happen, fall, occur
arhangēn   vb., wk. 3,   to hang
arhevan   vb., str. VI,   to lift (up), raise, set; undertake, begin; with reflex.: to set out on one's way
arliugan   vb., str. II,   to lie; abandon disloyally
arm   adj.,   poor, weak, miserable
arstēn   vb., VII,   to arise, raise oneself
arteilen   vb., wk. 1,   to judge; determine, decide
artruknēn   vb., wk. 1,   to dry up, out
arwartan (irwerten)   vb., wk. 1,   to injure, wound; ruin, destroy
augen   vb., wk. 1,   to see, observe, set eyes on
az   prep. (dat., acc.),   to, at, in, in front of, before
azstantan   vb., str. VI,   to stand (by), help

bald   adj.,   bold, strong, courageous; confident, assured, undoubting, hopeful
barn (parn)   noun, neut. str.,   child, offspring, descendent
beide   pron.-adj.,   both
beitōn   vb., wk. 2,   to remain; wait for, expect
betōn   vb., wk. 2,   to pray; request, ask for
bibot   noun, neut. str.,   commandment; tiding
bifindan   vb., str. III,   learn, find out, discover
biruahhen   vb., wk. 1,   to trouble oneself to, take pains to; be concerned
biscof   noun, masc. str.,   bishop, priest
biscofheit   noun, masc.-fem. str.,   priest's office
bithiu wanta   conj.,   since, because, for, namely, that
bit(t)en   vb., str. V,   to bid, ask, request

Old High German

blīden   vb. (+reflex.), wk.1 (+gen.),   to rejoice; be happy, joyful
blīdi   adj.,   happy, joyful; friendly
blīdida   noun, fem. str.,   joy, happiness
bouhnen   vb., wk. 1,   to beckon, give a sign, indicate
brennen   vb., wk. 1,   to burn, light
bringan   vb., irreg., wk. 1,   to bring, give
buachāri   noun, masc. str.,   scribe, writer, author
buah (buoh)   noun, masc.-fem.-neut. str.,   book, scripture
burg   noun, fem. str.,   city, town

chēren   vb., wk. 1,   to turn, lead, bring, steer
Christ   noun, masc. str.,   Christ
chrūci   noun, neut. str.,   cross
chunno (kunni)   noun, neut. str.,   line, genus, kind
cuning   (see <u>kuning</u>)

dar   (see <u>thar</u>)
dāraba   adv.,   from there (downwards)
daz   conj.,   that, so that
deota   noun, fem. str.-wk.,   people, folk
der, diu, daʒ   art., dem. pron., rel. pron.,   the; this, that; who, which
   pidiu - therefore, to/for this end, reason
dese   dem. pron.,   this, that
d(h)īn   poss. pron.,   2nd sg., adj.,   your
ding   noun, neut. str.,   judgment, judgment day; meeting; thing, affair
doh   adv., conj.,   however, although, but, nevertheless, in any case
drāto   adv.,   very, completely, exceedingly; quickly
dreso (treso)   noun, masc.-neut. str.,   treasure

droum (troum)   noun, masc. str.,   dream
druhtīn   (see truhtin)
duan   (see tuon)
durft   noun, fem. str.,   need, necessity, interest
duruh   prep. (acc.),   through, by means of, in consequence of

eigan   noun, neut. str.,   possession, property
eigin   adj.,   own, characteristic
ein   card. num., indef. pron., adj.,   one, someone, a certain one
eiscōn (eigiscōn)   vb., wk. 2,   to demand, ask; ascertain, find out, search
Elias   (see Helias)
engil   noun, masc. str.,   angel
enihc (einig)   adj.,   only, any, some(one), own
enti   adv.,   earlier, before
ēo   adv.,   ever, always, continually, now, then
ēr   adv., conj., prep. (dat., instr.),   earlier, once, before, until
er (her)   pers. pron., 3rd sg.,   he
erda   noun, fem. str.-wk.,   earth, ground, land
ēwarto   noun, masc. wk.,   priest
ēwo   noun, masc. wk.,   eternity

fallan   vb., str. VII,   to fall, sink
faran   vb., str. VI,   to go, proceed, travel
fardolēn   vb., wk. 3,   to suffer, bear, endure
farprennen (firbrennen)   vb., wk. 1,   to burn up, set fire to
farsenkan (firsenken)   vb., wk. 1,   to sink, to fall to ruin
farstantan   vb., str. VI,   to understand, grasp, perceive
farswelhan   vb., str. III,   swallow, devour, gulp down
fart   noun, masc.-fem. str.,   travel, journey, course, path, line, track, flight
fasta   noun, fem. str.-wk.,   fasting

Old High German

fater — noun, masc. str., father, abbot
fel — noun, neut. str., skin
ferro — adv., far (away); very
festi, feste — adj., strong, fast, certain
    festi duan - fortify; bring about, cause; confirm, substantiate
    in festī - truly
fījant — noun, masc. str., foe, enemy
filu — noun, indec., adv., much, great; very, very much, completely
fimf — card. num., five
finger — noun, masc. str., finger
finstrī — noun, fem. str., darkness
firiha (firaha) — noun, masc. pl. str., men, mankind
firina — noun, fem. str., sin, crime
firinlīh (uirinlīh) — adj., terrible, horrible
firnemen — vb., str. IV, hear, accept, receive; recognize; understand
firstantan — vb., str. VI, to understand, grasp; recognize, know, think
firwerdan — vb., str. III, to come to grief, go to (rack and) ruin, perish
fleisc(h) — noun, neut. str., flesh, body
folk — noun, masc.-neut. str., folk, crowd, people
fon(a) — prep. (dat.), from
for(a) — prep. (dat.), before, on account of, through, for, about
forasago — noun, masc. wk., prophet
for(h)ta — noun, fem. str.-wk., fear, worry, anxiety, terror, horror, astonishment
for(h)ten — vb., wk. 1, to be afraid, to fear
forna — adv., forward; before, earlier, once
frāgēn — vb., wk. 1, to ask, investigate, question
fram — adv., further, farther; very
fram-gangan — vb., str. VII, to proceed, to go out, to go before
framgigangan — adj., advanced
framhald(e) — adv., forward, down
frawalīcho — adv., with joy, joyfully
frōno — adj., holy, majestic, glorious

fruma   noun, fem. str.,   use, advantage; blessing, safety, blessedness
fuir   noun, neut. str.,   fire
furi   prep. (dat., acc.), adv.,   before, in front of
furimagan   vb., pret.-pres.,   to be able
furisizzan   vb., str. V,   neglect, miss, omit, avoid

Gabriel   prop. noun,   Gabriel
gāhūn   adv.,   suddenly, quickly
gangan   vb., str. VII,   to go, walk, step
gart   noun, masc. str.,   garden; circle; chorus
garwēn   vb., wk. 1,   to prepare, make ready
geba   noun, fem. str.,   gift, grace
geban   vb., str. V,   to give, give up
geist   noun, masc. str.,   Spirit, ghost, breath; heart, soul
geistlich   adj.,   spiritual, religious, sacred
gibāri   adj.,   behaving oneself; well-tempered, well-behaved; of good disposition; right
(gi)beran   vb., str. IV,   to bear, give birth to, bring forth
gibet   noun, neut. str.,   prayer, bidding, request
giburt   noun, fem. str.,   birth; lineage, race; generation, people
gidruaben   (see <u>gitruoben</u>)
giduan   vb., irreg.,   to do, make; create, act; cause, effect, complete, bring about, take place
    anawart giduan - to make known, make aware, reveal to
gieinōn   vb., wk. 2,   to unite, bind, decide, agree
gifeho   noun, masc. wk.,   joy
gift   noun, fem. str.,   gift; suggestion, inspiration
(gi)fullen   vb., wk. 1 (+gen.),   to fill, make full; end, complete
gihalōn   vb., wk. 2,   to get, obtain; summon, invite; bring, give
(gi)hōren   vb., wk. 1,   to hear, to listen to, acknowledge; obey
gikunden   vb., wk. 1,   announce, communicate; show
gilīcho   adv.,   in the same manner, in like manner, similarly

Old High German

gelīh	adj., similar, like, same; with gen. pl. as pron. or adj.: each, every
gilouba	noun, fem. str.-wk., belief
gilouben	vb., wk. 1, to believe, trust in
gimanōn	vb., wk. 2, to remind of, warn, admonish
gināda	noun, fem. str., grace, mercy
ginōzo	noun, masc. wk., companion, comrade, fellow
giordinōn	vb., wk. 2, order, appoint, arrange
(gi)rihten	vb., wk. 1, guide, lead, steer, send
girihtī	noun, fem. str., honesty, uprightness; righteousness
	in girihtī - straightaway, directly; simply, justly
girusti	noun, neut. str., preparation, equipment, armament; position, construction
gisamanōn	vb., wk. 2, to gather, call together; to come together
giscouwōn	vb., wk. 2, to look upon, see; give attention to
gisehan	vb., str. V, to see, look (at), observe
(gi)senten	vb., wk. 1, to send, to bring, to give
gisiht	noun, fem. str., sight; face, countenance; vision
gisizzen	vb., str. V, to sit
gistirri (gestirne)	noun, neut. str., Stars, constellation
githenken	vb., wk. 1 (+gen.), think, consider; to remember; to have in mind; to plan, intend
githingen	vb., wk. 1, to hope (for)
	tharazua githingen - to set one's hope on, put one's hope in, hope (for)
gitruoben (gidruaben)	vb., wk. 1, to confuse, to frighten, disturb, upset
giwaralīcho	adv., carefully, thoroughly
(gi)wenten	vb., wk. 1, to turn (around), move, lead, bring, change
(gi)(h)werban	vb., str. III, to turn, move, change
giwisso	adv., conj., certainly, undoubtedly, truly; but, also, namely, therefore
giwon	adj., used to, accustomed to

giwona	noun, fem. str.-wk., custom, use, order
gizellen	vb., wk. 1, to recount, tell, describe, report
gold	noun, neut. str., gold
gomen	noun, masc. str., man
got (kot)	noun, masc. str., god
gotman	noun, masc. str., theologian, man of God
guat	adj., good, righteous; pious, holy
guot	(see guat)

habēn	vb., wk. 3, to have, hold, own, possess
halingon	adv., secretly, in secret
hant	noun, fem. str., hand, arm; power; realm, scope, range; possession
	anan henti wesan - to be available, at one's disposal, at hand
hapēn	(see haben)
harēn	vb., wk. 3, to cry out (to), call (to)
harto	adv., hard, very, much, vehemently
hauar (aber)	adv., conj., but, however; again, namely
hebīg	adj., important, distinguished, great, powerful
heilag	adj., holy, blessed; pious, devout
heiz	adj., hot, glowing, burning
helfan	vb., str. III, to help, aid, assist
Helias	prop. noun, Elias
hēlig	adj., holy, blessed
hella	noun, fem. str., hell, underworld
heo	(see eo)
her	(see er - pron.)
heri	noun, masc.-neut. str., group, host; mass, throng; number, multitude
Herod	prop. noun, masc. str., Herod
herza	noun, neut. str.-wk., heart
heven	vb., str. VI, to raise, take, set; (+reflex.): rise, arise, to get oneself ready, make ready

Old High German

(h)ēwigo	adj.,	eternal, unending
hiar	adv.,	here
hilfa	noun, fem. str.,	help, aid, protection
himil	noun, masc. str.,	heaven, sky
himilisc	adj.,	heavenly, divine
himilzungal	noun, neut. str.,	stars of heaven; constellation
hinān	adv.,	from here, from now on; therefore
hintarqueman	vb. (+gen.), str. IV/V (past part.),	to be astounded, shocked, frightened (at)
hiowiht	(see iowiht)	
hōren	vb., wk. 1,	to hear; obey, follow
horn	noun, neut. str.,	horn; horn of plenty
houbit	noun, neut. str.,	head, chief, the highest
houpit	(see houbit)	
huckan	vb. (+gen.), wk. 1,	to think, remind oneself of, be aware of; pay attention, recognize
huldi	noun, fem. str.,	grace, favor, friendship
hūs	noun, neut. str.,	house, dwelling; family

iaman	indef. pron.,	somebody, someone
iawiht	indef. pron., adv.,	something, anything; somehow
ih	pers. pron.,	I
īlen	vb. (+gen.), wk.,	hurry; strive, to take pains
imbot	noun, neut. str.,	commandment, order, instruction, assignment
in	adv.,	in, into
in	prep. (+dat., acc., & instr.),	in, into; according to, among
induan (intuon)	vb., irreg.,	to open, uncover, unveil, reveal
ingangan	vb., str. VII,	to go, step in, enter
inprennen (inbrennen)	vb., wk. 1,	to ignite, set fire to; begin to burn
intfāhan	vb., str. VII,	to receive, get; grasp; conceive
inti	conj.,	and
ioh	adv.,	ever, once, always, further, then

(I)Johannis   prop. noun,   John
iolīcho   adv.,   always, continually
ipu   conj.,   if, whether, in the case (event) that; although
ir   pers. pron., 2nd pl.,   you
ir   poss. adj., 2nd pl., 3rd sg. fem., 3rd pl.,   your, her, their
irdwellen (irtwellen)   vb., wk.1,   neglect, omit, leave out
irkennen   vb., wk. 1,   recognize, see, perceive, notice; understand, know
irlesgen   vb., wk. 1,   to extinguish
irrōn   vb., wk. 2,   to wander, go; to be confused, err
     +gen. - to be uncertain of
irsagēn   vb., wk. 3,   to tell, express, report
irsuah(h)en   vb., wk. 1,   to seek, ascertain, inquire
irthuesben (irthwesben)   vb., wk. 1,   to destroy, kill
irzellen   vb., wk. 1,   to tell, recount, describe, report
Israhel   prop. noun, Israel
itiwīz   noun, masc. str.,   shame, reproach
iuwar   poss. pron., 2nd pl., adj.,   your
iz   pers. pron., 3rd sg., neut.,   it
     imo (dat. sg.)

Judeo   noun, masc. wk.,   Jew

kerno   adv.,   gladly, willingly, joyfully
khenfo (kempfo)   noun, masc. wk.,   warrior, soldier
kichunden   (see <u>gikunden</u>)
kifrumen   vb., wk. 1,   to do, make, bring about, cause
kihalōn   (see <u>gihalōn</u>)
kihuct   noun, fem. str.,   thought, mind
kilīh   (see <u>gilīh</u>)
kiluten   vb., wk. 1,   to sound

Old High German

kimarchōn   vb., wk. 2,   to set (a boundary), appoint, establish, ordain
kināda   (see <u>gināda</u>)
kind   noun, neut. str.,   child, offspring, son
kipāgan   vb., str. VII,   to oppose, fight against
kipannan (gibannan)   vb., red. 7,   summon, call
     daz mahal gibannan - call forth, summon, order the final judgment
kipuazan   vb., wk. 1,   to repent of, do penance for
kirahhōn   vb., wk. 2,   to tell, give an account
kirihten   (see <u>girihten</u>)
kisagēn   vb., wk. 3,   to say, tell, announce, make known, report, reveal
kisindi   noun, neut. str.,   people, following (disciples), kin
kispanan   vb. (+gen.), str. VII,   convince, move, urge, persuade
kistān (gistān)   vb., irreg. VII,   to stand, be situated, lie; to remain, stop, stay; rise; begin
kistantan (gistantan)   vb., str. VI,   to stand (fast), stop, place oneself; begin
kistarkan (gesterchen)   vb., wk. 1,   strengthen, make powerful
kitarnan   vb., wk. 1,   to hide
kitragan   vb., str. VI,   to carry, bear
kitriufan   vb., wk. 1,   to drip, fall
kiturran (giturran)   vb., pret.-pres.,   to dare
(ki)wāfanan (giwafanan)   vb., wk. 1,   to arm (with a weapon)
kiwaltan (giwaltan)   vb. (+gen.), str. VII,   to rule over, govern, have power over
kiwerkōn (giwerkōn)   vb., wk. 2,   to act, do, bring about
kiwinnan   vb., str. III,   to win, acquire (for oneself), obtain, reach, receive, get
kōsa   noun, fem. str.,   matter in dispute, cause
kot   (see <u>got</u>)
kreftic (kreftig)   adj.,   strong, powerful, mighty, great
Krist   prop. noun, masc. str.,   Christ, the anointed
kunden   vb., wk. 1,   to make known, reveal, announce, say, tell

kuning   noun, masc. str.,   king, ruler
kuniok (kinuok)   adj., adv.,   enough, adequate, much

ladōn   vb., wk. 2,   to invite, summon, call
lant   noun, neut. str.,   land, region, area
lastar   noun, neut. str.,   blasphemy; sin
lauc   noun, masc. str.,   fire, flame
lāzzan   vb., str. VII,   to leave, allow, let
lazzēn   vb., wk. 1,   to delay, tarry
leid   noun, neut. str.,   sorrow, misfortune, pain
leiten   vb., wk. 1,   to bring, guide, lead
lēo   noun, masc. str.,   grave (mound)
lepen (leben)   vb., wk. 3,   to live, be alive
lid   noun, masc.-fem.-neut. str.,   member, limb; servant
līd   noun, masc.-fem.-neut. str.,   fruit wine, drink
līhhamo   noun, masc. wk.,   body, flesh
likkan (liggen)   vb., str. V,   to lie, be situated, remain
liogan   vb., str. II,   to lie, speak falsely, prevaricate
lioht   noun, neut. str.,   light, brightness
līp   noun, masc.-neut. str.,   life, body; conduct, way of living
list   noun, masc.-fem. str.,   knowledge, craft, skill, art
listīc   adj.,   sly, clever
lōnōn   vb., wk. 2 (+person - dat.; +thing - gen.),   to reward, pay, repay
lossan   vb., wk. 1,   to loose, free, release
loug   (see lauc)
lōz   noun, masc.-neut. str.,   fate, destiny, chance, lot
luft   noun, masc.-fem. str.,   air, sky
luzil   adj.,   small, tiny, little

magadburt   noun, fem. str.,   virgin birth

Old High German

mahal	noun, neut. str., judgment, judgment place; last judgment
mahalstat	noun, fem. str., place of judgment
mahtīg	adj., mighty, powerful, great, majestic
māk (māg)	noun, masc. str., relative, kinsman
man	noun, masc. str., man
man	indef. pron., one, someone
manag	pron., adj., many a, many, innumerable
mancunni	noun, neut. str., mankind, humanity
manilīh	indef. pron., each, every; everyone
māno	noun, masc. wk., moon
mānōd	noun, masc. str., month
marg	noun, neut. str., the marrow of bones
marha	noun, fem. str., border; land, region
māri	adj., known, famous; thoughtworthy, well-regarded
	māri tuon - to make known, reveal
marran	vb., wk. 1, to cause offense; (+acc.) to disturb, injure, damage, hinder; (+dat.) to harm; (+gen.) to keep, prevent from
māsa	noun, fem. wk., scar
megin	noun, neut. str., power, strength; majesty, wonder
meisto	adj., the most, greatest, highest, most important
mendōn	vb., wk. 2, to be happy about, rejoice
menigī	noun, fem. str., crowd, multitude, throng
men(n)isco	noun, masc. wk., man, human being
menniskī	noun, fem. str., human, human form
mēra	adv., more, further, farther, besides
miata	noun, fem. str.-wk., reward, gift; bribe
mih(h)il	adj., great, important, powerful
mīn	poss. pron., 1st sg., my
minna	noun, fem. str., love
mit	prep., with
mittilagart	noun, masc. str., earth, world
molta	noun, fem. str., dust
mord	noun, masc.-neut. str., murder

mugan	vb., pret.-pres.,	to be able, to be possible; to have to
mund	noun, masc. str.,	mouth
muor	noun, neut. str.,	moor
muot	noun, masc.-neut. str.,	soul, heart, feeling; sense, understanding, spirit; passion, inclination, intention
muoter (muater)	noun, fem. str.,	mother
muozzan	vb., pret.-pres.,	to be able to, to be in a position to
muspilli	noun, masc.-neut. str.,	last judgment
myrra	noun, fem. wk.,	myrrh

nāhen	vb. (+refl.), wk. 1,	to draw near, come toward, approach
nals	adv.,	but not, in no way
namo	noun, masc. wk.,	name, designation, word
nemnen	vb., wk. 1,	to name, call, to call by name, to designate
neoman	indef. pron.,	no one, none
nesso	noun, masc. wk.,	worm
ni	conj., neg. participle,	no, not, but not, if not, that ... not, so that ... not
niazen	vb., str. II,	to use; accept, grasp; enjoy
nihein	indef. pron.,	no one
nioman	(see <u>neoman</u>)	
niun	num.,	nine
niuwi	adj.,	new, young
nohhein	(see <u>nihein</u>)	
nōt	noun, masc.-fem. str.,	need, necessity; urge, compulsion, coercion
	zi nōti - urgently	
nu	adv., conj.,	now, even, just; for, since, therefore

ōstana	adv.,	from the east

Old High German

ostar	adv., in the east, towards the east
ouh	conj., adv., also, likewise, besides, furthermore

pāgan (bāgan)	vb., str. VII, to battle, struggle, strive, contend
pald	(see bald)
palden	vb., wk. 3, to take courage, be comforted
palwīc	adj., bad, evil
pan (ban)	noun, masc. str., order, commandment
paradīs	noun, neut. str., paradise
parn	(see barn)
peh	noun, neut. str., hellfire
perg (berg)	noun, masc. str., hill, mountain
pi (bi)	adv., prep. (+gen., dat., acc., instr.), at, on, in to, instead of, for, next to, compared with, during, by means of, for reason of, concerning
pidingan	vb., str. III, to force, compel; conquer, overpower; to bind, make fast
pifallan (bifallan)	vb., red. 7, to fall, collapse
pimīdan	vb., str. I, to avoid, escape
pīna	noun, fem. str.-wk., pain, agony, torment, torture
piqueman	vb., str. IV (past part. 5), to come, come to pass, arrive, occur
piutan (biutan)	vb., str. II, to offer
pluot (bluot)	noun, neut. str., blood
poum (boum)	noun, masc. str., tree, wood
preit (breit)	adj., broad, wide, flat, great; proud
prennen	(see brennen)
pringan	(see bringan)
pū (bū)	noun, masc. str., dwelling, place
puazan	vb., wk. 1, to make better, good; to make amends

quedan   vb., str. V, to speak, say, tell, report, explain, maintain
quek   adj., living, alive
queman   vb., str. IV (past part. 5), to come, arrive, reach, go, follow
quena   noun, fem. str.-wk., woman, wife

rāhha   noun, fem. str., affair, thing, matter; condition, situation; activity; account, reckoning, reason; talk, gossip
rahhōn   vb., wk. 2, to say, tell, express
rātan   vb., str. VII, to advise, counsel
(h)ref   noun, neut. str., womb
reht   adj., righteous, just
reht   noun, neut. str., law, right; duty
rehta   noun, neut. wk., right, justice, law
rehtfestī   noun, fem. str., righteousness, steadfastness
rehtkern   adj., righteous, loving justice
rehto   adv., rightly, justly, truly; really, certainly, very
restī   noun, fem. str., peace, place of rest
rīchi (rīh(h)i)   adj., rich, powerful, high, fortunate
rih(h)i   noun, neut. str., majesty, ruler; authority, control; power; land, world, region; empire, kingdom
rihtunga   noun, fem. str., court
rouh(h)en   vb., wk. 1, to present an offer of incense, to offer incense
ruova   noun, fem. str., number, enumeration

sagēn   vb., wk. 3, to say, tell, speak
sālīg   adj., holy, blessed, happy
saman   adv., together, completely
sār(e)   adv., immediately, right away, quickly, suddenly, soon

Old High German

sārio adv., at once, directly, immediately; then, at all, in general
Satanas noun, masc. str., Satan, devil
scīn adj., obvious, clear, evident, distinct
scīnan vb., str. I, to shine, gleam, glow, stream, light
scōni adj., beautiful, glorious, shining
scōno adv., beautifully, majestically, wonderfully
scrīban vb., str. I, to write
sculan vb., pret.-pres., to be supposed to, to ought to, to have to
sehen vb., str. V, to see, look, glance, view, notice
sēla noun, fem. str.-wk., soul, spirit
selb pron., adj., (him-, her-, it-, etc.) self, the same, the very, this, these
selida noun, fem. str., house, dwelling, haven, refuge
seltsāni noun, neut. str., wonder, sign
seltsāni adj., wonderful, unusual, extraordinary, astonishing
si(a) pers. pron., 3rd sg. fem., she
sīd prep. (+dat., instr.), adv., conj., since, after; later; in consequence of, because
sigalōs adj., without victory, conquered, vanquished
sih refl. pron., 3rd pers., itself, herself, himself; themselves
sīn poss. adj., 3rd sg. masc.-neut., his, its
sīn vb., anom., to be, exist
sind (see sinth)
singan vb., str. III, to sing, praise, intone, speak, announce
sinth (sind) noun, masc. str., way, path, direction
  bī, in, zi themo sinde - thereby, in this way; at that time
siu (sie) pers. pron., 3rd pl., they
siuh adj., sick, ailing, ill
slāfen vb., str. VII, to sleep, fall asleep
sliumo adv., quickly, immediately; as soon as
sō adv., conj., so, thus, in this way
sō daz conj., so that
sorga noun, fem. str.-wk., worry, trouble, consternation
sorgēn vb., wk. 1, (sorgon - wk. 2), to worry, be troubled

sprehhan   vb., str. IV,   to speak, talk, say, express
stān   vb., anom.,   to stand, find oneself, remain, stop, to lie
stantan   vb., str.VI,   to stand, stand fast, stop; remain, be situated; to place, place oneself; rise, begin
stēn (stein)   noun, masc. str.,   stone, rock
sterro (sterno)   noun, masc. wk.,   star, constellation
strāza   noun, fem. str.,   street, path, way; course
strītan   vb., str. I,   to fight, contend, strive
stūatago   noun, masc. wk.,   day of judgment
stūēn   vb., wk. 3,   to atone, make amends for, do penance
stum   adj.,   dumb, speechless
suah(h)an   vb., wk. 1,   to seek, look for; ask for
suanāri   noun, masc. str.,   judge
suannen (suonnan)   vb., wk. 1,   to judge, pass judgment on
sum   pron., adj.,   a certain, another; some
sunna   noun, fem. wk.,   sun
suntīg   adj.,   sinful, guilty, godless
sunu   noun, masc. str.,   son
suona   noun, fem. str.,   atonement, reconciliation; judgment
sus   adv.,   thus, so, in this way
swīgēn (suigen)   vb., wk. 3,   to be silent, to be dumb
swilizōn   vb., wk. 2,   to burn up

tag   noun, masc. str.,   day, time
tāt   noun, fem. str.,   deed, action
teikin (zeihan)   noun, neut. str.,   sign, token; wonder; picture; constellation
tempel   noun, neut. str.,   temple
thanān   adv., conj.,   from there, thence; from then; therefore
than(n)e   adv.,   then, at that time, in this case
thar (dar)   adv., conj.,   there, here; then, at that time, in that case; when, while, where; who, which
   dar pi - there; thereby

Old High German

tharzua   adv.,   besides, in addition to; on it, in it
       tharazua githingen - to put hope in, hope for
t(h)az   conj.,   that, so that; since, because
thenken   vb., wk. 1,   to think, ponder; imagine; intend; notice, pay attention to
ther, thiu, thaz   article, dem. pron., rel. pron.,   the; this, that; who, which
       mit thiu - therefore; because
these   dem. pron.,   this, that
thiggen   vb., wk. 1,   to ask for, beg for, implore, entreaty
thīn   poss. pron., 2nd sg., adj.,   your
thingōn   vb., wk. 2,   to speak; negotiate, deliberate; hold court
thō   adv.,   when, as; then, lo
tho(h)   adv., conj.,   yet, still; although, but, inspite of, in any case
thū   pers. pron., 2nd sg.,   you
thunken   vb., wk. 1,   to seem, appear; think, believe, opine
thurfan   vb., pret.-pres.,   to need, to ought to, to be necessary
thuruhtīg   adj.,   prepared
thuruhwonēn   vb., wk. 3,   to remain
tiwal   noun, masc.-neut. str.,   devil, evil spirit
tōd   noun, masc. str.,   death
tohter   noun, fem. str.-wk.,   daughter
tōt (dōt)   adj.,   dead
       tōt werdan - to die
tougilen   vb., wk. 1,   to hide
touwen   vb., wk. 1,   to die
trinkan   vb., str. III,   to drink
truhti(i)n (druhtīn)   noun, masc. str.,   Lord, ruler
tulli   noun, neut. str.,   arrow, point of an arrow
tuon (don, duan)   vb., anom.,   to do, make, effect, bring about, deal (with)
       māri tuon - to make known, reveal
       in feste duan - to fortify, bring about, cause; confirm

IF NOT UNDER " U " SEE " F "

uazza	noun, fem. str.,	burden, weight, encumbrance
ubar	prep. (+dat., acc., instr.),	above, over, about, upon
ubil	noun, neut. str.,	evil, misdeed, sin
ūf	adv.,	upwards, up
umbi	prep. (+acc.), adv.,	around, from
unberenti (um)	adj.,	barren, unfruitful
ungerno	adv.,	ungladly, unwillingly
ungiloubfol	adj.,	unbelieving
unkust	noun, fem. str.,	falseness, evil, sin
untar	prep. (+dat., acc., instr.),	under, beneath; between, among
unz	conj., prep. (+dat., acc.), adv.,	until, while, as long as; up to now
unzan	prep. (+dat., acc.), adv., conj.,	until; how long; as long as; during
uppīg	adj.,	empty, idle, vain, meaningless
urmāri	adj.,	famous, renown, well-known
ūzgangan	vb., str. VII,	to go out
ūz(z)an	prep. (+gen., dat., acc.), adv.,	except for, outside of, without; if not, but, but rather
ūzze, ūze	adv.,	outside

wāhi	adj.,	fine, glorious, grand, splendid, extraordinary
(h)wanān	adv.,	whence, wherefore, where, how
wānen	vb., wk. 1,	to mean, intend, think, believe; hope (for); suppose
wankōn	vb., wk. 2,	to sway, reel; wander, stray; turn from
wanta	adv., conj.,	why, wherefore; for, because, since, namely, that, after
wār	adj.,	true, just, right

in wāra - truly, verily

Old High German

wār — adv., conj., where; somewhere; when
wār — noun, neut. str., truth, that which is true
wāra — noun, fem. str., truth
warch (warg) — noun, masc. str., the foe, the evil one
wārheit — noun, fem. str., truth, righteousness
warlīhho — adv., truly, verily, justly
wartēn — vb., wk. 3 (+gen., dat.), to see, look at, observe; follow
wartil — noun, masc. str., guard, warden; watcher, observer; informer, spy
wasal — noun, neut. str., earth
waz — inter. pron., what, what kind of
wē — interjection, woe
wechen — vb., wk. 1, to awaken, arouse
weder — inter. pron., conj., who, what, which (of two); if, whether
weg — noun, masc. str., way, street, path
wehsal — noun, masc.-neut. str., change, transformation, section, part, branch; course, office
welīh — inter. & indef. pron., who, which, what kind of; someone; each, every
wellen (wollen) — vb., anom., to want to, wish, desire; intend
wēneg — adj., unhappy, miserable, poor
werdan — vb., str. III, to become, to come to pass, happen, to take place, to grow
    tōt werdan - to die
werkōn — vb., wk. 2, to effect, bring about; work, do, complete, prepare, accomplish
werolt — (see worolt)
weroltrehtwīso — noun, masc. wk., one knowledgeable (experienced) in the law(s) of the world
wīcstat — noun, fem. str., place of battle
wie (wio) — adv., conj., how, in what way
wīg (wīc) — noun, masc.-neut. str., fight, battle, war

wī(h)rouh   noun, masc.-neut. str.,   incense
wīhrouhbrunst   noun, fem. str.,   incense offering
wiht   indef. pron.,   anything, something; (+neg.) nothing
willo   noun, masc. wk.,   will, wish, desire; intention, resolution
    mit willen - gladly, readily
wīn   noun, masc. str.,   wine
wir   pers. pron., 1st pl.,   we
wīs   adj.,   wise, knowing, knowledgeable
wīsan   vb., str. I,   to avoid
wīsōn   vb., wk. 2,   to seek, visit; plague, haunt, infest
wissan   vb., wk. 1,   to invite, summon, call
wīstuom   noun, masc.-neut. str.,   wisdom, insight, knowledge, understaning
wīzi   noun, neut. str.,   punishment, suffering; hell
wiz(z)an   vb., pret.-pres.,   to know, recognize, understand, experience
worolt (werolt)   noun, fem. str.,   time, age, eternity; world, earth
wort   noun, neut. str.,   word, speech, report
wunt   adj.,   wounded, injured
wuntar   noun, neut. str.,   wonder, astonishment; sign
wuntarlīch   adj.,   wonderful, extraordinary, astonishing
wuntorōn (wunt[e]ren)   vb., wk. 2,   to wonder, to be astonished, to marvel

yrscīnan   vb., str. I,   to appear, shine, be revealed

Zacharias   proper noun,   Zacharias
zeichan   noun, neut. str.,   sign, picture, image; wonder; constellation, sign of the Zodiac
zeigōn   vb., wk. 2,   to show, point out, indicate

Old High German

zeinōn   vb., wk. 2,   to show, point out, indicate
zellen   vb., wk. 1,   to count; tell, say, report, make known
zēn (zehan)   card. num.,   ten
zeso   noun, neut. str.,   the right, right side
zi   prep. (+dat., acc., instr.), adv.,   to, toward, until, on, at
zīt   noun, fem.-neut. str.,   time, period, age, era; season; hour

Old English Glossary

abbudisse   noun, fem. wk.,   abbess
ac   conj.,   but
æfest   adj.,   devout, pious
æfeste   adv.,   devoutedly, piously
æfestniss   noun, fem. str.,   devotion, religion
æfre   adv.,   ever, always
æfter   prep. (dat.),   after; according to; in the course of
ælmihtig   adj.,   almighty, all-powerful
ænig   adj., pron.,   any; anyone
ǣr   adv.,   ere, before, sooner, earlier, first, heretofore,
   formerly, already, some time ago, lately, just now, till, until
ǣrest   adv. (superl. of ǣr),   first, earliest
ǣrest(e)   adj. (superl. of ǣr),   first, earliest
æt   prep. (dat.),   at, in, by, to
ætsomne   adv.,   at once, together, likewise, also
āgifan   vb., str. V,   to give (back), return
āhrēowan   (see hreowan)
aldor   noun, neut. str.,   life
ān   adv.,   alone
and-   (see ond-)
andswaru   noun, fem. str.,   answer
ānforlǣtan   vb., str. VII,   to give up, forsake, relinquish
apostol   noun, masc. str.,   apostle
ārfæstniss   noun, fem. str.,   honor-firmness, piety, virtue
ārīsan   vb., str. I,   to arise, get up
āsingan   vb., str. III,   to sing
ātēon   vb., str. II,   to draw, lead out (away)
aweccan   vb., wk. 1,   to arouse, awake

bar	adj.,	bare, naked
batwa	adj.,	both, we two
be	prep. (dat.),	at, by; about, concerning; according to
bearn	noun, neut. str.,	child
bebēodan	vb., str. II,	to command, order, assign; offer
bedroren	past part. of bedreosan,	deceived, deluded, bereaved, deprived
beforan	prep. (dat., acc.),	before
bēgen	adj., pron.,	both
belimpan	vb., str. III,	to concern, regard, pertain to
bēon (wesan)	vb., anom.,	to be
beorht	adj.,	bright, light, clear, lucid
betst(a)	adj. (superl. of god),	best
betȳnan	vb., wk. 1,	to shut, close
bĭ	(see be)	
bīdan	vb., str. I,	to await, bide, wait, expect
biddan	vb., str. V,	to ask, pray, beseech, entreat
biter	adj.,	bitter, sharp, horrid
blīcan	vb., str. I,	to shine, glitter, dazzle, amaze
bliss	noun, fem. str.,	joy, happiness, bliss
bōcere	noun, masc. str.,	scribe, writer, author
booc (boc)	noun, fem. str.,	book
brēost	noun, masc.-fem.-neut. str.,	breast, mind
bringan	vb., wk. 1,	to bring, carry, bear
brōðor	noun, masc. str.,	brother
būtū (batwa)	adj.,	both, we two

canon	noun, masc. str.,	sacred canon
ceald	adj.,	cold
clǣne	adj.,	clear, pure
clyppan	vb., wk. 1,	to embrace, clasp
cræft	noun, masc. str.,	craft, art, skill; strength, power; ability, faculty

Old English

cuman	vb., str. IV, to come, happen
cunnan	vb., pret.-pres., to know (how)
cweðan	vb., str. V, to speak, say
cyme	noun, masc. str., coming; advent
cȳðan	vb., wk. 1, to make known, reveal

dǣd	noun, fem. str., deed, action
dæg	noun, masc. str., day
dēofol	noun, masc. str., devil
dēop	adj., deep
dōm	noun, masc. str., doom, judgment; praise, glory; power
dōn	vb., anom., to do, make
drihten	noun, masc. str., lord; God, Christ

ēac	adv., also, likewise
ēage	noun, neut. wk., eye
eal(l)	adj., all, every
ealdormon	noun, masc. str., alderman
ēastan	adv., easternly, from the east
ēaðmōdlīce	adv., humbly
ēce	adj., eternal, everlasting
efne	adv., even, just (as); precisely, exactly
eft	adv., again, afterwards; back
ege	noun, masc. str., fear
ellenwōdniss	noun, fem. str., ardor, zeal
ende	noun, masc. str., end
endebyrdness	noun, fem. str., order, turn
Engliscgereord	noun, neut. str., English language
eodorcan	vb., wk. 1, to chew, masticate, ruminate
eorðe	noun, fem. wk., earth

fæc	noun, neut. str.,	space, interval of time
fæger	adj.,	fair, lovely
fæste	adv.,	fast, firmly
faran	vb., str. VI,	to go, proceed, march, travel, depart
feallan	vb., str. VII,	to fall
fers	noun, neut. str.,	verse, sentence
fīras	noun, masc. str. (pl.),	men, mankind
firen	noun, fem. str.,	sin, crime, transgression
flōd	noun, neut. str.,	flood, deluge; river
folc	noun, neut. str.,	folk, people
folde	noun, fem. wk.,	earth, land
for	prep. (dat., acc.),	for, because of
forbrecan	vb., str. IV,	to break in two, break, bruise
forgeatan	vb., str. VII,	to expose, forget
forgifan	vb., str. V,	to give, grant
forhogdniss	noun, fem. str.,	contempt, disdain
forlǣran	vb., wk. 1,	to mislearn, deceive, seduce
forlǣtan	vb., str. VII,	to leave, abandon, let go
forst	noun, masc. str.,	frost
forð	adv.,	forth, away; forwards; henceforth
forþon	conj., adv.,	therefore; for, because, for the reason that
forwyrcan	vb., wk. 1,	to miswork, forfeit, lose
frēa	noun, masc. wk.,	lord; God
fremsumness	noun, fem. str.,	mercy, kindness
from	prep. (dat.),	from
fruma	noun, masc. wk.,	beginning, origin
frumsceaft	noun, fem. str.,	first Creation, beginning
fyrhtu	noun, fem. str.,	fright, terror
fyrnum	adv.,	with horror, horribly, intensely

gān	vb., anom.,	to go
gāst	noun, masc. str.,	soul, spirit; breath

    Hālig Gāst - Holy Spirit

Old English

gebed	noun, neut. str., prayer, supplication; command
gebēorscip	noun, masc. str., feast
gecēosan	vb., str. II, to choose, elect; determine, decide
gedafenian	vb., wk. 2 (usually dat.), to be becoming or fit; behoove
gedēman	vb., wk. 1, to deem, judge
geendian	vb., wk. 2, to end, complete, finish
gefultumian	vb., wk. 2, to help, assist, give aid
geglengan	vb., wk. 1, to adorn, embellish
gehātland	noun, neut. str., promised land
gehwā, gehwæt	pron. (+part. gen.), each, every
gehwilc	adj., pron., each, every (one), all; whoever, whatever
gehwyrfan	vb., wk. 1, to change, turn, convert
gehȳran	vb., wk. 1, to hear
gehȳrness	noun, fem. str., hearing, report
gelǣdan	vb., wk. 1, to lead, bring, conduct
gelǣran	vb., wk. 1, to teach, educate, instruct
geleornian	vb., wk. 2, to learn, inquire
gelīc	adj., like
gelīce	adv., in like manner, similarly, likewise
gelimplīc	adj., fit, suitable
gelȳfed	adj., advanced, weakened
gemǣran	vb., wk. 1, to celebrate, glorify
gemearcian	vb., wk. 2, to describe, appoint, determine
gemet	noun, neut. str., measure, manner
gemynd	noun, fem. str., mind, memory; thought
gemyndgian	vb., wk. 2, to remember, be mindful of
geornfulness	noun, fem. str., eagerness, zeal, diligence
geornlīce	adv., earnestly, zealously, diligently
gerisenlīce	adv., fittingly, suitably
gerœd	(see rǣdan)
gesceap	noun, neut. str., creation; fate
gesceapu	noun, neut. str., beauty, form; commands, precepts, destinies
gesēon	vb., str. (contr.), to see, look at, observe

gesettan   vb., wk. 1,   to set, place, occupy; establish
gesomnian   vb., wk. 2,   to assemble, collect
gesomnung   noun, fem. str.,   congregation, church
gesweorc   noun, neut. str.,   cloud, mist, smoke
getæl   noun, neut. str.,   reckoning, estimation; number, series
getenge   adj.,   heavy, grievous, troublesome
geþēodan   vb., wk. 1,   to join, unite
geþēodniss   noun, fem. str.,   joining, association
geweorc   noun, masc. str.,   work, creation
geweorðian   vb., wk. 2,   to honor, dignify
gewīsian   vb., wk. 2,   to instruct, inform, direct, command
gewītan   vb., str. I,   to go, depart; come
gewrit   noun, neut. str.,   something written, writ; a book
gewunian   vb., wk. 2,   to be accustomed, to be wont to
gewyrcan (gewyrcean)   vb., wk. 1,   to form, make,
                         construct, prepare; create
gīeman   vb., wk. 1, (+gen.),   to care for, regard, seek
gif   conj.,   if
gīfre   adj.,   greedy, covetous, voracious, anxious, desirous
gifu   noun, fem. str.,   gift, grace
gnornian   vb., wk. 2,   to grieve, murmur, groan, lament
gōd   adj.,   good
gōd   noun, neut. str.,   good (thing); possession
god   noun, masc. str.,   god, deity
godcund   adj.,   of the nature of god, divine
godcundlīce   adv.,   divinely, from heaven
grǣdig   adj.,   greedy, covetous
grēne   adj.,   green, flourishing
grētan   vb., wk. 1,   to greet, address
grimman   vb., wk. 1,   to rage
grund   noun, masc. str.,   ground, earth, the deep, abyss

habban   vb., wk. 3,   to have, hold

Old English

hægel, hagol	noun, masc. str.,	hail
hālettan	vb., wk. 1,	to greet
hālig	adj.,	holy, divine, blessed
hām	adv.,	home, homeward
hāt	adj.,	hot, fervent
hātan	vb., str. VII,	to command, order; name, call
hē, hēo, hit	pers. pron., 3rd sg.,	he, she, it
hearm	noun, masc. str.,	harm, hurt, damage, calamity
hearmscearu	noun, fem. str.,	vengeance, punishment
hearpe	noun, fem. wk.,	harp
hearra	noun, masc. wk.,	lord, master, leader
hefon	(see heofon)	
hell	noun, fem. str.,	hell; grave, tomb
hēo	pers. pron., 3rd sg. fem.,	she
hēo	pers. pron., 3rd pl.,	they
heofon	noun, masc. str.,	heaven
heofonlīc	adj.,	from heaven, heavenly
heofonrīce	noun, neut. str.,	kingdom of heaven
heonane	adv.,	hence, from here
heord	noun, fem. str.,	herd, flock
heorte	noun, fem. wk.,	heart
hēr	adv.,	here, now, at this time
hereness	noun, fem. str.,	praise
herigean	vb., wk. 2,	to praise, honor, glorify
herra	(see hearra)	
hete	noun, masc. str.,	hate, hatred, indignation
hider	adv.,	hither, to this place
hīeran	vb., wk. 1,	to hear; obey
hit	pers. pron., 3rd sg. neut.,	it
hlēo	noun, fem. str.,	shade, shelter; refuge
holt	noun, masc. str.,	wood, grove
hrēowan	vb., str. II,	to rue, repent, regret; impers. (+dat.): to grieve, distress
hrēowig	adj.,	penitent
hrōf	noun, masc. str.,	roof; sky

hū adv., conj., how, in what manner
hunger noun, masc. str., hunger, famine
hūs noun, neut. str., house, dwelling, abode
hwā, hwæt pron. (inter.), who, what, which
hwæt interj., lo, behold
hwæthwugu pron., something, somewhat, a little
hwæð(e)re adv., conj., yet, however, nevertheless
hweorfan vb., str. III, to turn, go away, depart, wander
hwīlum adv., sometime, awhile, for a time, once, now
hwonan adv., whence, from where
hwylc adj., pron., which, what
hyge noun, masc. str., mind
hyldo noun, fem. str., affection, favor, fidelity

ic pers. pron., 1st sg., I
īdel adj., idle, empty, vain
ides noun, fem. str., female, woman
ilca pron., adj., same
in prep. (dat., acc.), in, into, to
inbryrdniss noun, fem. str., in-breathing, inspiration
ingong noun, masc. str., entrance, entry
innan adv., prep., within, inwardly; in, into
intinga noun, masc. wk., cause, occasion

lǣran vb., wk. 1, to advise, teach, exhort
land (lond) noun, neut. str., land, country, region
lār noun, fem. str., lore, learning
lārēow noun, masc. str., teacher, master
lēaf noun, neut. str., leaf
lēasung noun, fem. str., lying, vain speech, false witness, hypocrisy

Old English

lēoht   noun, neut. str.,   light; time
leomu   (see lim)
leornere   noun, masc. str.,   learner, scholar
leornian   vb., wk. 2,   to learn, study
lēoð   noun, neut. str.,   song, poem
lēoðcræft   noun, masc. str.,   song-craft, art of poetry
lēoðsong   noun, masc. str.,   poetic song, poem-song
libban   vb., wk. 3,   to live
līchoma   noun, masc. wk.,   body
līf   noun, neut. str.,   life
līg   noun, masc. str.,   flame
lim   noun, neut. str.,   limb
lið   noun, masc.-neut. str.,   limb, member, joint
lond (land)   noun, neut. str.,   land, country, region
lufe   noun, fem. wk.,   love
lufigean   vb., wk. 2,   to love

mǣlan   vb., wk. 1,   to say, speak, converse
mǣst   adj. (superl. of micel),   most, greatest
magan   vb., pret.-pres.,   to be able, (can, may)
māndǣd   noun, fem. str.,   evil deed, crime
meaht   noun, fem. str.,   might, power
mearcian   vb., wk. 2,   to mark, point or mark out, describe; to assign, appoint, determine
medmicel   adj.,   not great, moderate, small
menniscness   noun, fem. str.,   human nature; incarnation
meotod   noun, masc. str.,   the measurer (god)
merestream   noun, masc. str.,   stream of the ocean, sea, ocean
mete   noun, masc. str.,   meat, food
micel   adj.,   great, much, many
mid   prep. (dat.),   with, by; amid, among
middangeard   noun, masc. str.,   earth, world

mihtig   adj., mighty, powerful, able
mīn   poss. adj., mine, my
mōd   noun, neut. str., mind, heart; will
mōdgeþanc   noun, masc. str., mind, counsel
mon (man)   noun, masc. str., man
moncynn   noun, neut. str., mankind, the human race
monian   vb., wk. 2, to admonish, warn, exhort
monig (manig)   adj., many
morgen   noun, masc. str., morning
mōtan   vb., pret.-pres., to be permitted
mūð   noun, masc. str., mouth; door, gate
munuchād   noun, masc. str., monkhood
mynster   noun, neut. str., religious house, monastery

nāht   (see nōht)
næfre   adv., never
nænig   adj., pron., not any, none; no one
nalæs   adv., not, not at all
nĕ   adv., conj., not; nor
neaht   noun, fem. str., night
nēalēcan   vb., wk. 1, (+dat.), to approach, draw near to
nēat   noun, neut. str., neat, ox, cow
nemnan   vb., wk. 1, to call, address (by name)
nēten   noun, neut. str., animal
niod   noun, fem. str., need, necessity
nō   adv., not
nōht, nāht   noun, neut. str., nothing
noma   noun, masc. wk., name
norðan   adv., northernly, from the north
nū   adv., now

Old English

o (see <u>on</u>)
of prep. (dat.),   from, of, out of
oft adv.,   often
on prep. (dat., acc.),   in, on, among, at; in, into, on, onto, upon; against, towards
onbærnan vb., wk. 1,   to enkindle, light; inspire
ond conj.,   and
ondswarian vb., wk. 2,   to answer, respond
ondweard adj.,   present, in attendance
onfōn vb., str. VII,   to receive, take; undertake, begin
Ongelþēod noun, fem. str.,   English people (nation)
ongemang adv.,   mixed in, among
onginnan vb., str. III,   to begin, attempt, endeavor
onslǣpan vb., wk. 1,   to fall asleep, sleep
onstellan vb., wk. 1,   to institute, create
onsundran adv.,   assunder, apart
ōr noun, neut. str.,   origin, beginning
orsorg adj.,   without care, secure, prosperous
oð prep. (acc.), conj.,   to, up to, until
ōðer adj.,   other, another; something else; next
oððe conj.,   or

rǣdan vb., str. VII,   to advise, counsel, persuade; consult, discuss, deliberate, plot, design; decree, decide; rule, guide, have control over, possess; provide for, bring, deliver, bring about
reccan vb., wk. 1,   to tell, speak of, reckon; care about
regollec adj.,   regular, in accordance with monastic rule
rest noun, fem. str.,   rest, quiet; resting place
rīce noun, neut. str.,   realm, kingdom, dominion

sǣ	noun, masc.-fem., (often indeclin., but sǣs, sǣwe), sea
sceatt	noun, masc. str., money, price, gain; treasure
sciene	adj., shining, clear, neat, fair, beautiful
scieppan	vb., str. VI, to create, shape, form
scīnan	vb., str., I, to shine, glitter, appear
scipen	noun, fem. str., cattle-stall
scomu	noun, fem. str., shame, confusion
scopgereord	noun, neut. str., language of poetry, poetic speech
sculan	vb., pret.-pres., to have to, to be supposed to, to be obliged to
scūr	noun, masc. str., shower
scūrsceadu	noun, fem. str., protection against storms; umbrella; storm shade
scyppend	noun, masc. str., creator
sē, sēo, þæt	dem. adj., def. art., pron., rel. pron. (often +rel. part. -þe-), that, the, that one; those, he, she, it, they; who, which, that; he, who, whoever
secgan	vb., wk. 3, to say, tell
self	(see sylf)
singan	vb., str. III, to sing, recite, chant
sīð	noun, masc. str., path, way; journey; moving, departing; time, occasion; part, lot, fortune, adversity
sittan	vb., str. V, to sit; remain, dwell
slǣp	noun, masc. str., sleep
slǣpan	vb., wk. 1, to sleep
slītan	vb., str. I, to slit, tear, bite, break through
sniomor	adv. (comp. of sneome), more readily
sōna	adv., soon, forthwith
song	noun, masc. str., song, poetry
songcræft	noun, masc. str., song-craft, art of writing poetry
sorgian	vb., wk. 2, to sorrow, grieve, to be anxious, solicitous
spell	noun, neut. str., story, discourse

Old English

sprecan — vb., str. V, to speak, say, talk to
stæf — noun, masc. str., staff, written character, letter
stǣr — noun, neut. str., history
standen — vb., str. VI, to stand; remain
sum — indef. pron., adj., (a certain) one; some
sunne — noun, fem. wk., sun
suðan — adv., southernly, from the south
swā — adv., conj., so, in such manner, thus; as, as if
    swā hwæt swā - whatsoever
    swā þæt(te) - so that
sweart — adj., black, swarthy, gloomy
swefen — noun, neut. str., sleep, dream
swelce — conj., adv., likewise; as if; like, as
    swelce ēac - likewise also
swēte — adj., sweet
swētniss — noun, fem. str., sweetness
swinsung — noun, fem. str., harmony, melody
swīþe — adv., very
sylf (self) — pron., adj., self
symbel — noun, neut. str., banquet, feast
syndriglīce — adv., specially, particularly
synn — noun, fem. str., sin, guilt, crime

tēon — vb., wk. 3, to create, make
tīd — noun, fem. str., time, period of time
tintreglīc — adj., torturing, hell-tormenting
tō — prep. (dat.), to, for, at
tōgan — vb., anom., to go (to), depart, go away
tōgeþēodan — vb., wk. 1, to join
tōweard — adj., approaching, impending
tunge — noun, fem. wk., tongue
tūngerēfa — noun, masc. wk., town reeve, steward
tweogan — vb., wk. 3, to doubt

þā   adv., conj.,   then, after that; when
      þā ... þā - then when, when ... then
þǣr   adv., conj.,   there, where; where, there where
þæs   adv.,   of this, for this, so far, so much so, thus, since, that, whereby, whereof, so
þæt   conj.,   that, so that, in order that; for, because
      swā þæt(te) - so that
þafian   vb., wk. 2,   to consent to, agree with
þanc   noun, masc. str.,   will, mind, thought, favor, the acknowledgment of a favor
þe   rel. pron. part., indecl.,   who, which, that
þēah   adv., conj.,   though, although, yet, still, however
þeccan   vb., wk. 1,   to cover, conceal
þegnscipe   noun, masc. str.,   service, valor
þēoden   noun, masc. str.,   people's ruler, king, chief, lord
þēodscipe   noun, masc. str.,   fellowship, association
þēow   noun, masc. str.,   servant
þēs, þēos, þis   dem. adj., pron.,   this
þīn   poss. adj.,   thy, thine, your
þonne   adv., conj.,   then; when, than
þrōwung   noun, fem. str.,   suffering, passion
þū   pers. pron., 2nd sg.,   you
þurh   prep. (acc.),   through, by means of, because
þurst   noun, masc. str.,   thirst
þus   adv.,   thus, so

uncer   adj.,   our two
underþēodan   vb., wk. 1,   to subject to, subjugate, reduce
unwered   adj.,   unprotected
ūp   adv.,   up
ūpāstīgness   noun, fem. str.,   ascension

Old English

ūt   adv., out
ūtgong   noun, masc. str., exodus, going out
uton   word of exhortation (+infin.), let us

wadan   vb., str. VI, to wade, go, proceed
wǣd   noun, fem. str., garment, clothing, apparel
wǣdo   (see wēd)
waldend   noun, masc. str., ruler, governor, lord
warian   vb., wk. 2, to beware, guard, ward off
wē   pers. pron., 1st pl., we
weald   noun, masc. str., forest, wood
weard   noun, masc. str., guardian, lord
wēd   noun, fem. str., garment, clothing
wel   adv., well, fully
weorc   noun, neut. str., work, deed, act
weorðan   vb., str. III, to become, to come, to come to pass
weoruldhād   noun, masc. str., worldly condition, secular life
werian   vb., wk. 2, to wear, put on, bear; fortify, protect, defend
westan   adv., westernly, from the west
wielm   noun, masc. str., boiling; fervor, zeal
wīf   noun, neut. str., woman, female
wiht   (see wuht)
willa   noun, masc. wk., will, mind, wish, disposition
willan   vb., pret.-pres. (anom.), to be willing, wish, desire
wind   noun, masc. str., wind
wine   noun, masc. str., friend, disciple, one beloved, dear, darling
wīse   noun, fem. wk., manner, way, custom
wit   pers. pron., dual, we two
wītan   vb., wk. 1, to blame, reproach, ascribe to
wīte   noun, neut., str., punishment, torture, torment, harm

wið	prep. (dat., acc.), against
wið þām þe	- when, at the time when
wliteg	adj., fair, beautiful, pure, shining, splendid
wǣdo	(see wed)
word	noun, neut. str., word, speech
woruld	noun, fem. str., world
woruldhād	(see weoruldhād)
wrāðmōd	adj., wrath in mind or mood, angry
wrītan	vb., str. I, to write
wuht (wiht)	pron., aught, anything
wuldorfæder	noun, masc. str., father of glory
wundor	noun, neut. str., wonder, glory
wylm	noun, masc. str., surge, stream; fervor
wynsum	adj., winsome, pleasant
wyrcan	vb., wk. 1, to form, make, prepare; create
wyrs	adv. (comp. of yfele), worse
wyrðe	adj., worthy

yfel	noun, neut. str., evil
yldu	noun, fem. str., age

Linguistic Technical Terms

abduction   A type of reasoning whereby the minor premise is derived from the major premise and the conclusion of a syllogism; an educated guess, an analogy.

ablaut   Vowel gradation. The meaningful systematic variation of vowels in the same or related roots or affixes, caused by the Indo-European accent system; apophony.

action of vocal folds   Vibration or nonvibration, yielding voiced and voiceless sounds, respectively.

acute   Distinctive feature used to treat variations in place of articulation. Opposite feature is *grave*. Acute sounds are those involving a medial articulation and a concentration of energy in higher frequencies.

affricate   In phonetic terminology, a sound articulated as a stop with a sharp homorganic fricative release. The duration of the friction is usually shorter than it would be for an independent fricative sound, e.g., English *ch-* in *chin*, *g-* in *gin*; German *pf-* as in *Pferd*, *z-* as in *zu*.

alliteration   The repetition of a sound or similar sound, usually word initially, in a close chain of words.

allophone   Phonetic, nondistinctive variants of the same phoneme.

alveolar consonant   Consonant articulated by the approach of the tongue toward the alveolar ridge.

amplitude   The furthest point reached in the sound vibration; yields loudness of sound.

analogy   Process by which a linguistic unit is abduced as similar or like another linguistic unit; linguistic iconism.

analytic   A type of language using structural criteria and using words and particles rather than inflectional endings to show syntactic relationships. The term stands in opposition to synthetic languages, where words usually consist of more than one morpheme.

anaphoric   A word which refers to a word already said or written in the text or discourse.

anaphoric pronouns   Pronouns referring back to some previously expressed unit of meaning.

anomalous   Antiparadigmatic.

apocope   Loss or deliberate omission of the last letter, syllable or part of a word.

apophonic   Cf. ablaut.

archigraph   Abstraction subsuming graphic dialect variation and free variation.

argument   In predicate calculus a nominal referring to a person, place, or thing which is part of the proposition.

argument constituent   In nonlinear syntax, the nominal together with its modifications (article, adjective, pronoun, quantifier, intensifier, clause).

Technical Terms

aspect A category of the verb indicating how an action or state is implemented, cf. perfective, imperfective; part of the modality constituent.

aspirated Audible puff of air which may accompany articulation of plosive consonants.

assimilation Total or partial absorption of a linguistic feature.

back vowel Vowel produced by the bunching of the tongue in the vicinity of the velum.

bahuvrihi A compound in which the constituents reciprocally complement one another; exocentric.

bilabial Impedance of the breath stream by the lips in the production of a consonant.

binary feature Basis of classification of linguistic units in phonology, as well as in grammatical and semantic analyses of lexical items. Utilizes mutual exclusion, e.g., the presence of absence of lip-rounding in the articulation of a sound.

biunique Cf. biuniqueness, isomorphic.

biuniqueness Phonological principle which states that any sequence of phonemes will be represented by a unique sequence of phones, e.g., phonemic /d+i+n/ will be phonetically [d+I+n]. This correlation does not always hold true, e.g., in cases of overlap. Cf. isomorphism, iconism.

bond Morphological, syntactic and/or semantic agreement between two of more grammatical structures; cf. concord, governance.

bound morpheme   A morpheme which cannot occur on its own as a separate word, usually prefixes or suffixes, e.g., inflectional endings.

case   Syntactic-semantic interaction or bond between predicator and argument.

close vowel   Vowel produced with the tongue bunched in the highest position possible without producing audible friction. Can also be used as a relative term to neighbouring vowel in continuum, e.g., close *e*, *bait*:open *e*, *bet*; cf. open.

coda   The phonological segment following the syllable nucleus.

compact   Articulatorily, sounds involving a constriction toward the front of the mouth; acoustically, sounds involving a concentration of formants in a central part of the sound spectrum.

complementary distribution   Occurrence of phonetically different phones in mutally exclusive phonetic environments. Sounds which are in complementary distribution are allophones of a phoneme, e.g., Eng. [p^h] and [p^-] are allophones of the phoneme /p/.

concord   Grammatical, inflectional agreement between predicator and subject argument.

consonant   Speech sound articulated with the whole or partial blockage of the breath stream enroute to emission through the mouth and/or nose.

constative   A proposition describing an event or state of affairs which reacts to truth value.

Technical Terms

content level   A term referring to the content or meaning plane of language as distinct from the expression plane or level. In word classification, those words which have a stateable lexical meaning (content words) as opposed to those relatively few words (function words) whose role it is to express grammatical relationships.

continuant   Speech sound in which the breath stream is not totally occluded but continues through the vocal tract and out of the mouth and/or nose.

contrastive distribution   Occurrence of two phones in similar phonetic environment with a resultant change in meaning.

copula(tive)   An equative verb, e.g., 'is,' 'become,' or the semantic feature equative.

deep structure   A term used in contrast to surface structure, with reference to the abstract syntactic representation of a sentence. An underlying level of structural organization specifying the factors which govern the manner of interpreting a sentence.

deictic   A term referring to features of language directly related to the personal, temporal, or locational characteristics of the context within which an utterance takes place, and whose meaning is therefore relative to that context.

deictic pronouns   A term used to refer to pronouns which refer to personal, temporal or locational characteristics of the situation in which the utterance takes place, whose meaning is therefore relative to that situation. All pronouns, specifically demonstrative pronouns.

dental Consonant produced with the tip of the tongue against the upper front teeth.

dependency (grammar) A formal grammar which establishes types of dependencies between the elements of a construction. Used as a means of explaining grammatical relationships. Dependency trees whose interconnections specify structural relations are used to represent syntactic structure.

dependent A term referring to a modifier constituent in a compound.

derivation In morphology a term used to refer to one of the two main processes of word formation, the other being inflection. Derivation results basically in a new word; inflection results in a different form of the same word. Derivational affixes may change the grammatical category of the word to which they are attached; inflectional affixes do not cause a change of category.

desinence An inflectional suffix.

determiner Used to refer to a class of words which co-occur with nouns to express semantic contrasts, e.g., quantity or number. Articles, *each/ every, this/that, some/any* are major sets of determiners in English.

diachronic grammar Data within at least two different time frames.

diachronic synchrony Synchronic variation studied as non-static.

dialect A variety of a language defined by a set of characterizing isoglosses.

diathesis   Grammatical binary category active:passive.

diatopic   Geographic distribution.

diffuse   Articulatorily, sounds involving a constriction toward the back of the mouth; acoustically, sounds involving a concentration of formants in noncentral parts of the sound spectrum.

directive   A command; an utterance intended to get other people to do something for the speaker.

discourse   In-text physical language data.

distinctive feature   A minimal contrastive difference, i.e., signalling a semantic difference in any component of the grammar which is discrete in the system is a distinctive feature.

drift   Refers to a consistent diachronic change in the pattern of a language, resulting in the breaking up into dialects because of specific linguistic tendencies.

dual   The grammatical number denoting *two*, which is used by many languages in addition to the singular and plural.

dvandva   A copulative compound; constituents united by *and*.

endocentric   A construction with a center which dominates constituents within its immediate syntagm.

embedded clause   The sentence included/inserted in another sentence.

epenthesis   An intrusive or inserted vowel or consonant sound medially in a word.

equative Indentity relationship.

essive A grammatical case which semantically indicates a state of being.

exocentric A construction without a center; one part does not dominate the other part linguistically.

expression level Level of linguistic organization of substance, physical lingutistic material, i.e., phonology and graphemics and their grammatical occurrence.

factive clause A clause, the truth of which is presupposed by the speaker.

final devoicing Change of a voiced to a voiceless stop or fricative consonant in voiceless contexts.

finite verb form Verb form inflected for person, number, tense, mood, aspect.

fit Division of a poem or a song, e.g., in the OS *Heliand*.

flat Distinctive feature used to describe lip-rounding. The opposite feature is *plain*. Sounds with a relatively narrow mouth opening and accompanied by velarization.

formant Concentration of acoustic energy of vertical bands of energy which reflects the vibration of air in the vocal tract as it changes shape.

free morpheme Any morpheme which can be used as an independent word, i.e., which has a distinct meaning of its own when used alone.

free variation   The occurrence of sounds which are substitutable for one another in a given environment with no resulting change in the meaning of a word, e.g., the *t* in *net* may be articulated with aspirated release or without this nondistinctive feature.

frequency   Number of sound waves produced per second by the vibration of the vocal cords.

fricative   A consonant articulated by a narrowing of the air passages, thus producing an audible friction as the air is expelled from the lungs.

front vowel   A vowel in which the point of articulation is in the front part of the oral cavity.

functional load   The amount of work done by a linguistic unit or item.

fundamental identifying form (FIF)   The basic lexical form of a word.

geminate   A double consonant or vowel.

generalization   A linguistic observation applicable to a wide range of data.

genetically, genetic grammar   Data viewed from Indo-European or Germanic origin.

gerund   Inflected infinitive, has the function of a substantive and at the same time shows the verbal features of tense, voice, and capacity to take adverbial modifiers and to govern objects.

glide A transitional sound produced by the shifting of the vocal organs from the articulation of one sound to the articulation of another sound.

glottal consonant A sound made in the larynx, resulting from the closure or narrowing of the glottis, which is the opening between the vocal cords.

governance The bond between nonsubject arguments and predicator.

government The case requirement by a predicator.

grammatical change Voiced:voiceless consonant alternation (genetically understood as Verner's law).

grave Distinctive feature used for variations in the place of articulation. Its opposite is *acute*. Grave sounds involve a peripheral place of articulation in the sound tract with a concentration of acoustic energy in the lower frequencies.

half-close vowel A vowel sound in which the tongue height is described as occupying an intermediate position on a range from close to open (close, half-close, half-open, and open).

haplology Syllabic dissimilation; omission of one of two similar sounds or groups of sounds or syllables.

head Lexical category around which a phrase is built.

heavy syllable A syllable is heavy if it contains a $\bar{V}$ or a $\check{V}$ followed by two consonants, the last of which may be the onset of the next syllable.

heteroclitic Inclusion of a nominal in more than one stem or gender set.

homophonous   Two forms which sound alike, but differ in meaning.

homorganic semivowel   A semivowel which has the same place of articulation as a contiguous phone.

hortative   In some languages a distinct mood used to express an exhortation, encouragement, or suggestion. Sometimes applied to imperative or subjunctive mood when used in such sentences.

hw-word   A question word such as *hwē* 'who', *hwat* 'what', *hwilīk* 'which'.

iconic/iconism   Factually similar in structure, cf. analogy, assimilation.

imperative   The verbal mood used in the expression of commands.

indicative   The verbal mood used in the expression of factual statements or questions.

infinitive   The fundamental identifying form for verb in lexicon; nonfinite form of the verb.

Ingvaeonic   Subdivision of the West Germanic branch of the Germanic group of languages. It consists of Old English, Old Saxon, Old Frisian.

inorganic   Refers in linguistics to a sound or letter which is lacking etymological justification, e.g., the *t* in English **oncet*.

intensity   Acoustic feature measured in decibels; in speech it is based on the size of the vibrations of the vocal cords. Corresponds somewhat to the auditory phonetic feature *loudness*.

interdental consonant   A consonant sound made with the tip of the tongue between the teeth, as in English /þ/ and /ð/, *thorn, this*.

interference   Influence of one language or dialect on another.

isogloss   A linguistic feature spatially and temporally peculiar to a language or a dialect, or to sets of languages or dialects.

isomorphic   A one to one form:meaning correspondence; cf. biunique, iconic.

juncture   The way in which the sounds of a language are joined together; phonetic boundary features in morphemes, words, clauses.

karmadharaya   A compound in which the dependent constituent describes the head constituent; endocentric.

kenning   A metaphorical compound word or phrase used particularly in Old English, Old Norse and Old Saxon poetry, e.g., *swan-road* for *ocean*.

labial consonant   Consonants produced with the involvement of the lips in the articulation.

labiodental   A consonant produced with the lower lip touching the upper teeth.

Technical Terms

labiovelar A consonant pronounced with the lips rounded and the back part of the tongue arched toward the soft palate (velum).

larynx A valve regulating the flow of air in the respiratory mechanism; housing for the vocal cords, which may be caused to vibrate during speech production, resulting in speech sounds with *voice.*

lateral consonant A consonant pronounced with complete closure in the front of the oral cavity but with incomplete closure at the sides (Lat. *latus*), permitting the air to escape.

lax vowel Distinctive feature used to deal with variations in the manner of articulation; lax sounds are produced with less muscular movement and effort and are relatively short and indistinct compared to tense sounds.

lexical category The natural classes into which the words of a language are divided according to their formation, nature, or functions, viz., nouns, pronouns, adjectives, numerals, verbs, adverbs, prepositions.

lexical meaning The meaning of a word as a dictionary item, in paradigm; the FIF or core meaning.

light syllable A syllable is light if it contains $\breve{V}(C)$.

linear syntax Word order within a sentence; sentence order within discourse; cf. macro- and micro(structure).

liquid consonant A term used to refer to all of the apico-alveolar sounds of the types [l] and [r].

long vowel   Length and shortness refer to the duration of articulation and usually are considered structural characteristics of the syllable as a whole.

low tongue height   Position of tongue-body below the level which it assumes in neutral position. As a distinctive feature, used to deal with variations in place of articulation; its opposite is nonlow.

macro(structure)   Cross-sentential; the domain of larger discourse or text in linear syntax. In nonlinear syntax, the domain of the phrase structures with subcategorization rules.

manner of articulation   Descriptive factor used for the physical articulation of consonants. Concentrates on the degree and type of obstruction of the air stream in the production of consonants.

marked   Not the neutral or most general feature.

matrix clause   The sentence within which another sentence is embedded.

megadialect   A sibling language of a Proto language, e.g., Old High German or Old English or Old Saxon or Old Frisian belonging to Proto-West Germanic.

medial voicing   Voicing of fricative consonants in voiced surrounds.

mellow   Distinctive feature used to deal with variations in place of articulation; opposite is *strident*.

metathesis (metathesize)   The transposition of the order of sounds within a word or between two words, e.g., English *aks* for *ask*; Latin *periculum* becomes Spanish *peligro*.

micro(structure)   Confined or delimited to an immediate structured string of word(s) yielding a complete thought in linear syntax. In nonlinear syntax the morphology.

mid-tongue height   Phonetic classification of vertical tongue movement in vowel sounds, along with high and low. Vowels made in the middle area of articulation.

minimal pair   A discovery procedure, also known as the commutation test, used to determine which sounds belong to the same class (phoneme). A method of establishing the phonemic inventory of a language. A pair of words in which a meaning distinction is effected by a minimal feature difference, e.g., *pin* vs. *bin*.

modal auxiliary   Verbs expressing modalities, e.g., permission, necessity, possibility (in genetic grammar, preterite-present verbs).

modality constituent   In nonlinear syntax, modifications on the verb (tense, mood, aspect, polarity, diathesis).

monophthongization   A compound phone changing to a simplex phone, i.e., one vowel quality.

mood   Category of the verb expressing speaker attitude toward the predicator, e.g., definiteness, indefiniteness, directivity as expressed morphologically by indicative, subjunctive, imperative, respectively.

morpheme   The smallest meaningful linguistic unit.

morphology   That component of grammar which studies the paradigmatic (derivational) and syntagmatic (inflectional) composition of all parts of a word.

morphophonemic alternation   The meaningful alternation of a phoneme within a morpheme.

mutually exclusive environment   Distribution of phones in such a manner that the occurrence in one environment dictates that the phones will not occur in the other environment.

narrative   The propositional and modal content of a text.

nasal   In phonetic terminology a sound produced with the velum lowered, allowing the air to escape through the nose.

natural class A set of segments for which fewer features are needed to specify the set as a whole than to specify any one member of the set.

neutralization   Suspension of distinguishing linguistic feature(s); cf. syncretism.

noise   Technical term in acoustic phonetics for nonperiodic vibrations represented by consonants.

nominal   Noun or noun-like grammatical category.

nondistinctive   Feature which is irrelevant in that it does not affect meaning.

nonfinite verb form   Verb form uninflected for tense, mood, or person.

Technical Terms

nonlinear syntax   Includes predicate constituent, modality constituent, and argument constituent; morphology. Cf. macro- and micro(structure).

number   The binary opposition singular:plural; in OS personal pronouns a ternary opposition: singular:plural:dual.

oblique cases   All inflectional cases but the nominative.

obstruent   Phonetic term referring to sounds that involve a constriction which impedes the passage of the breath stream through nose or mouth. In phonology it designates the opposition to sonorant.

onset   The phonological segment preceding the syllable nucleus.

open vowel   Refers to a vowel articulated with the tongue in the lowest possible position in the mouth. Part of the classification of vertical tongue movement in vowel sounds, the other members being 'close,' 'half-close,' and 'half-open.'

orthographic lag   Failure of the written language to keep pace with phonological changes in a language.

palate (palatal)   The roof of the mouth from the alveolar ridge to the uvula. Usually divided into the hard palate, the immobile bony area immediately behind the alveolar ridge, and the soft palate, or velum, the mobile fleshy part of the mouth from the hard palate to the uvula. Sounds articulated in the area of the hard palate are called palatal sounds; sounds articulated in the area of the velum are either velar or uvular sounds.

palatalization   The articulatory fronting of a speech sound; the front of the tongue contacts the hard palate.

paradigm   A set of linguistic units which have certain features in common, but which differ distinctively, e.g., an inflectional, conjugational, derivational paradigm.

patient   A term used to refer to the person, place or thing affected by the action of the verb.

performative   A proposition which per se is an action and which is neutral to truth value.

pharynx   Tubular cavity of the throat from the larynx upward. 'Pharyngeal' sounds are sounds made in the pharynx. Articulatory phonetics divides the pharynx into the oral pharynx and the nasal pharynx.

phoneme   A class of similar speech sounds which comprise a minimal bundle of relevant sound features. A minimum unit of distinctive sound feature.

phonological rule   A formal statement of the correspondence between phonological elements. Predictive rules which express a hypothesis about the relationship between sounds which reflect the native speaker's competence.

phonology   That component of grammar which studies sounds and their tactics.

phonotactics   In phonology, the specific arrangements of sounds or phonemes which occur in a language. Sequential constraints which may be stated in terms of phonotactic rules.

phrase structure   The semantic-syntactic configuration of a word with other words and, in turn, phrases in a sentence.

Technical Terms

plain Distinctive feature used to treat variations in manner of articulation. Refers to sounds articulated with a relatively wide mouth opening and a relatively strong high-frequency component of the sound spectrum. Opposite is *flat*.

polarity Grammatical category expressing positive or negative; part of modality constituent.

polysemous A set of closely related semantic features; having several, often quite different, meanings, all derived from the basic idea or concept.

pragmatics That superordinate component of grammar which studies speaker/hearer strategies as evidenced in the other components of the grammar.

predicate A potential predicator.

predicate calculus System expressing logical structure of a simple proposition.

predicate constituent In nonlinear syntax, the verb and its simple (case) or complex (sentential) components.

predicator In predicate calculus, word or words of varying grammatical categories (verb, noun, adjective, preposition) which ascribe to one or more arguments some property as an action or a state; cf. relation.

productive A term used with reference to the use made by a language of a specific feature or pattern. The pattern is productive when repeatedly used by the language to produce further instances of the same type, e.g., the past tense affix *-ed* in English.

proposition   Meaningful utterance consisting of a predicator or relation and one or more arguments.

prosodic phonology   Cf. suprasegmental.

quality   As used in phonology and auditory phonetics the characteristic resonance or timbre of a sound.

recursive   A rule or rules which are capable of repeated application in the generation of a sentence; also used in reference to the structures so generated.

register   The variety of language defined according to its use in social situations, e.g., formal English.

relation   Integral part of a proposition; cf. predicator.

resonance chamber   Cavities in the vocal tract, especially mouth, nose and pharynx which act to strengthen frequencies present in the source of sound, thereby producing the range of human sounds.

resonant   A sound that is both a vowel and a consonant, typically r, l, m, n, ŋ.

rewrite   A rule or statement of the type x —> y whereby x, the input, becomes y, the output.

root   Part of a word that contains the lexical meaning.

root shape   (C)V(C) that composes the root syllable.

rounding (rounded)   In phonetics, the visual appearance of the lips when they assume a rounded shape as opposed to a stretched position in the articulation of sounds.

Rückumlaut   Lack of mutation or umlaut; unmutation.

sandhi   Elision, phonetic conjunction.

scale of sonority   Proposed ranking of consonant or vowel sounds according to the degree of openness in the vocal tract through which the air travels and the vibration or nonvibration of the vocal cords during phonation.

schwa   Term usually given to the neutral vowel sound found in weakly stressed syllables, e.g., in the English word *amaze*.

secondary umlaut   The umlauting of those instances in which primary umlaut had been inhibited, e.g., before consonant + h, r, l, *mahtig*.

segmental phonology   Analysis of speech into articulatory/acoustic features which characterize an individual sound.

semantics   That component of grammar which studies grammatical, lexical and discourse meaning.

semivowel   A sound that is neither totally a vowel nor totally a consonant, typically *j, w*.

sentence   A grammatically structured string of one or more words yielding a complete thought.

servitude   Grammatical congruence of subconstituent with head constituent in a phrase, e.g., an adjective is in servitude to a noun in a NP.

short vowel   Length and shortness refer to the duration of articulation and usually are considered structural characteristics of the syllable as a whole.

sibilant Phonetic descriptor used to describe the manner of articulation of fricative consonants in which a narrow groove between the blade of the tongue and the back of the alveolar ridge produces a high-frequency hissing sound.

simplex consonant A single consonant.

sound spectograph Electronic instrument capable of visually displaying the acoustic properties of speech sounds: frequency, time, and amplitude. Properties are displayed on a spectogram or sonogram.

sound wave Longitudinal pressure waves which may or may not constitute audible sound. Specifically, waves in the air produced by the vibration resulting from various parts of the articulatory tract as they shape the respiratory air.

speech act An utterance defined from the point of view of the communicative dynamics between speaker action and listener reaction.

spread lips Phonetic reference to the appearance of lips when they are held fairly close together and stretched sideways. Contrasted with neutral, open, and rounded lip positions.

stem formant Noninflectional vowel/consonant joined to the root of a word.

stem A word root plus an affix other than inflectional suffix.

stop consonant Phonetic classification based on manner of articulation; refers to any sound produced with a complete closure in the vocal tract.

Technical Terms

stress Relative prominence given by the amount of energy in the production of a syllable in a word, or a word in a sentence.

strident Distinctive feature which deals with variations in the sibilance (= hiss-likeness) of a sound. Articulatorily those sounds marked by a constriction which is relatively complex; acoustically, those sounds marked by relatively high frequency and intensity. Opposite is mellow.

strong verb A verb which does not form its preterite by dental suffix.

subcategorization rules Selection restrictions; rules that bond predicators with arguments, expressed in the inflectional morphology.

subjunctive The verbal mood indicating that the action or state denoted by the verb is regarded as hypothetical or subject to another action or state.

substantive Cf. nominal.

superstratum The language of a culturally, economically, politically dominant nation, or of a military conqueror, introduced into a foreign national or geographical territory and affecting or even supplanting the native language, often labelled the substratum. Adstrata refers to coexisting strata without a value judgment.

suppletive Different roots, but shared meaning.

suprasegmental phonology Analysis of features such as pitch, stress, juncture of sound, but in particular of more than one sound thus words, phrases and the sentence; cf. prosodic phonology.

syllable nucleus   The central segment of the syllable; used in conjunction with the *coda* = closing segment of a syllable, and *onset* = the opening segment of a syllable.

synchronic grammar   Data studied within one time frame, i.e., as static.

syncope   Loss of a sound medially in a word.

syncretism   The merger of linguistic units through such linguistic causes as rule changes and their underlying causes, including analogy; cf. neutralization.

syntagm   A narrative chain in which linguistic units interrelate.

syntax   That component of grammar which studies the relationship of words to one another in syntagm (nonlinear syntax) and the order of words relative to one another in the sentence (linear syntax).

synthetic   A type of language in which words typically contain more than one morpheme and these morphemes are used for indicating syntactic relationships, e.g., inflecting languages, where inflectional suffixes are used.

system   Network of patterned relationships constituting the organization of language. For example, the language system is comprised of the phonological, grammatical and semantic systems; the phonological system comprises the segmental and suprasegmental systems.

systematic phonemes   Distinctive sounds which serve as input to phonological rules deriving the allophonic variation in terms of systematic phones.

Technical Terms

tatpurusha A determinative compound in which the dependent constituent is affected by the head constituent; endocentric.

tense Grammatical category of the verb expressing present and nonpresent time frames within which a state or action occurs. Phonetic descriptor referring to the muscular tension involved in the production of a speech sound. As a distinctive feature it is used to deal with manner of articulation; articulatorily the sounds produced display a relatively strong muscular effort; acoustically the sounds so labelled show a relatively strong spread of acoustic energy.

text The amalgamation of the physical (discourse) and the abstract (narrative) components of language data.

thematic vowel Cf. stem formant

tongue Organ of articulation most involved in the production of speech sounds. Usually described in terms of tip(apex), blade(front), center(top), back(dorsum), and root.

tongue height Relative bunching of the tongue toward the roof of the mouth in the articulation of speech sounds. Usually divided into three descriptors: high, mid, and low.

tongue position The configuration of the highly mobile articulatory organ in the production of a speech sound.

trill Phonetic classification of consonant sounds referring to sounds made by the rapid tapping of one organ of articulation against another. French and German are languages which have a uvular trill [R]. Friction may accompany the trill, and reference is then made to a fricative trill.

umlaut   Vowel of root syllable regressively mutated by vowel of following weakly stressed syllable.

universal principle   A language principle valid at all times and in all places.

unmarked   The neutral or most general feature.

unreleased   Phonetic term used to describe the non-movement of speech organs from the position of articulation to that of rest. Opposite is released. Used particularly in reference to the plosive consonants; e.g., English plosives may be released with or without aspiration.

uvular   Phonetic classification of a consonant on the basis of place of articulation. Contact by the back of the tongue and the uvula, e.g., French or German uvular *R*.

valence   Degree or number of actual or potential arguments of a given predicator.

velar   Phonetic classification of consonant sounds based on place of articulation. Contact or constriction effected by back of tongue against the soft palate or velum; e.g., Eng. [k], [g], [ŋ].

Verner's Law   The Germanic reflexes of IE *p *t *k *ph *th *kh *s are voiced in the coda of a nonprimary stressed syllable; cf. grammatical change.

vibration   In phonetics the interposition of some vibratile organ in the path of the moving air stream. Most commonly used for this purpose are the vocal cords, the uvula, the front and tip of the tongue, and the lips.

Technical Terms

vocal cords Also called vocal lips or bands. Folds in the ligament-covered inner wall of the larynx. These folds can be drawn together or apart by muscular contraction. When drawn together along the entire line of the folds, the vocal cords can be set in vibration, i.e., into a steady repetition of opening and closing movements. Together with the stream of expiratory air, these periodic vibrations produce a glottal tone or voice.

vocal tract The air passage above the larynx, which can be shaped into affecting the quality of speech sounds. Usually divided into the nasal tract, the air passage above the soft palate within the nose, and the oral tract, the mouth and pharyngeal areas. In more general usage the vocal tract is applied to the vocal organs and includes all the features of the respiratory tract involved in the production of sounds, i.e., lungs, trachea and larynx.

voice A term used in the phonetic classification of speech sounds; refers to the auditory result of the periodic vibration of the vocal cords during the production of speech sounds. Sounds so produced are called voiced sounds; sounds produced without the periodic vibration of the vocal cords are called voiceless or unvoiced sounds.

voiced consonant A consonant sound produced while the vocal cords are vibrating.

vowel Speech sound characterized by an open articulation, a lack of a complete, partial, or intermittent blockage of the supraglottal air passage through the pharynx and mouth.

weak verb A verb which forms its preterite by dental suffix.

West Germanic A branch of the Germanic group of the Indo-European family of languages, consisting of the Anglo-Frisian (Anglo-Saxon, its modern descendant, English, and Frisian), the German, and the Dutch (including Flemish) languages, with their numerous dialects and variants.

zero inflection The significant noninflection of a word.

Selected Bibliography

Behaghel, Otto. 1932. *Deutsche Syntax.* vol. IV. Heidelberg: Winter.
Behaghel, Otto. 1965. *Heliand und Genesis.* 8. ed. rev. by Walter Mitzka. Tübingen: Niemeyer.
Behaghel, Otto. 1984. *Heliand und Genesis.* 9. ed. rev. by Burkhard Taeger. Tübingen: Niemeyer.
Belkin, Johanna and Jürgen Meier. 1975. *Bibiographie zu Otfrid von Weissenburg und zur altsächsischen Bibeldichtung (Heliand und Genesis).* Berlin: Ernst Schmidt.
Berr, Samuel. 1971. *An Etymological Glossary to the Old Saxon Heliand* (= European University Papers I/33). Bern/Frankfurt: Lang.
Besch, Werner, Oskar Reichmann, and Stefan Sonderegger (ed.) 1985. *Sprachgeschichte: Ein Handbuch zur Geschichte der deutschen Sprache und ihrer Erforschung,* II, 2. Berlin: Walter de Gruyter.
Bischoff, Bernhard. 1979. Die Schriftheimat der Münchener Heliand-Handschrift. *Beiträge zur Geschichte der deutschen Sprache und Literatur* (Tübingen) 101: 161-170.
Bischoff, Bernhard. 1979. Die Straubinger Fragmente einer Heliand-Handschrift. *Beiträge zur Geschichte der deutschen Sprache und Literatur* (Tübingen) 101: 171-180.
Brewda, Lee A. 1981 *A Semantically-Based Verb Valence Analysis of Old Saxon.* Unpubl. diss. Princeton University.
Carr, Charles T. 1939. *Nominal Compounds in Germanic* (= St. Andrew's University Publications XLI). London: Milford.
Cordes, Gerhard. 1973. *Altniederdeutsches Elementarbuch.* Heidelberg: Carl Winter.
Cordes, Gerhard. 1980. 65. Altniederdeutsch. *Lexikon der germanistischen Linguistik,* 2. ed. by H. P. Althaus, H. Henne, H. E. Wiegand, 576-580. Tübingen: Niemeyer.

Cordes, Gerhard. 1985. 88. Morphologie des Altniederdeutschen (Altsächsischen). *Sprachgeschichte: Ein Handbuch zur Geschichte der deutschen Sprache und ihrer Erforschung*, II, 2, ed. by W. Besch, O. Reichmann, S. Sonderegger, 1079-1083. Berlin: Walter de Gruyter.

Drögereit, Richard. 1950. *Werden und der Heliand: Studien zur Kulturgeschichte der Abtei Werden und zur Herkunft des Heliand* (= *Essener Beiträge* 66). Essen: Fredebeul & Koenen.

Drögereit, Richard. 1970. War der Dichter des Heliand ein Friese? *Flecht op 'e koai* (= *Fryske Akademy* 382), ed. by T. Hoekema et al. 11-17. Grins: Wolters-Noordhoff.

Eichhoff, Jürgen and Irmengard Rauch. 1973. *Der Heliand* (= *Wege der Forschung*, CCCXXI). Darmstadt: Wissenschaftliche Buchgesellschaft.

Einhard 830/1960. *The Life of Charlemagne*, trans. by S. E. Turner. Ann Arbor: University of Michigan Press.

fon Wearinga, Juw. 1986. The Heliand and Bernlef. *Michigan Germanic Studies* XII: 21-31.

Gallée, Johan H. 1910. *Altsächsische Grammatik*. 2. ed. rev. Halle: Niemeyer.

Hannemann, Kurt. 1939/1972. Die Lösung des Rätsels der Herkunft der Heliandpraefatio. *Der Heliand* (= *Wege der Forschung* CCCXXI), ed. by J. Eichhoff and I. Rauch, 1-13. Darmstadt: Wissenschaftliche Buchgesellschaft.

Hartig, Joachim. 1985. 86. Soziokulturelle Voraussetzungen und Sprachraum des Altniederdeutschen (Altsächsischen). *Sprachgeschichte: Ein Handbuch zur Geschichte der deutschen Sprache und ihrer Erforschung*, II. 2, ed. by W. Besch, O, Reichmann, S. Sonderegger, 1069-1074. Berlin: Walter de Gruyter.

Haubrichs, Wolfgang. 1966/1973. Die Praefatio des Heliand. *Der Heliand* (=*Wege der Forschung* CCCXXI), ed. by J. Eichhoff and I. Rauch, 400-435. Darmstadt: Wissenschaftliche Buchgesellschaft.

Heyne, Moritz. 1983. *Kleine altsächsische und altniederfränkische Grammatik*. Paderborn: Ferdinand Schöningh.

Selected Bibliography

Holthausen, Ferdinand. 1921. *Altsächsisches Elementarbuch*. 2. ed. rev. Heidelberg: Carl Winter.
Ilkow, Peter. 1968. *Die Nominalkomposita der altsächsischen Bibeldichtung. Ein semantisch-kulturgeschichtliches Glossar*. Göttingen: Vandenhoeck & Ruprecht.
Jacobson, Roman, C. Gunnar M. Fant, and Morris Halle. 1952. *Preliminaries to Speech Analysis*. Cambridge, MA: MIT Press.
Jesperson, Otto. 1926. *Lehrbuch der Phonetik*. Leipzig: Teubner.
Juntune, Thomas W. 1969. *Comparative syntax of the verb phrase in Old High German and Old Saxon*. Unpubl. diss. Princeton University.
Klein, Thomas. 1977. *Studien zur Wechselbeziehung zwischen altsächsischem und althochdeutschem Schreibwesen und ihrer sprach- und kulturgeschichtlichen Bedeutung* (= Göppinger Arbeiten zur Germanistik 205). Göppingen: Alfred Kümmerle Verlag.
Klein, Thomas. 1985. 87. Phonetik und Phonologie, Graphetik und Graphemik des Altniederdeutschen (Altsächsischen). *Sprachgeschichte. Ein Handbuch zur Geschichte der deutschen Sprache und ihrer Erforschung*, II. 2, ed. by W. Besch, O. Reichmann, S. Sonderegger. 1074-1078. Berlin: Walter de Gruyter.
König, Werner. 1978. *dtv-Atlas zur deutschen Sprache*. Munich: Deutsches Taschenbuch Verlag.
Krogmann, Willy. 1948/1973. Die Praefatio in librum antiquum lingua Saxonica conscriptum. *Der Heliand* (= *Wege der Forschung* CCCXXI), ed. by J. Eichhoff and I. Rauch, 20-53. Darmstadt: Wissenschaftliche Buchgesellschaft.
Lasch, Agathe. 1979. Palatales *k* im Altniederdeutschen. *Agathe Lasch: Ausgewählte Schriften zur niederdeutschen Philologie*, ed. by R. Peters and T. Sodmann, 104-217. Neumünster: Karl Wachholtz.
Lehmann, Winfred P. 1956. *The Development of Germanic Verse Form*. Austin: University of Texas Press.
Lussky, Geoge F. 1921. *Die mit dem Partizip des Präteritums umschriebenen Tempora im Altsächsischen*. Leipzig: Borna.

Lyons, John. 1977. *Semantics* I, II. Cambridge: Cambridge University Press.
Magoun, F. P. Jr.1948. The *Praefatio* and *Versus* associated with some Old Saxon Biblical Poems. *Medieval Studies in Honor of J. D. M. Ford*, ed. by U. T. Holmes, Jr. & A. J. Denomy, 107-136. Cambridge, MA: Harvard Univ. Press.
Murphy, G. Ronald. 1989. *The Saxon Savior: The Germanic Transformation of the Gospel in the Ninth-Century Heliand.* New York: Oxford University Press.
Page, Carl Richard. 1952. *The Phonological System of the Old Saxon Language.* Unpubl. MA Thesis, Cornell University.
Penzl, Herbert. 1972. *Methoden der germanischen Linguistik.* Tübingen: Niemeyer.
Purdy, Karen K. 1986. *The Special Dative in the Old Saxon Heliand and Genesis.* Unpubl. diss. University of Pennsylvania.
Rankin, J. W. 1910. A Study of the Kennings in Anglo-Saxon Poetry. *Journal of English and Germanic Philology* 9: 49-84.
Rathofer, Johannes. 1962. *Der Heliand: Theologischer Sinn als tektonische Form. Vorbereitung und Grundlegung der Interpretation.* (= *Niederdeutsche Studien* 9) Cologne: Bohlau.
Rauch, Irmengard. 1968. The *Heliand* Versus 5-7 Again. *Folia Linguistica* 2: 39-47.
Rauch, Irmengard. 1970/1973. 'Heliand' *i* -Umlaut Evidence for the Original Dialect Position of Old Saxon. *Der Heliand* (= *Wege der Forschung* CCCXXI), ed. by J. Eichhoff and I. Rauch, 461-470. Darmstadt: Wissenschaftliche Buchgesellschaft.
Rauch, Irmengard. 1973. Old High German Vocalic Clusters. *Issues in Linguistics: Papers in Honor of Henry and Renée Kahane*, ed. by B. B. Kachru et al, 775-779. Urbana, IL: University of Illinois Press.
Rauch, Irmengard. 1975. What Can Generative Grammar Do for Etymology?: An Old Saxon Hapax. *Semasia: Beiträge zur germanisch-romanischen Sprachforschung* 2: 249-260.
Rauch, Irmengard. 1980. Between Linguistics and Semiotics: Paralanguage. *The Signifying Animal: The Grammar of*

Language and Experience , ed. by I. Rauch & G. F. Carr, 284-289. Bloomington: Indiana University Press.
Rauch, Irmengard. 1981 a. Inversion, Adjectival Participle, and Narrative Effect in Old Saxon. *Jahrbuch des Vereins für niederdeutsche Sprachforschung* 104: 22-30.
Rauch, Irmengard. 1981 b. Semiotics in Search of Method; Narrativity. *Semiotica* 34: 167-176.
Rauch, Irmengard. 1983a. Evolution of a Semantic Set: Text, Discourse, Narrative. In *Language Change,* ed. by I. Rauch & G. F. Carr, 28-38. Bloomington: Indiana University Press.
Rauch, Irmengard. 1983b. On the Modality of the Article. *Monatshefte* 75: 156-162.
Rauch, Irmengard. 1985. 90. Syntax des Altniederdeutschen (Altsächsischen). *Sprachgeschichte: Ein Handbuch zur Geschichte der deutschen Sprache und ihrer Erforschung*, II. 2, ed. by W. Besch, O Reichmann, S. Sonderegger. 1089-1093. Berlin: Walter de Gruyter.
Rauch, Irmengard. 1986. Review of *Der Heliand. Studienausgabe in Auswahl* by Burkhard Taeger. *Colloquia Germanica* 19: 330-332.
Rauch, Irmengard. 1987. Old Saxon *hell*, Drawl and Silence. *Althochdeusch*, ed. by H. Kolb, K. Matzel, K. Starkmann, 1145-1151. Heidelberg: Carl Winter.
Rauch, Irmengard. 1988. The Saussurean Axes Subverted. *dispositio* XI: 35-44.
Rauch, Irmengard. 1990. Evidence of Language Change. *Research Guide for Language Change* , ed. by E. Polomé, 37-70. Berlin: Mouton de Gruyter.
Rauch, Irmengard. 1991. Early New High German *e*- Plural. *Beiträge zur Geschichte der deutschen Sprache und Literatur* 113: 367-383.
Rauch, Irmengard. 1992. Another Old English-Old Saxon Isogloss: (REM) Activity. *De Gustibus: Essays for Alain Renoir*, ed. by J. M. Foley. In *Albert Bates Lord Studies in Oral Tradition* 10: 480-493.

Rauch, Irmengard. forthcoming a. Linguistic Polygraphy and Linguistic Polyphony: Old Saxon /ie, uo/. In XVth International Congress of Linguists (Quebec City, Canada) 1992.

Rauch, Irmengard. forthcoming b. The Old English *Genesis B* Poet: Bilingual or Interlingual? *American Journal of Germanic Linguistics and Literatures.*

Ries, John. 1880. *Die Stellung von Subjekt und Prädicatsverbum im Heliand, nebst einem Anhang metrischer Excurse.* (=*Quellen und Forschungen* XLI). Strassburg: Trübner.

Rooth, Erik. 1956/1973. Über die Heliandsprache. *Der Heliand* (= *Wege der Forschung* CCCXXI), ed. by J. Eichhoff and I. Rauch, 200-246. Darmstadt: Wissenschaftliche Buchgesellschaft.

Sanders, Willy. 1973. Altsächsische Sprache. *Niederdeutsch: Sprache und Literatur*, ed. by J. Goossens, 28-65. Neumünster: Karl Wachholtz.

Sanders, Willy. 1985a. 89. Lexikologie des Altniederdeutschen (Altsächsischen). *Sprachgeschichte: Ein Handbuch zur Geschichte der deutschen Sprache und ihrer Erforschung*, II, 2, ed. by W. Besch, O. Reichmann, S. Sonderegger, 1083-1088. Berlin: Walter de Gruyter.

Sanders, Willy. 1985b. 92. Die Textsorten des Altniederdeutschen (Altsächsischen). *Sprachgeschichte: Ein Handbuch zur Geschichte der deutschen Sprache und ihrer Erforschung*, II, 2, ed. by W. Besch, O. Reichmann, S. Sonderegger, 1103-1109. Berlin: Walter de Gruyter.

Scheuermann, Ulrich. 1985. 93. Die Diagliederung des Altniederdeutschen (Altsächsischen). *Sprachgeschichte: Ein Handbuch zur Geschichte der deutschen Sprache und ihrer Erforschung*, II. 2, ed. by W. Besch, O. Reichmann, S. Sonderegger, 1109-1114. Berlin: Walter de Gruyter.

Sehrt, Edward H. 1966. *Vollständiges Wörterbuch zum Heliand und zur altsächsischen Genesis.* 2. ed. Göttingen: Vanderhoeck & Ruprecht.

Sehrt, Edward H. 1940/1973. The Long Forms of ōn-Verbs in Old Saxon. *Der Heliand* (= *Wege der Forschung* CCCXXI), ed. by J. Eichhoff and I. Rauch, 14-19. Darmstadt: Wissenschaftliche Buchgesellschaft.
Sievers, Eduard (ed.) 1878. *Heliand* (=*Germanistische Handbibliothek IV*). Halle: Buchhandlung des Waisenhauses.
Simon, Werner. 1965. *Zur Sprachmischung im Heliand* (=*Philologische Studien und Quellen* 27). Berlin: Erich Schmidt.
Taeger, Burkhard. 1979. Das Straubinger 'Heliand' Fragment. Philologische Untersuchungen I. *Beiträge zur Geschichte der deutschen Sprache und Literatur* (Tübingen) 101: 181-228.
Taeger, Burkhard. 1981. Das Straubinger 'Heliand' Fragment: Philologische Untersuchungen II. *Beiträge zur Geschichte der deutschen Sprache und Literatur* (Tübingen) 103: 402-424.
Trager, George. 1958. Paralanguage: A First Approximation. *Studies in Linguistics* 13: 1-12.
Trubetzkoy, N. S. 1939. Gedanken über das Indogermanenproblem. *Acta Linguistica* I: 81-89.
Van Ginneken, J. 1956. Roman Jakobson: Pioneer of Diachronic Phonology. *For Roman Jakobson*, ed. by M. Halle et al, 574-581. The Hague: Mouton.
Vennemann, Theo. 1988. *Preference Laws for Syllable Structure (and the Explanation of Sound Change)*. Berlin: Mouton de Gruyter.
Vickrey, John F. Jr. 1960. *"Genesis B": A New Analysis and Edition*. Unpubl. diss. Indiana University.
Voyles. Joseph B. 1970. The Phonology of Old Saxon (1). *Glossa* 4: 123-159.
Voyles. Joseph B. 1971. The Phonology of Old Saxon (2). *Glossa* 5: 3-30.
Wurzel, Wolfgang U. 1987. II. System-dependent morphological naturalness in inflection. *Leitmotifs in Natural Morphology* (= *SLSS* 10), ed. by W. U. Dressler, W. Mayerthaler, O. Panagl, W. U. Wurzel, 59-96. Amsterdam: Benjamins.
Zanni, Roland. 1985. 91. Wortbildung des Altniederdeutschen (Altsächsischen). *Sprachgeschichte: Ein Handbuch zur Ge-*

schichte der deutschen Sprache und ihrer Erforschung, II, 2, ed. by W. Besch, O. Reichmann, S. Sonderegger, 1094-1102. Berlin: Walter de Gruyter.

Index

Reference is to section numbers, except for the Introduction, which is referenced by roman numeral page numbers.

ABLAUT xxv, 3.3, 3.3.1, 3.3.2, 7, 8.2.1, 25, 26.1.4, 28.1, 28.2, 28.2.1, 29.1, 29.2.2
acoustic(s) (see phonology)
adjective: 10.1, 22.8; 26, (see also complement); comparative/superlative 25.1, 26, 26.1.3; intensifier 23.4; noun phrase expansion by 23, 23.4; (trigender) strong 26.1.1, 26.1.2, 26.1.4; (trigender) weak 26.1.2, 26.1.3, 26.1.4
alliteration/alliterative (verse): 6.4, 17.3.1, 19.4.13; Germanic 17.3.1, 25.2; (see also stress: metrical)
Anglo-Frisian 19.3.3, 19.4.29
argument (see grammatical constituent)
article: definite, indefinite (see determiner)
articulatory (see phonology)
aspect: 20; 24.1, 24.3, 24.5; durative-perfective effec-tive 24.1, 24.3; durative-perfective ingressive 24.1, 24.3; imperfective 24.3; lexical 24.1, 24.3; major sets 24.3; perfective 24.3; primary 24.1; (see also grammatical constituent: modality), (see also tense)

barred vowel xxxv, 14.1, 15.1
base form inflection xxxv
Behaghel's Rules 6.4

case(s): 20; as prepositional phrase(s) 22.3, 22.4, (see also syntax: nonlinear), (see also semantic feature[s]/categories)
cognition: abductive reasoning 14.1
cognitive: center-periphery schema xxxviii; constituents 1; strategies xxv.

complement(s): 20; adjective 22.8, (see also sentence: adjective as); adverbial 22, 22.4; complex nominal 22, 22.2; infinitive 22, 22.5, (see also sentence: infinitive as); present participle 22, 22.6, (see also sentence: present participle as); preposition 22, (see also case: as prepositional phrase); preterite participle 22, 22.7, (see also sentence: preterite participle as); sentence 22, (see also sentence); simple nominal 22, 22.1; (see also phrase: noun, prepositional)

compound(ing): xxxviii, 7, 25, 25.1, 25.2; copulative 25.2; determinative 25.2; nominal 25.2; possessive 25.2

congruence rules: occasional optional 30.2

consonant: 16.1.1; acoustically 16.2, 16.2.1; alliterating 17.3.1; articulation/production of 16.1, 16.1.1, 16.1.2; geminate 3.3.2, 8.2.1, 11.2, 12.2, 14.2, 19.4.31, 28.2.2; in initial, medial, final position 19.4; position in syllable 19.4; simplex 3.3.2; 8.2.1, 12.2, 28.2.2; vowel division 16.1

dental preterite 28.1, 28.2.2, 28.2.3, 29.2.2, (see also verb:anomalous), (see also verb: modal auxiliary), (see also verb: weak)

derivation: xxxviii, 7, 25, 25.1; prefix(al) 25, 25.1; sufix(al) 25.1

determiner: 23; article 23, 23.1; deictic pronoun 23, 23.1; possessive pronoun 23, 23.3; quantifier 23, 23.2

diachronic synchrony xxvi, 4, 11.2.1, 12.1, 13.2

dialect(s) (pervades the data; see also interference)

diathesis/voice 20; 24.5, (see also grammatical constituent: modality)

dictionary finder chart (see verb)

diphthong-s/-ization xxxvi - xxxviii, 17.1, 19.3.3, 19.4.31, 19.5

directive (see mood: imperative)

discourse: xxv, xxvi, 5, 6.4, 24.1, 24.5; backgrounding 24.1; factors 19.4.26; (see also text)

Index

English xxv, 26.1.2

final devoicing 3.3.1, 3.3.2, 11.2, 12.2, 14.2, 18, 19.5; 26.1.2
fundamental identifying form xxxv, 3.1, 3.3.1, 4, 6.4, 7, 8.1, 8.2.2, 11.1, 13.2, 14.1, 15.1, 26.1, 26.1.2, 26.1.3, 28.1, 28.2.1

Genesis: OS xxxix, 19.3.3 (see also *Heliand*); OE *Later* or *B* 19.3.3
generalization (linguistic) 4, 6.4, 14.1, 22, 26.1, 26.1.1, 28.2.2
genetic: fact/grounding xxvi; sound provenance xxxv; phonological rule 3.3.1; grammar 4; reconstruction 13.2; stem class/set/type xxvi, 11.1, 11.2, 11.2.1, 12.1, 14.1, 14.2.1, 15.1
German xxv, 26.1.2
Germanic: xxv, 4, 19.3.3; East 4; (North-) West 4, 18; 19.3.3, 26.1.2
Gothic 4
grammatical category: 25; of noun 10.1; of verb 8
grammatical change 3.3.1, 3.3.2

grammatical constituent(s): predicate/predicator/relation 2, 4, 7, 9, 10; 10.1, 21, 22; argument 2, 4, 7, 9, 10, 21, 23; modality 2, 21, 24, 24.3, 24.4; (see also aspect, diathesis, mood, polarity, tense)
graph(em)(ic): 13,19.4; evidence xxxv, 16, 19.4.26; variation xxxv, 3.3.2, 11.1, 11.2,12.1, 12.2, 13, 13.1, 13.2, 14.1, 15.1, 17.3.3, 18, 19.4.31, 26.1.1, 26.1.2, 26.1.3, 27, 28.1, 28.2.2, 28.2.3, 29.1; sound fit 18; (see also phonology)

Heliand: xxxix; manuscripts 19.1, 19.4; narrative epic 1, 19.2; poet(s) 19.2, 25.2; numerical/architectonic structuring 25.2; time of composition 19.2, 19.4; verse form (see alliteration/alliterative verse); register 19.3.2

Indo-: European 4, 7; Hittite 4
infinitive: 26, 26.1.4, 28.1 (see also verb); inflected 22.5, 26.1.4
Ingvaeonic (see Anglo-Frisian)

intensifier: (see adjective), (see pronoun)
interference: (mega)dialect 3.3.2, 13.2, 18, 19.3, 19.3.2; 19.3.3; 19.4, 19.4.7, 19.4.8, 19.4.13, 19.4.21, 19.4.22, 19.4.26; 19.4.27, 19.4.29, 19.4.30, 19.5, 22, 26.1.1

"Lay of Hildebrand" 25.2
Latin: 19.4.13; Vulgar 4
lexical/lexicon: xxxvi, 2, 3, 4, 5, 7; categor-y/-ies 7, 9; 10.1, 11.1, 25.2; change in category 25
lexical category phrases: linear order of 30.1.2

medial voicing 3.3.1, 3.3.2, 11.2, 12.2, 14.2, 19.5, 26.1.2
Middle Low German 13.2, 19.3.1
Middle Netherlandic 13.2
modal (verb): in nonauxiliary function 22.5; -like 22.5; (see also verb: modal auxiliary)
modality 20; (see also grammatical constituent)
monophthongization 3.3.2
mood: 20; 24.2; imperative/hortative 24.2, 29.1; indicative 24.2; subjunctive 24.2, 29.2; (see also grammatical constituent: modality), (see also verb)
morpheme: bound 25, 25.1; free 25, 25.1; 25.2; productive 25; (see also derivation; compounding)
morphology: 2,7; derivational 7, 25; independent reflexive 26; inflection(al) xxvi – xxxiii, 5, 7, 9; 10.1, 14.1, 20. 25, 27

narrative: sequence 6.4; speech scenario/situation 6.4; (see also text)
negative: derivational morphology 24.4; lexicon 24.2; intensifiying morphemes 24.4; (see also polarity)
nominal(s): 10.1, 25.2; phrase 9, (see also complement); forms (see infinitive), (see participle: present), (see participle: preterite)
nondental preterite (see verb: strong)
nonnoun nominal: 26; trigender strong 26.1, 26.1.1
noun: 23, 26; feminine strong 14., 14.1, 14.2, 14.2.1; masculine strong 11, 11.1,

Index 413

11.2, 11.2.1, 12.1, 12.2,
14.1, 14.2; neuter strong
12, 12.1, 12.2, 14.1, 14.2;
possessive 23.3; strong
10.1, 26.1 15.2; trigender
weak 15, 15.1, 15.2,
26.1.3; weak 10.1
numerals: 26; cardinal 26.1.2;
ordinal 26.1.2

Old English xxxix, 4, 18,
19.3.3, 19.4.8, 19.4.13,
19.4.26, 19.4.27, 19.4.29,
19.4.30; 25.2, 26, 26.1.1
Old Frisian 13.2, 19.3.3,
19.4.21, 19.4.22, 19.4.26,
19.4.29, 19.4.30, 26
Old High German xxxix, 4,
19.3.1, 19.3.3, 19.4.7,
19.4.8, 19.4.13, 19.4.26
"Old Low German" 19.3.1
Old Low Franconian 19.3.1
Old Norse 25.2
Old Saxon: speech area:
19.3.1, 19.3.2; *limes saxonicus* 4; era/period
xxxv, 19.3.1
orthographic lag 18

Panini 25.2
participle: 26; (inflected)
present 26.1.4; (inflected)
preterite 24.1, 24.3, 24.5,
26.1.4; (see also aspect),
(see also diathesis/voice),
(see also verb)
performative 6.4
phone-s/-mes: allophone/
grapheme 19.4; schwa
17.1, 17.3.3, 19.4.26,
19.4.28, 27, 29.2.2;
systematic 17.2, 19.5;
systematic segmental
17.2 & chart, 19.5; (see
also stress: word), (see
also stress: syntactic)
phonetics (see phonology)
phonology: xxvi, xxxv – xxxviii,
2,7; acoustic phonetics
16.2; acoustic/articula-
tory analysis 16, 17;
articulatory phonetics
16.1; segmental 16.1,
17.3.1; suprasegmental
16.1, 17.3, 24.3; supra-
segmental rule 17.3.2,
17.3.3; (see also conso-
nant), (see also vowel)
phrase: noun 20, 22, 23; noun
phrase expansion (see
adjective), (see sentence);
prepositional 20; verb 20,
24.1, 26.1.4, (see also
case), (see also comple-
ment); structure rule 20,
22.8; verb 20, 22
pitch 16.1, 16.2, 17.3, 24.3

polarity 20; 24.4; (see also grammatical constituent: modality), (see also negative)
pragmatic(s): xxvi, 5; strategies 6.4, 7, 9; (see also discourse: factors)
predicate/predicator (see grammatical constituent)
Prefaces (Latin) xxxix, 19.2, 25.2; *vitteas* 'fits' 19.2; Caedmonian metaphor 19.2; (see also *Heliand*)
prefixation (see derivation)
present participle (see verb)
preterite participle (see verb)
preterite-present (see modal verb), (see also verb: modal auxiliary)
pronoun: 26.1; (trigender) anaphoric 26, 26.1.1; (compounded) (interrogative) *hw-* 26, 26.1, 26.1.1; inflection 26.1; (intensified) (trigender) deictic 26, 26.1.1; intensifier 23.3; personal 26, 26.1.1; possessive 26, 26.1.1, (see also adjective: strong); reflexive 26; trigender quantifying 26.1.1; (see also determiner)
proposition(al) 2, 9, 10

quantifier: trigender 26; (see also adjective: strong), (see also determiner), (see also pronoun)

recursive characteristic 22.8, (see also phrase: structure rule[s]), (see also sentence: nonfinite series of)
reference (see cognitive constituents)
relation (see grammatical constituent: predicator)

scale of sonority 16.1, 16.1.2; (see also sonority continuum)
scribal error 3.3.2, 13.2, 18, 19.4.7, 19.4.8, 19.4.11, 19.4.23
semantic feature(s)/categories: 22.3; agent 22; essive 22; intransitive 22; object 22; of VP 22; patient 22; transitive 22; underspecification/adumbration of 22
semantic focus: of *OSL* xxv
sentence: 20; adjective as 22.7, 22.8; as surface complement 22.8; dependent 30.1.1; imperative

Index

6.2, 6.3; independent: 6, 6.3; independent declarative 6, 6.3, 6.4; independent interrogative 6.2, 6.3, 6.4; infinitive as 22.5, 22.8; nonfinite series of 22.8; noun phrase expansion by 23, 23.5; present participle as 22.6, 22.8; preterite participle as 22.7, 22.8; (see also proposition)
sequence (see cognitive constituents)
sonority continuum xxxv, 16.1.1, 19.4; (see also consonant: vowel division)
sound(s): 16; production (physiology) 16.1; natural(ness) (class) 16.1.1, 17; spectrograph 16.2; symbol fit (see grapheme: sound fit)
stress 16.1, 16.2, 17.3; 17.3.1, 24.3, 27; metrical 17.3.3; word 17.3.2, 25; syntactic 17.3.3, 19.4.22, 19.4.23, 19.4.26, 26.1.1
subcategorization (rules) 7, 20, 21, 22, 23, 24.1, 30.1
suprasegmental (see phonology)
syllable: 17.4; position 19.4; shape/structure 7, 17.4; long/short, heavy/light 11.1., 12.1, 14.1, 17.4, 26.1.2; division/schemas 17.4
syntax: xxxviii; linear xxvi, 2, 5, 6, 6.4, 7, 30. 30.1; nonlinear 2, 10.1, 14.1, 30, 30.1; nonlinear macro- 7, 9, 20, 21, 22.3; 24.4, (see also subcategorization [rules]); nonlinear micro- 7, 20, 25

tense: 24, 24.1, 24.3; future 24.1; present 24.1; present perfect 24.1; preterite 3.2, 3.3, 8.2; preterite perfect 24.1; primary 24.1, 24.3; (see also verb), (see also grammatical constituent: modality)
text: xxvi; narrative discourse 1
topicalization (see cognitive constituents)

umlaut conditioner: semantic disambiguation 19.4.26, 29.2.2

umlaut: historic[al]/palatal xxvi, 3.3.2 4, 11.2, 14.2, 19.4.21, 19.4.23, 19.4.25, 19.4.26, 19.4.27, 19.4.29, 19.4.30, 19.5; prehistoric xxvi, 3.3.1, 3.3.2, 4; prehistoric palatal 19.4.29; Rückumlaut (unmutation) 19.4.29, 28.2.2; secondary (palatal) 19.4.26

valence (see verb)
verb: ABLAUT (see ABLAUT); anomalous 3.2, 8.1, 8.2.3, 26.1.4, 28.1, 28.2, 28.2.1, 28.2.3, 29.2, 29.2.1, 29.2.2; indicative 3.3; infinitive 3.1, 3.3.2, 7, 8.1, 28.1, 28.2.2, 29.1, 29.2.1, 29.2.2 (see also complement); modal auxiliary 3.2, 8.2.2, 28.2, 28.2.2, 29.2.1, 29.2.2; present participle 3.3, (see also complement); present tense indicative 8.1, 8.2; 8.2.1, 8.2.2, 8.2.3, 28.1; present tense subjunctive 29.2.1; preterite participle 3.3, 3.3.2, (see also complement); preterite tense indicative 28; 28.1, 28.2, 28.2.1, 28.2.2, 28.2.3; preterite tense subjunctive 29.2.2; strong 3.2, 3.3, 3.3.1, 3.3.2, 8.1, 8.2, 28, 28.1, 28.2, 29.1, 29.2.1, 29.2.2; strong verb dictionary finder 3.2, 8.1, 8.2; 8.2.1; weak 3.2, 28, 28.1, 28.2, 28.2.2, 29.1, 29.2.1, 29.2.2
Verner's Law (see grammatical change)
vowel: acoustically 16.2, 16.2.2; alliterating 17.3.1; articulation/production of 16.1, 16.1.1, 16.1.2; consonant division 16.1; in root syllable under primary stress 19.4

word: 2; production 25, 25.1

Berkeley Models of Grammars

This series invites an array of grammar types useful both as learning devices and as research tools. The freedom to break away from Latin and Greek grammar models, traditionally required, in particular of Indo-European historical languages, is respected and even urged where appropriate. On the other hand, the valuable genetic study of a language should remain a sought-after, well-developed endeavor, and should not be lost to the present and future world of learning. Accordingly, the *Berkeley Models of Grammars* series seeks forward-looking, theoretically sophisticated methodologies which are at the same time relatively exhaustive or complete grammars of a given language at any period of its existence.

> Irmengard Rauch
> Department of German
> University of California-Berkeley
> Berkeley, CA 94720